Multilingual Law

This book introduces and explores the concept of multilingual law. Providing an overview as to what is 'multilingual law', the study establishes a new discourse based on this concept, which has hitherto lacked recognition for reasons of complexity and multidisciplinarity. The need for such a discourse now exists and is becoming urgent in view of the progress being made towards European integration and the legal and factual foundation for it in multilingualism and multilingual legislation.

Covering different types of multilingual legal orders and their distinguishing features, as well as the basic structure of legal systems, the author studies policy formation, drafting, translation, revision, terminology and computer tools in connection with the legislative and judicial processes.

Bringing together a range of diverse legal and linguistic ideas under one roof, this book is of importance to legal-linguists, drafters and translators, as well as students and scholars of legal linguistics, legal translation and revision.

Colin D. Robertson is a member of the Law Society of Scotland and worked for many years as legal-linguistic expert on EC and EU legislative texts at the Council of the European Union, Brussels. He has published on issues related to law and language.

Law, Language and Communication
Series Editors:
Anne Wagner, Lille University – Nord de France, Centre for Legal Research and Perspectives of Law, René Demogue Group, France and Vijay Kumar Bhatia, City University of Hong Kong

This series encourages innovative and integrated perspectives within and across the boundaries of law, language and communication, with particular emphasis on issues of communication in specialised socio-legal and professional contexts. It seeks to bring together a range of diverse yet cumulative research traditions related to these fields in order to identify and encourage interdisciplinary research.

The series welcomes proposals – both edited collections as well as single-authored monographs – emphasising critical approaches to law, language and communication, identifying and discussing issues, proposing solutions to problems, offering analyses in areas such as legal construction, interpretation, translation and de-codification.

For further information on this and other series from Routledge, please visit: www.routledge.com.

Multilingual Law

A framework for analysis and understanding

Colin D. Robertson

LONDON AND NEW YORK

First published 2016
by Routledge
2 Park Square, Milton Park, Abingdon, Oxon OX14 4RN

and by Routledge
711 Third Avenue, New York, NY 10017

First issued in paperback 2018

Routledge is an imprint of the Taylor & Francis Group, an informa business

© 2016 Colin D. Robertson

The right of Colin D. Robertson to be identified as author of this work has been asserted by him in accordance with sections 77 and 78 of the Copyright, Designs and Patents Act 1988.

All rights reserved. No part of this book may be reprinted or reproduced or utilised in any form or by any electronic, mechanical, or other means, now known or hereafter invented, including photocopying and recording, or in any information storage or retrieval system, without permission in writing from the publishers.

Trademark notice: Product or corporate names may be trademarks or registered trademarks, and are used only for identification and explanation without intent to infringe.

British Library Cataloguing in Publication Data
A catalogue record for this book is available from the British Library

Library of Congress Cataloguing in Publication Data
Names: Robertson, Colin D., author.
Title: Multilingual law : a framework for analysis and understanding / by Colin D. Robertson.
Description: Farnham, Surrey, UK England; Burlington, VT, USA: Ashgate, 2016. | Series: Law, language and communication | Includes bibliographical references and index.
Identifiers: LCCN 2015045527 (print) | LCCN 2015046157 (ebook) |
ISBN 9781409421887 (hardback: alk. paper)
Subjects: LCSH: Law–Language. | Law–Translating. | Law–European Union countries–Language. | Law–Translating–European Union countries.
Classification: LCC K487.L36 R63 2016 (print) | LCC K487.L36 (ebook) |
DDC 340/.14–dc23 LC record available at http://lccn.loc.gov/2015045527

ISBN 13: 978-1-138-60643-2 (pbk)
ISBN 13: 978-1-4094-2188-7 (hbk)

Typeset in Times New Roman
by Out of House Publishing

To Michèle

Contents

Preface xiii
List of abbreviations xvii

PART I
Introduction 1

1 The concept of multilingual law 3
Introduction 3
Field of enquiry: multilingual law 5
Multilingual world 8
Defining multilingual law 11
Law and language: two complex fields 15
Summary 18

2 Framework of models and an overview 20
Introduction 20
Legal-linguistic modelling 20
Structuring the field of enquiry 23
Overview of the chapters 24
Summary 28

PART II
Law 29

3 Viewpoints of law 31
Introduction 31
Legal viewpoints 32
What is law? 34
Rules, norms and principles 38
Legal systems 42
Branches of law 43
Substantive and procedural law 45

viii *Contents*

    States and legal orders   46
    Summary   47

4 Legal texts   51
    Introduction   51
    Sources of law and legal texts   52
    Different types of legal text   61
    Legal texts as sites for actions   62
    Facts, evidence and proof   67
    Enforcement   68
    Summary   69

5 Law of language(s)   72
    Introduction   72
    Law of language   73
    Linguistic regimes   76
    Variations in linguistic regimes   83
    Summary   84

PART III
Language   87

6 Viewpoints of language   89
    Introduction   89
    Linguistic viewpoints   90
    What is language?   92
    Oral and written language   93
    Linguistics: searching for what is useful   95
    Summary   111

7 Language(s) for legal purposes   113
    Introduction   113
    Legal language   114
    Official languages   116
    Classifying languages by use and status   118
    Language policy   124
    Summary   124

PART IV
Signs   127

8 Law and language as signs   129
    Introduction   129

Sign as comprising two elements 129
Sign as comprising three elements 132
The mental dimension to signs 134
Semiosis: creating new signs 135
Objectifying the subjective 135
Summary 136

PART V
Meaning 139

9 Texts, terms and meanings 141
Introduction 141
Sites of engagement 142
Semiotic meaning 143
Linguistic meaning 144
Legal meaning 145
Four viewpoints: law, language, policy, and action 146
Role of terminology 148
Summary 149

PART VI
Translation and revision 151

10 Viewpoints of translation 153
Introduction 153
Translation viewpoints 154
What is translation? 155
Translation as a process 162
Seven scenarios for legal translation 164
Summary 168

11 Revision 170
Introduction 170
Revision viewpoint 170
Revision 171
Legal-linguistic revision 173
Summary 174

PART VII
Back-up, support and training 175

12 Tools and technology 177
Introduction 177

x *Contents*

    Technology viewpoint 177
    Tools and aids for specialists 178
    Summary 182

13 Education and training   184
    Introduction 184
    Training viewpoint 184
    Specialist knowledge and skills 186
    Summary 189

PART VIII
Framework, models and applications   191

14 Framework for analysis and understanding   193
    Introduction 193
    States, languages and official languages (Appendix I) 194
    Legal-linguistic models (Appendix II) 194
    Searching for rules, practice and guidance on language(s), drafting and
        interpretation (Appendix III) 194
    Classifying languages by use and status (Appendix IV) 195
    Drafting and revision checklist for multilingual acts (Appendix V) 195
    Making a presentation or writing a paper on multilingual legal language
        (Appendix VI) 195
    Training questions on law and legal language (Appendix VII) 195
    Framework for analysis and understanding (Appendix VIII) 196
    The appendices as tools of enquiry 201
    Summary 201

15 Multilingual law   202
    Introduction 202
    Matrices of law(s), language(s) and culture(s) 203
    Themes and patterns 205
    Pros and cons of multilingual law 207
    Multilingualism implies respect 208
    Problems and solutions 208
    Specialist knowledge, training and education 209
    Areas for study and research 209
    Conclusion 210

    Appendices
    Appendix I   States, languages and official languages   211
    Appendix II   Legal-linguistic models   212

Appendix III Searching for rules, practice and guidance on language(s), drafting and interpretation	215
Appendix IV Classifying languages by use and status	222
Appendix V Drafting and revision checklist for multilingual acts	224
Appendix VI Making a presentation or writing a paper on multilingual legal language	227
Appendix VII Training questions on law and legal language	231
Appendix VIII Framework for analysis and understanding	237
Bibliography	250
Index	264

Preface

Why does one need a book on the concept of multilingual law? Surely it is just a matter of translation? Maybe; but what is 'translation' and what is its place in a legal order that functions in 24 languages as in the European Union? Personal experience in the past was that many questions and problems arising on a daily basis in multilingual EU legal-linguistic work did not find answers and explanations in the literature. In the absence of guides one starts to construct one's own. Where does one start and how does one proceed? What should one look for? How can one organise the information? How can one facilitate access to specialist literatures? These questions led to this book.

The idea pursued is to take the concept of multilingual law, analyse it and search for component elements, and then explore them and see where the threads lead. The legal and linguistic work that is undertaken every day does not take place in a vacuum; it is real, concrete and specific. It takes place within systems of law through language and languages as codes for communication. To be relevant, the concept of multilingual law must be pinned down and connected to a real-world environment. However, it soon becomes apparent that that environment is phenomenally complex. So either one abandons the task early on, or one seeks a strategy to cut a pathway through the complexity. One way is to attempt a conceptual approach, with emphasis on structures and methods. However, this risks emptying law and language of its everyday living substance and content.

The concept of 'framework' is an organising device. If one can identify the main fields of activity that underpin multilingual legal systems, and therefore multilingual law as a concept, perhaps one can set down signposts which in turn help one to understand, analyse and find solutions for pragmatic problems that arise – perhaps one can see how different activities dovetail together; perhaps one can see the possibilities of alternative strategies and approaches? Such an approach implies stepping outside any single system, and it implies adopting a conceptual and somewhat theoretical approach, taking a broad 'bird's eye' view, as it were. It means venturing into unfamiliar territory, looking at unfamiliar specialist fields and trying to work out how they are relevant. Immediately one is surrounded by details and complexity. However, adopting the concept of multilingual law as the unifying notion supplemented by the concept of 'framework' as an organising tool helps to create a counterbalance. This book sets out the results of the enquiry.

The formal starting point for the investigation was a presentation given at the 12th European Symposium on Language for Special Purposes (LSP '99), which took place in Brixen/Bressanone (Italy/South Tyrol) from 30 August to 3 September 1999 and had as its theme 'Language for Special Purposes: Perspectives for the New Millennium' (Mayer 2001). A presentation given entitled 'Multilingual Law: A Framework for

Understanding' (Robertson 2001) set the course which has led to this book. Ideas sketched out then have been developed through undertaking the daily work of an EU legal-linguistic expert (lawyer-linguist) but also through having the opportunity to present and participate in seminars and linguistic conferences and explore individual themes, building the framework concept step by step over the years.

The academic audiences have been helpful and tolerant, quietly guiding a practitioner with a four-year law degree from Aberdeen University in Scots Law, followed by legal experience in Scottish law firms, UK governmental legal service, the European Commission Legal Service, and then translation experience in the Court of Justice of the European Union and over twenty years as legal-linguistic reviser in the Council of the European Union until retirement in 2013. Each of these institutions provided solid training, experience and support. In recent years the door of time and opportunity opened to permit more reflexive activity to develop ideas, as well as to learn some of the methods of academic presentation and text-writing. This book is a fusion of these influences. Yet behind them all lies a more personal one, for being Scottish means being infused with a particular culture and philosophy, and apparently the philosophy is one of 'common sense' (Broadie 2000: 17).

This book has been constructed with three readerships in mind: first, the general reader, with no or little background in law or languages. The aim here is to present multilingual law as a picture comprising many elements, and to make a journey around topics – as in a museum – describing, explaining and attempting to show how each one contributes to the larger picture and interrelates. That has meant selecting examples from a handful of languages out of many possible ones, and it has meant restricting the legal systems discussed to a representative few. The task has been to search for common threads and patterns and to bring them together within a framework of questions that can be asked of any legal system from a legal-linguistic point of view.

The second readership is academic, primarily researchers in legal language and legal linguistics, perhaps also of legal theory. The discourse style has in part been learned from them. Throughout the text individual topics have been summarised and it is hoped that they retain the essential gist in each case. Personal insights and viewpoints offered are drawn from practitioner experience and moulded into an outline that may perhaps be of some assistance for further researches. The appendices have been included with such interests in mind. They are dry technical lists intended to summarise technical information. They draw on the chapters, but go beyond them and are self-standing. Together they constitute the framework of the book.

The third readership is dear to the heart: former colleagues and future colleagues working in practice in drafting, translating, revising and putting together legal texts in whatever languages. This book is for them especially. They need assistance in discerning the 'wood from the trees', orienting themselves, understanding legal ideas, understanding linguistic ideas, seeing how their work fits in with the work of others, and in asking the 'right' questions to elicit information needed. It is hoped they will be encouraged to make contact and work with academic researchers to mutual advantage. They will probably not agree with everything written here and will see the flaws, but it is hoped they will be encouraged to put forward and develop their own ideas and viewpoints to correct such errors. For them the appendices serve as a shopping list of ideas they can draw on in that respect.

This book has been a long time in gestation since 1999. It has been a slow process; drawing strands from different locations in private and public legal practice in Britain and EU institutions. Countless experiences, countless conversations, countless influences – they have all been formative. Thanks go to everyone, though they are too numerous to name. Yet there are persons whose influence have been of direct significance and impact: first my wife Michèle, who introduced me to the finer points of French language and culture as well as to linguistics, and who started me thinking more concretely about law in linguistic and semiotic terms. She drew my attention to Ferdinand de Saussure and Charles Sanders Peirce, and gave me practical help in teaching myself translation skills to pass the lawyer-linguist competition for the Court of Justice.

Within EU institutions John Forman and Joe Morgan gave particular support and guidance. Lawyer-linguist, translator and terminologist colleagues from within the EU institutions contributed to the development of the ideas through discussions and by making invitations for presentations on particular themes. Maria Tynell and Klavs Skovsholm were always ready to listen and discuss ideas. Gérard Losson, originator of the Council Manual of Precedents (*Formulaire*), granted many hours of conversation. He expressed the wish to write his own book, but did not live to fulfil it. Perhaps this one goes some of the way, although in English and not French.

On the academic side I owe a particular debt to Emerita Professor Susan Šarčević. She has been a constant source of inspiration, encouragement and collaboration since we first met in Zagreb at a seminar on EU legal language given at the start of the millennium. Through her the door to the academic side of legal-linguistics was opened, something that has been hard for a pure practitioner to follow. Subsequent invitations to conferences, seminars and round tables to participate and give presentations led to a gradual widening of exposure to applied linguistics and have left their mark on this book, as many topics were individually explored. In that connection, thanks are extended, among others, to: Thomas Watkin, Anne Wagner, Stanislaw Roszkowski, Lelija Sočinač, Christopher Williams, Vijay Bhatia, Ingrid Simonnæs, Jørn Øyrehagen Sunde, Barbara Pozzo, Ross Charnock, Sebastian McEvoy, Anne Lise Kjær, William Bull, Igor Dizdarevic, Nikolaos Anagnostopoulos and Fernando Prieto Ramos for their invitations. The results of some of their invitations appear in the bibliography at the end of the book. Appendix VI arose following a request by Melisa Okicic for assistance. The experience of a lesser-used language was enhanced by the invitation by Elaine Morton to become a contributor, working with Kenneth Farrow, to the Scots language magazine *Lallans* produced in Scots lowland speech (Lallans) by the Scots Leid Associe (Scots Language Association).[1] An example of the language has been included in Chapter 6 as part of a reflection on historical linguistics.

I wish to give particular thanks to Ashgate for agreeing to take the risk of a contract to publish this book when others feared to 'confuse' their scholars. Alison Kirk has been courteous, encouraging and patient through the years. Alex Buckley's assistance has been invaluable. It has been a long time coming but I hope it has been worth the wait.

Then came the news of the transfer of the assets of Ashgate to Taylor & Francis. New collaborations arose and thanks are extended to Nick Craggs, Gail Welsh and Lorraine Slipper for bringing this book to fruition. While sad to see the demise of a valued and respected name in academic publishing, I am heartened that their heritage continues under very capable hands and appreciate the continuity.

Lastly, I must mention the encouragement by my father Professor Forbes Robertson, who read and advised on early drafts of initial chapters in his last year.

I extend my warmest thanks to each and every person who has contributed towards this book. That said, this work has been a personal project and reflects solely my own views and opinions. I am alone responsible for its errors, weaknesses and infelicities.

Note

1 www.lallans.co.uk/index.php/lallans (operational as at 2 April 2016).

Abbreviations

AU	African Union
CAT	computer-assisted tools
EASA	European Aviation Safety Agency
EC	European Community
ESP	English as specific, special, specialist or specialised language
EU	European Union
FAO	Food and Agriculture Organization
ICAO	International Civil Aviation Organization
ILO	International Labour Organization
IPA	International Phonetic Alphabet
ISO	International Organization for Standardization
LGP	language for general purposes
LSP	language used for specific, special, specialist or specialised purposes
NASA	National Aeronautics and Space Administration
NGO	non-governmental organisation
OAU	Organisation of African Unity
SL	source language
TEU	Treaty on European Union (post-Lisbon)
TEAEC	Treaty establishing the European Atomic Energy Community (EURATOM Treaty)
TFEU	Treaty on the functioning of the European Union
TL	target language
UN	United Nations
UNESCO	United Nations Educational, Scientific and Cultural Organization

Part I
Introduction

1 The concept of multilingual law

Introduction

The theme of this book is multilingual law. It seeks to draw together in one volume many threads and strands that have a bearing on law and languages in a multilingual context. The purpose is to organise information from a variety of disciplines in a way that brings them together as a conceptual tool to analyse and understand different types of multilingual legal systems from a legal-linguistic point of view. The conceptual tool proposed takes the form of a 'framework', set out in appendices. The purpose of this book is to describe fields and activities that have a bearing on the practice and theory of multilingual law and to link them together conceptually within a frame of reference that can be used as a tool for enquiry. A secondary purpose is to reflect on the language(s) of law, and the law of language(s), in a multilingual context. No prior knowledge of any of the disciplines covered is assumed.

There is nothing new about multilingualism in law or making and applying laws in several languages. It is a phenomenon that is as old as civilisation. In the ancient Near East multilingualism was widespread among peoples. Ostler observes that 'unlike Egypt, China or India, its cities and states had always been consciously multilingual, whether for communication with neighbours who spoke different languages, or because their histories had made them adopt a foreign language to dignify court, religion or commerce' (Ostler 2005: 34).

The sacred texts at the roots of world religions, and legal systems, also bear witness to multilingualism. The texts comprising the Old Testament of the Bible were first written in Hebrew and Aramaic and translated into Greek, the language of the New Testament. Both Old and New Testaments were translated into Latin,[1] followed by many other languages. One estimate is that the Bible has now been translated wholly or partly into at least 2,287 languages and dialects (Biblica 2013). The Roman Empire at its height used Latin in the West and Greek in the East (Herrin 2008, Kirby 2014). The inscription on the Rosetta Stone, a decree of 196 BC by a council of priests, was in hieroglyphic and demotic Egyptian and also in Greek, and provided the key to decipherment of the hieroglyphs by Jean-François Champollion.[2]

Why does one need a book on multilingual law? If multilingualism is so ancient, there seems little to say. It is just a matter of translation and little more, surely? Maybe; but the reality of modern life is that there is an intensification of proximity in every direction. We travel more often abroad. We have the Internet, which allows us to consult and communicate round the world instantly. We have immigration and emigration and movement of goods, services and capital throughout the European Union and the world. We are told that climate and weather patterns are changing in disadvantageous ways. The social, economic and political consequences of all these circumstances need to be managed and organised somehow. This is done in part through making rules in the form of laws and these are made using language. People need to be employed, paid and told what to do – in a language they can understand. People speak different languages and come from different cultures, so organising everything requires taking that into account. Is single language use preferable, as a lingua franca, or many languages, and if so how many and which ones? Is every language suitable and adapted for the purposes of law with respect to any matter? If not, why not and how could it be made suitable? How does one produce complex legal texts in different languages? How does one decide on such matters? What are the methods?

These questions raise deep issues and they are charged with emotion and identity. Yet they are important and urgent because technological and environmental factors are forcing the pace of international, intercultural and interlingual cooperation. Industrialisation, trade, urbanisation, population growth and movement are taking place in a context where the climate is changing, weather patterns are changing, water resources are becoming a source of pressure and there is an ever-growing need for closer international cooperation to tackle a multitude of problems. That implies methods of negotiation, shared rule-making and acting in coordination. These processes cut across cultures, legal systems and languages. Making rules in many languages is not new, but understanding the processes involved is acquiring an unprecedented urgency.

The concept of multilingual law provides a starting point for organising and structuring information we already have about law and language. We can try and shape what we know, bring it together and make a picture to help more of us to see how different parts fit together and to actively plan for further cooperation and coordination across languages and cultures. Exploring the concept allows us to reflect in a structured way and to make informed choices. It draws on the knowledge of specialists in different fields and opens doors to information-sharing across cultures. It is a living field and it is undergoing constant change. This book draws on many specialist strands and brings them together. The unifying and organising factor is the concept of multilingual law. The objective is to create a picture of the different strands and how they fit together in a legal-linguistic way, that is to say drawing on concepts from law and linguistics. Each of the fields is introduced successively in as non-technical language as possible and gradually an overview is built up. The picture, or overview, is presented in lists of topics as a 'framework'. The picture is a linguistic image. It is in the mind, like law, and is a legal-linguistic image.

The main difficulty encountered is that study of the concept of multilingual law embraces many disciplines: law, languages, language theory, translation and terminology, to mention only the main ones. Each of these involves different specialist knowledge, and it is difficult to bring them together under one roof. We can use the theory of signs, semiotics, as a tool to that end, but doing so involves adding yet another discipline to the study. A full picture should also take into account back-up and support arrangements such as computerisation and training. So a rather large number of technical fields soon impose themselves for attention. That makes things difficult to describe and explain. Lawyers generally work in their own, usually single, language and are not often called on to deal with issues which involve other languages. Linguists, on the other hand, generally lack training in law. Terminology work is specialised and relatively few people have knowledge about it. There are demarcations between specialist activities that are difficult to overcome.

Modern research in linguistics, in particular applied linguistics, has been moving steadily into the study of language used for special purposes (LSP). It differs from general language (language for general purposes: LGP) in various ways, most notably in the use of technical forms of language connected to particular jobs and professions (Swales 1992). Legal language is one of the fields of research of applied linguistics and LSP, and goes by the name of legal linguistics (Mattila 2006, 2013). By extension multilingual legal language comes within the scope of legal linguistics and LSP, since it implies a study of multilingual legal texts from a language point of view. Adopting an approach that draws on linguistic as well as legal knowledge and experience makes it possible to achieve new insights into both law and language for special purposes; this is the 'legal-linguistic' point of view, that of the lawyer-linguist. The concept of lawyer-linguist as such is to a certain extent a product of the 60 years of the European Community/Union and stems from the need to have specialised lawyers translating, revising and checking language versions of EU legislative and court texts to ensure as far as possible that each of them contains the same message (Šarčević and Robertson 2013).

Analysis and understanding are both made easier if it is possible to simplify and categorise into abstract groups. This implies proposing a series of models of legal systems, with different combinations of languages as variants. If a legal system falls within a given model, then it becomes less necessary to recount all the details of the system for comparison with other systems, since simply to indicate the model and variant could be enough to give a broad initial picture, subject to detailed analysis. This approach is introduced. It has a link with the theory of signs, semiotics, because a model stands for or represents something else, the real thing. These ideas will be raised in the course of the narrative. This book is offered as a journey of exploration, encountering phenomena and reflecting on what they involve and how they fit into the picture. The fruit of the journey is summarised in the appendices, and these in turn are starting points for further studies and researches into individual systems of law and language. This is semiosis, the making of new signs.

The rest of this chapter introduces the theme, provides background and explains how the subject matter is to be handled, together with inevitable limitations. Chapter 2 continues the introduction by setting out how the field of enquiry is to be structured and providing an outline of the chapters. Part I gives a broad introduction to serve as background and overview. Parts II to VII examine individual fields, disciplines and activities. Part VIII introduces the appendices which comprise the framework and reflects on their use and application. It concludes with some observations of a general nature.

Field of enquiry: multilingual law

The theme of this book is multilingual law. The focus of attention is on the concept as an abstract idea separate from, but reflected in, each and every multilingual system of law. There are many legal systems that function in more than one language. We can cite a few examples:

Belgium: three official languages (Dutch, French, German);[3]
Canada: two official federal languages (English and French);[4]
Ireland: two official languages (Irish and English);[5]
Switzerland: four official languages: (German, French, Italian, Romansh).[6]

However, the concept of multilingual law does not apply solely to states; it extends to international organisations and any forms of law-making in more than one language. Thus, for example, it embraces the United Nations with six official languages (Arabic,

Chinese, English, French, Russian, Spanish)[7] and the European Union currently with 24 languages (Bulgarian, Croatian, Czech, Danish, Dutch, English, Estonian, Finnish, French, German, Greek, Hungarian, Irish, Italian, Latvian, Lithuanian, Maltese, Polish, Portuguese, Romanian, Slovak, Slovene, Spanish and Swedish).[8]

International relations are conducted in languages chosen by the negotiating participants. They make agreements and contracts that bind themselves like laws, and these too form part of the picture. One could go further and include all forms of agreements and contracts between private individuals, commercial corporations and non-government bodies (NGOs) and organisations, but it is preferable to draw a line and reserve these for a separate study. There is also a formal reason to hold back on them. Private individuals, corporations and NGOs are generally subject to the rules of individual legal systems and act according to the rules created by those systems, including the rules on languages. Attention is placed in this book mainly at the system level and on the rules and methods of systems as a whole. Nonetheless, the concept of rule-making through contract does form part of the picture and needs to be addressed, notably in the international context.

Another way of expressing the foregoing is to say that attention here is principally on what lawyers refer to as 'public law', the field of law that addresses the exercise of public authority by governmental and public authorities, as opposed to 'private law', which is the field addressing individual people and their businesses. Public law addresses the exercise of public power by institutions connected directly with state power and the constitutional relationships of legislature, executive and judiciary, whereas the agreements of private persons and bodies are connected to the exercise of rights that are conferred by the system and remain governed by the system. That said, there seems no reason why the concepts and methods explored in this book may not also be applied to private contracts and arrangements. It is something to explore.[9]

Having identified some multilingual legal systems, should we not then dive into each of them and make analyses of their use of language in each of their languages? Indeed, one can do that, and it has to varying extents been done, since each system of law has its own specialist literature. But what do we study? Is it the whole system as expressed in each of the official languages, or is it the rules on languages, or both? Is it the subject matter contents of the rules of law, or the linguistic way in which the rules are expressed? Each system is different and uses language differently, as Mattila (2006, 2013) makes clear among others for legal Latin, German, French and English. Each system constitutes its own world of ideas, concepts, terms and culture. How can one handle such a vast array of information in a way that can give meaning from a multilingual perspective?

Put differently, how do we 'jump' from one system to another where everything may look and feel different, as well as be in a different language? What should be our points of reference? Can one say that one system is better or preferable? What are the criteria for selection? If one wishes to be objective and non-partisan, one needs to search for criteria that transcend each and every system. They materialise at a deeper level within the structure of systems, and then we can explore how the different deeper forms are shaped and adapted at the surface level in accordance with local factors. Are there constant or universal strands? One can explore and test and see what emerges. What started out as the exploration of a concept seems to ripple out in all directions.

A preliminary question is whether the subject is not already well covered in the literature. At the time of writing there is indeed extensive literature on multilingualism in the law,[10] but the problem is that it is specialised and not always easily comprehended by the non-specialist reader. That hinders a wider function. There appears to be no single source that exposes in relatively simple words, accessible to non-specialists, the different activities and issues that underpin the concept of multilingual law. For a person working, for example, as a legal-linguistic expert in EU law and language, this has been a handicap. There is a wealth of information on particular legal aspects of particular systems and on particular linguistic forms and methods, but as yet there seems to be no overall legal-linguistic map to structure and organise this knowledge in a way that is accessible to the layperson. This book addresses the gap.

One can perhaps see two different but linked needs: first, the search for a theoretical overview, and second, developing practical guidance for everyday multilingual work. The words 'framework for analysis and understanding' in the title serve to emphasise this double requirement. A framework can be utilised as a source of questions to ask of legal systems and legal language from a research point of view, but it can also be used for practical purposes in training future practitioners in the field, or for the formation of language policy by administrators. The important thing, it is suggested, is to create for oneself one's own mental image and then to build on it and enlarge on it as new items are added. It is like learning a language, or learning law. Indeed, it is both, and it is also a prerequisite for management and administration of multilingual legal systems. Let us now start to think about how to construct a mental image for a framework for the concept of multilingual law.

The juxtaposition of the words 'multilingual' and 'law' in the concept suggests an examination of legal and linguistic ideas. Law and language are both large and complex fields of knowledge. Yet without embracing them, it seems impossible to make any progress. Both involve specialist knowledge: knowledge of law, legal theory, legal systems and legal practice, on the one hand, and knowledge of language, linguistic theories, languages and modes of language applied to legal purposes. That is all rather daunting, and it is precisely a reason for progressing slowly and cautiously. First, one has to learn the basic concepts and ideas that are embedded within legal systems, then one has to learn the basic concepts and ideas that lie within linguistics. Third, one has to learn the ideas, concepts and approaches that make legal systems function linguistically, first in one language and then in many languages. A step-by-step gradual progression is thus called for and the way in which that is done in this book can already be seen from a glance at the sequence of the chapters and themes set out in the list of contents.

The culture of multilingual law is interdisciplinary, combining the knowledge of lawyers and linguists and in particular that of specialists such as translators, language interpreters, legal drafters, judges and academic researchers on law and language. Yet one must not forget that law exists to serve society at large and all citizens are involved in one way or another, and there are experts, administrators and politicians to give structure, guidance and direction to all the diverse facets of a legal, economic and political culture. Their interests must also be borne in mind. This diversity makes it difficult to decide how to pitch the level of discourse: whether more technical to match the discourse of subject matter experts, or more general for the lay reader. Subject matter experts in one discipline are often lay persons in another. That suggests a broader and less dense approach, with an emphasis on developing an area of 'shared understanding'. In turn it implies the need to explain concepts and to show how they are used in multilingual systems of law. It also implies a minimal reliance on assumed knowledge. The method runs the risk of error from over-simplification, but it has the advantage of creating a common space of shared knowledge between diverse specialists and providing a basis for future refinement and fine-tuning. Thus, experts for each field will scan

8 *Introduction*

the text for accuracy in their discipline and, it is hoped, draw attention to errors and infelicities that may inadvertently arise; for the author is not a subject matter expert in every discipline covered, despite best endeavours.

With the foregoing words in mind, we will move on to introduce some general ideas about multilingualism in legal systems and start to develop some conceptual tools. When exploring a new topic it is often simplest to start with the widest possible view and gradually progress towards finer details. With that in mind, we will begin with some background realities about multilingualism and the number of languages in the world. Later we will consider who speaks them and for what purposes, and which languages are used for the purposes of the law, government and officialdom. Some languages are used for legal purposes and others are not. We may wonder why there are differences in use and status between languages. It is an important question, but it is not pursued here, except indirectly, as the answers involve politics, economics, sociology, history and so on, as documented in the literature relating to individual languages and the countries in which they are spoken. The emphasis in this book is technical, structural and conceptual, taking a look at things as they are, or appear to be, without enquiring particularly *why* they may be like that, although reasons may emerge incidentally. The aim is primarily descriptive and not prescriptive. While the underlying stance is broadly in favour of multilingualism in the law as befits the theme, it is not intended to proselytise for any particular law/languages combination. Each context is different and choices are made according to local circumstances. The viewpoint is neutral. With those preliminary comments, let us move on and ask: How many languages are there in the world?

Multilingual world

How many languages are there in the world? An estimate of 7,102 living languages in 2015 is given by Ethnologue,[11] broken down by area of origin as follows:

Africa	2,138 languages
Americas	1,064 languages
Asia	2,301 languages
Europe	286 languages
Pacific	1,313 languages

(Lewis *et al.* 2015)[12]

Extinct languages and languages used only as a second language are excluded. The criterion for inclusion is that each language has at least one speaker for whom it is their first language. A language is counted only once by its area of origin. Ethnologue provides information about each language: its three-letter ISO (International Organization for Standardization) code,[13] alternate names, population, location, language maps, language status, classification, dialects, typology, language use, language development, language resources, writing and other comments (Lewis *et al.* 2015).

Other sources of information exist which provide information regarding world languages. Ethnologue covers only living languages. The *Dictionary of Languages* (Dalby 2004) gives a description of over 400 languages, both living and dead. The *Dictionnaire des Langues* (Bonvini *et al.* 2011) provides a wealth of information of past and present world languages placed in a historical and language-family context, together with information on specific linguistic features. *The Atlas of the World's Languages* (Asher and Moseley 2007) gives visual information in the form of maps on the distribution of languages around the world. These are a few examples.

It seems there are still undiscovered languages in parts of the world, and the number of languages listed by Ethnologue each year seems to increase for some regions, while diminishing for others. The work of describing and analysing languages goes on steadily and every so often the discovery of a new language catches attention. Yet in part the number of languages depends on what one regards as a language as opposed to a dialect of a language. What is the difference between a language and a dialect? Oxford Dictionaries online says that a language is 'a system of communication used by a particular country or community'[14] and a dialect is 'a particular form of a language which is peculiar to a specific region or social group.'[15] A language is a broad system of grammar, spelling and words used to communicate with another person. English, French and German are languages. Dialects are subsets of a language.

At times the borderline can seem almost arbitrary and linked to politics, economics and social dynamics. Danish, Norwegian and Swedish are closely related and mutually understandable, but each is a language and not a dialect. Scots language is regarded by some as a dialect of English, but it is included by Ethnologue in its list of world languages with a note that it is most similar to English and Frisian (Lewis *et al.* 2015) and it has been recognised as a language by the UK for the purposes of the European Charter for Regional or Minority Languages (1992).

Whatever the exact number of languages, it is clear that it is huge. It also seems to be clear that many of them are threatened with extinction through language death. This happens when the speakers die out, or they switch to other languages. This process is described by Crystal (2014). Language change has been a constant feature of human civilisations, and Ostler (2005) gives a vivid picture of how this has happened over the past millennia in all the continents of the world. He incidentally shows how linguistics comes to the support of historical and archaeological research, when for example he speculates on why, against linguistic expectations, Germanic languages took precedence in Britain after the Roman army left in the fifth century AD: the indigenous population may have been decimated by plague in the sixth century (Ostler 2005: 313). This event is relevant to modern times as the descendant language English has spread to play a major role in international discourse today. A significant part of modern legal translation is from English and it is one of the key languages in modern multilingualism, being seen as a lingua franca, that is to say a 'language that is adopted as a common language between speakers whose native languages are different.'[16] This role of English is a recent phenomenon. One can trace back though time other languages which have performed a similar role as lingua franca. Ostler lists the following: Akkadian, Arabic, Aramaic, 'Atlantic Celtic', Chinese, English, Italian, French, Greek, Latin, Malay, Nahuatl, Pali, Persian, Phoenician, Portuguese, Russian, Sanskrit, Sogdian, Swahili, and Turkic (Ostler 2005: 604). It is important to see the role of a lingua franca not as a displacer of other languages but rather as a supplement and an additional means of communication internationally. It can be seen as a strand in the pattern of multiculturalism; it can enhance and support it. However, it can also undermine smaller languages.

Let us now indulge in an arbitrary exercise. Suppose the 7,102 languages listed in Ethnologue were spread evenly between countries around the world; if one takes, for example, the 193 member states of the United Nations plus 2 observer states as a reference,[17] that would give 195 states and just over 36 languages per state, regardless of size.

The exercise is fanciful and erroneous because some countries have fewer and others far more languages, and languages spread over borders, but it serves to emphasise the scale of linguistic variety. Suppose each of us had to master 36 languages? The first step towards analysing multilingualism in the law is to embrace consciously the reality of linguistic plurality. This is the psychological dimension.

Let us explore further why the foregoing exercise is erroneous. First, not every territory in the world is a state that is a member of the United Nations. There are countries, independent nation states and dependent territories, which are not members of the UN.[18] Second, languages are not spread evenly round the world; for evidence of that we can consult the *Atlas of the World's Languages* (Asher and Moseley 2007) or Ethnologue (Lewis *et al.* 2015). So some countries must manage many languages and others few languages. However, what is the status of each language in each country? Does it matter that some of the languages are spoken by ethnically indigenous people and others by recent immigrants? If we bear in mind trends in migration, even for countries with a small range of languages, one cannot always be sure that there are no immigrants speaking languages which have not been noted in the official statistics.[19] Within the EU there is a policy of freedom of movement across borders for EU citizens (Article 45 of the Treaty on the functioning of the European Union (TFEU)). Thus in each EU member state there may be speakers of any EU language present.

Another factor is to take into account languages learned as second or third languages by children and adults as part of their education.[20] Indeed, part of the complexity of multilingualism is that there are many people in the world who are polyglot. They may speak two, three or many more languages. That raises the question of whether to include second and third language speakers within the statistics on language size, with evident implications for the results. Multiple language knowledge raises the question of the overlapping of language territories. Some language territories are larger and others smaller. Larger languages tend to be used by several states and their legal systems, but smaller languages can also cross frontiers. Ethnologue includes information on the number of speakers of the languages listed, and also regarding their use as first or second languages. It also notes where languages are spoken in more than one country. It includes a table[21] of the world's largest languages according to numbers of speakers, the first dozen of which are as follows:

Language	*Number of speakers*
Chinese	1,197 million
(Mandarin	848 million)
Spanish	399 million
English	335 million
Hindi	260 million
Arabic	242 million
Portuguese	203 million
Bengali	189 million
Russian	166 million
Japanese	128 million
Lahnda	88.7 million
Javanese	84.3 million
German	78.1 million

(Lewis *et al.* 2015)

Of those, the following languages are spoken in more than one country. We can take them in the same order as above:

Language	Number of countries
Chinese	33
(Mandarin	12)
Spanish	31
English	101
Hindi	4
Arabic	60
Portuguese	12
Bengali	4
Russian	16
Japanese	2
German	18

(Lewis *et al.* 2015)

French is placed fourteenth in terms of speakers with 75.9 million in 51 countries (Lewis *et al.* 2015). Other sources of information provide different numbers and sizes.[22] One should therefore probably treat such statistics with caution, but they do nonetheless present a general picture, which is sufficient for the present purpose. The world is highly multilingual; many languages are spoken in many countries, and languages are spread across political frontiers and shared by speakers living in different countries. Within most languages there are also dialects; sometimes these can be understood widely, and sometimes not, as visitors to different parts of the UK will no doubt have found out when confronted with regional variations in words, speech forms and accents.[23]

The evidence does seem to point in the direction of widespread multilingualism in some form or other throughout the world. How does this circumstance impact on law and legal language? The answer broadly depends on how each language is treated by the relevant legal system, whether used as an official language, not used and left to its own fate, or actively repressed. Within those categories there are gradations that can be marked out. Broadly, when a language has status as an official language that means that it is used by organs of the state for legal purposes; it is a language of the law and is used to express legal language. As such it enters into the scope of the present study. It may be a 'big' language spoken by millions of people or a 'small' language spoken by just a few thousand or even a few hundred or even fewer. What matters is not the number of speakers but the status of the language; it is used for purposes of the state, whether law, administration or education. However, we are interested here in multilingual law; there must be more than one single official language in a given territory in order to invoke the concept of multilingual law.

Defining multilingual law

What is 'multilingual law'? How should we define it? What does it entail? Let us start with some examples. When a state enacts a law in the form of a legislative text in two parallel language versions – for example one version in English and one in French,

12 *Introduction*

as in Canada for a federal law, as set out in the Official Languages Act 1985 – then one can say that they are part of a two-language, or bilingual, legal system. In such a system laws are made in duplicate, with a version in each language, and the citizen is free to decide which language version to use. However, the implication is that both versions carry the same message and have the same consequences, because otherwise citizens who use language version A may be in a better or worse position than citizens who use language version B. How can one make 'identical' texts in two or more languages? We have here a fundamental issue for any multilingual system of law, and different strategies are adopted with respect to it. But is it always necessary for every law to be duplicated in each language? And what about private disputes and cases brought before courts? Must they be conducted in two languages, and if only one language, how does one know which one is to be used? What about contracts? These are all areas to explore.

A state may choose to recognise three official languages. For example, Article 2 of the Belgian Constitution states:

> La Belgique comprend trois communautés: la Communauté française, la Communauté flamande et la Communauté germanophone. / België omvat drie gemeenschappen: de Vlaamse Gemeenschap, de Franse Gemeenschap en de Duitstalige Gemeenschap. / Belgien umfaßt drei Gemeinschaften: die Deutschsprachige Gemeinschaft, die Flämische Gemeinschaft und die Französische Gemeinschaft.[24]

In the case of Switzerland, Article 4 of the Federal Constitution of the Swiss Confederation states:

> Die Landessprachen sind Deutsch, Französisch, Italienisch und Rätoromanisch. / Les langues nationales sont l'allemand, le français, l'italien et le romanche. / Le lingue nazionali sono il tedesco, il francese, l'italiano e il romancio. / Las linguas naziunalas èn il tudestg, il franzos, il talian ed il rumantsch.[25]

There is no obvious logical upper limit to the number of languages that may be used in a legal system. Section 6(1) of the Constitution of the Republic of South Africa 1996 states:

> The official languages of the Republic are Sepedi, Sesotho, Setswana, siSwati, Tshivenda, Xitsonga, Afrikaans, English, isiNdebele, isiXhosa and isiZulu.[26]

The same Section goes on in subsection (3)(a) to state:

> The national government and provincial governments may use any particular official languages for the purposes of government, taking into account usage, practicality, expense, regional circumstances and the balance of the needs and preferences of the population as a whole or in the province concerned; but the national government and each provincial government must use at least two official languages.

A greater number of languages is also possible. The European Union, a supranational regional organisation, currently works in 24 official languages. The foundation provision is set out not in a constitution, as with a state, but in a treaty negotiated between the Member States and amended each time a new state joins and brings a new language with it. Article 342 TFEU states:

> The rules governing the languages of the institutions of the Union shall, without prejudice to the provisions contained in the Statute of the Court of Justice of the European Union, be determined by the Council, acting unanimously by means of regulations.

This provision is implemented by Regulation No. 1 determining the languages to be used by the European Economic Community as amended by the addition of new languages following accessions. Article 1 (as amended) lists the 'official languages and the working languages of the institutions of the European Union.'[27] The treaty texts and laws created by the EU institutions are drawn up in those languages[28] and published in the Official Journal of the European Union online[29] and in paper format. Any language version may be consulted and in principle the same information is to be found in the same location at the same page number in each language version of the edition. This is the 'synoptic approach'.

While there is no upper limit to the number of languages for a multilingual legal system, is there a lower limit? This raises the question of what we mean by 'multilingual'. It becomes an issue of definition: does 'multi-' include two as well as three or more? It evidently excludes a single-language, monolingual, legal system. What about two languages? There is nothing to be gained by excluding bilingual legal systems from the scope of the study, and a lot to be gained by including them, since countries such as Canada have extensive experience in bilingualism through making laws in more than one language and this is a major source of guidance and advice. So it is proposed to 'stretch' the definition and include 'two' within 'multi', for pragmatic reasons. By adopting this comprehensive approach and including 'two' within the concept of 'many', we can then define multilingual law simply as *law expressed in two or more languages*. That introduces the central opposition, or contrast, against legal systems expressed in a single language (monolingual).

So, in principle, monolingual legal systems are excluded from the present scope. However, there are reasons for not excluding them altogether: first, they provide the base system against which multilingual legal systems can be contrasted and compared; making comparisons renders the diverging features of multilingual systems more apparent. Second, if one thinks in terms of law/language models, the one-language model is the simplest type of legal-linguistic model; it can be used to explore basic themes and then complexity can be added through adding languages to the model. Third, one of the reasons for adopting a multilingual legal system is where the national territory is inhabited by people speaking different languages and many of them are monolingual in one of those languages. Multilingual law enables them to manage their legal and administrative affairs effectively within a single-language environment if they so wish. Thus a multilingual legal system serves, among other things, to allow people to live as if the legal system was monolingual and to use 'their own language' whenever they wish. This paradox within multilingual law means that the context of the single-language legal system also needs to be addressed, since multilingual law can be seen in terms of monolingual systems running side by side but bound together in legal and semantic unity.

The third and last-mentioned factor provides a reason for creating a multilingual system of law, on the view that different languages are spoken in the community and

14 *Introduction*

everyone is entitled to equal treatment before the law; this includes language equality and the right to have access to the law in a language one understands.[30] There are several levels to this: first, a level of fact, linked to the languages spoken in the population; second, a level of law and morality, linked to principles of justice and equal access to law, being able to know one's rights and obligations and being in a position to secure them; third, a level linked to participation in the economic and political activities of the country. Ensuring different language communities participate fully in the life of a community creates opportunities and confidence, which in turn encourages and stimulates commitment to institutions, structures and systems, thereby leading to material well-being through stability and reliability. In a word: it's good for business. However, in each case the precise balance and choices are a function of national circumstances and no opinion is expressed on such matters here.

We have now arrived at the paradoxical conclusion that a study of multilingual law embraces all types of law and legal system in whatever number of languages. Yet even a pure monolingual system is not immune from a multilingual element. There are foreign elements such as evidence in foreign languages required by courts, as well as witnesses or accused persons who do not speak the national language, and so on. Nonetheless, the primary focus remains on multilingual legal systems. What then is the object of the enquiry? What are we looking for and how do we organise and structure the information? It is necessary to restate these questions because we find ourselves having to take into account all types of legal system and any number of combinations of languages. At this juncture we are searching for methods and techniques to open the field of multilingual law to a broad-based conceptual enquiry. We are on the edge of hyper-complex realities and risk losing our bearings in the face of a mass of details. It is here that the concept of 'framework' comes to hand. It is impossible to describe everything in every legal system, but one can identify certain key features of multilingual legal systems and use them to construct our framework, which is then available as a point of reference for analysis, understanding and comparison of different systems.

For the present, if we accept the idea of multiplicity, represented by the prefix 'multi' in 'multilingual', we can move on to the aspects of 'language' and 'law' which are also present in the concept of 'multilingual law'. This in turn leads us to think of a field of enquiry with two dimensions: linguistic and legal. We can imagine two centres of focus in a combined field. Metaphorically, we can envisage an ellipse with two foci, or a coin with two sides, or a double-yoked egg (Robertson 2001, 2009) – two points of reference indissolubly connected to each other, but which each generate a different way of looking at the same information. We can refer to this way of looking as a 'viewpoint', a concept derived from Ferdinand de Saussure, who was a founder of the study of signs, semiotics (Saussure 2005). We will reflect on that in more detail in Chapter 8.

How far are these metaphors of ellipse, coin or egg accurate? They imply a fusion of the fields of law and language, yet language is used in many domains unrelated to law, for example in science, medicine, politics, art, culture and so on, extending far beyond legal usage. Legal language is just one area of language use, an area or field of applied language, albeit a highly specialised one. On the other hand, is all law related to language? Is law solely a linguistic phenomenon or does it extend beyond language? Law uses language as a tool for its ends. Legal texts, whether contracts, legislation or court decisions, are made manifest through written language. Discussions between judge and lawyer in court or between lawyer and client are forms of oral legal discourse conducted through language. But is that all? What about the clothes worn by lawyers in court?

Judges wear special robes and these have meaning and significance (connected to status and power) which do not involve language. Gestures convey legal meaning, as when traffic is directed by a police officer. Traffic lights and road signs also convey legal meanings for road-users. These go beyond language, so there is an extra-lingual dimension, but the meaning of gestures and signs is nonetheless generally laid down in a written text, so that one does not 'escape' entirely from language.

On another level, when lawyers think about law and legal problems, do they have thoughts and ideas which in some way 'precede' their communication through language? And if so, what is the nature of these thoughts? Do lawyers form a 'picture' of the legal system and individual laws in their minds? Is it an image of interconnections? Is it like a mathematical image? Is it a visual memory of texts and cases? It need not be the same for everyone. We need not concern ourselves with these questions here, but we need to bear in mind that lawyers from different languages, systems and cultures tend to have different images, networks and concepts in their minds and these differences come to the surface in the multilingual legal environment when making laws and when interpreting and applying them.

While law uses language as its principal tool for communication, it also uses other methods. That should be borne in mind throughout because it implies that there is not an absolute identity between law and language. In the multilingual context it may sometimes be useful to 'bypass' language through the use of non-linguistic symbols and images. We see this in the supermarket with special diagrams on products that indicate toxicity if swallowed or adherence to an 'organic' method of production. Nonetheless, since this book addresses multi*lingual* law, the focus will be on the areas in which there is an overlap between law and language. Following up the idea of two foci which lead to different viewpoints, which should one take first, and why?

Law and language: two complex fields

We can start with a linguistic observation: the term 'multilingual law' has 'law' as the noun/substantive element and 'multilingual' as the adjective/qualifying element, but the whole term is a composite expression. In searching for an organising principle, we could build on this grammatical observation and take 'law' as the primary context and language as the ancillary context. On this view language is a means for creating and furthering law. However, we should also ask the contradicting question, whether law is a means for creating language. The answer here is relevant to multilingual law because, while language seems to be innate to human beings and so is not as such 'created' by law, it is the case that law can make rules about language use – for example, by regulating the alphabet to be used, the spelling conventions for words, grammatical forms, and so on. The fact that the English language is not overtly subject to such formal rules does not mean they do not exist, as they can also arise by custom and usage and become intrinsically linked to meanings constructed by courts. Further, law can make rules about which languages – let us call them 'language codes' – are to be used (or not used). In that connection, we noted above the linguistic regimes (rules on languages) for Belgium, Switzerland, South Africa and the EU, without entering into details.

There is, however, another factor that must be mentioned at the outset, which is that the terms 'law' and 'language' are both polysemic, having more than one meaning. The term 'language' can cover language in general or a specific language code such as English, French or Italian. We have a similar problem with 'law', where the term can

16 *Introduction*

apply to law in general or a specific act called a 'law'. This phenomenon is not restricted to English. To take this a stage further, let us look at some dictionary definitions, first of 'law' and then of 'language'.

The online Oxford Dictionaries[31] give four classes of definition for the term 'law' as a noun. The first class refers to the 'system of rules which a particular country or community recognizes as regulating the actions of its members and which it may enforce by the imposition of penalties'. Within this class there is first the 'individual rule as part of a system of law', second, the 'systems of law as a subject of study or as the basis of the legal profession', third, 'statute law and the common law', fourth, 'something regarded as having binding force or effect', and fifth, an informal reference to the police. The second class is connected to sport as 'a rule defining correct procedure or behaviour in a sport'. The third class involves a 'statement of fact, deduced from observation, to the effect that a particular natural or scientific phenomenon always occurs if certain conditions are present' or a 'generalization based on a fact or event perceived to be recurrent'. The fourth class is connected to religion and refers to the 'body of divine commandments as expressed in the Bible or other religious texts', more specifically the Pentateuch.

The first class of definition is the broadest and most of the variants are included in this book, except the informal usage as a synonym for the police. The second class of definitions is connected with games and is not followed up here. The third class is connected to science, for example physics and chemistry. It is not followed up here as such, but scientific laws are mentioned in Chapter 3 when dipping into some philosophy of law. The fourth class of definition is also not followed up here, but it raises an important cultural point. Behind legal systems and legal ideas and concepts there tends to lie a deeper dimension linked to religion, philosophy, ethics and how societies relate to the natural environment in which they live. The European tradition is predominantly Judaeo-Christian. Other parts of the World have a different culture centred on Buddhism, Hinduism, Islam, Shintoism to name just four religions.[32] The concepts and ideas in each religion carry through into the legal systems and into legal language. Where a country has populations who embrace different religions as well as different languages, there is a multicultural as well as a multilingual dimension to cope with. One of the most complex situations to contend with is where there is a crossover of languages, religions and cultures within a single legal environment. It is an issue of daily reality for non-European countries which have taken over a European-derived legal system, whether common law or civil law, alongside more ancient indigenous methods of law. It is also a daily reality for negotiating international agreements between states with different cultural and religious traditions.

Let us now turn to definitions of 'language' as a noun from the same online Oxford Dictionaries.[33] Here we find three classes of definition. The first class concerns the 'method of human communication, either spoken or written, consisting of the use of words in a structured and conventional way', including 'a non-verbal method of expression or communication'. The second class refers to 'a system of communication used by a particular country or community'. Computing language is included as 'a system of symbols and rules for writing programs or algorithms'. The third class relates to 'the style of a piece of writing or speech' and includes 'the phraseology and vocabulary of a particular profession, domain, or group' such as legal language. It also includes bad, foul, or strong language such as 'coarse or offensive language'.

The first class of definition will be retained while excluding non-verbal methods of expression or communication (although these may have legal effects). The second definition raises the idea of language as a code, which is useful because it makes us think about what goes to make up a code and takes us into the study of languages and linguistics. The third definition is interesting as it refers to 'style'; legal texts are written according to a particular style or register in terms of degrees of formality or informality, prose as opposed to poetry, third person as opposed to second or first person, and the simplicity or complexity of the sentences. This third class of definition broadly covers the linguistic features of written and oral language. The three definitions thus point towards three linguistic levels which are directly relevant to multilingual law: first there is communication of information through language; second, there is the specific language code; third, we have pieces of writing and oral speech (written and oral utterances); fourth, we have the linguistic features of these utterances. We will here leave in the background computer language and 'bad' language. Sign language is another form of language, but we will also leave that in the background, even though it is one of the official languages of New Zealand, alongside English and Maori.[34]

We can now start to link up the law and language dimensions; for example, a 'law' is a piece of writing that uses the language of a language code and exhibits linguistic features. In a multilingual legal system one has a 'law' reproduced in a plurality of language codes, each of which exhibits linguistic features. Are those linguistic features similar or different? In order to answer such a question, one needs to have knowledge about languages, but also about law, types of legal system and the sort of problems that law addresses, as well as the ways in which it addresses them. One also needs to think in terms of communicating messages through language and the effects of the messages. In brief, one needs an introduction to legal theory and linguistic theory. One also needs to understand the ways in which information is transferred across languages through translation and oral interpretation.[35] It is clearly impossible to provide detailed expositions of all these fields, but one can nonetheless seek to sketch out some principal themes that are of particular relevance to the concept of multilingual law. These themes can be used to construct a conceptual framework.

The chapters in this book take us through some of the key themes in multilingual law. First there is an exploration of basic ideas and concepts so as to ensure a minimum level of knowledge, and then the ideas are gradually developed and refined through the addition of further information. To that end an approach based on 'viewpoints' is adopted as it provides a method to accommodate different tasks and actions that arise in respect of legal texts. Broadly, we will take a legal viewpoint and then a linguistic viewpoint. We will ask questions about the nature of law, legal systems and legal acts and we will also ask questions about the nature of language, the branches of linguistics and the linguistic nature of legal acts. We will also consider what it means for a language to be a legal language and we will reflect on how legal texts are drafted, translated and interpreted. Each time we will think about the monolingual dimension first and then add a multilingual dimension. As we proceed, other topics will come to the surface; multilingual law is a 'hedgehog' of prickly little points that have to be resolved. We cannot mention them all, but we can mention many. The appendices add to, and go beyond, the discussion in the chapters. They are concise, technical, open-ended and intended to encourage and stimulate further studies in the field.

Multilingual law is a shared interdisciplinary field and knowledge from one specialism joins with knowledge from other specialisms to lead to a combined approach and viewpoint. There is an overlap between legal and linguistic knowledge and we can refer to this combined viewpoint as 'legal-linguistic'. The aim throughout the chapters

18 Introduction

is to progress towards the legal-linguistic framework for multilingual law set out in Appendix VIII. The first task is to ask whether it is possible to build 'simplifications' or identify repeating patterns that can be handled as a class, where the members of the class have similar characteristics, rather like models.

Summary

This chapter has opened the enquiry into multilingual law. It has set the scene, explained that multilingualism is widespread in the world, considered the numbers of languages in the world and noted there are many multilingual legal systems. The concept of 'multilingual law' has not been sufficiently explored and there is an absence of guidance materials on it. This book aims to fill that gap. It does so by taking the concept of 'multilingual law' and defining it as law expressed in two or more languages. However, the multilingual law paradox is that such systems aim to allow speakers to act monolingually in law, and it implies including monolingual systems as the 'simplest' basic model. The chapters in this book explore different themes with an aim of introducing concepts and basic information. Appendices set out additional technical summaries. Appendix VIII contains the framework, but it is supplemented by the preceding appendices. The appendices are directed towards specialist practice. They can be taken as starting points for making legal-linguistic analyses, or linguistic profiling, of systems of law in any number of languages, as well as other forms of research. The next step is to see whether one can make legal-linguistic models as a means to simplify the complexities and facilitate analysis and understanding.

Notes

1. See the Introductions to the Old and New Testaments in The New English Bible (1970). MacCulloch (2010) provides extensive contextual information.
2. See, among others, http://discoveringegypt.com/egyptian-video-documentaries/mystery-of-the-rosetta-stone/.
3. Article 2 of the Belgian Constitution.
4. Official Languages Act 1985 as amended.
5. Article 8 of the Constitution of Ireland.
6. Articles 4 and 70 of the Federal Constitution of the Swiss Federation.
7. See for example Article 51 of the Rules of Procedure of the General Assembly of the United Nations.
8. Regulation No 1 determining the languages to be used by the European Economic Community as amended.
9. Business contracts in English in Indonesia have been held invalid; see *English Language Contract Deemed Void by Indonesian Court* (2013). [Online]. Available at: www.out-law.com/articles/2013/november/english-language-contract-deemed-void-by-indonesian-court/; *Court Nullifies an Agreement due to Breach of Language Law* (2013). [Online]. Available at: www.legal500.com/c/indonesia/developments/24183.
10. See for example Peruginelli (no date) and the references listed therein.
11. The Ethnologue website at www.ethnologue.com is constantly updated and its information regularly published in book form.
12. In 2013 the figures were: Africa 2,146, Americas 1,060, Asia 2,304, Europe 284 and Pacific 1,311 languages respectively, with a total of 7,105, three more than in 2015.
13. Languages are represented by codes standardised internationally under ISO 639 and are two or three letters long. The EU uses two-letter codes.

14 See www.oxforddictionaries.com/definition/english/language.
15 See www.oxforddictionaries.com/definition/english/dialect?q=dialect.
16 See www.oxforddictionaries.com/definition/english/lingua-franca?q=lingua+franca.
17 See www.un.org/en/members/. Surprisingly, there seems to be uncertainty as to the total number of states in the world; see http://geography.about.com/cs/countries/a/numbercountries.htm.
18 See, for example, www.nationsonline.org/oneworld/territories.htm.
19 Information about languages may be included within periodic population censuses.
20 Luxembourg is an example of multiple-language speakers: the national languages are Luxembourgish, German and French, plus Portuguese and English.
21 See www.Ethnologue.com/statistics/size.
22 See, for example, http://listverse.com/2008/06/26/top-10-most-spoken-languages-in-the-world/.
23 See, among others, *An Atlas of English Dialects* (Upton and Widdowson 2006).
24 [Belgium comprises three communities: the Flemish Community, the French Community and the German-speaking Community]. Note that each language places itself in first position; when translating into English, one is forced to make a choice as to sequence. This situation is typical in legal translation and is frequently resolved by adopting some neutral formal approach, such as alphabetical order in the target language, as followed here.
25 [The National Languages are German, French, Italian, and Romansh.] Same order in each language here.
26 Act No. 108 of 1996. English text signed by the president.
27 Bulgarian, Croatian, Czech, Danish, Dutch, English, Estonian, Finnish, French, German, Greek, Hungarian, Irish, Italian, Latvian, Lithuanian, Maltese, Polish, Portuguese, Romanian, Slovak, Slovene, Spanish and Swedish.
28 Subject to any temporary derogations.
29 See http://eur-lex.europa.eu/oj/direct-access.html.
30 Linguistic rights are not addressed here directly, except in part in Chapters 5 and 7. See Universal Declaration on Linguistic Rights 1996, European Charter for Regional or Minority Languages 1992, individual national constitutions and laws and, among others, May (2011).
31 www.oxforddictionaries.com/definition/english/law.
32 Religion, philosophy, ethics and morality are kept in the background in this book.
33 www.oxforddictionaries.com/definition/english/language.
34 On New Zealand sign language, see Te Keti Ipurangi (2015).
35 The term 'interpretation' is used for translation of speech and also for extracting meaning from legal texts. To reduce confusion the expressions 'oral interpretation' and 'oral translation' will sometimes be used to distinguish from 'legal interpretation'.

2 Framework of models and an overview

Introduction

This chapter continues the introduction. Its purpose is to clear away some ground and set out a pragmatic method for making an enquiry into the different dimensions and fields of activity that come together to make a system of multilingual law function. The first step is to identify a conceptual structure around which to organise the study. Chapter 1 started the process. This chapter takes it further by proposing a series of conceptual models and then reviewing how to organise information through structuring the field of enquiry and fitting them around the models. In order to fully comprehend the models and be able to develop and extend them in their scope and variations, it is necessary to have extensive specialist knowledge of law and language. That is essential if one is to understand the framework and be able to apply, extend and develop it further. However, no specialist knowledge is assumed for the present study, and that means that it is necessary to introduce the fundamental concepts, describe and explain them, and endeavour to show how they fit together in the larger picture. Unfortunately, that implies a course on law and a course on language. Not only that, a knowledge of translation of legal texts also comes into the picture, since multilingual systems function in a multiplicity of languages. It is easy to become lost in the details, but if one can develop a simplified set of orientations in one's mind, things become clearer. The purpose of this chapter is to provide such a simplified overview. Subsequent chapters explore details. The Table of Contents at the start and Appendix VIII represent the structure and framework of the present enquiry. It is primarily conceptual. The author takes a range of elements from familiar systems, using the English language as means of communication, and the reader extends, applies and adapts them to systems with which they are familiar using their preferred language. That is how multilingual law functions. It means in practice that examples will be drawn from a narrower range of systems than one would ideally like, but it reduces confusion through seeking to embrace too many systems at the same time. We will start by introducing the concept of modelling that sets things in motion.

Legal-linguistic modelling

Law, legal systems, language and languages are all complex, so it assists if one can find ways to simplify matters. Complexity is commonplace in scientific research and one of the responses is to seek to make simplified representations through the development of models of whatever phenomenon is under examination. It assists in visualisation and further research, as well as in teaching and informing the general public. We can think of the periodic table for chemistry, models of DNA for genetics and the numerous mathematical formulae that have been devised over the centuries. Each of them provides a representation of reality. Making models makes it easier to ask and find answers for questions that arise. Once established and validated by analysis and experience, a model can subsequently be adapted and modified to take account of new information that comes to hand. Can one do something similar for law and multilingual legal systems? Can one make legal-linguistic models, and, if so, how? What might they look like?

We will start with some definitions of the term 'model' as a noun so as to be clear as to what is being aimed at. The online Oxford Dictionaries provide several definitions.[1] They include artistic models and product designs, but also a 'three-dimensional representation of a person or thing or of a proposed structure, typically on a smaller scale than the original' and a 'simplified description, especially a mathematical one, of a system or process, to assist calculations and predictions'. In them we see a reference to the words 'representation', 'smaller scale', 'system' and 'process'. Law contains both the latter two concepts, as we speak of a 'legal system' and of the 'due process of law'. We also see a reference to 'description'. Thus we are not searching for an explanation, but just a way to inform ourselves about certain elements as a description. This description is 'simplified', so we will not cover every nook and cranny, but seek broad representative themes. Lastly, the model may be mathematical. This is interesting as it suggests we can enter variables to see what effect they have on the model. Whether everything can be turned into mathematical formulae is left for mathematicians to advise on. Ferrara and Gaglioti (2012) make suggestions on mathematical modelling for the quantitive analysis of law and putting legal values into numbers. However, the intention here is to remain with language and to create models using language.

Frydman (2011) presents a series of models of law from the point of view of the history of legal interpretation in his book *Le Sens des Lois*. He refers to these as rhetorical, biblical, patristic, scholastic, geometric, philological, sociological and economic, linguistic and normative, and the pragmatic model of interpretation. These are historical contexts, linked to the development of legal culture in Europe. We are searching for simpler structural models that in some way represent modern realities. If we find variations in them, we wish to be able to adapt the models to fit. What are the possible variations and how might we express them in models?

Before proposing answers, we might add a semiotic note to the effect that a model stands for something else. We see that with the word 'representation' in the first definition mentioned above. A model is a 'sign' or 'token' that represents something. One advantage of a semiotic approach, that is to say an approached based on signs,[2] is that it places all information on the same level as an indicator of something else. Thus it matters not whether the sign points to legal information or linguistic or cultural information; there is no 'better', 'worse' or 'correct' interpretation but just what the sign represents, which implies thinking about the way in which the mind of the viewer of a sign reads and gives meaning to it. That could imply that models could be constructed taking any set of criteria one wished, but then they must be made to reflect reality. They are imagined for a purpose and to reveal certain types of information.

Applying these ideas to multilingual law implies the construction of models which create a simplified, abstract view of a complex world, and to that extent are 'scientific'. They should seek to depict structural elements, but also leave room for variable and subjective elements and conceptual constraints within multilingual law. Different relationships and conceptual views need to be explored. How does one construct these models? It is not possible to make a physical object like a mini Eiffel Tower, as law and language are abstract. Nor is it clear (at present) how to make mathematical models, as law is not generally constructed through maths. Pictorial images seem possible, but then it would seem to be a case of mental images in the form of ideas, patterns and connections created in the mind through words and phrases, since these are the tools of law and language. This seems nearest to what we are searching for, and we should perhaps bear in mind that we could potentially have to express our models in up to 7,000 languages if every language were to become a language of law.

Who are the models made for and what is their purpose? These questions feed into how they are made. It raises the question as to whom multilingual law is made for, as well as the participants and professionals who work in the field. Each of these has a viewpoint and a need. For example, there is the viewpoint of the lawyer and that of the linguist, but on closer inspection we also encounter different types of lawyer (advocate/barrister, notary, solicitor, judge, law drafter, law clerk), as well as different types of linguist (language researcher, linguistics theoretician, translator, lexicologist, terminologist, language teacher). For each specialism there are different viewpoints, for example an 'internal' viewpoint of the participant in a process and an 'external' viewpoint of the observer. In that respect, the lawyer is an external observer of language theory and the linguist is an external observer of legal theory. The legal-linguistic viewpoint implies having an internal view of both law and language, and that suggests that legal-linguistic modelling would call for an internal viewpoint for both domains. This in turn requires extensive information to establish a shared common 'insider' space extending to both law and language. It represents the internal viewpoint of the lawyer-linguist. On the other hand, since the law applies to everyone, including linguists and the general public, everyone can be said to have an 'internal' approach to it since they are bound by it. It is a question of degree of knowledge and familiarity with the underlying mechanisms and methods and being tasked with a legal activity.

Taking legal concepts and linguistic concepts, we can construct models. Should they be legal models of language or linguistic models of law? Multilingual law is about law in different languages and so the latter would seem apt here. If law is the primary element, then we need to identify different types of system of multilingual law first and then consider their linguistic variations. The most immediate linguistic variation concerns the linguistic regime and the number of languages. Thus we can create models of types of legal system against numbers of languages. It provides an outline structure within which to work, and one can add details to each basic model, study differences and adapt. As the models are intended to reflect reality, we search for real systems that fit within the description of the models, and adapt the models to what we find.

The appendices at the end of this book are connected to the concept of making models. Some of them aim at the macro-level and others at the micro-level connected to specific tasks and activities. In that respect, the latter come within a further definition of 'model' as a 'thing used as an example to follow or imitate'.[3] Each appendix is introduced in the chapter where first mentioned, and they are all summarised in Chapter 14. For the present, the first two appendices will be introduced. Appendix I serves as a token model. It is entitled 'States, languages and official languages' and sets out the idea of creating a table that lists all states with their spoken and written languages and official languages identified, together with legal sources and other information. At present such information is scattered in different sources. Ethnologue contains lists and, for example, the National Aeronautics and Space Administration (NASA) website includes a list of nations of the world and their languages listed by country and major languages.[4] The United Nations and individual country databases are other sources. The task of compiling a full appendix greatly exceeded available resources, and so it remains as a token entry. The purpose is to provide factual background for adapting and refining the models proposed in Appendix II.

Appendix II proposes legal-linguistic models. These underpin the framework concept. They are technical and imply specialist knowledge. This is imparted through the subsequent chapters, so that by the conclusion they should almost become self-evident. This appendix consists in ten models, arbitrarily allocated a letter. Each model represents a type of law, which can be a type of legal system, or a type of legal order. These are concepts to be explained. Each model is presented as a legal structure which may contain variations at different levels. These variations create individualised contexts for legal terminology and meanings. In this way the language dimension is built into the legal fabric. However, to take account of multilingualism, each model is subject to variants in terms of the number of official languages. These variants may arise at different levels within a system, so that a form of coding is introduced to reflect such differences. Behind the structure of Appendix II lies the concept of 'state', which also needs to be introduced. The models are at a high level of generality. They can be developed, refined and adapted according to different systems. However, they provide a broad method of categorizing systems for comparison purposes.

It is one thing to propose static models that represent a structural reality, and it is another thing to take account of the dynamic reality in terms of method that lies behind, and has generated, the models. Appendix II by itself does not address this dynamic dimension. For that, other appendices and models to follow are required. Since we are in specialised technical territory where no prior knowledge is assumed, it is necessary to provide descriptions of the underlying concepts and methods. That is the task of the subsequent chapters. But the immediate question facing us is, what is relevant? What does one need to know? How should the information be presented and in what order? In short, how to structure the enquiry.

Structuring the field of enquiry

The starting point was with law expressed in more than one language. To construct legal-linguistic models in Appendix II different types of legal system were identified, along with linguistic variations. We wish to reflect on the whole range of legal possibilities where multilingualism may arise. For that we need to understand some legal concepts. We are aware that law uses language as its main tool for communication. That implies that we need to think about the forms of language that law embraces, but also the nature of the documents in which language is used. How do such documents arise? What makes a document a legal document? What happens if one has legal documents in different languages? How are they made? How does one know whether the information in different language versions is the same or not? These are all questions that go to method and are a vital part of multilingual law. So they need to be addressed.

On the other hand, if law uses language as a tool, one needs to know something about the languages so used. What is language? What are all the dimensions of language that come together in a legal text? How is legal language different from other forms of language? How does one transfer information from one language to another? And so on. There are thus many questions that arise, and these are mostly questions of detail, often of a subtle nature. For example, how can one know whether two persons read and understand a text in the same way? What happens if each is reading a different language version and lives in a different region or country? This is multilingual reality and systems of multilingual law, as law generally, has developed methods for handling such questions. These will be explored in subsequent chapters.

Searching for a way to structure the field of enquiry, it is proposed to return to the starting point of conceiving multilingual law in terms of two points of focus. We need to build up knowledge of specialist concepts. We can start with concepts of law and then shift to concepts of language. In that way we equip ourselves with a minimum shared basis. Then we can look at how legal language functions and ways in which legal information is transferred across languages through oral interpretation and translation of written texts. We enter into specialist working environments, such as that of the European Union, so we can draw on pragmatic experience and illustrate problems faced and methods developed in response.

Different systems and languages view information differently. This is a constant feature of multilingual environments. In order to enter into this subtle and difficult-to-grasp context, it is useful to reflect on information in terms of signs and analyse the nature of signs. This involves an excursion into semiotics, but an understanding of semiotics facilitates the handling of legal concepts and terms, especially across languages and legal systems. It thus becomes an important entry point to the multilingual context.

Underpinning the approach to be followed is the concept of 'viewpoints' derived from Ferdinand de Saussure. Each topic is prefaced by a reflection on the range of viewpoints connected to it. These viewpoints are, in turn, linked to tasks, on the view that a task, or activity, creates a viewpoint which in turn creates a way of looking at reality and developing a philosophy connected to it. Perhaps it is an approach rooted in economics. The advantage of this approach is to shift emphasis from an abstract world of theory to that of the factory floor and production, where problems have to be solved and one needs to develop theoretical methods to that end. So, a practitioner-rooted viewpoint.

For each task or activity one can add those little 'wh?' questions which form part of discourse analysis (Paltridge 2006): what, when, which, why, where, who, but also how. Who are the persons who undertake it? What are the tasks? When are they undertaken? Which tasks? Why are they undertaken (or not)? Where do they take place? How are they done? With these questions we enter the workplace. Each is different. We cannot cover them all, but we can nonetheless explore a few themes. To obtain a clearer idea of this, let us now pass the chapters to come in brief review.

Overview of the chapters

The chapters have been organised under parts, each of which reflects a viewpoint linked to professional activity and function. The objective is to pass in review conceptual information necessary for a study of multilingual law and for the appendices. Chapter 1 and this chapter come within Part I as general introduction and background. Part II takes the viewpoints of law as the point of reference. The aim here is to provide information on a broad range of legal issues that are directly relevant to constructing legal-linguistic models and the framework.

Chapter 3 commences by presenting different legal roles and viewpoints and goes on to ask: what is law? This takes us into legal philosophy, but it is necessary as it leads on to fundamental legal concepts such as rules, norms and principles, as well as states and legal orders. One finds that one keeps on returning to these fundamental concepts at different stages in the enquiry. It is important for linguists working with legal texts to have some knowledge of legal theory as it helps to clarify some of the language and terminology issues that arise. It is rare for legal texts to contain information that is redundant and without purpose, but it is frequent for legal texts to omit information that impacts on meaning because the information in question is to be found elsewhere in the legal system and is not to be duplicated needlessly. Each text is part of the whole system for drafting and interpretation and is read together with all the others; this is what linguists refer to as 'intertextuality'.

Chapter 4 shifts attention to the level of the legal text, variously referred to as 'legal act' or 'legal instrument'. Each legal text is created within a context. It is one document within a whole system that comprises branches and sub-branches. The document must fit within that matrix if it is to achieve its full effects. The first step is to pick up on legal theory and identify how legal texts can arise, in terms of their sources. One legal system is selected as example and its sources and types of legal document are briefly summarised. These can be seen in terms of genres. Each legal act can be seen as a site for actions and one can explore them. This leads to reflection on the activities of drafting, interpretation, amendment and repeal. In order to link the abstraction of legal texts to the everyday world of people and fact, the chapter includes a mention of the role of facts, evidence and proof in legal thinking, as well as the enforcing of legal acts against those under obligation through methods that may involve the use of force.

Chapter 5 shifts attention to the more specifically linguistic and multilingual context. Most of the time attention is paid to the ways in which law uses language, which is the language of law, but there is the converse side, which is the law of language and of languages. Here language is seen as a phenomenon that is itself regulated by law and legal rules. There is the way in which each language is organised to achieve legal purposes, but there are also the ways in which law regulates the choice, or use, of languages through the rules of its linguistic regime, a term which has already been introduced in Chapter 1. Frequently when thinking about multilingual law, attention is primarily paid to this aspect. However, the types of linguistic regime may vary, and one of the factors here concerns the nature of the system of law in question. It is at this point that the concept of 'legal order' is elaborated on. By this time Appendix II is becoming clearer and one can identify variations in types of linguistic regime. The aim is that, by the end of Chapter 5, a broad legal picture of the context of multilingual law has been presented. From there attention shifts to the linguistic side of the coin.

Part III places the focus on language. Chapter 6 presents some viewpoints of language. Its purpose is to mirror Chapter 3, this time as regards language theory, and to draw out some key concepts from linguistics that appear relevant, or useful, for a study of multilingual law. Unlike with law where the formal branches are backgrounded in favour of some structural concepts, it is necessary to enter the branches of linguistics in order to make an assessment. The chapter unavoidably takes the form of a list of topics. Each has a certain value and relevance, and the opportunity is taken to make suggestions in that respect. In order to provide some degree of structure to the sequence, other than an alphabetical list, two ideas are drawn on which overlap: first, the concept of circles proposed by Aitchison (2003), and second, the distinction by Ferdinand de Saussure between 'language' *'langue'* and *'parole'* (Saussure 2005). This implies a shift of attention from broad issues of the biology of language and sound production towards individual language codes and the everyday forms of oral and written utterances. Each forms part of the picture; legal rules openly or tacitly regulate the form of code and a study of legal discourse engages attention on the utterances. In the multilingual context comparisons and alignments come into play, circling around the problem of meaning.

Chapter 7 stays within a linguistic frame of reference but adds the dimension of legal language as special language (LSP). It first picks up threads from Chapter 6 and introduces the concept of legal language, addressing some typical features. This is the language of law, and in multilingual systems such language is reproduced in two or more languages. From there, the chapter enquires about what it is that makes language specifically legal, and this leads on to the view that it is a matter of status, as well as forms of style. The concept of official language is then introduced. This leads on to enquiring whether it is possible to classify languages in terms of being a language of law or not. A table of classification of languages is proposed in terms of their use and status. The classification is different from the one in Ethnologue, as it is solely devoted to the context of legal systems and aims to provide a method for exploring different permutations, as well as terminology implications. The chapter concludes with the topic of language policy and language planning.

With Part IV we start to move towards the exploration of meaning. This part is devoted to the concept of signs as indicators of meaning. What meaning? Well, that depends on the senses, experiences and cultural associations of the person enquiring. Chapter 8 presents an introduction to certain aspects of the study of signs, semiotics – a strange subject, as it seems to shadow everything and makes one wonder if it is real or fantasy. Yet there are theories which are of pragmatic utility. Two of these are explored; they both relate to the concept of the sign. One theory, proposed by Ferdinand de Saussure, sees signs as essentially comprising two elements. A second theory, proposed by Charles Sanders Peirce, sees signs as essentially comprising three elements. It is argued that the triadic conception assists with analysing meaning in a multilingual context. The chapter emphasises the mental element to signs, and reflects on the creation of new signs, a process referred to as 'semiosis'. Lastly, semiotics is seen as a means for objectifying the subjective. This not only implies relativising all viewpoints, but also that there is another mind observing the subjective activities under study. Semiotic analysis underpins the analysis of terminology and primary and secondary term formation. The latter especially is of paramount importance for multilingual systems of law, since a key objective is to reproduce the same ideas and concepts across a range of languages.

Part V takes the reflections on meaning into a legal context involving the use of language in legal utterances, whether oral or written texts. Chapter 9 seeks to clarify different aspects of meaning that arise within a context of law. There is sometimes a tendency to regard law as being solely linked to language, but this needs to be nuanced. The chapter commences by identifying sites of engagement for the creation of legal meaning. It picks up on Chapter 8 with respect to semiotic meaning, and takes that further into linguistic meaning as a specific category. This is the field of semantics. Legal texts draw on linguistic meanings, but the meaning that is constructed in particular situations does not always tie in clearly with the language of texts. This opens the door to the concept of 'legal meaning' as something different. This is explored. The significance for multilingual texts is that it provides an explanation of how it is possible for meanings to be drawn from multilingual texts, sometimes contrary to the actual wording of individual texts. Different ranges of meaning may be searched for in legal texts. The chapter presents four viewpoints that can be used as tools to this end. They have practical significance for the work of legal-linguistic revisers and for assessing the function of particular terms in texts. Based on the foregoing, the chapter then reflects on the multilingual context and the processes of creating meaning through drafting and of constructing meaning through reading and interpretation. Is there alignment between the two sides? Selection of appropriate terminology by the drafter is a key part of the answer, and the chapter concludes with a mention of the role of terminology with respect to meaning.

Part VI makes another shift of focus and takes us into the activity of transferring information, that is to say meanings, across languages. There is the dimension of oral language through oral interpretation and the dimension of written language through the translation of written texts. Chapter 10 explores the translation process with particular emphasis on legal translation. First, it presents some translation viewpoints to provide an indication of the breadth of the field of translation and the vast array of types of texts that are translated. It asks the question: what is translation? This serves to draw out some different ideas about the nature of the activity. The focus is then shifted to think about translation in terms of a process. This is relevant to multilingual law, as thinking in terms of process makes one think about the steps involved, the individual stages in production, and from there about what is needed in order to achieve a quality product fit for service. It also provides an entry point for marking a distinction between translation and revision. That in turn paves the way for thinking about the role of legal-linguistic revision, which is an established function in organisations such as the institutions of the EU.

Chapter 10 does not aim at a theoretical exposition of translation or legal translation. Instead it seeks to identify particular types of problem and open the door to reflection on strategies for finding solutions. In that connection it presents seven scenarios for legal translation, which serve the purpose of drawing one from 'simpler' legal translation contexts into 'more complicated' ones. In particular, the purpose is to show how terminology can become a difficult issue in multilingual, multicultural contexts. Individual legal texts may be destined for different legal contexts at the same time and that creates the idea of there being a legal matrix in respect of meanings.

Chapter 11 is an extension of Chapter 10, but it suggests that the task of translation can be split into two facets: the first phase linked closely to source language author and a second phase which is more closely linked to readership, usage, client needs and fitness for service. Drawing this distinction makes it possible to reflect on the revision viewpoint. That in turn allows us to introduce another dimension to multilingual law, which is that not infrequently in international contexts legal texts are conceived and drafted by persons who are not native speakers of the language in question. This is an issue for languages that serve as a lingua franca. It is an issue for English and also for French. One response is to arrange for revision of draft texts by native-speaker experts. With respect to legal texts, these experts are typically legal-linguistic experts and the chapter includes a mention of the work of EU lawyer-linguists working in a 24-language environment, by way of example.

By this stage, many of the substantive dimensions of multilingual law in system terms have been covered. One could stop here, but the everyday work of practitioners in multilingual legal systems involves additional considerations of a practical nature. These are referred to generically in Part VII as back-up, support and training. This part is intentionally short and brief, and its only objective is to draw attention to certain matters as requiring attention. Each system has its own tools and methods of support

28 *Introduction*

and training, and the purpose is not to enter into these. Chapter 12 accordingly selects a range of roles as lawyer, linguist and lawyer-linguist and, taking the EU context by way of example, briefly discusses some of the technology available.

Chapter 13 continues the review of support issues, this time in the context of education and training of practitioners in multilingual systems. Its sole purpose is to draw attention to the range of knowledge and skills that are involved and invite reflection. That brings the exposition of topics to a close.

In the course of the chapters certain topics are identified and given specialised technical treatment in a series of appendices. Appendices I and II have been mentioned in this chapter. The appendices comprise the framework for analysis and understanding, while the chapters serve as conceptual introduction. Chapter 14 passes the appendices in review, introducing each of them and drawing attention to links between them. It suggests how the appendices may become tools for further analysis and enquiry. However, given the extreme levels of complexity and variation that arise, one needs to proceed with care, as it is easy to become overwhelmed. Appendix VIII seeks to minimise this by drawing threads together and presenting criteria in a structured sequence that reflects the sequence of the chapters. It constitutes the framework of analysis and understanding.

Chapter 15 concludes this book. It addresses a range of broad issues. Multilingual law can be seen in terms of matrices of law, language, languages and cultures. There are repeating themes and patterns, involving matters such as terminology, context, technology, the size of a language and the boundary limits of legal systems and their attached languages. Multilingual law has its pros and cons, which vary in their weight according to individual circumstances. An integral part of a multilingual system is a minimum degree of respect for the 'other'. Technology is playing an increasing role and facilitating the employment of increasing numbers of languages in systems, such as that of the EU. However, it is specialist work and requires specialised solutions, training and knowledge. The last point which it is wished to emphasise concerns the need, and role, for study and research into multilingual law and language. Practitioners need assistance. Research lawyers and linguists can assist them, but they need to be informed about the practitioner environment and problems. If this book can help remove a few barriers to communication, it will have served its purpose.

Summary

This chapter has continued the introduction to multilingual law. It has introduced the concept of legal-linguistic modelling. It has introduced Appendices I and II. It has suggested the way in which it is proposed to structure the field of enquiry and it has entered into a brief overview of each chapter. The next step is to dive into the details, starting with some viewpoints of law.

Notes

1 See www.oxforddictionaries.com/definition/english/model.
2 See Chapter 8.
3 See www.oxforddictionaries.com/definition/english/model.
4 See http://oeop.larc.nasa.gov/lap/nwlanguages.html.

Part II
Law

3 Viewpoints of law

Introduction

This chapter starts the descent into detail. Its purpose is to introduce a few legal concepts which are essential for organising information on multilingual law in a legal-linguistic manner that can lead to developing a framework. The simplest approach is to commence by reflecting on legal roles and viewpoints that flow from them. This provides a backcloth for entering into the philosophy of law, which is entailed by asking the question: what is law? Different theories are sketched without going beyond the most superficial level. The purpose is to evoke the diversity of opinions on the matter. Issues of legal theory are of fundamental importance as they condition the ways in which legal texts are created, as well as the ways in which they are read and interpreted. Lack of awareness and understanding on this matter represents a barrier to full comprehension of the meanings attributed by lawyers to legal texts in the construction of the law. This applies in the monolingual environment, but equally in a multilingual and multicultural context as there may be divergences in the theoretical legal philosophies behind the respective texts.

A reflection on philosophy leads on to canvassing legal concepts. The ones selected in this chapter are important for the structure of law and legal systems. They link abstract legal ideas with the everyday world of fact. Thinking along the twin tracks of legal concepts and the facts to which they relate helps in the analysis of legal terminology and in making comparisons between languages and legal systems. There is a field of legal study, comparative law, which is devoted to analysing and comparing legal systems and concepts. It forms part of the background to the harmonisation and unification of law which underpins international organisations such as the European Union.[1] This and the following chapters do not propose comparisons directly, but aim to explore at a conceptual level some of the broad underlying strands that are present in different forms and variations across and between legal systems that follow European models with roots in civil law or common law. The 'backcloth' is the existence of the European Union and its developing multilingual system of law, and the ways in which a multicultural and increasingly integrated continent functions through law on different levels. There are other systems of law, notably Chinese, Hindu, Jewish and Muslim law. They merit an attention which the author is currently unable to provide. It is hoped the framework approach adopted here may, however, be of some relevance in that respect.

It helps understanding if one can put ideas in a 'real-life' context, and one of the ways of doing that is to place an emphasis on the tasks that are performed and the roles of persons called on to perform them. Theory and concepts take on their significance when seen in that light, as they are the materials that are worked with to achieve the actions, objectives and effects sought by the clients for whom lawyers work. With that thought in mind, this chapter opens with a brief reflection on different legal roles and suggesting legal viewpoints associated with them. Each role has a core activity and these activities find their counterpart when one inquires into the nature of law.

What is law? This question lies at the heart of the concept of law. There is no single answer and one can only summarise a few of the theories that have been put forward over the centuries to give a flavour of the nature of the debates. The enquiry, however, leads on to exploring what law does and how it does it. That in turn leads on to a wealth of topics, in particular the concept of rules, or norms, and how they differ from principles; the concepts of state, legal system, legal order; and the ways in which law is structured into branches. The difference between the substantive law of rights and duties and the procedural law that serves their implementation and application is also an important distinction for law. The selection of topics and concepts in this chapter is small, but each topic is presented as a structural element for understanding multilingual law and making conceptual legal-linguistic models of legal systems and organisations. Each finds a place in the concept of the framework that is contained in Appendix VIII, supplemented by the preceding appendices. We will commence with a range of legal viewpoints.

Legal viewpoints

There are different legal roles. They cluster round particular tasks and activities. First, we have courts with their officers and staff. The primary function of the court is to regulate and settle disputes (civil law) and oversee certain important activities such as the repression of undesired conduct and behaviour (criminal, or penal law), as well as to provide a means to review whether administrative bodies have acted correctly (administrative law). The most prominent figures are the judges, who are called on to decide. They deliver judgments and opinions that are usually set down in writing and form the case law that later lawyers study as 'precedents'. It is a viewpoint that implies making decisions on questions involving facts and how they are established through evidence, interpreting legal and all kinds of texts, and making connections between the facts established and the legal rules and principles that comprise law and apply to the facts. Judges declare what the law is and how it is applied in cases before them. They supervise the application and enforcement of law as part of the system of administering justice. The judicial viewpoint is the reference point for lawyers as it is the one which ultimately determines legal meanings.

A second viewpoint is that of the barrister/advocate[2] pleading a case in court in public before a judge on behalf of a paying client, or as a prosecutor on behalf of the public interest to repress, punish and deter crime. The role involves oral and written skills in pleading, argument, forensic examination of witnesses and leading evidence to establish the facts, in order that an application of the legal rules will benefit their client (Du Cann 1993). Advocates use rhetorical skills to convince the judge, or in a criminal case the jury, that their view of the facts should prevail (Fish 2012). They present arguments as to what the law is and how the legal texts should be interpreted and applied. They discuss cases with their clients, give advice and take instructions; and in this context we can note the use of legal language adapted to the non-professional (Heffer *et al.* 2013). Within the courtroom there is professional discourse between lawyers, witnesses giving evidence and judges, which has to conform to certain patterns (Goodrich 1990: 179–208). Witness evidence is usually oral, but there may be written texts that have to be described and explained. The study of legal language, the language of law, by linguists bears the name 'legal linguistics' or 'forensic linguistics', though this carries an inference of emphasis on courtroom language. Legal linguistics is raised in Chapter 7 in the context of legal language. Linguists also study how law is constructed through language (Gibbons 1994). This is relevant to legal philosophy, since it too is constructed through the use of language.

A third viewpoint is that of the solicitor, notary or law agent involved with transactions relating to land, commerce, companies, families, wills and succession. They generally work in their offices away from courts and have paying clients who seek advice and legal products in the form of texts and acts, as well as advice and guidance. These professionals create legal documents to record and implement all kinds of legal transactions and advise and guide clients on to how to organise their affairs in accordance with the rules of law. Depending on the legal system and other factors, a solicitor may plead in court, or be involved in instructing barristers/advocates in connection with court cases, but that role may be allocated to other legal specialists such as the former French *avoués*.

A fourth legal viewpoint is that of the 'in-house' lawyer employed by government, local authorities, business and industry to advise, defend and generally protect and further their employer's interests. The tasks include drafting legal documents such as commercial contracts (business and industry) or drafting legislative texts (government and parliament), as well as providing advice and guidance. Legal acts such as laws or statutes made by parliament, or ministerial or government decree, are generally drafted by specialist legal drafters. As such, they express the viewpoint of the authors of legislative texts, the legislative viewpoint. The ways in which they draft is affected by whether the system is one of civil law or common law. In the former, all law is essentially written and derives from a legislative body; the role of the judges is to interpret and apply the rules to the facts of cases before them. In the latter, the heart of the system is previous decisions by judges, originally unwritten, and the role of the legislator is to correct deficiencies and regulate immediate and necessary matters. These ideas underscore methods not only of drafting but also of reading and interpretation.

All of these legal specialists work with the law and legal documents and have a shared understanding about law that is developed over many years of intensive training and working together. Their knowledge is specialised and their activities centre on the use of language for specialist legal purposes (LSP). Yet law is not a matter merely for lawyers; it exists for society at large, and in that respect everyone is involved, layman as well as expert. Non-lawyers have an important role, for example as representatives elected to parliament to make laws. Ordinary people participate in the legal process as members of juries to decide on guilt and innocence in criminal trials. Not all judges in courts and specialised tribunals (courts) are legally qualified. For example, there are lay magistrates in England and Wales (Courts and Tribunals Judiciary 2015). Non-lawyers are frequently at the origin of creating new laws and legal texts, acting in response to changes in society, changes in technology, disasters to be avoided, and so on. Changes in the law come about through the creation of new legislative texts, or new interpretations by the courts of the previous case law.

Running as a thread through the above activities, there is a 'public' dimension, represented by public institutions acting on behalf of everyone, and a 'private' dimension represented by the personal interests and activities of individual persons and companies: public law *versus* private law. While the concept of multilingual law covers everything, when it comes to searching for the rules establishing the linguistic arrangements for legal systems and legal orders, it is primarily to the public law dimension that one looks. Private affairs are undertaken in accordance with the rules laid down and within the scope of flexibility permitted by the rules of the system. Our attention will be primarily on the public law context, since rules on language form part of the foundation of a legal system, but the private law dimension will continuously be present in the background.

For each of the foregoing areas of legal work specialised knowledge and experience is required. Legal experts within a system share a common legal culture and training, but even where systems are quite different, there is generally a shared way of thinking, constructing and organising information, and approaching the solving of legal problems. This is the 'legal culture' and it reflects certain ways of thinking and reasoning.[3] It is taught by law professors to students and theorised by philosophers, and these provide yet more viewpoints on law.

What is law?

At the outset it is important to form some clear ideas about what we mean by 'law', as it is a foundation concept. As one investigates further, the ideas change and adapt as it becomes evident that there are different ways of looking at, and thinking about, law. Thus one can take dictionary definitions of the term 'law'; one can examine philosophical theories about the concept of law; one can study the history of law – or rather of legal systems and ideas about law; and one can go oneself to see law in action in courtrooms and legislatures. Indeed, one is already participating in it through a myriad of daily ways, whether it be going shopping, making a will, marrying, getting divorced or going on holiday. All social life is regulated in some way or other by law and all our actions have legal consequences. To make that clearer, we need to study legal texts and examine the words, terms and concepts used to talk about law and see how these relate to our everyday affairs.

Ideas about law are not static and unchanging, and that is evident if one compares a mediaeval law with a modern law, or reports of court cases from different periods.[4] So our everyday actions may be subject to different legal implications and consequences at different times. The same applies to different places, for habits and customs vary from place to place, and so does the law. Thus the idea of law is a very broad notion. There must be large differences between the law of a small tribal illiterate hunting-gathering society and that of a modern bureaucratic state, for example.[5] Yet behind all ideas about law lie the culture and broader ethical, moral and religious ideas and concepts of each human society. The concept of multilingual law embraces all cultures, all types of law and all languages. However, for the purpose of this book and piecing together a reference framework, the principal background point of reference is that of European legal history, philosophy and culture seen from an authorial Scottish viewpoint (Friedrich 1963, Kelly 1992, Robinson *et al.* 2000, Meston *et al.* 1991).

However, even narrowing the cultural parameters in this way, there is no single universal vision of law. Perhaps it is a reflection of the sheer range of legal viewpoints: philosopher theorising a just society, lawyer wanting to win a case, ruler wanting order and obedience, judge having to decide cases, citizen wanting protection for life, limb and property, and so on. Each may have a different theory on law. We will canvas some legal theories, but before doing so, it is useful to reflect on a few issues, so as to be able to place the theories in a context. Law has a pragmatic dimension; theory has to relate in some way to everyday life, either drawing on it or guiding it. Matters have to be organised in some way, whether it be through positive action or a choice of inaction. Law is closely connected with how people behave, or rather how they 'ought' to behave if they observe the rules of law in force. That is its primary purpose, though it has others, such as to guide and educate through rule-making. The mere fact of not acting as obliged by law, such as driving through a red stop-light, does not itself invalidate a rule of law as a 'norm' to be observed, but if no one ever observes a particular rule, one can wonder if it still exists.[6] There is 'enforcement' through punishment by fines or imprisonment to make sure law is obeyed. Legal systems exist to establish and maintain order and set standards of conduct to be observed. Harris (1997: 56) describes four principles applied by English courts in respect of punishment through judicial sentencing: retribution, deterrence, prevention and rehabilitation.

One of the difficulties with modern law is that there is so much of it. There are so many legal texts, and they are all so detailed and complicated that no one can know it all. That might mean it should not apply, but legal systems get round this problem by declaring that everyone is deemed to know the law and cannot plead ignorance. It is a foundation concept and therefore in Latin: *Ignorantia juris neminem excusat* [ignorance of the law excuses no one].[7] Otherwise the rule of law would collapse. If we then proceed to search for law, to inform ourselves, we can ask knowledgeable persons for information, but we must be aware that they are expressing opinions, and the source itself lies in legal texts by parliament, the courts and in other law books. We learn through reading and decoding the information, and it is an exercise in abstract mental thinking. The substance of law is abstract, in the mind, shared through society by teaching and learning. There is an individual psychological dimension and a social collective dimension, as law regulates both individual and collective action. It does that through rules, or norms, and principles. We need to expand on these concepts, but first let us take an ultra-brief look at some philosophical ideas about law. The viewpoint here is culturally anglocentric and one must take into account that if this book were written in a different language and from a different cultural perspective, it might have placed a different emphasis. That too forms part of multilingual law.[8]

Legal philosophy in Britain and the United States goes under the name of 'jurisprudence',[9] a term which in civil law countries such as France signifies 'case law'. Ancient Greeks and Romans, from whom so many of our ideas derive, distinguished between 'natural law' and 'human law' (also referred to as 'man-made', or 'positive law') (Fitzgerald (1966), d'Entrèves (1970), Friedrich (1963), Harris (1997), Kelly (1992), McLeod (2012), Robinson *et al.* (2000)). Natural Law comprised the immutable 'laws' underpinning all life, and was linked to the deities (divine law). It had to be interpreted by humans for application to human society – a role for a priesthood, but later for philosophers and lawyers using logic and reasoning. Much of this body of knowledge subsequently developed into sciences such as physics and chemistry, and we routinely talk about scientific laws, and the laws of physics or thermodynamics, as we saw from the definitions above. If something happens, then something else happens in a particular immutable way, such as dropping an apple leads to it falling to the ground. Natural law as divine law sets an ideal standard of justice against which human/positive law is measured. Religions such as Christianity see this as the law of God and seek for its principles and rules in religious texts such as the Bible. Other religions similarly derive principles and rules from their religious texts for application to everyday life. People sought, and still seek, to live in accordance with divine law.

In a secular society, the concept of natural law remains important, but it tends to be linked to ideas of morality, ethics and utility. Notions of natural law lie behind prosecutions for genocide and war crimes, which may perhaps not be prohibited under purely human positive law in some places.[10] They also lie behind charters of human and fundamental rights, such as the Universal Declaration of Human Rights of the United Nations and the Charter of Fundamental Rights of the European Union, and include the UN Educational, Scientific and Cultural Organization (UNESCO) Universal Declaration on Linguistic Rights (1996). For the purposes of the creation and interpretation of law and legal texts, the principles of natural law must always be borne in mind, even when not mentioned explicitly, because issues of equality, fairness, due process of law and so on can directly influence meaning. A text may be declared invalid if it is in breach of a fundamental principle of law, which means it ceases to exist in law and carries no legal meaning. The concepts of law and justice are closely connected. Indeed, one of the perceived functions of law is to apply justice among people: hence the title 'Court of Justice'. What is 'justice'? For the moment let us settle for the idea that it is 'fairness', and not become engaged in the difference between 'distributive justice' and 'corrective justice'.[11] Some core ideas are of balance and impartiality; the image of a blindfolded female figure holding scales of judgment comes to mind.

If we shift attention to human law, also called positive law, we find other views. One of them sees law in terms of commands by a superior (a sovereign) to an inferior to do or abstain from doing something, under pain of punishment. Law is seen as commands, backed by threat of sanctions, from a sovereign to whom people have a habit of obedience. This view was put forward by the nineteenth-century English philosopher John Austin (Harris 1997: 28–35).[12] If we think of the sovereign writing the commands in written codes and legislative texts, it gives us an idea of the civil law approach that places an emphasis on written texts.

Another view, again simplified, sees law in terms of prophecies of what the courts will do (Oliver Wendell Holmes cited by Harris 1997: 99). This is a viewpoint that takes decisions by courts as the centre of legal action and it is the heart of the common law approach. Yet another view sees law in terms of magic, emotion and psychology (Axel Hägerström and Karl Olivekrona, per Harris 1997: 103–108). This view looks at facts and behaviour relating to law and sets it in a factual context in terms of reality. Law takes on the aspect of a psychological phenomenon. To an external viewer some legal results can seem magical, as one cannot explain them through observation.

A fourth view sees law in terms of statements about what 'ought' to be done (Hans Kelsen, per Harris 1997: 64–69) and each of these 'ought' statements is called a 'norm'. This view separates behaviour that actually happens from what 'ought' (by law) to happen.[13] The norms are organised hierarchically and there is a foundation norm called a '*Grundnorm*'; there are some who doubt the existence of the *Grundnorm*, and a linguistic view of law might suggest thinking more in terms of bundles and foci of connections. But perhaps it is just that our ideas of law reflect the current social order and change as societies change, and we now have much more international cooperation along with international multilingual rule-making organisations.

A fifth view looks at law in terms of being a concept that is connected to social life and takes a linguistic point of view (Herbert Hart, per Harris 1997: 117–121; Hart

1997[14]). How does one know when law is present? One can study how people behave. On the one hand there is the 'external' view of an outsider watching people behave and the 'inside' view of the person acting. The internal view may be based on feelings of obligation or compulsion. A difference is made between people acting from habit, such as walking the dog each morning, and those acting under the compulsion of a rule – which may be to walk the dog; indeed, it should be.

The foregoing gives a whiff of some issues in what is a large, extensive and complex array of ideas about law, and we will gradually explore more legal concepts as we proceed. Yet for the moment let us pause and consider what if anything might be relevant so far to multilingual law. The first point is that everything noted about the concept of law also applies to multilingual law. Second, if we wish we can find a foundation for multilingual law and multilingual legal systems in natural law on divine, ethical or moral grounds, or on utilitarian grounds as being of benefit. For example, ideas about equality and the right to have access to, and to be able to know and understand, the law lead to the view that the rules should be in a language that one knows and understands. That implies both that the 'language' as language code (English, French, German) used is known and that the words, terms and expressions used within the particular language code can be understood. So two levels of implication arise. The first level leads to questions concerning language regime and choice of languages, and the second leads to questions concerning making the law accessible to all by being simpler to access and understand and using language that is plain and accessible.[15] From a point of view of linguistic rights one could also add the degree of official recognition of lesser-used languages as part of social justice and equality.

Arguments in favour of multilingualism can be based on justice and fairness as moral issues, or on economic, social, psychological or utilitarian grounds. Very often legal issues run along two lines of thought, one based in legal reasoning and abstract theory and the other in the everyday world of reality, behaviour and psychology. The different theories and viewpoints on law can be seen in this light. However, having given arguments in favour of multilingualism, one must be aware of counter-arguments, such as perhaps a perceived weakening of overall national linguistic cohesion, or extra costs needed to manage the system leaving less funds for other urgent social needs. In the case of a society of massive immigration, such as the United States, a single official language is perceived as being a unifying factor (Crawford 2015). Law is a balance.

Let us now return to the dictionary definitions of the term 'law' that were highlighted in Chapter 1 and select some salient elements. Thus in English the word 'law' refers to the concept of 'law' as a whole, but also to specific written legal acts or particular sets of 'rules'. Further, it can refer to: first, an individual rule as part of a system of law; second, systems of law as a subject of study or as the basis of the legal profession; third, statute law and the common law; fourth, something regarded as having binding force or effect; fifth, informal – the police; sixth, a rule defining correct procedure or behaviour in a sport; seventh, a statement of fact, deduced from observation, to the effect that a particular natural or scientific phenomenon always occurs if certain conditions are present; eighth, a generalisation based on a fact or event perceived to be recurrent; ninth, the body of divine commandments as expressed in the Bible or other religious texts (Oxford Dictionaries 2015). The same source observes that the origin of the word 'law' is from Old English *lagu*, from Old Norse *lag* (something laid down or fixed), of Germanic origin, and related to *lay*.

In English the word 'law' refers to the concept of law as a whole but also to specific rules. There is a dichotomy here that is reflected in other languages. In French the general concept is rendered by '*le Droit*'. There is also the term '*la Loi*' that can refer to the rules as a whole,[16] and the concept of a specific rule as in '*une loi*', '*une règle*',[17] or '*une norme*'[18] (law, rule, norm). There is also the legislative document '*une loi*' (a law). In German there are the general terms '*Jura*',[19] '*das Recht*'[20] and for the individual rule '*eine Regel*',[21] '*eine Norm*',[22] as well as the legislative act '*ein Gesetz*'.[23] English also uses different names for legislative acts, such as 'statute'.

The term '*droit*' in French also carries the meaning of specific entitlement, which is rendered as '*Recht*' in German. It reminds us of the English word 'right' (that is my right) and, by extension, of 'rights' as in 'Bill of Rights' or 'Human Rights'. To say that I have a right is to assert that there is a rule or law that allows me to do something in certain circumstances. Alternatively, someone else has a 'duty' or 'obligation' to allow me to do it. Law is concerned with making rules which impose obligations or confer rights on people. These are expressed in legal language through terms such as 'shall' and 'must', while the term 'may' implies a choice of doing or not doing something. They all connect with a further aspect of law which is linked to the idea of 'power' and the counterpart of 'liability' or obligation, being subject to the exercise of power by someone else. These terms are deeply embedded in legal theory, practice and the texts. It is part of the structure of relationships created by law. Note that we have moved from a broad concept of law as a phenomenon towards specific instances of it. We will take this further.

Rules, norms and principles

We have seen that the term 'law' may refer to a collective system of rules, a rule itself, or be the name given to a written legislative act. The terms 'rule' and 'right' figure prominently, as does the term 'norm'. These need further elucidation. Moreover, in the discussion on 'natural law' above there was a mention of 'principles'. What is the difference between these concepts, and is there any implication for multilingual law? The concept of 'rule' or 'norm' seems to be so central to the notion of law that it is worth dwelling on it for a moment. In particular, how does it differ from a 'principle'? And what is the relationship with 'rights' and 'duties'?

The Oxford Dictionaries online give among others the following entries for 'rule' as a noun: first, 'one of a set of explicit or understood regulations or principles governing conduct or procedure within a particular area of activity'; second, 'a principle that operates within a particular sphere of knowledge, describing or prescribing what is possible or allowable'; third, 'a code of practice and discipline for a religious order or community'; fourth, 'control of or dominion over an area or people'; fifth, 'the normal or customary state of things'. On the other hand, Curzon's Dictionary of Law defines 'rule' as first, 'a regulation, principle, direction', and second, 'a standard by which to judge an individual's conduct' (Curzon 1993: 341; Richards and Curzon 2011: 415). These definitions provide a general picture, but they blur the distinction, if any, between 'rule' and 'principle'. The distinction is useful in practice, because if the former is seen as being narrower and directly linked to facts, the latter can be seen as broader and not necessarily linked to specific facts but more abstract and at a deeper level in the structure of a legal system.[24] We will come back to this in a moment, but first we should mention the term 'norm', which it was suggested might be seen as a synonym of 'rule'.

For the term 'norm' as a noun in English, the Oxford Dictionaries gives among others the following entries: first, '(the norm) Something that is usual, typical, or standard'; second, '(usually norms) A standard or pattern, especially of social behaviour, that is typical or expected'; third, 'A required standard; a level to be complied with or reached'. These can be compared with the technical definition in Curzon's Dictionary of Law: 'An authoritative standard or rule of behaviour' (Curzon 1993: 262). We can set these definitions of norm against a philosophical theory of law which sees laws entirely in terms of norms. It is summarised by Curzon as follows:

> Law is a coercive order of human behaviour and is built from 'legal norms' which are valid only if authorised by legal norms of a higher rank. The norms rest ultimately upon the force of a 'basic norm' (*Grundnorm*) e.g., that the British Parliament is sovereign. The basic norm is 'a juristic presumption or postulate implicit in legal thinking'; it gives the quality of validity to a legal system.
> (Curzon 1993: 220 under the entry: law, pure theory of.)[25]

The concept of the 'norm' and of the '*Grundnorm*' are associated with the legal philosopher Hans Kelsen, mentioned earlier. The 'norm' is seen in terms of being a statement of what 'ought to be done' (Kelsen, per Harris 1997: 65). The terms 'rule' and 'norm' overlap and to that extent are synonyms, but the legal concept of norm appears more technical and scientific. In English it is less usual to talk about 'norms' and the term 'rule' is more common. Linking the concept of norm not to fact and what actually happens but to what 'ought' to happen helps to make it clear that there is a difference between facts and rules. One of the aspects legal philosophers discuss, and take different views on, is how far ideas of natural law are or should be included in the concept of law and the system of norms/rules. For the present purpose it is not necessary to delve into this background, beyond being aware that there are different views regarding the nature of law and of rules and norms, which remain nonetheless key concepts.

One of the definitions of 'rule' above included a reference to the 'customary state of things', but it was qualified as '*the* rule'. There is a difference between the concept of 'rule' and that of 'custom'. If behaviour is 'customary', is that because there is a rule that obliges the behaviour (and a social expectation), or is it merely that there is a habit of repeating certain behaviour, without a legal obligation (Hart, per Harris 1997: 118)? Viewed externally, one sees repeated action, but viewed internally there may be a rule and an obligation. We come back to the example of walking the dog: habit or rule?[26] The existence of a rule implies an obligation, and an expectation by others that something will be done, so that they can rely on it in organising their activities (a function of law being predictability and certainty). On the other hand, habits are actions repeated without any formal legal obligation to do so. The issue is relevant to multilingual law in the context of custom, through repeated habit, as a source of law.

Does a beneficiary of a regular habit, or practice, become entitled to expect it and rely on it as a right? In trade and commerce a habit, or custom, may become regarded as an unwritten rule, especially if something is done in reliance on it, but does dog-walking come in that category? For the dog, there is an expectation and maybe the dog thinks there is a rule that should be obeyed; but alas, the dog has no means to enforce such a viewpoint by testing it before the courts. A habit becomes a rule when declared as such by a court, which in effect means that rules are created by persons or bodies who have been given authority by the law to make (or declare) them.

Rules, and rule-making, are thus surrounded by, and governed by, other rules. Nothing exists on its own within a system of law. We cannot opt out (a rule), nor can we say we did not know (a rule). Whether a rule exists or not is subject to other rules. Could we say a legal system ceases to exist? That would also require a rule at a level high enough, or powerful enough, to override other rules, for there is also hierarchy. We can add that enforcement does not change the status of a rule, but looks at its application in practice. Lack of access to courts can impede enforcement of rights, which would be the dog's problem.

There are a number of implications from all of this for multilingual law. First, since rules interconnect with each other in a network, so must the texts that express them linguistically also be organised so as to interconnect with each other (intertextuality). That means that the terms and concepts between legal texts must match up and merge together in a seamless web semantically within each language and also across all the languages of a legal system, otherwise there are different implications according to the language version selected. Second, the use of particular languages for legal purposes may arise from habit, that is to say usage becoming custom, or from a formal rule creating language rights or obligations. English as a language of the law seems to be broadly based on usage and custom de facto[27] in recent centuries, particularly by the courts and Parliament. Here practice would create the rule. In France, Article 2 of the French Constitution states: 'La langue de la République est le français' [The language of the Republic is French]. Third, habits may become customary and declared to be obligatory even though not written down in texts. This carries the implication that law entails a dimension that goes beyond language, and therefore beyond multilingual law. What about written and oral language? There is no reason why laws cannot be oral only, and in a society without writing one must rely on the knowledge and memories of individuals, supplemented by other signs in the form of clothing, body-marking and physical objects (Qiyao 2009). How does one produce oral-only multilingual law?

There are other ways of looking at legal rules. We noted the school of thought that sees law and rules as something in the mind, a psychological phenomenon which gives it existence in the world of fact (Harris 1997: 103–108). This is useful because it reminds us that law is generally abstract and intangible. We cannot touch a 'rule'. We can touch the paper where symbols, or signs, that represent language and meaning are printed, but not the 'concept' itself. That stays in the mind and is interpreted from the signs. On the other hand, we can see the effects of law being applied (a thief in prison, for example). So law has reality, and it has effects in the real world of 'facts'. We can use these effects as a method to test rules and also to test whether a translation of a legal text from a 'source' into a 'target' language leads to the same effects as the 'source language'.

On the other hand, while law is a mental phenomenon, and psychological, it is also shared culturally by members of the same group or society, which brings one to the social dimension of law. We live in communities and societies of greater or lesser complexity. The function of law and rules is to influence and direct how we act individually and how our societies and communities function collectively. It can be seen as a sort of organisational 'glue' that holds everything in society together, like the 'bones' which in a body give structural support to the whole – hence its importance. However, like bones it can become rigid and inflexible. When circumstances change, rules may cease to be relevant. For example, we would expect rules about the pulling of weights by horses to be changed when harnesses were introduced, and then further rules on pulling weights would be introduced following mechanisation and motorised transport. So constant review and updating is required. Another factor to bear in mind is that there may be gaps in rules and matters that are not regulated, since it is very hard to anticipate everything until it happens. In situations where the rules are no longer adapted or where unforeseen circumstances arise for the first time and decisions on how to respond are required, it is necessary to have methods to fall back on to assist in deciding on appropriate responses for making new rules.

All of these factors lead towards introducing 'signposts' in a legal system which point to certain approaches as being desirable or undesirable. These are abstract propositions and are not attached to any particular facts. They are generalisations, useful as ready-to-hand axioms to assist in making decisions. Proverbs serve this role in ordinary general language: 'a bird in the hand is worth two in the bush', 'count your blessings' and so on in English.[28] The Bible sets out the well-known Ten Commandments (Exodus 20). They provide a general framework for living in a society. They are rules, but they are also principles. For example: 'You shall not steal' (Exodus 20:15). It is framed as a rule in command form, but it does not define what constitutes stealing. It is general, like a principle, unattached to particular circumstances. However, it acts as a guide for making specific rules as it indicates a certain type of conduct as wrong. Legal systems have similar broad expressions. They may be referred to as 'rules' or 'principles' as there seems to be a degree of overlap between these terms, as can be seen from the dictionary definitions. However, for the present purpose it is suggested that it is useful to think of principles as being broader, deeper and more abstract than rules and norms.[29]

The Oxford Dictionaries online give among others the following definitions of 'principle': first, 'a fundamental truth or proposition that serves as the foundation for a system of belief or behaviour or for a chain of reasoning'; second, '(usually principles) a rule or belief governing one's behaviour'; third, '[mass noun] Morally correct behaviour and attitudes'; fourth, 'a general scientific theorem or law that has numerous special applications across a wide field'; fifth, 'a natural law forming the basis for the construction or working of a machine'; sixth, 'a fundamental source or basis of something'; seventh, 'a fundamental quality determining the nature of something'.

In law a principle[30] points towards conduct as desirable, or to be avoided. Its precise status and force as obligatory (binding) is determined by the law, whether in legislative enactments or judicial decisions. Principles are 'the authoritative starting point or basis for legal reasoning wherever legal provision must be made for a situation not governed by a strict or precise rule of law' (Walker 2001: 92). Some principles are stronger than others. Some principles have overriding force and can override and disapply rules. Important principles are often expressed in Latin: *ne bis in idem* (a person may not be prosecuted twice for the same offence);[31] *ignorantia legis neminem excusat* (ignorance of the law is no excuse); *pacta sunt servanda* (contracts between states are binding), 'reciprocity' (between states). Two modern examples from environmental law are 'polluter pays'[32] and the 'precautionary principle'.[33] Circumstances can give rise to conflicts between principles, just as between rules. Choices have to be made, sometimes hard ones, and it is the role of the courts and judges to decide in these circumstances. *Dura lex, sed lex* (The law is hard, but it is the law).

In civil law codes it is common to find an exposition of general principles at the start of a code, as this sets the basic orientation of the text and places it in a philosophical and semantic context.[34] Readers and interpreters understand the general direction and way of thinking of the text, its 'spirit' and broad approach. They are able to apply this in cases not precisely covered by the rules set down elsewhere in the text in order to arrive at a solution to cases before them, thereby creating new rules *ad hoc*. It is part of the concept of 'discretion': empowering persons to make decisions in the light of the information before them. Within each legal system and each domain a balance needs to be struck between regulating for minutiae and allowing discretion to judges to adapt the law to circumstances and do justice.

Legal systems

Ideas about law may be abstract, but people live in communities in town and country, and affairs have to be organised and structured in some way on a daily basis. Even basic things have to be regulated, such as the standard weights and measures, which side of the road to drive along, or what happens to their property when people die. These do not necessarily raise issues of justice, although they may do; but it is often more a question of having some commonly accepted set of standards to apply, and knowing what criteria to use to decide. People need to know what they may and may not do, as well as how, or how not, to do things. Complicated and dangerous processes need to be regulated and managed according to best practice in the light of the latest knowledge. New technology may need to be standardised so that all manufacturers can participate in a market for products and spare parts, while the state ensures certain minimum levels of safety and security for producers and users of consumer goods. Since markets are global, this is an area where national law cannot reach sufficiently as it is limited by the extent of its territory in the application of its rules, and to remedy this problem, recourse must be had to techniques of cooperation through international and supranational law, which in turn leads to making multilingual legal texts.

Making rules is a role for the law, lawmakers and lawyers, working with technical experts and society at large. There needs to be structure and consistency. Law must reflect the society it regulates. There is a need for consistency, coherence, predictability and certainty, and that leads to efforts to harmonise the rules across the range of fields and make them compatible with each other. In that way, a network of interrelationships is developed and continually adjusted. This network takes the form of concepts, and terms expressing those concepts. Each concept occupies a certain 'space' in the system and sometimes there is overlap. Much of the task of judicial interpretation is taken up with determining the limits and boundaries between concepts and the meaning of terms, so as to determine which rules should be applied. For example, in France whether a 'person' acts in a civil or commercial capacity may determine whether the civil code or the commercial code applies (Lawson *et al.* 1966: 342).

The idea being followed here is that law needs to express a set of coherent responses to problems. That in turn leads to 'systematisation' and to thinking about the concept of law in terms of a 'system'. Indeed, we routinely talk about a 'legal system' or 'system of law(s)'. A legal system represents a conceptual unit (in semiotic terms a 'sign' or 'token', see Chapter 8), with an inside and an outside, and a boundary between it and other systems. Which system applies: French law or English law? We need rules to give answers. Each system has its own rules and they may align and lead to the same results, or they may lead to opposing results and be in conflict. For example, French law may say it applies to a matter and so may English law; or alternatively both may say neither applies to it. The ideal is where the rules on such matters are coordinated between the systems and lead to the same results on similar facts. There are many scenarios, for example the rules applying to people who move abroad and are subject to taxation in different countries or die with property in different countries to be distributed to heirs in succession. The way out of different approaches and dilemmas that arise is through coordinating the rules in different systems by means of special agreements, often called conventions. This is the field of private international law[35] and one of the functions of EU law is to deal with such questions and provide solutions.[36] It forms part of international law and supranational law, while frequently regulating matters of private law; hence the title of the field. Yet, while it is regularly recognised that there is a legal boundary between systems of law, and a branch of legal study is devoted to such questions, it is not so often noticed that there is also a linguistic boundary. Words take their meaning from context, and a legal system creates a context of meaning for law and also for language. This is important when it comes to translation, as words in different languages and legal systems occupy different spaces and may not match up. Reality, including legal reality, is 'chopped up' in different ways in different legal systems, even between those having the same language.

Branches of law

While a legal system provides an overall cultural, legal and linguistic context of its own, there are subdivisions and sub-systems within it. These are the branches of law and they match with linguistic domains as they constitute specialised contexts for meaning. Each system has its own structure of branches and individual features, and what is true for one system may not apply to another. One can take a general textbook introducing any legal system and obtain an idea of how the system is structured. Here it is proposed to select one system and trace a few strands from the general to the specific for the purposes of illustration. The system is Scots law and the branch selected is contract law. Scots law is a hybrid common law/civil law system. In a civil law system one would look up the relevant code and see how the text is structured, but in a common law system things are not so 'simple'. Contract law has been selected as an example of this, and also because contracts are a foundation for international and supranational rule-making where states enter into agreements. Contracts are the foundation of businesses and organisations. The European Union is founded on contract, as is the United Nations. We will be making reference to contracts in Chapter 4 when we consider the foundations for making legal texts, so it is useful to have a general idea about them from the outset.

Let us trace the levels in the Scots system from the most general to the most detailed, placing a focus on the law of contract and working our way from the most general and abstract level down to the level of a specific rule. As the system is not codified, we start with a general textbook on the Scottish legal system for guidance. Walker informs us that the great body of doctrines, principles and rules comprising the system 'can be grouped so as to form a logical structure with major divisions, subdivisions, branches, headings and sub-headings' (Walker 2001: 199). Understanding this helps in understanding the principles and rules, as well as in finding and applying the law. The Scots system follows the common pattern of modern Western legal systems, but it has its own nomenclature for many of the categories. Codified systems of law are given structure by the codes and their chapter headings, but 'in an uncodified system it is for the jurists to develop a structure' (Walker 2001: 199).

While Scots law is not codified, its history and deep-level structure is heavily influenced by Roman law (Robinson *et al.* 2000: 228–248). Modern everyday reality, in the form of legislation and court decisions, resembles a common law system. As a jurist, Walker

44 *Law*

therefore proposes a structure for the system, while noting that alternative approaches such as being linked to facts (for example, the law of road traffic or the law of animals) are possible (Walker 2001, footnote 2). The highest-level branches are as follows: public law and private law; administrative, criminal and civil law; civil and commercial law; common law and equity; common law and statute law; substantive and adjective law (Walker 2001: 200–206). These are broad abstract classifications and they do not tell us about the actual rules to be followed. For that we need to move to lower levels of classification where we come to more specific areas of law. The law of contract is situated under private law and under the heading of law of obligations, which covers 'all those sets of circumstances when two persons come to be so placed that the law imposes a legal link or bond of obligation between them from which flow rights, duties, liabilities, privileges, disabilities and powers as between one and another' (Walker 2001: 221). This branch is divided into sub-branches. contract law comes within them.

For the purpose of continuing with lower levels of classification in the system we will turn to another textbook on the Law of Scotland (Gloag and Henderson 1995),[37] which addresses among others contract law. Under 'contract' we find a range of sub-branches which include headings such as: capacity to contract, formation of contract, rules of evidence in relation to contract, agreements void or voidable, agreements defective in form, agreement improperly obtained, *pacta illicita* (unlawful agreements), unfair contract terms, title to sue, assignability, impossibility of performance, breach of contract, extinction of obligations and prescription. The headings provide a flavour of the range of issues involved as part of contract law (Gloag and Henderson 1995: 65–221). We are not at the level of principles or rules but still in legal and linguistic domains. The titles to these fields also provide us with information that is relevant to legal texts, legal language and legal meanings, for if the text of a contract is unlawful or contains unfair terms, the courts are not going to ignore this circumstance.

Let us proceed a stage further towards detail. In the above list the first item was 'capacity to contract'. Under it we find further sub-headings: young persons, persons under 16, persons between 16 and 18, insanity, aliens, corporate bodies, law of *ultra vires*, companies, methods of contracting, trade unions, and building societies (Gloag and Henderson 1995: 65–71). We note that attention is placed on specific categories. We are coming into the realm of circumstances, facts and the variable factors that influence the precise rules. In the background is the idea that there is basic capacity to contract by persons, but that different rules apply to different categories. 'The capacity of certain persons to enter into contracts is limited. The contractual power of persons under the age of 16 years, lunatics, aliens and corporate bodies are the points which have to be considered' (Gloag and Henderson 1995: 65).

We are coming closer to specific rules. We find ourselves being directed towards specific legislative enactments and cases and being informed of rules which have been laid down. Thus, under the first heading 'Young Persons' we read: 'The Age of Legal Capacity (Scotland) Act 1991 abolishes the division of children under the age of 18 years into pupils and minors' (Gloag and Henderson 1995: 65), and under the heading 'Persons under 16' we read that the 'general rule is that persons under the age of 16 have no contractual capacity' (Gloag and Henderson 1995: 65). At this point we are directed to section 1(1)(a) of The Age of Legal Capacity (Scotland) Act 1991.[38] So now we have reached the level of the rule. It is expressed in a legislative act. It might have been expressed in a court decision as case law. Moreover, we note the words 'general rule', which implies that there may be exceptions and specific rules for particular cases. Legislative drafting is all about setting general rules and then listing exceptions. Section 1(1) of the 1991 Act states:

1 Age of legal capacity.
   (1) As from the commencement of this Act –
      (a) a person under the age of 16 years shall, subject to section 2 below, have no legal capacity to enter into any transaction;
      (b) a person of or over the age of 16 years shall have legal capacity to enter into any transaction.[39]

We see two rules in subsection 1(a) and (b). They apply to facts: a person wants to buy a house. If aged 16 or over then they may; if under 16 they may not. We find analogous rules on the same question in other systems of law, *mutatis mutandis*. For the present purpose we are not concerned with the qualifications and methods for circumventing incapacity through the intervention of a guardian, which entails other rules.

If we were legal specialists with expert knowledge, we could have gone straight to the 1991 Act and examined how it is structured and the rules it contains. We might also have started with case law and the court decisions, and considered how the Act affected those decisions. We must check on subsequent cases and newer legislation to see how the rule has been interpreted, changed or amended. The function of a legal textbook is to facilitate access to the detailed rules, a bit like an internet browser searching for websites, and to provide an introduction and detailed coverage of the field, but in the final analysis there is no substitute for working with the legislation and the case law directly as primary sources. That said, legal textbooks and legal articles frequently propose relevant and significant interpretations that can be pleaded in court. They explore fields in detail and place issues within broad and narrow contexts. In the absence of written codes they are indispensible. In a codified system one can look to the code directly for rules, supplemented with textbooks to fill in details, such as interpretations and applications given by courts and interlinkages between different parts of the code and with other codes and the constitution, as well as with other legal orders.[40]

Substantive and procedural law

Let us now return to ideas of structure and the highest levels of classification, as there is a conceptual distinction that we can use for building models and the framework. Walker draws a distinction between 'substantive law' and 'adjective law' (Walker 2001: 205). This is of interest because it marks two dimensions of law which can be used to structure a method of analysing multilingual legal systems and legal language. 'Substantive law' denotes the rights, powers and privileges or the duties, liabilities and disabilities of persons and bodies under the branch of law in question, whereas 'the adjective law of each branch comprises the rules as to how rights are vindicated and duties enforced' (Walker 2001: 205). Stated simply, the difference is between having rights and applying or enforcing them. Enforcement generally involves a court case conducted in accordance with the court's rules of procedure, stage by stage, leading to an outcome. For example, we can analyse a court process in its various stages and, thinking multilingually, ask how the process functions when a legal system is multilingual. One can take each stage in the procedure and ask what documents are required and in what language(s). Each text then takes its place within a sequence of stages within the procedure. Translation and terminology have their roles here. The issues that arise include: jurisdiction of courts, rules of procedure, rules on evidence and proving facts, and enforcing court judgments. Each of these, as well as the texts of substantive law, has a multilingual and translation dimension. For the present purpose, the term 'procedural law' will be retained rather than 'adjective law', as it is more widely used and understood.

Adopting a viewpoint based on procedures and processes facilitates enquiry into multilingual law, because like language, a procedure is linear with a start and a finish, and each step can be explored individually. It reminds one of a production line with actions performed on a product at different stages. Procedures exist everywhere in legal systems, as they reflect the way laws are made (legislative procedure) and contracts made through negotiations, and how legal rights and obligations are applied and enforced through court or arbitration procedures. Translation can also be seen in terms of procedural stages. We thus have a background structure for deconstructing and analysing legal processes and texts in terms of their function in specific contexts of time, place and purpose. At the most simple level, one has a series of steps, from a starting point to a conclusion where the desired result (it is hoped) is achieved. If we apply that to the way we view multilingual law, we start by looking at a set of texts (corpus) written in various languages as a 'static' end product, and mentally shift towards a 'dynamic' view where we see the corpus as part of a process of continuous construction and adaptation. We move from external viewer of the static text to insider participant in the dynamic process, and towards the legal-linguistic viewpoint. In our mind's eye, before us is the whole system in all its branches of concepts and procedures as a single unit or system, but we also think of the machinery of the system in each part in the way the wheels turn and the cogs interlock. In a multilingual system these processes take place in two or more languages.

States and legal orders

We have looked briefly at the structure of a legal system and traced a rule, relating to capacity to contract, within one branch of it, but we need to introduce another set of concepts that underpin the models in Appendix II. There are different types of systems of law, in particular: systems of national law,[41] international law and supranational law.[42] This needs expanding on as there are important implications for the concept of multilingual law. While national systems of law may, or may not, be multilingual, the contexts of international and supranational law are almost always multilingual, even where only one language is selected for use. Each of the three types of system listed above is referred to as a 'legal order'. A central concept which links the three types of law (legal order) is that of the 'state'. The basic political point of reference in national law is the state. It is the organisational pivot around which law and the legal orders turn. Thus there is the law internal to the state, which is organised by and through the organs of the state. Modern legal systems are managed politically and administratively by states and the concept of 'official language' is intimately bound up with the functioning of the state. The state is the political, legal and management unit around which social life is organised. It controls a territory, and its organs and bodies administer the system of justice. There is an 'inside' the state, controlled by it, and an 'outside' the state, where it is in contact with other states and external realities. These areas of external contact give rise to two other legal orders: international law and supranational law.

States are organised in different ways; some have a single set of laws applying to their whole territory, with central institutions of government, parliament and judiciary to control the legal system (unitary state). Others (federal states) have a centre with law applying to the whole territory (federal law) and regions or provinces with a degree of autonomy and their own laws (province law).[43] We can think of these as 'models' and consider the possible language variations. Appendix II does that by setting out a range of models with language-regime alternatives presented as variants. The simplest model is where the same legal system applies throughout the whole territory. Typically, that refers to a unitary state with a single centre in the capital city. With federal states there are different systems of law: one covering the whole territory at the federal level, administered by federal institutions (federal government, parliament, judiciary), and a system of law for each province, which has its own capital and province institutions. Those are the basic conceptual (political and legal) models. With the federal model there are boundaries of law between federal and province and also between each province. So one needs rules to indicate which set of rules applies to whom and to what, as well as how to deal with matters that 'cross' the borders, such as for trade or personal relationships. One also keeps in mind that terms may have different meanings in different provinces and in federal law.

Not all states fit the two role models precisely. One exception is the United Kingdom, which has features of both models. The Westminster Parliament asserts full sovereignty over the territory of the UK like a unitary state, but there is devolution of powers to Scotland, Wales and Northern Ireland resembling a federal state to some extent although with significant differences. In Appendix II the UK is placed under a heading of 'hybrid model'.

All matters relating to the internal legal organisation of a state constitutes one type of legal order. It is the 'internal', 'domestic' or 'national'[44] law applying within the boundaries of the state to its territory and citizens. On the other hand, there are practices, customs, arrangements, agreements and treaties that each state enters into with other states for the regulation of affairs between them and which come under the name of 'international' law[45] as a second legal order. A third legal order is where states use the methods of international law to create an internal legal space between themselves for the purpose of making rules applicable to themselves and their citizens, rather like national law but at a higher hierarchical level. This is 'supranational' law and it is typified by the law of the European Union. Each of the legal orders makes law, but as the context and purpose of each are different, the precise rules developed are also different. The concept of multilingual law embraces all of the legal orders and looks at each from a point of view of the range of languages involved, the effects on texts and the interrelationships and legal-linguistic interactions between them all. One can think of this in terms of matrices of systems of law and their languages, and explore the infinite variations as they affect the legal texts and their meanings. However, for that one needs first to reflect on the nature of legal texts and where they come from.

Summary

This chapter has looked at some issues of legal theory in order to provide a foundation for making a framework and to explain the basis for the models proposed in Appendix II. It first rooted the discussion in professional legal activities and viewpoints in order to suggest a link between functions, viewpoints and philosophies of law. It asked about the nature of law and canvassed a range of different answers that have been proposed, each of which reveals a facet of the philosophy of law. While law is largely made up of rules and principles,[46] the question of justice, fairness and natural law play a significant role. Behind law stand ethics, morality, philosophy and religion.

The difference between rules and principles was touched on. The chapter then moved on to consider how legal systems are structured 'horizontally' into branches and 'vertically' from high to lower-level details within each branch. The example of Scots law was drawn on for this purpose, using the concept of contract. The concept of 'legal order' was introduced and linked to that of the state as the pivotal element between the three legal orders identified. While there was discussion of certain features of national law, the features of international and supranational law were not covered, for reasons of space.[47] The distinction between substantive law and adjective law (procedural law) that buttresses it was mentioned, and it was suggested that placing a focus on the procedural side of law and seeing legal texts in terms of a series of sites of action, or engagement, could be useful for organising information about multilingual law.

From the foregoing, there is material to construct models in terms of types of legal order and types of state and to consider linguistic variations for each of them, as set out in Appendix II. From there, one can study how systems with similar numbers of official languages tackle particular issues, and one can make comparisons. One can also extend the range of models beyond states to cover international organisations or other kinds of organisations, as indicated in Appendix II. With these observations, we have an initial outline structure for developing the framework approach in Appendix VIII. The next step is to turn attention to further details. For that it is proposed to reflect on the principal vehicles of law, namely legal texts, their different types and how they come into being as sites of engagement and effects.

Notes

1 Comparative law is not discussed in this book. For an introduction, see among others Norman (2006), Muir Watt (2015) and publications of the British Institute of International and Comparative Law.
2 In Scotland, a 'barrister' is an 'advocate'; hence the double usage here. French has *'avocat'*.
3 For a cultural introduction aimed at law students, see Benjamin and Templin (2003).
4 An example of a Scots fifteenth-century Act, The Lawburrows Act 1429, is given in Chapter 6 in connection with historical linguistics.
5 Gibbons (1994) provides examples of this in the context of court cases.
6 This is the concept of 'desuetude', known in some legal systems but not in others (Walker 2001: 258).
7 See www.merriam-webster.com/dictionary/ignorantia%20juris%20neminem%0excusat. Alternatively, *ignorantia legis neminem excusat* or *ignorantia juris non excusat*.
8 The reader will no doubt find examples of the propositions in this chapter from their own culture and language and make comparisons.
9 See www.law.cornell.edu/wex/jurisprudence and http://legal-dictionary.thefreedictionary.com/jurisprudence.
10 See Alvarez (2001) on ways used to justify genocide, for example.
11 On these concepts derived from Aristotle, see among others Kelly (1992: 26–28) and McLeod (2012: 40–44). Harris discusses the link between law and justice (Harris 1997: 277–298).
12 See also the entry on John Austin in the *Stanford Encyclopedia of Philosophy* (2014).

13 The distinction between and 'is' and 'ought' was 'in the long run inspired by Hume' (Kelly 1992: 356).
14 This book is a starting point for the present study.
15 This has led to codifying the law, which means writing all the laws in books in a systematic way; it has also led to the plain language movement (Balmford 2015).
16 See www.larousse.fr/dictionnaires/francais/loi/47700.
17 See www.larousse.fr/dictionnaires/francais/r%C3%A8gle/67653.
18 See www.larousse.fr/dictionnaires/francais/norme/55009.
19 See www.duden.de/rechtschreibung/Jura_Rechtswissenschaft_Fach.
20 See www.duden.de/suchen/dudenonline/recht.
21 See www.duden.de/rechtschreibung/Regel.
22 See www.duden.de/rechtschreibung/Norm.
23 See www.duden.de/rechtschreibung/Gesetz.
24 Note that each court has its 'rules of court' which regulate the practice and procedure of a court (Richards and Curzon 2011: 415). Language issues may be included in them.
25 Interestingly, entries relating to norms are not included in the most recent successor edition: Richards and Curzon 2011. That suggests that English-language usage of the term is regarded as insignificant, as opposed to Continental practice.
26 We note in passing that the law tends not to ask the dog for its views on the matter. This is important for those interested in rights for nature.
27 On the history of English, see among others Barber *et al.* (2012), Bragg (2003), Crystal (2003), Jones (2002), McCrum *et al.* (2011).
28 On a translation note, consider how these would be translated: literally or by an equivalent proverb in the target language?
29 There are also 'doctrines' which include principles established through past cases, such as the doctrine of self-defence. The distinction between doctrines, principles and rules is discussed by Walker (2001: 91–93). They can be seen in terms of a hierarchy of degree of breadth and abstraction. In French, '*la doctrine*' covers academic opinions and writings (Braudo 2015).
30 To be distinguished from 'principal'.
31 For application in an EU context, see Pîrnuţă, and Arseni (2011).
32 See www.theguardian.com/environment/2012/jul/02/polluter-pays-climate-change.
33 See COMEST/UNESCO (2005).
34 See, for example, the French *Code de l'environnement* [Environmental Code], which sets out general principles in Article L 110–1 of Title 1 of Book One.
35 See the Hague Conference on Private International Law and their conventions, available at: www.hcch.net/.
36 See, for example, the *Practical Handbook on European Private International Law* (EU 2010).
37 For the purpose of this exposition, the 1995 edition is retained as it serves the purpose more conveniently than the most recent 2012 edition (Gloag and Henderson 2012), which places the topic of capacity under the heading of the Law of Persons rather than the Law of Contract. This illustrates how a particular topic may be shared between different branches and also how different branches interconnect.
38 We check the provision is still in force and for any amendments, and we check for cases applying the provision to see how terms have been defined and applied.
39 See www.legislation.gov.uk/ukpga/1991/50/section/1.
40 On branches of law in different systems, see among others: James (1989), James *et al.* (1996) on English law; Walker (2001) on Scots law; Lawson *et al.* (1966) on French law; Crawford (2012) on international law; TEU and TFEU on EU law.
41 The discussion on Scots law is an example of national law.
42 Other types of law, such as religious law, are not addressed in this book, but they are provided for in the models in Appendix II.

43 The term 'province' is retained here to refer to units of territory in federal states which bear many names according to the country: state, province, Land, region etc. In a general narrative such as here, it is less confusing to use a generic term, albeit slightly artificial. The term 'state' is reserved here for the whole unit, for example represented in the United Nations.
44 These terms are largely synonymous, but used in different legal contexts.
45 Private people and businesses also transact internationally, but they do so using the rules of law made available to them under the legal orders and systems.
46 Close analysis of legal texts leads one to ask whether every provision contains a rule or principle. Consider recitals in EU directives or international agreements, or the first article of legislative instruments stating what it deals with in terms of scope and application; these more resemble assertions of legal-fact.
47 On international law, see among others Starke (1989), Akehurst and Malanczuk (1997), Kaczorowska (2003), Feltham (2012), Cooper *et al.* (2013); on EU, formerly European Community, law, see among others Louis (1980), Kapteyn and VerLoren van Themaat (2008), Chalmers *et al.* (2014), Hartley (2014) and the Europa website: http://europa.eu.

4 Legal texts

Introduction

In this chapter we turn from abstract legal theory towards the everyday application of law. This mainly takes place through the creation, interpretation and application of legal texts. For simplicity, and to introduce further concepts, the discussion is couched primarily in terms of one language, but throughout the discussion we bear in mind that in multilingual systems the processes discussed are taking place in several languages in parallel. We also bear in mind that law arises through oral language (oral utterances) and from actions by persons and from physical states of being and events that occur.[1]

An initial question is to enquire how legal texts arise. Where do they come from, how do they come into being and what is their purpose? These questions influence the form and structure of a legal act, the contents, and the way in which it is drafted in terms of style and register. They also influence the ways in which the text is read, interpreted and acted on. Each legal system has its own rules about legal acts, and so we will again take one system as representative to explore ideas and concepts. By asking where legal texts come from, we are in effect asking where law comes from. Lawyers refer to this as the 'sources of law'. Different legal systems and different legal orders can have different sources.

Identifying different sources of law leads on to thinking about the types of legal texts that are associated with them in different languages. There can be many types of text within each category of source and infinite variety in the finer details. Nonetheless, there are certain patterns and regular features. Certain sources of law and types of text have particular relevance to multilingual law as they set out the rules on language.

Once one has identified types of text, the next step towards approaching the detailed operation of a multilingual legal system is to reflect on legal texts as sites of action and to see how far the texts in different languages match up in what they say. Linguists talk about texts as 'sites of engagement'; they study how language is used. Lawyers, however, are more interested in the actual actions and legal effects of the texts they draft and read. For them, language is a tool, a precision tool, that is used to achieve specific, and specialist, purposes. Words and sentences create mental images and relationships, and that is what they are after. So the viewpoint is different and there is a difference in the emphasis. Each text can be viewed as a site where a range of different forms of action arise. First, the text is created through drafting; second, it is read and interpreted for meaning; third, it is acted on and given effect (or not).[2] However, other events occur: the text may be changed through amendment, cancelled through repeal or integrated with other acts and consolidated into a single larger text. Each of these forms of action should be canvassed, as they too are fundamental to multilingual law.

With legal texts one has to be aware of the link between law and the world of fact and reality. We have seen that law is abstract, in the mind, and the existence of a rule is not necessarily affected by whether it is complied with or not, as it is a statement of what 'ought' to happen. Legal texts differ from texts in other disciplines in so far as they deal with power relations and have implications that can lead to individuals being deprived of cash, property, liberty or life. That is serious and it impacts on all aspects of legal texts, whether it be their drafting or their interpretation, or in a multilingual context their translation. It is therefore important to ensure as far as possible that all the facts are known and that they are established as being true and correct, otherwise the rules in the legal acts will be applied wrongly and create injustice. In such cases the law fails in its purpose. There are accordingly rules about how facts are established through evidence and become 'proved' as being true, and there are procedures to be followed to maximise the probability that the true facts and circumstances are uncovered. These needs lie at the heart of any court process and court rules of procedure are devised with them in mind, as well as fairness between the parties. The relevant branch of law is that of evidence and procedure, and to it one can add enforcement of judgments to ensure that the rules of law are obeyed. In the end, force is the link between law and obedience to it.

Sources of law and legal texts

Formal sources of law

We will start by taking the different branches of law for granted. They were touched on in Chapter 3, and for the present purposes the individual fields can be largely back-grounded as the focus is on method and technique. Legal texts generally deal with some branch or other, usually of substantive law, but perhaps of some aspect of adjective law: for example, the rules of procedure of a court.[3] However, what interests us here is not so much what the texts are about (family law, commercial law, civil law, etc.) but rather who is making the texts and how they make them – what body and under what authority or powers, which is a legal question. Since legal texts convey law, the question comes close to asking about the sources of law itself. This takes us back to theory, but it makes a bridge between theory and practice. It helps explain why particular legal texts take the shape and form that they do in each system. In multilingual legal systems we cannot exclude the possibility that texts in different language versions have different appearances; indeed, to a certain extent the mere fact of being in a different language and observing its conventions creates of itself a difference, a strangeness. How much deeper than surface appearance do differences go? Each language version must remain coherent and consistent within its own language and cultural environment of texts. However, before exploring such issues one needs to develop familiarity with the nature and main types of legal texts and see their role as sources of law. The range of texts is large, as they constitute the vehicle for all branches of law and their implementation. So we will restrict attention to a few broad categories. First, though, we take a step back towards theory and consider where law comes from in terms of its sources.

The simplest approach to reflecting on sources is to select one system, identify its methods and then build on that to compare with other systems. With that in mind, we return to Scots law and briefly make reference to sources in other legal systems and legal orders. As regards Scots law, Walker observes that: 'the phrase "sources of law" has several meanings which have to be carefully distinguished' (Walker 2001: 407).

First, there are the 'historical sources, which are the events and incidents in legal history which have given rise to the principle or rule in question' (Walker 2001: 407). He gives examples: 'Common historical sources include ancient customs, the Roman law, the Bible and the Christian church, the canon law, feudal law, the medieval law, merchant and maritime law, foreign (including English) rules and many of the major events in constitutional and legal history' (Walker 2001: 407).[4]

A second meaning is connected to social, political, economic, moral or religious sources that have given rise to a principle or rule. For example, race riots have given rise in the past to rules on racial discrimination (Walker 2001: 407). A third meaning is of direct interest for the present context as it covers the 'statements in enactments, decisions, books and documents and the usages of persons from which a court may derive a principle for the decision of a case'. These are 'material sources' and 'every principle or rule has such a source'. However, 'these are better described as the materials for formulating a decision and which determine the content of a principle or rule derived from them' (Walker 2001: 408).

Walker prefers not to talk of the foregoing in terms of formal sources, but rather as being the 'historical origins of rules, philosophical bases of rules and material grounds of rules' (Walker 2001: 408). What is interesting in the third formulation is that the sources are perceived as the 'raw materials' from which a court or judge creates (constructs) the law. We have a clue here that a judge is not merely studying texts for their linguistic meanings, but is also engaged on a wider and more active search for materials on which to build a solution to the legal case before them. It is an active role of adaptation and creation. This is significant for understanding legal interpretation, and by extension the interpretation of multilingual legal texts, which just involve a greater number of raw materials to draw on.

That brings us to a fourth meaning. Walker explains that 'The only true "sources" of legal principles and rules are the legal or formal sources'. Further, 'It is to these legal sources only that one may resort to find a rule or principle of law for the application to and solution of a legal controversy or problem raised by certain facts' (Walker 2001: 408). What, then, are these true sources? The answer is significant because we are seeking to establish a link between sources of law and sources of legal texts, which in turn we hope may lead us on to questions of form, layout, structure, contents, effects and methods of interpretation applied to different types of legal text; and by extension to translation and multilingual legal texts. Walker lists, and analyses, seven sources for Scots law: legislation, judicial precedents or case law, literary sources – books of authority, standard textbooks and other legal literature, custom, equity and extraneous sources (Walker 2001: 407–485). But he also observes that the ultimate source is the power of the state (Walker 2001: 408). So we have a link to legal texts, but we also have a problem because it is not obvious how custom, equity and extraneous sources fit into a pattern of texts. We will pass each of these sources briefly in review.

Legislation
Of all the formal sources, legislation and case law seem to be the most significant. The former comprises written rules made by the Westminster Parliament in London for the UK[5] and by the devolved Holyrood Parliament for Scotland.[6] Then there are the rules made by the EU institutions[7] for the EU Member States, including the UK. Strictly speaking, the EU forms part of a different legal order (supranational law), with its own sources deriving from the EU Treaties and the case law of the Court of Justice of the

European Union, but EU legal acts such as regulations, directives and decisions are binding on Member States (Article 288 TFEU), as are judgments of the Court of Justice of the European Union (Mikelsone 2013). To that one could add the final judgments of the European Court of Human Rights in Strasbourg under the European Convention on Human Rights, since Article 46(1) thereof says that 'The High Contracting Parties undertake to abide by the final judgment of the Court in any case to which they are parties'.[8] We have here an exception to the general approach (in some legal systems) that international texts are not formally binding in national law, though politically they are generally observed (Craig Barker 2004: point 3).[9]

Let us pause and consider what it means for a legislative act to be a source of law. First, the act sets out rules to be observed. Second, law-making is hierarchical, because there are higher- and lower-level acts (statutes, regulations, bye-laws, etc.). A higher-level act is a source of authority for a lower-level act, because the higher-level act expressly provides for the existence of the lower-level act as a part and extension of itself with respect to some matter of finer detail. The lower-level act needs to make its parentage explicit as the higher-level act is its source of power,[10] and the terms and expressions in the lower-level act reflect those in the higher-level act.[11] The higher-level act 'controls' the domains and meanings of terms in the lower-level act. Definitions of terms in the higher-level act apply equally to the lower-level act.[12] This approach is systematic and functional and a method for controlling legal meanings. In a civil law system the constitution would be at the highest level. There are codes and laws, and lower-level regulations and ordinances (subordinate legislation) made under them (Lawson et al. 1966: 14; Weston 1991: 59–65). In the case of Scots law, as Scotland is part of the UK, there is no formal written constitution and the laws (statutes) made by the Westminster Parliament stand at the highest level, with regulations and 'statutory instruments' being made under them. In the case of EU law the foundation treaties (TEU and TFEU) are the primary source of law. Article 288 TFEU provides for secondary-level legislative acts: regulations, directives, decisions, and recommendations and opinions. In each language there needs to be consistency in the terminology and language of the lower-level act with respect to the higher-level act.

Each time when one searches for law, or the legal rule on a matter, one turns to the relevant legislative act to read what it says, and that is what it means for it to be a source of law. The lawyer takes the legislative text as a source of information on the law, interprets it for meaning and advises the client on what it means for them. As a site of action, different scenarios arise: a lawyer may consult the act to tell a client what to do (or not do) or for guidance in drawing up a contract or house transfer deed. The text may be relied on in a submission to a court by a barrister/advocate, and the court may pronounce on its meaning in law. On the other hand, there may be a need to amend the act, or to draft a subordinate act to implement a detail in it, such as when the act is to come into force and have legal effect (commencement order). Perhaps the act must be cancelled through repeal, which implies a new repealing act at the same or a higher level. Or perhaps administrative guidance must be prepared on how a legislative act should be implemented, and so on.

We can see the emergence of different types, or genres, of legal text linked to these different actions. In a multilingual legal system each operation takes place in parallel in each language version of the act. It is like a rainbow of colours with each colour representing a language. South Africa with 11 official languages is the 'rainbow nation'. The language editions of the EU Official Journal in paper are colour-coded. The acts must be consistent and coherent within each language internally or 'vertically' and also across the language versions 'horizontally'. This creates a legal-linguistic matrix for terminology.

Judicial precedents and case law
Case law as a source consists of the reports of the courts (Walker 2001: 433–475). The courts in this context are the Scottish courts, but also other UK courts for matters, such as tax, that apply broadly to the whole UK or where there are cases that have raised similar issues to the ones at issue. For the same reason, decisions by courts in other countries may be consulted. The court system is hierarchical and the highest court for many matters is the Supreme Court of the United Kingdom[13], though not for criminal law, as that remains with the Scottish courts. Each legal system similarly has its hierarchy of courts.[14] The Court of Justice of the European Union, based in Luxembourg, is the highest EU court.[15] Its decisions on EU law are a source of law for all EU member states and their courts. Similarly the International Court of Justice based in the Hague makes rulings which are a source of international law.[16] The European Court in Strasbourg issues rulings on the European Convention on Human Rights.[17] If we reflect, in passing, that a particular matter may be touched on in legislative texts at any level in any legal order and by decisions of any of the above-mentioned courts, then we can begin to appreciate the potential complexity of deciding on the law and legal meaning in certain (rather complicated) sets of circumstances. Which act or which court decision should prevail if there are differences between them? Conflicts in rules arise and they must be resolved in order to maintain coherence and certainty. We come back to the idea of a matrix of sources for the making of meaning and determining what the law is on a particular matter.

Using case law as a source means knowing how to read and interpret cases, transferring information obtained from past cases and comparing it with the circumstances of a case in hand. Past cases are a source of guidance as courts follow their previous decisions. This is the concept of 'precedent'. The concept of 'binding precedent' means that no deviation is permitted, epitomised in the phrase '*stare decisis*' [to stand by decided matters] (Perell 1987). Yet one can ask what part of a decision is binding. Here we enter into the details of how to interpret cases, and there are differences between civil law and common law systems (Lawson *et al.* 1966: 14–17). In the former, the basic rules are generally found in the code or a legislative act and the decision is an application of the rules to particular circumstances before the court. The decision is not necessarily binding for other courts, though a lower court is unlikely to depart from the approach of a higher court, since a diverging judgment would probably be overturned on an appeal.[18] In a common law system there may be a legislative act and a similar circumstance as described, but there may be only previous cases and judicial rulings covering a matter and these need to be analysed to identify what rules they might contain. The rule is to be constructed out of the circumstances of the case and the judgment. That means making a general proposition out of particular circumstances and applying it to the case in hand. Lawyers identify different parts of a judgment (Walker 2001: 457–471) and attribute different weightings to them; for example, the part of the judgment that is decisive as the reason for a decision (*ratio decidendi*) and the part that is more general comment and observation (*obiter dicta*), and they use these concepts to construct arguments for resolving the case in hand.

From this brief indication, one can glimpse how case interpretation can become complex as a later court searches for the rule to be extracted from previous cases to apply to the case before it. That reminds one of the legal expression: 'the rule in [such and such case]'. Take, for example, the 'postal rule' in English law that an offer made by post becomes a contract when it is accepted by post, which derived from the case of *Adams v Lindsell* (1818) 1 B & Ald 681. For common law lawyers, citing the name of a court case is tantamount to stating the rule of law deriving from it. It is an example of how legal meaning can be different from linguistic meaning and how expert knowledge is required in order to understand the significance of the reference to a previous case.

How does all of this function in a multilingual legal system? If a court case in a multilingual system takes place in a single language, whether imposed or chosen by the parties, there is a possibility of imbalances arising between languages if there are many cases in a large language and few in a smaller language. How is a balance maintained? Ideally we should study the details of each legal system, but for reasons of space we will take one example. The EU Court of Justice publishes its court reports in all EU languages. The language of the case (the language in which the case is heard) is technically the authentic version.[19] It is, however, possible for a multilingual system also to be multi-legal in the sense of incorporating more than one type of legal system within its territory. For example, Canada embraces provinces with common law traditions but also civil law traditions, notably in Quebec province, which uses the French language.[20] In the UK there are also different traditions between Scots and English law. It means that one must enter within the particular system and follow the rules and methods of that system and in the language that applies.

A lawyer uses the interpretations and decisions in past cases to advise clients and draw up private contracts and documents. We can place attention on the actual court documents. How are these drawn up, how are they structured and how is the information in each of them organised? We can ask which are the documents that are generated by a court, and for what purpose as legal texts. Each court case involves a process that follows methods and procedures laid down by law (court jurisdiction, rules of procedure, etc.). Thus, for example, a court case, or process, is started by a complaint by a person aggrieved and may be followed by a defence, a hearing of facts and evidence and arguments, judgment and possibly subsequent enforcement procedures. The names for each type of document differ according to the legal system and also according to the type of process that is involved, but there is a broad underlying model here. The names of each act, the sequence of steps and the variants are set down in rules of procedure of the court in question, accompanied by guidance if available. In a multilingual system one expects all those documents to be available in all the official languages, and one can take the Rules of Procedure of the EU Court of Justice as an example of this.

Each stage in a process implies a type of legal document, to be constructed according to particular formulae, using language adapted to the context and dedicated to setting out the point of view of client, advocate/barrister or court, or indicating a procedural stage. In general terms, three elements are present in a court judgment: the facts of the case as presented by opposing parties and as determined by the court; the rules of law relevant to the facts of the matter under contention (whether in legislation, case law, etc.); and the specific application of those rules and texts to the particular facts of the case decided by the court. The judge 'constructs' the law applicable to the facts and gives meanings to terms. It is a creative act which is generally set down in a written judgment that follows patterns and styles that differ from those of legislative acts, as can be readily seen from a perusal of any law or case report in any language. In a multilingual context the court may need to draw on texts from the different languages in the system and compare them for their meanings in order to construct the law applying to the case in hand.

Literary sources and legal literature
Books of authority, standard textbooks and other legal literature are sources of law in Scotland[21] (Walker 2001: 475–480), but their precise status depends on the legal system and also the degree of development of a given branch of law. For example, in a highly regulated branch such as tax law the legislation and case law are the primary sources, but textbooks provide an overview and interpretations and arguments to put forward. In other branches which are new and complex and there are few cases, the legal literature may be the only source of detailed examination of a field and will be relied on heavily to analyse issues and construct legal rules. The example of international space law comes to mind as an area for future development.[22]

Legal textbooks elucidate, document and draw attention to cases, legislation and international and supranational texts. In a codified civil law legal system they may tend to follow the structure of codes and comment on their provisions, cases and related materials. In a common law system where the centre is judicial decision-making and court reports, although certain fields (such as company law) are largely regulated by statute, textbooks play an important role in providing a broad overview and structure and in looking at how case law and legislation fit together. They provide a means of placing everything in a wider context. That can be difficult to do within individual cases. Textbooks provide training for lawyers as well as information for general readers. The books referred to in this chapter, such as Walker (2001), who provides deeper legal-philosophical reflections that have been drawn on, are examples of this. For the lawyer and linguist, textbooks and literary works also provide a source of terms and expressions linked to context.

From the point of view of multilingual law, textbooks tend to be written in one language. They may be translated, but that is mainly a commercial matter. On the other hand, official guides and publications are expected to be issued in the official languages. For EU law, as well as the Official Journal, there are books published by the Official Publications Office in Luxembourg[23] in the EU official languages. In each case legal textbooks are a source of information and guidance on terminology for the purposes of translation, as they generally make the context of terms and concepts clear.

Custom
Walker's fourth category of source is 'custom'. This is an interesting source as it can be non-linguistic. Where there is a habit or practice reflected in behaviour, action and conduct, it may be treated as a custom and be a source of law, provided that it meets a number of criteria, such as that it is fair and reasonable and has been generally accepted for a long time (Walker 2001: 480–481). In itself, a 'mere habit' does not create a rule, but through repetition over time it can give rise to an expectation on the part of others, leading them to take actions that depend on it, and that can in turn lead to the possible creation of a rule of law. In effect a habit becomes a rule under certain circumstances. For example, walking the dog can be seen as a habit, but not as giving rise to an expectation, entitlement or rule of law.[24] One can wonder about the dog's viewpoint on the matter; but the dog has no means to bring its wishes before a court

of law. In commercial law and practice many activities can take place tacitly, without a formal agreement, as custom.

How far it is possible for custom to give rise to a rule depends on each legal system. It is possible in Scots law. However, to become clearly established as law, a custom needs to be identified and declared as such by an authorised body, such as a court. This brings us back to language and to the context of a court case and a judicial decision recorded in a document. Custom as a source of law seems to be most relevant to systems of law that are less developed, or where there are specialised activities such as commercial activities.

One of the problems of life in society is that not everything can be foreseen in advance in legal texts, and people then need to find everyday solutions that work for them. The issue takes on a degree of importance in relation to gaps in legal texts, legal holes, *vides juridiques*, and such like. Daily administration requires implementation of law to wide varieties of situations not always anticipated. The texts may not cover particular facts precisely, and 'creative' interpretation is required. Here it may be necessary to fall back on principles of law and general method and adapt them to the problem in hand, perhaps also applying a particular rule by analogy. The actions and solutions adopted may be regarded as similar to custom, until validated or rejected by a formal legal act. Finding meaning from legal texts can also lead to constructing meaning from other sources when there is a gap in the information in a text. One aspect relevant to multilingual law is that there may be an apparent gap in one language version, but not in another; alternatively, the nuances of the language versions may differ.

Custom is important in international law in relations between states as a source of law. Other sources of international law include the International Court of Justice, law-making treaties, general principles of law, judicial decisions, writings of publicists, considerations of humanity and legitimate interests (Crawford 2012: 20–47). Custom is important in international trade and commerce. Rules on languages can also arise through custom. In the case of English in the UK, this could be regarded as one of the foundations. It is important to be aware of custom as a source of law and a factor in the construction of legal meanings.

Equity
Walker includes equity as a source of law. The concept has a range of meanings: 'as natural law, as fairness or justice, as flexibility and discretion opposed to rules of strict law, and as a body of principles distinct from those of law administered by separate courts' (Walker 2001: 481–482.). This is a source that ties in with legal theory and the concepts of natural law and justice, and it takes us back to Chapter 3. We can see how theory becomes embedded into practice. Scots law has a unified system, different from England. English law has developed equity into a major division of the legal system. To understand English law one must bear in mind its history: the original common law courts were supplemented by courts of equity, and the English concept of equity is highly technical and goes beyond relatively simple notions of 'fairness'.[25]

It follows from the foregoing, in Scots law, that legislative texts should conform to equitable principles and be drafted in accordance with them, and courts should act according to equitable principles and interpret legal texts in the light of them. One implication, however, is that courts may give a different meaning to a legal text from the one intended by the drafters and written into the text. For the linguist, we have here a signal that there can be divergence between the linguistic meaning of a text and its meaning in law. This arises through the action of interpretation rather than of drafting.

In a multilingual context we can note the possibility of different perceptions as to what is 'equitable', particularly where different languages are identified with different cultures. That can arise in national law with different ethnic and religious groups, but it also arises in the international and supranational legal orders where the divergences may be on a larger scale. On the other hand, a significant purpose of supranational law, such as EU law (formerly EC law), is to narrow down the differences and to enlarge the area of shared cultural perceptions through harmonisation of laws and creating common rules in many spheres of economic activities, using legal and linguistic means and creating common institutions (Hartley 2014). That thought leads us to embark on an examination of individual systems and their internal dynamics and viewpoints, but it takes us beyond the present scope.

Extraneous sources

Walker's last category of source, referred to as 'extraneous' sources, covers any other source that may be drawn on, whether it be a foreign system of law, or the judge's 'own moral conscience, his beliefs as to what is fair and right and reasonable in the circumstances, in short, on his idea of what justice requires' (Walker 2001: 483–485). This serves as a reminder that in law, as in life, for every exercise in categorisation and anticipation of every possibility there is something overlooked – the unknown unknowns. We will leave it at that.

Formal sources in different systems

Before leaving the subject of formal sources of law, we can make a few observations. The Scots law sources have been listed as examples for the purpose of setting up a conceptual framework of reference. Every system of law has its sources. Sources of French law include codes, laws, subordinate legislative acts, presidential decrees, administrative ordinances, *travaux préparatoires* (preparatory documents) that precede and accompany legislative texts, court decisions and learned annotations to them, textbooks, monographs, commentaries by writers of repute and decisions of foreign courts applying a similar system (Lawson *et al.* 1966: 14). Sources of English law include legislation, case law, law reporting, custom and books of authority (James 1989: 6–23). Sources of international law include the International Court of Justice, custom, law-making treaties, general principles of law, judicial decisions, writings of publicists, considerations of humanity, legitimate interests (Crawford 2012: 20–47). Sources of EU supranational law include the primary treaties, law enacted by EU institutions and 'Member States meeting in Council', the case law of the three courts comprising the Court of Justice of the European Union (Court of Justice, General Court, Civil Service Tribunal), general principles of law (principles shared by European legal systems), international agreements with third countries, cases of international courts, textbooks, monographs and commentaries by writers of repute, *travaux préparatoires*, and so on (Hartley 1994: 95–97).[26] To assist in searching for sources of rules relating to language and languages, Appendix III sets out some practical suggestions organised according to legal order and types of text. These can be adapted, enlarged and extended in the light of the particular system under enquiry.

Contracts

In the lists of formal sources set out above there is a genre of legal text which is not included but nonetheless figures prominently in legal life, and that is contracts. The concept of 'social contract' of Jean-Jacques Rousseau[27] underpins modern political theory, but contracts are not generally seen as a formal source of law. In domestic or national law contracts are made between persons or 'parties' to arrange matters between themselves. The parties may be private individuals, business corporations or government departments, or whoever. Their agreements apply essentially to the relations between themselves, although there can be an impact on others. The law of contract applies, and in Chapter 3 we made a short overview of some of its component elements in one system. Contracts can arise through written texts, or oral utterances, or even from tacit behaviour, such as, for example, buying flowers from a vendor: flowers in exchange for money.

From the point of view of multilingual law, parties can, to the extent permitted by the legal system governing the matter (not necessarily a simple question), make their contracts in any language they choose and in as many language versions as they wish, and specify which version(s) is/are binding between them. But this apparent freedom will turn out on closer inspection to be hedged in by many factors, such as the rules on language of the system and the alignment of the terminology. How does one treat a contract in French using concepts of French civil law that is declared to be subject to English law and therefore its system of concepts? With difficulty, using semiotic techniques discussed in Chapter 8. On the other hand, parties to a contract are usually able to select the methods and procedures they wish to follow in order to negotiate and sign their contract, within the limits of the legal system governing their capacity to act and the law governing contracts they may make. The contracting parties are subjects of law and not law-makers unless they have the powers of a state.

The foregoing represents a simplified view of a domestic national law context, but in the international and supranational orders the role of contract takes on a different character, including that of being a source of law if, for example, it comprises a 'law-making' treaty in international law (Crawford 2012: 31–32). For example, the TEU and TFEU are both international treaties, made in accordance with international law, but they also create the internal order of EU supranational law with direct effect on the national domestic law of the Member States. They are a source of EU law, national law and international law; yet they are in essence contracts between states, with effects on third parties, including EU citizens and businesses. International treaties, agreements, conventions, protocols and exchanges of letters[28] are all different names for what are in essence agreements, or contracts, between states and international organisations such as the UN or the EU that they have set up contractually between themselves. Of course, the technical details are different from those of national law, such as capacity to contract. So whenever there is a treaty or other international act, it is in essence a contract and the details are agreed between the parties.

Treaties and agreements are methods for creating international organisations. We expect to find rules relating to languages mentioned somewhere in the foundation texts, either in the primary texts or in subordinate implementing texts, but it is quite conceivable that no mention is made explicitly and a practice develops spontaneously through tacit agreement backed up by habit and custom. The mere fact of producing texts in language by itself reveals the linguistic choices made: *res ipsa loqitur*, the facts speak for themselves. The founding texts are written in language and it is evident which languages have been selected for them. One would generally expect a clause in a foundation text that indicates the status of particular languages and the relationship between them where there are more than one. The TEU is written as a single text in 24 language versions (as a result of amendment), each of which is equally valid (authentic) (Article 55 TEU as amended). The linguistic regime for the EU organisations is set up by the TFEU (Article 342 as amended) and provides (currently) for 24 official languages. The practical details are set out in subordinate (secondary) acts.[29]

In the case of EU supranational law, contract underpins the system through the treaties which create the primary level of law and the internal EU legal order, which has been organised so as to take on features of a classic domestic legal system. However, whereas a domestic national system of law must regulate 'everything', both international and supranational law can be selective in the subjects treated and in the way they are treated. Thus, for example, the EU legal order takes an economic viewpoint and aims at creating and regulating markets for goods and services. This is done through contracts between states which create organisations to manage the system on their behalf and on their instructions.

Different types of legal text

There are many types of legal text. Lawyers do not use the term, but linguists refer to 'genres', which is French for 'kinds' or 'sorts'. Generally the term is used in art and literature, as well as linguistics, but we can borrow the concept to make the point that there are an infinite variety of legal documents on all sorts of matters and they can be classified according to their legal order, their subject matter or branch of law, their status, the number of signatories or parties to them, their function, and so on. For example, at one end we have a simple unilateral handwritten will by a person to designate heirs. At the other end we have a complex multiparty treaty on an important diplomatic matter, comprising many texts and a final act. In between there is infinite variety. We can use the concept of genre to link legal texts to the concept of sources of law, as one method of classification. That would broadly take us into written laws, case law, textbooks and, we added, contracts. The handwritten will could be seen as a sort of unilateral contract, and the multilateral treaty as another form of contract. Legislative acts are written laws and judgments in cases comprise case law, and so on. There is probably no limit to the range of genres of legal texts, and for each category that we create, we can no doubt imagine variations and refinements such as sub-genres. In legal offices it is normal to have copies, styles and models of standard, frequently used or rarely used legal texts as an aid to practice. These are texts which have been successful in the past, have been accepted by clients, courts and/or authorities, and their effects are broadly known in advance from experience. Typically, they contain standard clauses or text to be included in all acts, with variants for different scenarios, and blank parts to be filled in with the individual specific information. We are all familiar with administrative forms to fill in for this or that matter, and these too can be seen as genres of legal texts.

Within each genre we find sub-genres, for example different types of legislative text such as constitution, higher-ranking laws, lower-ranking laws and regulations. We can take each of these subdivisions and make further classifications, such as different types of higher-ranking law according to context, function, signatory, and so on. Taking such an approach leads to the creation of patterns, like trees or family relationships. It is classification work, useful for organising information, but also useful for clarifying relationships and degrees of closeness and difference, as well as hierarchy and which takes precedence. For lawyers and linguists there is a benefit because it is important to identify which types of terms belong to which types of text, and also the ways in which different types (genres, discussed in Chapter 6) of text are written, or drafted, and read, interpreted and acted on. For example, a law is generally written using formal impersonal language and follows certain conventions and styles in its layout. The styles and conventions, as well as the precise range, can vary between legal systems and legal orders and languages. In a multicultural and multilingual system, such as for EU law, it is necessary to reflect on the different practices and conventions in Member State legal systems in order to arrive at a shared set of types of text and shared concepts and terminology across the languages. These are necessary to help ensure that all the language versions are fully aligned and convey the same messages.

One could devote a whole book to the topic of the different types of legal texts, classified according to author, subject matter domain, level in the legal hierarchy, whether public law or private law, civil or criminal or administrative law (or other branch), whether linked to substance or to procedure, and all that in an unending range of different types of legal process across systems and languages. To that one can add the dimension of the different legal orders, as well as the dimension of time: documents taken from any time in the past or present, bearing in mind that social and technological changes are constantly leading to the creation of new types of acts and their variants. For the present purpose it is sufficient to be aware of the background diversity in legal texts. They all use language, but not necessarily all the same language. The legal and linguistic question is how they all interrelate and combine to form a system of law.

Legal texts as sites for actions[30]

We have by now identified a broad range of sources of law and noted that many sources take the form of written texts, and there is a huge variety in the types of legal text. That said, all legal texts can be seen as sites of linguistic engagement and of legal actions. We can ask ourselves about the actions that typically surround a legal text. Here are a few: drafting, interpretation, amendment and repeal. They all apply to legislative enactments. Court judgments are not generally amended or repealed, though they may be 'overturned' or 'reversed' on appeal. We will take the example of legislative texts and reflect briefly on the actions mentioned. As they involve language, they can involve one, two or more languages. Legislative texts are important for multilingual law as each of them is at the heart of law-making. We will supplement them with two further matters that are central to law-making: the relationship to facts, evidence and proof, and the question of enforcement. These form part of the contextual environment of legal texts.

Drafting

It can be imagined that drafting different genres of legal text requires different knowledge and skills. Drafting is an art as well as a science (Bowman 2005). Let us sketch out some factors on the technical scientific side. First of all is the question of legal context: which legal order applies? Within a legal order, which legal system or particular regime? Is the text part of Scots, English, French, German (etc.) law? Is it an international law text? Is it an EU supranational law text, or one of another international

Legal texts 63

organisation? Whichever applies, the context contains rules and elements such as standard wording and terminology that need to be observed and adapted to. These have effects on many features of the legal text from the outset and determine their form and content by virtue of logic, common sense, consistency and coherence generated as a result of relationships: first, within the text; second, with related texts in the same field; third, with past texts of the same genre; fourth, between the text and the legal system in all its branches; fifth, between the text and the grammar, syntax and other features of the language in question.

Users become accustomed to certain styles and formats and develop techniques to interpret and use them. The courts develop techniques of interpretation based on a consistent use of language. Thus a Scottish legal act follows methods devised for such an act and uses relevant legal language, concepts and approaches, and an English, French, German, and so on, legal act likewise follows the prescribed methods.[31] An international law act follows the styles and conventions for such acts[32] and similarly with EU legislative acts.[33] Within each system, different types of act are drafted according to the type of act and its purpose. Yet certain types of act may have similar features across systems. For example, in legislative acts one could expect a core structure along the lines reflected in the guidance for EU multilingual acts in the Interinstitutional Agreement of 22 December 1998 and the accompanying Joint Practical Guide (EU 2013), which are both based on shared European practice. The foundation parts may be summarised as: title, author, citations, recitals, enacting provisions (articles) and annexes. Each part of a new text is constructed according to past precedents, standard wording and obligatory clauses for certain issues addressed, as well as standard terminology agreed across all language versions. The rest of the text is adapted to the policy sector and the intentions and objectives of the act. Different legal systems treat each part of the act in different ways. For example, in UK acts the recitals are reduced to a minimum, as one can see by looking at any statute, and this fits in with the common law system. The intention is for the meanings to be obtained from the enacted provisions analytically. Compare that with the number of recitals in an EU directive, which can be numerous.

Second, one can ask about the type and status of the act to be created. This links with genre: legislative act, court act, contract, or other type. If a legislative act, is it a high-ranking primary level act or a lower-level secondary act made under a primary act, or is it an administrative act? In each case the structure and much of the language to be used will already be well established, with manuals of drafting guidance and well-established precedents.

Third, which branch of law is involved? For each branch there is specialised language in the form of terms and expressions that carry specific meanings and must be used in order to avoid confusion and uncertainty. The implicit legal assumption is that different terms carry different meanings, so care is needed to be consistent as errors can become magnified through translation. There may be certain types of act (laws, regulations, etc.) that have become standard in a branch of law and certain types of structures and standard clauses may need to be inserted.

These questions, however, are all merely the starting point for creating the act, the empty box of form to be filled with substance. This substance goes under the name of 'policy' and it represents the changes in the legal system and specific actions and effects that the legal text is intended to bring about. There is the broad policy background of a text, in terms of the domain or field of action, and there are the detailed actions and effects to be brought about through legal means using language. One can seek out the different dimensions to a legal text by looking at it from different points of view. It is a method of checking, revising and analysing and it can be used to review the function of terminology used in drafting. For example, there are aspects that are primarily of a legal nature and relate to legal relationships, formal structure, powers, and so on (legal viewpoint); second, there are aspects that concern the policy field in question (policy viewpoint); third, there are aspects that concern the specific actions and effects intended by each word, sentence and article (action viewpoint); fourth, there is the way in which language is used to construct the text and achieve its purposes, including grammatical, spelling and syntactic conformity to the official language code (language viewpoint) (Robertson 2010).

In order to draft a text, the drafter needs to know the formal requirements, standardised language and terminology, policy context and effects being sought. These include existing laws, court decisions, day-to-day practice and the history of the field; all of this is imagined in terms of patterns and relationships, causes and effects, as well as desired and undesired activities. A drafter needs to know (or be informed about) the general policy environment, the specific wishes of the instructing client and the legal environment which is to be worked on (for legislation) or within (for a private contract). In practical terms this implies participation by a person who is expert in the policy field (or who knows the business) and a person who is expert in writing legal texts: client and lawyer, though the two viewpoints may be present in the same person. For very complex fields and texts there may be several persons occupying particular roles, each of whom has particular specialised knowledge and skills to contribute. They then form a team.

In a multilingual context, the legal text must be drafted in all the languages of the system. There are different ways of achieving this. We will take the example of a legislative text. The simplest is to draft a text in one language and to translate the final text into other language(s) (target languages). This is understood to be the method in Ireland for English and Irish (*The Irish Times*, 21 February 2015). The method is pragmatic, but it places a target language at a relative disadvantage, as it must follow the source language and concepts as best it can and it is moulded by the source language in terminology. In cases of doubt as to meaning, the source text is likely to carry the most prestige. It also implies arrangements for creating terms (secondary term formation) in target languages to match those created through primary term formation in a source language.

A second way of drafting multilingual legislation is to translate the source texts while still at an early stage in drafting, and then to translate each revised version. This method allows linguistic and terminological problems encountered by target languages to be raised and the source draft can be adjusted to accommodate them. There is a need for primary and secondary term formation for concepts, but there is scope for aligning them together across all the language versions early on in the drafting process. This blurs the distinction between 'source' and 'target' languages. A variant on this approach is that either the same language is used all the time as the source language, or there can be switching between languages as to which is the source language, which mixes things up somewhat. The EU broadly follows the approach of continuous translation and adjustment of language versions as they progress through the stages of preparation. It allows everyone involved in each language to consult, check and take instructions in anticipation of the next meeting of the negotiators. Any language can in theory act in the role of 'source' or 'base' language, but in practice one or two languages tend to take the lead: currently English and French. The EU method is seen in terms of co-drafting (Gallas 1999).

A third approach is to take the concept of 'co-drafting' a stage further and to draw up each language version separately from scratch, with separate drafting persons for each language, and then compare texts and revise the language versions together. This is understood to be the method followed for federal laws in Canada for English and French (Levert 1995, 2011). This method is sophisticated and places the languages on a level of equality, at least in theory. It requires good back-up, and the role of term creation, formation and alignment between languages must figure prominently. This raises issues of lexicology and terminology, topics that are included in Chapter 6 from a language point of view. However, where more than two languages are involved, things become more complicated.[34] Where there are very many languages, it helps if there is in the background at least one language which has complete linguistic consistency, because there are often different ways to translate a given text and variations can and do occur between translations over time.[35] So drafting in a multilingual context means juggling with all the languages that form part of the system in an effort to align them to achieve the same desired legal effects, while at the same time complying with all the formal requirements for drafting within each language. Appendix III contains some suggestions regarding sources in respect of drafting.

Interpretation

The purpose of drafting a legal text is to bring about changes and effects. The drafter tries to ensure the results desired through careful wording, but in the end it is the person reading the text who has the task to work out what is meant, apply it and produce the effects. If there is disagreement over the meaning of a text, then it is the courts, in the context of a court process, who must decide what a text means.[36] So courts are the ultimate deciders on what legal texts mean. However, legal interpretation is not merely a question of reading a text. There are different ways of reading texts. We are entering complex territory, but to illustrate some of the methods we will take a brief look at some approaches that apply with respect to legislative texts. Each system has its own methods, and in a multilingual context one must check whether language versions are aligned or carry divergent readings, as well as apply the armoury of methods and techniques of interpretation. At the outset it is useful to recall that the purpose of interpretation is to 'construct' the law. A text is an element in this process.

Interpretation of legal texts is not simply a matter of identifying and applying the literal (plain) meaning of words in a text. Words in legal texts do not always have a single meaning, but may have a variety of meanings and these are linked to context. (McLeod 2011: 231). While a starting point would be with the literal meaning of words (in all language versions), the courts have devised methods to handle texts where there is uncertainty. These include: looking at the whole text (golden rule) (McLeod 2011: 233–236); looking at the mischief being addressed (mischief rule) (McLeod 2011: 236–238); looking at the purpose of the text and the intention of the author (McLeod 2011: 238–247). However, these are aids to construction and do not constitute binding rules (McLeod 2011: 246–247). In a Scottish context, Walker distinguishes between the 'literal approach' and the 'liberal approach' (Walker 2001: 415–418): 'the need for the courts to try to appreciate the overriding intention of the legislation, the general policy behind the Act, and the need to further remedies and not take refuge in pettifogging verbal objections' (Walker 2001: 417).

The issue of interpretation thus becomes a matter of justice and raises issues of natural law mentioned in Chapter 3. That leads to the view expressed by Bennion (2001: 84), quoted by McLeod, that an enactment is to be construed 'according to the numerous general guides laid down for that purpose by law' and 'where these conflict (as they often do) the problem shall be resolved by weighing and balancing the interpretative factors concerned' (McLeod 2011: 248). In addition to using dictionaries, analysing context and the structure of the act, and other factors, there is a series of presumptions that come into play in interpretation: against injustice, absurdity, retrospectivity (retroactivity); strict interpretation of penal provisions; relating to 'and' and 'or'; compliance with international law and EU law; against gaining advantage from wrongdoing; against binding the Crown; and so on. (McLeod 2011: 248–291; Walker 2001: 419–432; Bennion 1990, 2009). One of the formal guides in UK law is the Interpretation Act 1978. It also serves as drafting guidance. EU law has no equivalent interpretation act, but in international law there is the Vienna Convention on the Law of Treaties 1969, which serves a similar purpose of setting standards. Articles 31–33 address interpretation of treaties. The general rule is that a treaty is to be 'interpreted in good faith in accordance with the ordinary meaning to be given to the terms of the treaty in their context and in the light of its object and purpose' (Article 31(1)). Where the meaning is ambiguous or obscure, or leads to a manifestly absurd or unreasonable result, Article 32 provides that recourse 'may be had to supplementary means of interpretation, including the preparatory work of the treaty and the circumstances of its conclusion'. Article 33 addresses the multilingual dimension and the interpretation of treaties authenticated in two or more languages. Here, 'the text is equally authoritative in each language, unless the treaty provides or the parties agree that, in case of divergence, a particular text shall prevail' (Article 33(1)). Additional language versions are considered authentic 'only if the treaty so provides or the parties so agree' (Article 33(2)). 'The terms of the treaty are presumed to have the same meaning in each authentic text' (Article 33(3)). Lastly, in the case of continuing uncertainty, 'the meaning which best reconciles the texts, having regard to the object and purpose of the treaty, shall be adopted' (Article 33(4)). The founding texts of the EU are in the form of treaties, in particular the Treaty on European Union and the Treaty on the Functioning of the European Union. As such they therefore come within the scope of the Vienna Convention on the Law of Treaties 1969. Various approaches to multilingual interpretation by the Court of Justice of the European Union are set out in Case C-265/03 *Igor Simutenkov v Ministerio de Educación y Cultura and Real Federación Española de Fútbol* in the Opinion of Advocate General Stix-Hackl, discussed in Robertson (2012b). Derlén (2009) places EU multilingual interpretation in context.

The drafter needs to be aware of the judicial methods of interpretation so as to 'steer' a draft text towards the intended reading. The problem for the drafter is to anticipate how the courts might interpret particular words, based on knowledge of past judicial approaches, and then adjust the wording of the legal text accordingly, or perhaps insert definitions to give terms precise meanings. The situation is more complex for multilingual texts because different language versions are in play and the problem arises as to whether they all convey the same meanings to everyone in each language. A broad 'acid test' is to analyse for legal effects; where they are the same for all languages in each part of the text, there may not be a particular linguistic issue on the face, but where wording has different effects between languages, the court must decide what meaning to attribute. In effect it means deciding which language versions are 'correct' and which are not.

The subsequent reader is presumed to have read all the cases interpreting the language versions and to be aware of the divergences and the interpretations given.[37]

It is important to understand how judges approach legal texts and interpret them to determine the law through the construction of legal meanings. Legal meaning is different from linguistic meaning. This is important for understanding multilingual law and the creation of meaning through different languages, because the lines of reasoning may vary between language versions of texts (and cultures) and each multilingual legal system needs to find ways of ensuring that the law treats citizens equally regardless of language, as part of the concept of justice; or if it is intended to treat them differently, then the reasons are clear and open to analysis and review. We will return to the question of meaning in Chapter 9. Appendix III contains some suggestions regarding sources in respect of interpretation.

Amendment and repeal

At this stage in the analysis we are exploring factors affecting legal texts. We have noted drafting by the 'utterer' and interpretation by the 'receiver', to use the linguistic language of communication. However, legal texts are also subject to later actions; in particular, legal texts are amended by adding or deleting words, sentences and clauses, and if a whole text is cancelled completely, it is 'repealed'. These operations take place in structured environments and involve two levels of language usage. The operation of amendment or repeal involves a new legal text, with its own legal structure and form, but the content, or message, is devoted to changing or terminating the previous act and fits within the structure and content of that act. For an amending act, the changes operate as part of the original act. There is a framework in the new act (first level) which delivers amended text in the form of part of the original (second level). The linguistic style at each level may be completely different, and one can see examples from EU amending texts published in the EU Official Journal in 24 languages. A formal method that clearly separates the levels facilitates 'consolidating' an act with all its amendments into a single comprehensive text.[38]

In the case of repeal, the previous text is cancelled by a simple formula such as: 'The [name of act] is [hereby] repealed.' With those words, set in an act that is formally valid and signed and published, the repealed act ceases to exist in law, although it remains as a physical linguistic document. We see again that the world of law is different from the world of fact. It is a virtual world, mental in nature, abstract, full of interconnections and networks which create patterns and pictures, connected intertextually, but interpreted also through other factors such as logic and 'common sense' (the man on the Clapham omnibus), along with ideas of justice, equity, principles and theory, as discussed in Chapter 3.

Facts, evidence and proof

Legal texts are written so as to have effects in the world of reality and fact. There is a difference between the world of law and the world of fact. Legal texts aim at influencing the world of fact, but they operate as part of the world of law. The link between the two 'worlds' is in the human mind, both individual and collective. It is psychological and social, as well as legal, political and economic. Legal acts take facts as conditions for the operation of rules and prescriptions contained in them. They can be seen as conditional propositions: if such and such facts occur or exist, then such and such rule applies, and the operation of that particular rule leads to other rules applying, again linked to facts, perhaps prescribing particular behaviour. The problem for lawyers is how to know what the facts are on which to base, or invoke, the rules. A whole branch of law is devoted to this issue: the law of evidence. Rules and methods exist for determining how facts are established as 'existing' and testing the truth of witnesses, where there may be temptation to tell falsehoods, or memory may be unreliable, and so on. Court procedures and methods are adapted to that end.

One form of 'evidence' is comprised by documents. A legal question is whether a court is entitled to read and interpret a document directly (authentic document such as a law) or whether it must invite expert witnesses to tell it what they think the document means as 'fact', such as a contract or a foreign law (because it is outwith the judicial knowledge of the court). All of these considerations may apply equally to multilingual law, depending on the rules of the system, but one question could be whether a court that works in one language can interpret a text in another language directly itself or requires evidence as to its meaning as a matter of 'fact'. The answer to this question involves legal rules and is specific to the circumstances of each system and each case. Nonetheless, a court would no doubt expect detailed submissions by each party's lawyers on every aspect of the case, including alternative interpretations to be given to the meanings of legal acts and all the evidence brought forth. Perhaps it should be mentioned in passing that the details of court processes, the types and forms of written and oral submissions made by lawyers and the precise ways in which judgments are structured are not discussed in this book. The emphasis is placed more on the legislative side of law, as this is the domain where the rules on languages tend to be more evident.

Enforcement

Before closing this chapter, we should consider a topic that is of vital importance for lawyers and their clients, but which does not necessarily figure at all on the purely linguistic level of a legal document. This is the concern to ensure that the legal effects intended are achieved in the real world. One may enact wonderful laws, or make excellent contracts, but if they are not read or followed, it is as if they had never been created in the first place. Why bother to go to the effort? We thus enter the dimension of enforcement of the legal act. It is a technical field, so we will treat it very lightly.

Some acts can be enforced directly (authentic instruments), such as certain civil law notarial instruments, but in general for a legal act to be enforced, it is necessary first to go to court to obtain a court order. Subsequent failure to comply with the order may lead to seizure of goods and/or bank accounts, and in the past imprisonment for debt. Within a national system the rules will be unified and enforcement of a court order may take place directly, but in the international and EU supranational environments, enforcement may need to be undertaken through the courts and methods of the national legal systems. That implies proving the original court order is valid, perhaps translating it, and obtaining a national court order for enforcement (*exequatur*). Within the EU legal arrangements have been introduced to simplify and streamline the procedures in this area. One of the most significant acts in that respect is Council Regulation (EC) No 44/2001 of 22 December 2000 on jurisdiction and the recognition and enforcement of judgments in civil and commercial matters. Enforcement is an area of 'lawyer's law' concerned with which court has jurisdiction (competence), which system of law applies to the matter in hand (applicable law), and the enforcement of judgments between different systems (private international law, conflict of laws).

Summary

This chapter has looked at the practical side of law through a focus on written legal texts. Connections between legal theory and legal acts have been made, and differences between the world of law and the world of fact highlighted. A range of sources of law have been identified, and these are starting points for making legal texts. Different types of text (genres) have been identified. Each has their own specific features and serves as a site of engagement and actions. Typical actions are drafting, interpretation, amendment and repeal. Legal texts are abstract but they are embedded in a world of fact that includes establishing the truth of facts through rules of evidence and procedure. Lastly, legal acts may be enforced.

The basic ideas and methods of a monolingual system apply also to multilingual legal systems and legal orders, but there are the individual legal and linguistic contexts that must be tracked all the time. There is the 'vertical' dimension within each language and 'the horizontal' dimension between and across languages, and one must have regard to the legal order in question. Is the legal system self-contained or is it connected with other legal orders? Within a European context having regard to EU supranational law, the national systems of the member states and international law, there is a matrix of legal and linguistic relationships between them all. It means that within a European context, when examining any given legal order in any given language, regard must be had to the possible impact of the other two legal orders, both in the same language and as between each and every language in operation in each related legal order. This impacts, for example, on terminology and the selection of appropriate terms to use.

Should the foregoing be insufficiently complex, we can add that within each language context there may be dialectal and terminological variance at work, as where the legal English in Scotland differs from that in England and Wales, Ireland, Malta or Gibraltar, if we mention territories within the EU. English is used for many international texts and we find further variations in form and style, such as with EU English. Similar questions arise for all major languages, such as French, German, Spanish and Portuguese among European languages used in different legal systems and orders. However, we are now shifting imperceptibly towards more specifically linguistic questions. We will soon shift attention to the focus of language, but before doing so, there is an important legal issue relating specifically to language as a policy area that needs to be addressed. This is the law of languages, the law of language and the types and implications of linguistic regimes.

Notes

1 The following all generate legal consequences: birth, death, accidents, drought, famine, floods, illness.
2 Law as a statement of what 'ought' to happen means that something different may in fact happen, but then other rules come into operation that anticipate this, and so on in a chain of causality.
3 For a multilingual example, see the Rules of Procedure of the Court of Justice of the European Union.

70 *Law*

4 On historical sources in different systems, see among others: James (1989), James *et al.* (1996) on English law; Meston *et al.* (1991), Walker (2001) on Scots law; Lawson *et al.* (1966) on French law; Akehurst and Malanczuk (1997), Crawford (2012), Kaczorowska (2003) on international law; Hartley (2014), Chalmers *et al.*(2014) on EU law.
5 See www.legislation.gov.uk/.
6 See www.legislation.gov.uk/browse/scotland.
7 See http://europa.eu/eu-law/index_en.htm.
8 See European Convention on Human Rights. [Online]. Available at: www.echr.coe.int/Documents/Convention_ENG.pdf.
9 However, there are two approaches – 'monist' and 'dualist' – on this question and the matter is not clear-cut (Kaczorowska 2003: 35–48).
10 This is its *vires*: *intra vires* (within the powers) and *ultra vires* (outwith the powers).
11 So we could expect to see the source of power mentioned in a legislative act early on in the text.
12 A different approach would undermine the higher-level act and create conflicts and divergences in terminology and concepts. Logic and consistency form part of legal method.
13 See www.supremecourt.uk/.
14 See *European Judicial Atlas in Civil Matters* (European Commission 2015), which contains names and addresses of all courts in the Member States competent in civil and commercial matters and geographical areas in which they have jurisdiction, and also *Judicial Systems in Member States* (2015), which contains information on EU member state legal systems.
15 See http://curia.europa.eu/. Note that there are three courts under this heading: Court of Justice, General Court and Civil Service Tribunal. See, however, REGULATION (EU, Euratom) 2015/2422, concerning the merger of the latter two courts.
16 See www.icj-cij.org/homepage/.
17 See European Court of Human Rights. [Online]. Available at: www.echr.coe.int/Pages/home.aspx?p=home.
18 An example of how external factual circumstances may influence legal interpretation of a text.
19 See http://curia.europa.eu/juris/recherche.jsf?cid=28940. Note the box for language in the top right corner of the site and select accordingly.
20 See www.justice.gouv.qc.ca/english/sites/lois/quebec-a.htm.
21 English law is more restrictive (James 1989: 23) and French law less restrictive (Lawson *et al.* (1966: 14–15).
22 See www.space-institute.org/ and www.iislweb.org/, but also the Agreement Governing the Activities of States on the Moon and Other Celestial Bodies.
23 See http://publications.europa.eu/en/web/about-us/who-we-are.
24 Although the law may require proper treatment of dogs; or a person may have contracted to walk a dog.
25 In English law equity is a branch of law that is juxtaposed to common law; see James (1989: 32–35).
26 See, however, REGULATION (EU, Euratom) 2015/2422, concerning the merger of the latter two courts.
27 *Du contrat social ou Principes du droit politique.* 1762.
28 Note the different genres of international agreements; each has its characteristic features.
29 Regulation No. 1 of 15 April 1958 determining the language to be used by the European Economic Community; Protocol (No. 3) on the Statute of the Court of Justice of the European Union, and the Rules of Procedure of the Court of Justice as amended. See also Regulation No. 1 of 15 April 1958 determining the language to be used by the European Atomic Energy Community.
30 Pluralising here is an example of EU international English to facilitate alignment with 23 other languages.
31 The texts on legal drafting around the world are numerous. The following represents a handful of examples in different spheres: Wilson (2007); Barr *et al.* (2009); Office of the Scottish

Parliamentary Counsel (2006); Bennion (1990), (2009); Bennion and Jones (2013); Eversheds (2011); Thornton and Xanthaki (2013); Wilson (2004); McLeod (2011); *Circulaire du 30 janvier 1997*, Gilder (2009); Dale (1986).

32 For examples of texts, see among others: Brownlie (1985), Evans (2011).
33 Interinstitutional Agreement of 22 December 1998, Joint Practical Guide (2013), Council of the European Union Manual of Precedents (2002), European Commission Manual on Legislative Drafting (1997), Interinstitutional Style Guide (2015), Morgan (1982).
34 On Belgian legislative drafting with three languages, see Conseil d'État (2008), and on Swiss federal drafting with four languages, see Swiss Confederation Federal Chancellery (2015).
35 For EU texts being translated into a new language where English is used as a main source, the original four EC languages must be checked for early texts because English was a translation.
36 Or it could be in an arbitration.
37 Good practice is to correct errors that are discovered; see the corrigenda of EU acts in the EU Official Journal.
38 In EU terminology this is 'codification', a term from French retained for EU languages, and an example of specialist EU legal terminology.

5 Law of language(s)

Introduction

In this chapter we remain within a legal frame of thinking but take language and languages as the field of policy that is regulated by law, legal rules and legal language. For just as law uses language as a tool to organise matters relating to society, individuals and their activities, so language itself can be the subject of regulation and rules of law. Many aspects of a language are not generally perceived in terms of law. For example, the spelling of words or the relationship between oral sounds and written symbols to represent them are not generally perceived as being the stuff of law. But why not? They are vital elements in creating, transmitting and receiving information and meaning. For legal texts, precision is essential and that in turn means organising, standardising and specifying the linguistic tools that are used.

For this chapter it is proposed to concentrate on two aspects: first, the question of the choice of language as applicable linguistic code, which takes one into the rules on choice of language and the linguistic regime in a given system; second, within each language, the rules, conventions and arrangements that structure and organise a language for its practical daily use. The second dimension is treated first and paves the way for a broader and deeper reflection on the nature of language in Chapter 6. On the other hand, the question of choice of language implies that there are two or more official languages. We can explore permutations and implications here by returning to the concept of legal system, legal order and state in order to project variations of linguistic regime. The approach implies placing languages within a legal framework which creates contexts for the creation of meanings through terminology, grammar and syntax. One of the questions is as to what makes language specifically legal, but that question is reserved for Chapter 7. Languages can be used for different purposes in legal systems, which raises implications for terminology.

There are many issues to be explored. The purpose of this chapter is to open the door to them by starting with a broad conceptual reflection on a range of permutations as regards law of language and languages. First, the concept of law of language is introduced. That is followed by moving to the question of choice of language codes, implicit in the concept of linguistic regime. From there, attention moves to rules on languages within the three legal orders discussed in Chapter 3: national law, international law and supranational law. The discussion is aligned on the structure of models in Appendix II. Thus the models of unitary, federal and hybrid states are explored in the context of particular systems. Similarly, the models of international law and international organisations are discussed, taking as examples the African Union and the

United Nations to illustrate their linguistic regimes. Lastly, the supranational model is evoked and illustrated by the Convention for the Protection of Human Rights and Fundamental Freedoms of 1950 and the European Union as a supranational organisation. In each case the rules on languages are expressed through sources of law as discussed in Chapter 3, whether by means of a particular genre of legal text or through custom. Appendix III is relevant in this connection. Linguistic choices may vary between territorial units, branches of law or the status of groups of persons, so these aspects need to be included in the reflection. The discussion opened in this chapter is continued in Chapter 7 in that respect.

A further dimension is to look at ways in which a language is adapted for use for legal purpose as the language of law. One can ask how legal language differs from general language (LGP) and from other language forms. This takes one into the field of language for specialist (or special or specific) purposes (LSP). It is an area of importance to multilingual law as it leads on to questions of multilingual drafting, interpretation and translation of texts in specialised legal language using specialist terminology. Behind these activities lies the question of meaning. To place that in a wider setting, one needs to make a review of linguistic theory and the range of discrete fields of focus that comprise it – a task for Chapter 6. For the present, to keep matters as simple as can be managed, in this chapter we continue to take a broadly monolingual approach rooted in English, and then introduce a multilingual dimension. Once a conceptual method has been developed in one language, it can be adapted to other languages. We turn to reflect on the internal or 'vertical' language dimension.

Law of language

What is necessary for a language to be used as an official legal language? One answer is 'standardisation', so as to create regularity, predictability, stability, reliability and a point of reference on which everyone can align and be taught. It allows people to conduct their business with peace of mind, secure in the knowledge that they know what the law is, what their texts mean and that others share that knowledge; that at any rate is the ideal. The education system comes into operation to set standards and inculcate them from an early age in children so as to ensure a shared language, but also a shared culture and way of seeing the world, thinking and acting.

From the point of view of language, the meanings of words become settled or 'fixed' through the use of dictionaries. Words and sentences are written according to conventions in grammar, spelling and syntax that also become settled and 'fixed' in textbooks, teaching and guidance.[1] The general features of a standard language can be summarised as including: authoritative dictionaries that record the language vocabulary, terms and expressions; authoritative grammar books which record the forms, rules and structures of the language; a recognised standard of pronunciation; making mention of the language in legal documents such as the constitution; using the language in public life in parliament and in schools; a body of literary texts expressing, supporting and extending it; formal instruction and research into the language and its literature in institutions of higher education; an institution promoting the use of the language and its educational institutions abroad; and translation of key religious texts such as the Bible or the Koran (UCL 2015).

Some languages are subject to express regulation, others less so. English has tended to develop without active intervention by the state, but that is not the case for other languages. Language is personal and emotive. There is often social resistance to language change, as people are unwilling to change ways of writing learned since childhood at personal cost. The link with the past becomes weakened as new generations become unable to read the script or understand the words in old texts. Language reforms come with a price attached in that respect and reform of Turkish with a shift from Arabic to Roman script is an example of this (Lewis 2002, Metz 1995). To this one may add that the ambition of 'language control' is not always fully achieved, as languages are living things and have a habit of moving in directions that are not anticipated and are difficult to control, as where new words arise and old words acquire new meanings, or ways of speaking change by themselves – something we notice with age or by looking at old books and films, but also learn about from literature on the history of languages. Historical linguistics is mentioned in Chapter 6.

The concept of legislating for language takes one into the realm of the sounds of the language and the signs (alphabets or characters) used to represent them, as well as the rules on grammar, syntax, proper usage and spelling. Some legal systems leave these questions out of the formal arena of legal regulation. For example, English in the UK and the USA is not formally regulated by law. Instead it is left to educationalists, writers, experts, publishing editors and society at large to set standards.[2] There are millions of legal texts in English (in UK and US form) and they rely on such usage, which becomes adopted and adapted for use in legal texts, legislation, court texts and contracts, and in so doing becomes legal language. In legal terms we can see this as a form of custom created through habitual use. Other languages are subject to more formal regulation. The German language has been subject to linguistic reforms, most recently in 1996.[3] Spelling reform has been an ongoing issue for the Dutch language in the Netherlands and Belgium.[4] The Chinese language underwent reform in the twentieth century,[5] as did Russian[6] and Turkish, as already noted. Updating spelling and the written script figured prominently, as well as enhancing mass literacy.

There is another dimension to the language of law that it is important to mention. This is where the same language is shared by different legal systems. In the case of Dutch, the Netherlands and Flanders in Belgium set up a language union (*Taalunie*) by signing the 1980 *Verdrag inzake de Nederlandse Taalunie* (Treaty concerning the Dutch Language Union). 'The Treaty stipulates that the governments will set joint policy with respect to the Dutch language. In 2004 Suriname joined as an associate member. In addition, the *Nederlandse Taalunie* also collaborates with Aruba, Curaçao and St Martin. The *Taalunie* is a unique organisation. Nowhere else in the world does such a treaty exist between countries with the same language' (Nederlandse Taalunie 2015).

English is used in many countries, notably in Commonwealth countries,[7] as the first language and as a language of law. What are the implications of sharing a language? If a language is the subject of legal rules, then different legal systems can have different rules regarding the 'same' language. We see that with English in differences between British English and American English, where 'colour' is spelled 'color' and 'standardise' is 'standardize' – small differences created after independence to mark out a separate identity (Kemmer 2009). This is only a difference in spelling, but divergences can go wider and words can have quite different meanings in different systems. There are frequently words which exist within one legal system and not in another.

Older examples can be seen in the language of Scots law as compared with the language of English law, where each system has concepts and terms unknown to the other, yet the common language is English. 'Heritable proprietor', 'not proven' and 'lawburrows' are three Scots terms; we will meet the last one in Chapter 6 in connection with historical legal language. 'Bocland', 'damage feasant' and 'scutage' are three old English concepts. Every system has its own unique concepts. The older branches of law relating to land law, succession law and court procedures are rich hunting grounds for such differences. However, where terms appear the same, the legal implications differ as they tie into the rest of the system through intertextuality.

We find analogous situations of shared usage with other languages. French is an official language in 29 countries[8] including France (Article 2 of the 1958 Constitution), Belgium (Articles 2, 3 and 4 of the Constitution), Luxembourg[9] and Switzerland.[10] German is an official language in Germany,[11] Austria (Article 8 of the Constitution), Belgium (Articles 2, 3 and 4 of the Constitution), Switzerland (Article 70 of the Constitution), Luxembourg[12] and Liechtenstein (Article 6 of the 1929 Constitution), as well as in South Tyrol (Special Statute for Trentino-Alto Adige). In Namibia, German ceased to be an official language in 1990 but remains widely used (Shah 2007). Portuguese is an official language in nine countries including Portugal (Article 9 of the 1976 Constitution), Brazil, Mozambique and Angola.[13] It has been subject to language reform by the *Acordo Ortográfico da Língua Portuguesa* of 1990 intended to standardise usage in all Portuguese-speaking countries (Portal da Língua Portuguesa 2015). Spanish is an official language in 20 countries including Spain,[14] Argentina and Mexico.[15] It is regulated internationally by the *Asociación de Academias de la Lengua Española* (Association of Spanish Language Academies). Arabic is a language spoken in many countries (Ridout 2014), as is Russian.[16] Each of these languages is a language of internal national law, international law and international organisations. In the case of the European languages mentioned, except Russian, each is an official language of the European Union.

In the case of Dutch, the formal language unification pursuant to the 1980 *Verdrag inzake de Nederlandse Taalunie* stipulates that the respective governments will set joint policy with respect to the Dutch language (Nederlandse Taalunie 2015). A formal agreement has similarly been agreed for Portuguese by the *Acordo Ortográfico da Língua Portuguesa* of 1990. Such patterns of shared usage of languages across countries and legal systems oblige one to draw a distinction between a language as a general code of communication and the precise form of the language code in operation within each individual legal system – or part of it, as there may also be internal regional variations, such as between provinces or local territories. These nuances and differences are generally taken into account in computer word-processing software and form part of the general picture of multilingual law. They have impacts on terminology in drafting, translation and interpretation. In the modern globalised world of communication there is evidently a benefit from ensuring standardised forms for languages and high levels of efficiency in communicating information, but one is aware of the risk of losing contact with past texts when changes become significant.

This brings us to the concept of 'dialects' of a language. Legal language can perhaps be seen as a form of specialised dialect, but it is more a case of a specialised variant since it adheres to the standardised official forms. There are practical implications, since a drafter or translator of legal texts needs to reflect on which variant form to use: which spelling conventions, which terminology. In the absence of formal guidance, the answers become essentially pragmatic: who are the readers, what is the purpose of the text? This raises the idea of translation within a language. It mainly arises where a language is shared by different systems and there are divergences, for example in spelling, terminology or standard expressions. The issue is not of importance within a given legal system as the context tends to be clear, but it assumes importance for international and supranational law texts where participating countries share languages but diverge on the details of practice. To that we can add that linguistic usages in international law and EU supranational law texts also depart from individual national linguistic usages since they must adapt to cope with diversity. This is the international 'legal-linguistic matrix'. For the moment we can note that elements of 'multilingualism' seem to arise even within a 'monolingual' environment; a curious paradox.

It is not proposed to dwell at length on the question of the difference between a language and a dialect. However, if we look at the question from a legal viewpoint, a language is what is declared by a rule of law to be a language. A legal system through its rules (express or implied through custom) indicates the language of the system and gives it a name. A legal system may use a language shared with another system or a language of its own. It may select what a linguist might see as a dialect and name it a language. For example, an outsider might regard the families of European languages as dialects: Romance (French, Italian, Portuguese, Spanish), Germanic (Danish, Dutch, English, German, Swedish), Slavic (Bulgarian, Czech, Russian, Slovak). The dialects have been given different names and erected into languages, with differences built on and emphasised to underscore national and political identities and values. In this connection, it is interesting to follow the linguistic developments following the break-up of the state of Yugoslavia at the end of the twentieth century, leading to accessions to the EU and linguistic adaptations of the individual successor states in connection with the process of accession (Bugarski and Hawkesworth 1992; Greenberg 1998; Požgaj Hadži 2013). To that may be added the functioning of the languages using two alphabets and scripts: Cyrillic and Latin (Ronelle 2006). A legal system may function in a plurality of languages, but also in a plurality of scripts to express a language – an extra dimension for exam markers to take into account. Who chooses the script to use? This brings us to consider the rules on choice of language, as part of a 'linguistic regime'. It is the dimension between and across languages, the 'horizontal' dimension.

Linguistic regimes

A formal linguistic regime sets out rules on the use of a particular language or languages within a legal system. There are different ways to approach the topic; first, one can consider the context in which the rules on the official languages are enunciated, such as the type of legal order – national, international or supranational – and then within that consider the details and variant themes. Second, one can examine the rules on language applying to different types of legal text: legislation, court judgments, textbooks, and so on. There is no logical need for the same rules to apply to all types of legal documents; for example, in a multilingual system legislation might be published in several languages, but court cases might take place in one language, the language of the parties. Third, one can look at particular domains, fields or branches of law and see what rules on language apply to them. There is also no logical need for all branches of law to be subject to the same language regime; variation is possible. Fourth, one can explore the possibility of different rules on languages applying to different regions or localities covered by a system, or indeed for particular groups of persons to benefit from different treatment in favour of their language. These latter situations link in with the recognition and protection of minority and lesser-used languages. Here we will limit ourselves to a

Law of language(s) 77

broad conceptual overview and explore implications by reference to some contexts and organisations. The framework in Appendix VIII goes into details.

National law

In the context of legal orders, the one which is closest to people and their languages is the domestic or national law context, discussed in Chapter 3. The concept of the state, and types of state, was introduced in that chapter in order to provide background for exploring different ways in which rules on languages – linguistic regimes – are ordered. We classified states as unitary, federal and hybrid, and saw that within each type of state there was also a local and regional dimension. If we know all the details of a system, we can enter them into the models in Appendix II, as well as Appendix I and Appendix VIII. However, it is assumed that we do not have this information and need to work it out step by step through reflection and research. That is the approach being followed in this book.

One can take each type of state and consider a range of possibilities in terms of languages and rules on languages. For example, a unitary state/system may prescribe a single official language, which is thus the sole language used for all official purposes. We see an example in Article 2 of the French Constitution, which declares French as the language of the Republic. Thus everything is in French for all official purposes. That does not mean that other languages are not spoken in the national territory; in the case of France there are many, including Alsatian, Breton, Corsican and Occitan.[17] Similarly, there can be a general rule for the whole territory, but local exceptions and variations, as with Alsace and Lorraine in France where there is local law, which includes texts in German, that applies (Glenn 1974).

With unitary states, while they may generally use a single language, it is also possible for them to function in two languages, bilingually, throughout their territory, as is the case in Ireland with Irish and English,[18] and Malta with English and Maltese.[19] However, in a bilingual system the question arises as to when and where one or the other language is to be used and the relationship between them. In theory, in a unitary system promoting equality one would expect each language to set down the same rules and obligations. That raises the question of how that is to be achieved in practice. For example, if one is making legislation, one must decide on the methods for creating the two language versions that are to run in parallel. How can that be done? The simplest method is to produce a text in one language and translate it into the other. This is understood to be the method in Ireland. The downside is that this can create an imbalance between the two languages as the translated language becomes tied to the terms, form and style of the first or source language. To remedy this tendency, one can consult informally between the languages in the drafting of the source text, as is understood to take place in Ireland. A second approach is to draw up the two language versions at the same time and adjust and align them while at draft stage. A third variant is co-legislation (co-drafting), where each language version is drafted in parallel from scratch and revised and adapted together. This third variant, followed in Canada, may not be so necessary where there is no cultural divergence lying behind the languages. For example, Ireland has a common law system, whereas Canada embraces both civil law and common law systems and needs to merge them within a single set of rules.

What applies to legislation does not necessarily apply to court cases, where there is an issue under debate between contending parties. Why impose extra costs for translation if they are not necessary? Typically a multilingual system has rules not only about the language(s) of legislation and administration, but also as regards court cases. One would look for them in the constitution, a law or secondary act, or the rules of procedure of courts. In the case of Malta, according to Article 5 of the Constitution the national language is Maltese, but Maltese and English and such other languages as prescribed by parliament are official languages and any may be used by the administration for official purposes. The language of the courts is Maltese, but provision may be made for the use of English. The parliament determines the language(s) used in parliamentary proceedings and records.

In Ireland the use of languages is regulated by the Official Languages Act 2003. Section 8 deals with court cases and provides for the use of either language in a case. In proceedings involving the state, it is the language chosen by the other party. In other cases the parties can choose, and if they cannot agree, the court decides. However, legislating is one thing and what people do is another; it seems that there is a general reluctance to litigate in Irish (Enright 2009). In the background there no doubt lie many factors in such a situation. One is the level of knowledge of the professionals and the parties. Translation of documents and interpretation of oral evidence may be needed, and it can be a question of whether judges are required to master both languages or just one of them. Which language does a court work in internally? These are a few of the questions which arise.

It seems less likely that a unitary state will have many more than two official languages in operation equally within the same system,[20] and where that is the case, it is likely that the state will prefer to take a federal format, with a federal centre and shared federal law, on the one hand, and devolved provinces for local administration on the other. The considerations and variations just noted with respect to a unitary state apply analogously to a federal system and to the system of each province within it, adapted to local circumstances. Belgium is a federal country with three languages: Dutch, French and German. However, there are four language areas: 'the Dutch language area, the French-speaking area, the bilingual region of Brussels-Capital (19 municipalities of Brussels) and the German language area' (Council of Europe/ERICarts 2015). Linguistic arrangements are set out in the Law Governing the Use of Languages in Administrative Matters Coordinated on 18 July 1966 as amended, among others.[21] The country is zoned on the basis of linguistic areas, with the capital Brussels being bilingual Dutch–French. The federal level involves making laws in the three languages.[22] The overall context is one of freedom to speak one's language of choice enshrined in Article 30 of the Belgian Constitution, which states: 'The use of languages spoken in Belgium is optional; only the law can rule on this matter, and only for acts of the public authorities and for judicial affairs.'

Within a federal state, provinces may have a shared language or different languages. One would perhaps expect laws at the federal level to be in all the languages that are official languages in the provinces, but that need not be the case. We noted that in multilingual Luxembourg the laws are only in French. In Canada, a federal multilingual country, most provinces have English as the official and spoken language. In Quebec, French is the official language according to the Charter of the French Language 1977, though English is also widely used. Under the Charter laws are made in French and English and a party can ask for a court judgment to be translated into French or English. New Brunswick is bilingual French–English.[23] The Canadian Official Languages Act 1985 provides for federal law and institutions to be bilingual English–French and every effort is taken to ensure linguistic equality and access to the law through methods of co-legislation in the two languages. However, there are also over fifty languages of aboriginal First Nation peoples in Canada (Huang 2009). The Inuit Language Protection Act 2008 and the Official Languages Act for Nunavit 2008 recognise three official languages for Nunavit: Inuit (Inuktitut and Inuinnaqtun), English and French.

The relationship between European-derived languages and legal systems with those of indigenous aboriginal peoples is a particular theme that raises many issues that need urgent attention for a variety of reasons, not least those linked to loss of cultural identity and languages. There are also complex issues that relate to the interplay of European-derived concepts and terminology and non-European indigenous concepts and terminology within national legal systems. They arise in a multitude of legal systems around the world, perhaps in the majority. The example of South Africa comes to mind, where 11 languages are official, and most of them are non-European: Sepedi, Sesotho, Setswana, siSwati, Tshivenda, Xitsonga, Afrikaans, English, isiNdebele, isiXhosa and isiZulu (Section 6 of the Constitution of South Africa). For the present, we can note that issues of cross-cultural dialogue and conceptual and linguistic alignment arise. These can be made clearer by thinking about the characteristics and lexicological range of each language involved, as well as clarifying the ways in which information is perceived and worked on. Chapters 7 and 8 address these issues by classifying languages according to use and status and reflecting on the way signs are perceived. Multilingual law is not just about differences in law and languages; it is also about differences between the cultures and concepts behind languages and finding ways to reconcile and bring them together in an environment of shared understanding and cooperation: unity in diversity. This is not easy. Here is a quote from Chief Philip Brochet in Manitoba:

> When the white man first seen us, when they first said, 'Well, there's something wrong with these people here. They don't have no religion. They have no judicial system. We have to do something for these people.' I guess that must have been what they thought because they totally screwed up what we already had.
>
> They introduced new religion and there was nothing wrong with our old religion. They just didn't understand it. We had our own ways of teaching our children, like the Elders and everything. There was nothing wrong with that way of teaching children. They just didn't understand it.
>
> The same thing with our judicial system. We had that judicial system and the white people, when they came here, they didn't see that. They said, 'These guys have nothing. We have to introduce all these different things to them so they can be one of us.' That's exactly the problem that we have.
> (The Aboriginal Justice Implementation Commission 1999)

The third category of state mentioned in Chapter 3 was referred to as 'hybrid', as being a state which is neither fully unitary nor fully federal, but something in between.[24] The example of the UK was mentioned: it has a central Parliament in Westminster and devolved powers for Scotland, Wales and Northern Ireland. The UK is often perceived in terms of having a single language, but the reality is more complex and multilingual, even leaving aside the number of new languages introduced in the twentieth century through immigration. There is the 'universal' language of English for all parts of the UK and this is the language in which all laws are written, with variations for each constituent system (there is more than one legal system present, as we have seen in connection with references to Scots law). In Wales, the Welsh language has been recognised as an official language for use in public affairs by laws that include the Welsh Language Acts of 1967 and 1993 and the National Assembly for Wales (Official Languages) Act 2012. In earlier days English was imposed by the Laws in Wales Acts 1535 and 1542. In Scotland, the Gaelic Language (Scotland) Act 2005 gave formal recognition to Gaelic (Sutherland et al. 2011).

In the background of many legal systems lie vestiges of other languages that were formally legal languages. For example, in Scotland Gaelic was formerly a legal language (McLeod 2001) and Latin was a principal language of law, alongside the everyday vernacular Scots (Lallans), which was overtaken after union with England and Wales and replaced by English as a language of law, while preserving many expressions and terms, as well as a number of pre-union laws. Lawyers adapted to the linguistic diversity.

International law

The second legal order identified in Chapter 3 is international law, the law between states. Here we can identify two aspects: first, the linguistic practices between states in conducting their affairs; second, the linguistic arrangements established for the international organisations they create. This covers their formal texts and the activities, tasks and texts they are required to perform or produce, as well as the daily internal language of discourse as working language(s). In the first context of state practice, it seems to be essentially a question of convenience and practice as custom. States communicate and make legal texts in whichever languages they wish. For texts such as agreements between two parties, one would expect language versions in the respective languages if these differ, and if they share the same language they will agree on the applicable conventions for orthography, terminology, and so on. If a state is itself multilingual, it will decide whether all or some of its official languages are to be used. Where many states come together to make an international agreement, they may decide to limit the number of language versions. There may be a single language version that is the signed and official version (authentic), or two or more authentic language versions. Translations into other languages may be made, but if so, they are likely to be labelled as translations and overridden by the authentic text(s) for the purposes of interpretation where there is a doubt as to meaning. Drafting and interpretation guidance is available in certain treaties such as the Vienna Convention on the Law of Treaties of 1969. The International Court of Justice has jurisdiction in respect of disputes between states. 'The Court's role is to settle, in accordance with international law, legal disputes submitted to it by states and to give advisory opinions on legal questions referred to it by authorised United Nations organs and specialized agencies'.[25]

International (governmental) organisations are created by several states coming together through an international agreement, which may have one of several different names (treaty, charter, agreement, convention, protocol). Typically the founding acts create a body or organ for making decisions on behalf of the members, an organ where the members meet, a secretariat, and a list of the objectives of the organisation and the tasks and activities to be performed by it on their behalf.[26] Each organ needs provisions on how it is constituted and on the procedures that it will follow in undertaking its activities (rules of procedure) The organs work in the languages specified by the founding texts or secondary acts made under them (linguistic regime), and a distinction may by drawn between formal official languages and the day-to-day languages of internal communication (working languages). The founding texts usually indicate the languages they are written in and say which are authentic. There are many international organisations. The Yearbook of International Organizations (undated) lists over 68,000 international organisations (over 38,000 active and 30,000 dormant), but these include both governmental and non-governmental organisations. We will take two international organisations by way of example: the African Union and the United Nations.

The African Union (AU) is an international organisation. It was established in 2001 and signed up to by 53 African countries (Constitutive Act of the African Union 2015). It has its headquarters in Addis Ababa and was formerly the Organisation of African Unity (OAU). The AU is established by the Constitutive Act of the African Union of 2000, as amended by the Protocol on Amendments to the Constitutive Act of the African Union of 2003. These foundation acts form part of international law. Matters of interpretation arising from the application or implementation of the Act are decided, after an initial transitional period, by the Court of Justice created by the Act. The objects of the organisation are to further unity, solidarity, defence of sovereignty, political and social integration, and promote a common position, international cooperation, peace, security, stability, democratic principles, good governance, human and peoples' rights, sustainable development, health, participation of women in decision-making, and so on (Article 3 of the Constitutive Act as amended by the Protocol).

The activities of the AU are linked to those of its organs: the Assembly; Executive Council; Pan-African Parliament; Court of Justice; Commission; Permanent Representatives Committee; Specialised Technical Committees; Economic, Social and Cultural Council; and Financial Institutions. The organs take decisions, adopt internal rules of procedure, give advice, and so on. The foundation Constitutive Act is drawn up and authentic in four languages: Arabic, English, French and Portuguese (Article 33(5)).[27] Article 25 has been amended by the Protocol (Article 11) to read:

1. The official languages of the Union and all its institutions shall be Arabic, English, French, Portuguese, Spanish, Kiswahili[28] and any other African language.
2. The Executive Council shall determine the process and practical modalities for the use of official languages as working languages.

As at 2015 the AU website[29] is provided in three languages: Arabic, English and French. It also includes the text of the Constitutive Act in those languages. To obtain further information on linguistic arrangements, one studies practice, in particular the languages of the texts produced, drafting guidance, terminology databases, translation methodology, interpretation methods, linguistic profiles for recruitment and so on. Thus, for example, a vacancy for a senior legal officer contained the following language requirements: 'Language requirement: An excellent command of, and good drafting skills in, one of the AU working languages (Arabic, English, French and Portuguese). Knowledge of any of the other three will be an added advantage.' The same notice listed the range of activities, tasks and texts to be worked on.

The United Nations is an older international organisation. It was founded in 1945 by the Charter of the United Nations, which is an international law text. The UN currently has 193 member states. The main organs are the General Assembly, the Security Council, the Economic and Social Council, the Trusteeship Council, the International Court of Justice and the UN Secretariat. The instruments and acts of these organs form

82 *Law*

part of international law. The UN encompasses the whole world and provides a background legal-linguistic environment for international legal acts and organisations generally. The objects of the UN include: international peace and security; prevention and removal of threats to the peace; suppression of acts of aggression or other breaches of the peace; friendly relations among nations; international cooperation in solving international problems of an economic, social, cultural, or humanitarian character; and to provide a centre for harmonising the actions of nations (Article 2 of the 1945 Charter).

The activities tasks and products are numerous and each organ needs to be considered separately. In addition, there are many specialised agencies, which include the Food and Agriculture Organization (FAO), the International Civil Aviation Organization (ICAO), the International Labour Organization (ILO) and the United Nations Educational, Scientific and Cultural Organization (UNESCO).[30] The UN Charter is authentic in five languages: Chinese, French, Russian, English and Spanish (Article 111). These are also official languages.[31] Arabic was added as an official language in 1973.[32] The working languages are English and French. Recruitment as translator or interpreter in a notice in 2015 required 'perfect knowledge of one of the official languages, usually but not always their mother tongue, and an excellent knowledge of at least two others'.

There is, of course, much more to say in respect of those organisations, and they are just two out of many. The preparation of international law texts generally involves translation, first of incoming documents that are used to prepare draft texts in the official languages, and then of the draft texts produced by the organisation so as to make them available in the authentic languages, in order that each can be checked and compared. The final versions need to be revised and proofread together to ensure they are aligned in what they say. If they create legal obligations on member states, there may be a secondary requirement on the part of those states to change their national laws to implement the obligations agreed to. This circumstance in turn creates a relationship between the international legal text for each language version and the legal texts made in each national legal system implementing the obligations. The texts in the two orders need to match up with each other in terms of meanings and effects. That reminds us of varying forms of speech within a language and intra-lingual translation between them, since the international and national contexts are different. In addition, there is a need for translation with respect to national legal systems that have a language that is different from those of the official languages of the international text. We will return to this matter in Chapter 10 in connection with translation.

Supranational law

The third legal order mentioned in Chapter 3 is supranational law. It builds on and develops the international law approach. Rights and duties are created that have direct and automatic effects within the national legal systems of member states. This arises because the national systems authorise compliance with the supranational obligations, so that in effect it is a national law rule that orders rules of an international organisation to have direct, supranational effects within its system, thereby overriding any contrary national rule. This means that, for any matter, it is necessary to be aware whether it is subject to rules at national, international or supranational level. The Convention for the Protection of Human Rights and Fundamental Freedoms of 1950 contains provisions that have binding force on the 'high contracting parties' (ratifying states), as

Article 46(1) states: 'The High Contracting Parties undertake to abide by the final judgment of the Court in any case to which they are parties.'

However, the leading example of supranational law is with the European Union. This is an international organisation founded by treaties. The current principal primary law texts are the Treaty on European Union (TEU) and the Treaty on the functioning of the European Union (TFEU). These are international law texts, but they create an internal legal order of EU law. The main institutions are: European Parliament, European Council, Council of the European Union (Council), European Commission, Court of Justice of the European Union, European Central Bank and the Court of Auditors (Article 13 TEU). There are many other EU bodies and agencies, each with a specific task, such as the European Aviation Safety Agency (EASA), which has responsibility for aviation safety. The activities of each institution, body or agency create sub-contexts that require separate study.

The objects of the EU include: to establish a union; promote peace, its values and the well-being of its peoples; offer its citizens an area of freedom, security and justice without internal frontiers; establish an internal market; combat social exclusion and discrimination; promote social justice and protection; establish an economic and monetary union, and so on (TEU Articles 1 to 3). The TFEU 'organises the functioning of the Union and determines the areas of, delimitation of, and arrangements for exercising its competences'. The two treaties have 'the same legal value' (TFEU Article 1).

The institutions and bodies produce many types of text. Of particular importance as supranational law texts are the regulation, directive, decision, recommendation and opinion (TFEU Article 288). The texts of the TEU and TFEU are authentic in 24 languages (TEU Article 55 and TFEU Article 358) as a result of amendments made by accession treaties for new Member States which adjusted EU law to include them. Article 342 provides for the linguistic regime as follows: 'The rules governing the languages of the institutions[33] of the Union shall, without prejudice to the provisions contained in the Statute of the Court of Justice of the European Union, be determined by the Council, acting unanimously by means of regulations.' Regulation No. 1 determining the languages to be used by the European Economic Community, as amended, provides for 24 official and working languages. Articles 36 to 42 of the Rules of Procedure of the Court of Justice of the EU set out rules on languages.[34] The 24 languages are languages of the case. Subject to certain exceptions, in a direct action the applicant chooses the language of the case. That language is used for written and oral pleadings and texts in other languages are translated into it. Court publications are in 24 languages. The Court has 'a language service staffed by experts with adequate legal training and a thorough knowledge of several official languages of the European Union'. EU texts can be accessed from the EU website[35] and are published by the Official Publications Office of the EU.

Variations in linguistic regimes

All sorts of permutations can arise in respect of linguistic regimes, and can be adapted to the relevant circumstances. For example, different language rules may apply in different areas on a territorial scope. One sees this in Belgium with its three language communities and Canada with mono- and bilingual provinces. On the local level particular provision is made in Germany with respect to Schleswig-Holstein in respect of Danish

(Voss 2000), and South Tyrol in Italy is bilingual Italian–German (Special Statute for Trentino-Alto Adige). On the other hand, as people and not territory speak language, special rules may apply to communities and groups in relation to their personal identity as members of a group and part of their status, such as nationality, being a member of a religious group or being blind or deaf. For example, special rules exist in New Zealand for deaf persons to use sign language (New Zealand Sign Language Act 2006).

Variation may also take place in respect of branches of law. We have seen the example of different rules on language between federal law and province law in Canada, but within a system there may be variations. For example, in the UK Welsh is recognised for use in relation to public institutions (Welsh Language Act 1993). Other areas, such as company law, would appear to be primarily in English. Thus it is a partial regime and not a full regime. These rules constitute language policy, and one element of it can be to maintain and preserve the existence and identity of speakers of minority or lesser-used languages. Behind such a status lie questions of the vocabulary and range of terminology, or lexicology, of such languages and whether and how they adapt to match the more widely used languages, taking into account that they also have official status as a language of the law and must adapt to fulfil the role. These are pragmatic matters, for behind a desire to follow a certain linguistic policy in respect of a language, it is necessary to consider the practicalities: what do the speakers of a language themselves want for it, what are the resources to support it, what are the methods available and how far will the language actually be used, which can be expressed in terms of the motivation to learn and use it. We will come back to the question of the relative size, status and use of languages in Chapter 7.

Summary

This chapter has taken a look at the existence of law in relation to language and languages. It reflected on ways in which the details of a language may or may not be laid down by law and noted how language use can vary in different systems that use the same language. In the case of some languages that has lead to agreements to coordinate or unify a language. The concept of linguistic regime was introduced and some examples were canvassed within the contexts of national law, international law and supranational law. There has been no attempt to describe the rules of any particular system, but rather through selecting a few examples the purpose has been to give a flavour of some of the issues that are encountered.

With these words we conclude Part II with its focus on law. We next shift attention to a linguistic focus in which the language of law comprises just one form of specialised language among many others. It is a point of view of linguistics and applied linguistics, in particular legal linguistics. The territory of exploration remains the same as hitherto, but the terminology, language and ways of thinking are different. Perhaps this difference is best expressed by suggesting that one moves away from a view on law and towards a (scientific) view on language used by lawyers and others in oral utterances and written texts. Nonetheless, the hybrid lawyer-linguist view offered up to now will be maintained, and the emphasis will also remain essentially on legal language and texts in view of their centrality in multilingual law. In the following chapter we will start with a broad overview of linguistics and work towards identifying areas that appear of most relevance for understanding multilingual law and constructing a framework of

Law of language(s) 85

reference. Appendices I to III, which have been introduced up to now, go some of the way to achieving this, and each can serve as an aid to enquiry on a range of matters. However, they reflect only a part of the overall multilingual canvas.

Notes

1. Take, for example, deciding on the form and gender of new words entering a language. At the time of writing, the term 'Bitcoin' is entering languages. What gender? Lower case or capital first letter? What meanings? Does one keep the same word or invent another term in other languages? This is terminology standardisation work.
2. See Kemmer (2009). She notes how American English is gaining ground around the world in English-speaking countries, notably in Canada and Australia.
3. See, among others, Learn German Online, *The German Spelling Reform*. [Online]. Available at: www.learn-german-online.net/en/learning-german-resources/german-spelling-reform.html.
4. See Van der Horst (2011); www.valerieyule.com.au/wdutchref.htm.
5. See Society for Anglo-Chinese Understanding (SACU) (2006). Mills (1956).
6. See Greenberg (2014).
7. For a list of the 53 Commonwealth member countries see: http://thecommonwealth.org/member-countries.
8. See www.worldatlas.com/french.htm.
9. Article 29 of the Constitution of the Grand Duchy of Luxembourg; Loi du 24 février 1984 sur le régime des langues, in particular Articles 2, 3 and 4 thereof. Luxembourgish is the first official language (Article 1 of the 1984 Law).
10. Article 70 of the Swiss Constitution. The cantons decide on their official languages.
11. The German constitution Grundgesetz (Basic Law) 1995 is in German, but it appears that German is not enshrined formally as the official language. Article 3 says that 'No one may be prejudiced or favoured because of…his language'.
12. German is an administrative and judicial language, but not a legislative language, which is restricted to French: Loi du 24 février 1984 sur le régime des langues.
13. See www.ranker.com/list/countries-where-portuguese-is-the-official-language/best-world-journeys; www.mapsofworld.com/languages-of-the-world/portuguese.html; Lancashire (2015).
14. Article 3 of the Constitution of 1978. Castilian Spanish is the language of the state and other languages are decided by the autonomous communities.
15. See for example www.worldatlas.com/spanish.htm
16. Article 68 of the constitution of the Russian Federation.
17. Available at: www.ethnologue.com/country/fr/languages.
18. Article 8 of the Constitution of Ireland. The same Article provides for exclusive use of either language for official purposes throughout the state or in any part of it.
19. Article 5 of the Constitution of Malta. Provision is made in that Article for the adoption of other languages as official languages.
20. In Luxembourg the Loi du 24 février 1984 sur le régime des langues declares three languages (French, German and Luxembourgish) as administrative and court-case languages, but legislation is only in French.
21. De gecoördineerde wetten van 18 juli 1966 op het gebruik van de talen in bestuurszaken; Loi sur l'emploi des langues en matière administrative coordonnée le 18 juillet 1966, Koordinierte Gesetze über den Sprachengebrauch in Verwaltungsangelegenheiten. 18 July 1966.
22. For a comparison of the Belgian and Canadian linguistic regimes, see Domenichelli (1999).
23. See History of Language Rights in New Brunswick. On language policies in different provinces see Vaillancourt *et al.* (2012).
24. Territorial entities such as protectorates, trusts and dependent territories are not specifically addressed here, but an analogous approach can be taken to them.

25 See www.icj-cij.org/court/index.php?p1=1.
26 On international organisations see, among others, Archer (2015).
27 Of those, the Arabic, English and French versions are currently available on the AU website: www.au.int/en/about/constitutive_act.
28 For information on Kiswahili see www.glcom.com/cyberswahili/swahili.htm.
29 See www.au.int/en/about/constitutive_act.
30 For a list see www.un.org/en/sections/about-un/funds-programmes-specialized-agencies-and-others/index.html.
31 General Assembly Resolution 2(1) of 1 February 1946, Annex, paragraph 1.
32 Decision of the General Assembly in its Resolution 3190 (XXVIII) of 18 December 1973.
33 Note: the reference to institutions implies that other bodies may have different rules.
34 Available at: http://curia.europa.eu/jcms/upload/docs/application/pdf/2012-10/rp_en.pdf.
35 See http://europa.eu.

Part III
Language

6 Viewpoints of language

Introduction

In Chapter 1 it was suggested that a study of multilingual law could be seen as a combination of two centres of focus: one of law and the other of language. After an introduction and overview in the first two chapters, attention was placed on legal viewpoints, and now it is time to shift to take account of viewpoints which take language as their starting point. Doing so makes it possible to proceed further into the details, minutiae and fine-tuning of legal texts and multilingual law, since multilingualism is very much a matter of language.

As regards the question of method and approach, it seems reasonable to follow along the same lines as hitherto, aiming at a non-specialist introduction of issues and topics that form part of a linguistic view of the world and searching for those elements that may have a particular relevance for a study of multilingual law and legal systems. Viewpoints are introduced in terms of practical activities connected to language. This leads on to identifying branches of linguistics as the principal field of investigation. As it is a vast and complex field of research, it is necessary to find a means to thread a path through it in order to identify topics that seem particularly relevant and should be retained for piecing together the conceptual framework being aimed at.

As we progress, we will make use of information about law derived from Part II, while extending and refining it to build up a more complex picture. We become aware of a constant process of reiteration, coming back to topics previously touched on, but each time from a different angle in order to elucidate different information and add another layer of information. A broad conceptual approach will be maintained, not attempting to describe 'everything', but selecting one or two examples and sources that illustrate a point, drawn from widely different contexts. In the background are the appendices, which are introduced in the chapters and are intended to be more specialist summaries. It helps in navigating through the details to have an overall 'site plan' in one's mind, while being aware that it is provisional and to be constantly adjusted as new information is encountered. In that respect we need to take into account that in this chapter we switch from a legal frame of reference to a linguistic one. This leads to different ways of thinking about what appears to be the same material.

Given the levels of detail and complexity in the topics to be traversed, it is not possible to undertake much more than a sketch of ideas and outline some principal concepts. The aim is not to expound individual fields of linguistics, but simply to draw attention to them, indicate what they cover and provide a subjective assessment as to how far knowledge of them may assist in understanding multilingual law. This chapter proposes a broad canvas and subsequent chapters develop some themes identified for further attention.

Accordingly, this chapter first introduces some linguistic viewpoints. It then asks 'what is language?' and moves on to distinguish oral and written language. Other forms of language, such as sign language for the deaf or Braille for the blind, are noted, but not taken further. The bulk of this chapter is devoted to reviewing a long list of topics in linguistics with an eye to their focus of emphasis and their degree of relevance for a study of multilingual law. The distinction between language for general purposes (LGP) and language for specialist (or specialised/specific) purposes (LSP) is also covered, and that prepares the way for a reflection on legal language as LSP. However, by this stage we have moved from a context of 'language in general' to one where attention is placed within a specific language as a code containing prescriptions about the way in which meanings are created, read and interpreted. In this way languages such as English, French, German, and so on, are seen as codes of communication, each with their specific rules, methods and habits, with variations. Ideally we should describe each language and make analyses and comparisons between them, but that would take us beyond the present scope. It is what translators must do in order to perform their tasks, and translation lies at the heart of multilingual law, so it is a fundamental issue and falls to be included within the conceptual framework.

Linguistic viewpoints

Everyone uses language: we speak to each other using sounds to communicate information orally; we write letters and communicate in writing; and we communicate by other means, such as gestures or sign language. So there is the 'everyone' viewpoint of the citizen and member of society. This rather resembles the way in which law applies to everyone, and it means that for both law and language there is a general layperson non-specialist point of view. It is a viewpoint that does not seek particularly to analyse the subtleties but is content to use and live with what is there, so long as it functions reasonably well; a viewpoint of 'habit'. It represents the core 'common sense' centre of gravity of law and language in terms of broad general social and family relationships. It is a lay general user viewpoint of language; language for general purposes (LGP).

From this shared ordinary person viewpoint we can shift attention to persons who specialise in language, or earn their living from it in one way or another. Writers such as journalists, novelists and authors come to mind. Then there are those who teach language, whether as schoolteachers or university professors. They may teach a foreign language, or the refined forms of literature of the mother-tongue first language. Then come other categories, such as professionals in fields of science, medicine, engineering and law; they work with forms of language adapted to their specialist functions. Their language is specialist (LSP) and adapted to their needs and contexts. Another category of specialists comprises persons who take language as their subject of study. They analyse and study language in all its forms and patterns scientifically for the purpose of gaining knowledge, understanding and developing applications. It is here that this book can perhaps be seen to fit, having as its purpose the study of language applied to legal purposes within a context of multiplicity of linguistic codes as vehicles of communication.

These are all viewpoints which relate broadly to persons using their 'own' language (first language or mother-tongue speakers), but one must also take into account the viewpoints of those who work between and across languages. Multilingualism is their domain of action. In multilingual communities there is more than one form of linguistic code in operation and people switch language code according to the persons with whom they communicate. However, not everyone possesses or has need of such skills as they are not in contact with other languages, or they are able to impose their own language, and so they remain tied to a single language; they need the intervention of an interpreter for speech or a translator for written texts when occasion arises. These language specialists look in two directions, reflecting the languages brought together for the transfer of information between them. Typically, one of the languages has been learned as a second language, or the person has been brought up bilingually. Second-language learning and use differs from first-language learning and use in various ways and frequently involves learning later in life, in a classroom and with a more or less extensive cultural knowledge brought along through the first language. There may also be a tendency to speak and write in the second (which includes here third or more) language using the forms and patterns of the first language, and this is one of the features of multilingual utterances in international and supranational texts written by non-native speakers. Thus we have the viewpoints of interpreter, translator and drafter in first or second language to add to the list.

All of these activities confer viewpoints on language use, and each of them needs to be taken into account in some way in an enquiry into multilingual law. The problem is how to do that in a meaningful way and how to be able to identify patterns and render what is complex less so. The method here is to start with the concept of language, distinguish oral from written language, and then both of these from other forms of communication through signs that do not lend themselves to multilingualism in a linguistic sense, for example gestures, symbols and pictures (but which represent a form of language in other senses). The second stage is to take a look at the scientific study of language and somehow steer a course through the large and complex field of linguistics, with the aim of searching for a limited range of 'useful' topics.

In a sense the whole field of linguistics[1] is relevant, but from the point of view of multilingual law some topics are more relevant, or useful, than others. This again involves the idea of 'fore-grounding' and 'back-grounding'; rather like when mending something broken, attention is paid to immediate factors to effect the task, and other matters are left in the background as they do not alter what needs to be done to effect the repair. The background issues are important as a *sine qua non* and we may discover later we do in fact need to bring them up front, but it helps to try to simplify at first and construct an outline mental image of what we are dealing with, using the signs of language. Once we have a mental image, it can be refined and made more complex.

With words like 'mental image' and 'sign' we are inadvertently invoking another field of study, one that lies behind the study of language and other phenomena. It sees the world in terms of signs and goes by the name of 'semiotics'. Its viewpoint is to draw attention to relationships between things and the ways we think about and represent them in our minds. It is relevant to multilingual law because when people speak different languages, they use words in different language codes to communicate their thoughts. How do we know whether speakers in different languages are talking about the same thing? How are translators able to know whether their translations are accurate? What meanings are created by legal texts in different languages and how do we analyse different language versions of a legal text and compare them to see if they carry the same information? What are the implications if readers of legal texts in different languages have different cultures and different cultural assumptions? Do they read the texts in the same way or obtain the same information? These questions are crucial and they go to the heart of a multilingual legal system, and the concept of multilingual law. However, they are complex and subtle and it is best to lead up to them gradually. For the moment, we can start with a few general observations on language to set the scene.

What is language?

What is language? In Chapter 1 we noted a general definition which included the following: 'The method of human communication, either spoken or written, consisting of the use of words in a structured and conventional way' and 'A system of communication used by a particular country or community'.[2] We will draw on these definitions for the purpose of this chapter: language as a means of communication and as a specific system of communication. As regards the former, we can view it as the phenomenon of sounds, or utterances, which are used to convey meanings. As regards the latter, we can think of it as being a specific form of speech or 'language', here referred to in terms of a code as it involves creating meanings in structured and organised ways. One of the founders of the science of linguistics Ferdinand de Saussure distinguished three dimensions: language, *langue* and *parole*, with the last being the actual, concrete ways of speaking and writing (Crystal 2010: 431). It is useful to bear these distinctions in mind as we will return to them.

Linguists have more specialist definitions for language. Thus it is the 'specialized sound signaling system which seems to be genetically programmed to develop in humans' (Aitchison 2003: 13). Signalling conveys information from one person to another ('utterer' to 'receiver') and vice versa. This is the domain of communication and communication studies. Distinctions are made from other methods of conveying information, such as through body language. Braille-writing for the blind (Crystal 2010: 290; Kimbrough 2015) and sign language for the deaf (Crystal 2010: 229–235; Yule 2014: 200–208)[3] are adaptations and should also be seen as part of a linguistic regime. There is no reason why law does not also make use of these forms of communication. They play a part in matters of evidence as to actions and attitudes in court cases, or as methods for communicating with blind or deaf persons in connection with legal matters. Sign language is one of the three official languages in New Zealand.[4] The other two are English and Maori.

It is quite common for legal texts to contain non-linguistic signs as where they contain maps or signs for road-use, or in industry and commerce for the purpose of labelling, such as eco-labels or signs warning of toxicity.[5] These are also forms of communication, but they are broadly non-linguistic and to that extent are not subject to multilingual treatment. Like a picture, these signs can be read, interpreted and described in any language, which makes them useful for multilingual texts, as on the face of it there is no need for translation. On the other hand, cultural knowledge is required to know what they mean, such as road markings in different colours. Furthermore, where signs are used for legal purposes, they need to have their meanings defined somehow and that is generally through language, so we are back to words and language after all. Mathematical formulae are another category that appears to be non-linguistic and universal, but conventions on notation and ways of expressing formulae can vary across cultures and languages. In legal texts meanings, including those attached to signs and symbols, are explained through language. We will therefore narrow the scope of enquiry by setting aside gestures, signs and mathematical formulae while recognising that they are also the subject of law and are found represented in legal texts. We will take a similar approach as regards 'computer language' and 'programming languages'.

Oral and written language

An oral culture without writing has to have recourse to memory and techniques of memorisation, and makes use of physical objects as markers of status and events. Objects, signs and symbols are important cultural aids in that respect. Boundary stones mark territorial limits. Handing over a clod of earth in front of witnesses as part of a ceremony of transfer of land provides a visual memory for witnesses. Going through a social ritual such as a marriage ceremony, or wearing special clothes to indicate status or function are other forms. Body tattooing and heraldic signs also convey information. In the event of a legal dispute, memories are drawn on, objects brought forth, and persons knowledgeable in the law consulted. Memorisation through repetition of important information from generation to generation is important. Genealogies of rulers and tribes have been carefully maintained over centuries in this way. In New Zealand, Maori children learned everything orally until the arrival of literacy, and some of them had to be capable of memorising vast amounts of information (Calman 2013). It is said that in the past in rural Norway, children memorised farm boundaries through a song learned in infancy and could be asked to sing it in the event of a dispute. The language of the law need not be in writing, nor necessarily in prose. From a point of view of multilingual law, a lack of writing means an equivalent lack of translation, not to mention lack of computers and their programs. The conception of law is likely to be different in an oral society and one can ask whether the concept of 'multilingual law' actually carries any meaning.

Oral language is an important feature of law, as is writing. There have been studies of both by lawyers and linguists, under headings such as 'language of the law' (Mellinkoff 1963), 'language and the law' (Gibbons 1994), 'languages of law' (Goodrich 1990), 'legal language' (Tiersma 1999), and more recently 'legal linguistics' (Mattila 2006, 2013), as well as 'forensic linguistics', which embraces language and law – language in the legal process and language as evidence.[6] In the narrower sense, forensic linguistics is 'concerned with the provision of expert linguistic evidence, usually in court' (Gibbons 1994: 319). Another name for it is 'legilinguistics'.[7] These studies look at the history of legal language (here primarily English and American legal language) as well as the ways in which language is used for legal purposes. However, before going into such topics, it is desirable in a multilingual context to tackle some of the nuts and bolts issues of language. Like taking a car and removing all the pieces that when assembled make it work, we can examine the component parts that taken together make a language function, and by extension legal language and multilingual law. Then, to continue the metaphor, just as we learn how to drive a car and make it take us where we want, so we can reflect on how language is used in everyday life through discourse to convey the information and meanings that we wish to convey. That takes us into the applied side of language: pragmatics, applied linguistics, discourse analysis and language for special purposes (LSP), which is the subject matter of the studies mentioned above.

Written language provides many advantages. It is more permanent than oral language (but we now have recordings). It facilitates the conveying of high levels of precision, detail and complexity more efficiently than oral language, where memory of words said even just a short time previously may be variable and uncertain. Law needs precision and certainty. Writing permits unrestricted diffusion of information. Oral language

94 *Language*

is restricted to those present, told by those present and passed on by word of mouth.[8] Written texts facilitate more complex social organisation. For these and other reasons most of modern law primarily takes a written form. That said, oral language always accompanies written legal texts, for example when they are being created, analysed, discussed, referred to or acted on. Each written text can be seen as embedded within an oral environment, as well as within a particular culture. A legal text may make explicit reference to oral language, as where an oral agreement is recorded in writing, or implicitly through the choice of particular words that reflect oral usage. A transcript of court proceedings is an official record of oral speech.

Of the two paradigms of language, 'oral' and 'written', it seems natural that the spoken word should come first. There are still many languages which have not been written down. However, the written form is not simply a transcription of the oral form. Each has its own forms and patterns, as linguists have demonstrated (Crystal 2010: 186–189). Written language seems more rule-bound and subject to prescription and regulation, as the numerous books on grammar, spelling and correct usage seem to testify. Words are collected and recorded in dictionaries and given definitions, and writers must take heed. Specialised words are created with single meanings (terms) for use by specialists. These forms carry over into oral usage, which is otherwise fleeting.

Many different writing systems have been devised over the centuries (Daniels and Bright 1996, Ager 2015b). They have been classified in different groups according to whether they mark events or represent objects, ideas or abstract concepts, and whether they represent sounds. These sounds may be whole syllables or individual elements of sound, such as just consonants or including vowels. There are many systems, but there seems to have been a broad movement over time in some parts of the world from pictorial representation (pictograms), to representing conceptual ideas (ideograms), representing words (logograms), syllables (syllabic writing), consonants (phonograms) or single sound types that include vowels (alphabetic writing) (Yule 2014: 212–220; Dobrovolsky and O'Grady 1997: 591–624; Crystal 2010: 206–213). Ancient Egyptian hieroglyphs have ideograms representing 'real-world entities or notions', but also phonograms that represent consonants (Crystal 2010: 209).

Chinese uses logograms, known as characters, to represent words, as does its derivative Japanese kanji. However, characters can also represent sounds. This occurs because a sound, such as a word, is attached to each character, since one has to be able to read and pronounce each of them. The particular sound may occur in another, perhaps more complicated or new word, and characters may be borrowed to represent the sounds making up the new word rather than inventing a completely new single character for it. A simple example is with the Chinese character for big: 大. It looks like a person with arms outstretched, as opposed to the character for small with arms closer: 小. The sound attached to 大 in Roman alphabetical *Pinyin* script is *dà*. So if we take the Chinese word for Australia 澳大利亚, *Àodàlìyà*, we can see the role of the character 大 as representing the sound *dà* in the pronunciation; this is known as 'rebus writing' and occurs frequently. It seems that rebus writing occurred in ancient times where the Sumerian cuneiform script was borrowed and used for languages such as Akkadian Elamite and Hurrian (Ostler 2005: 50). The sounds attached to the Sumerian words came along with the script.

It might be thought that an ideographic script should be able to serve as a universal script for all languages and therefore be useful for a multilingual system. In China, the script has allowed speakers of different languages to communicate through writing using the same signs. However, it does not work in practice as a universal multilingual script for a variety of reasons. We can glimpse this though Japanese, which adopted the Chinese script as kanji but supplemented it with two syllabic scripts: *katakana* and *hiragana* (Dobrovolsky and O'Grady 1997: 607; Ager 2015a). They also have an alphabetic Roman script *romaji* for foreigners. Languages which are inflected, such as European languages with declensions of nouns, conjugations of verbs, as well as definite and indefinite articles, do not fit neatly into the structure of Chinese script, and vice versa. There are other issues, such as length of sentences.[9] So the idea of a single multilingual script for all languages seems to be unrealistic. The nearest is perhaps the phonetic International Phonetic Alphabet (Ager 2015b).

European languages use alphabetical scripts where symbols represent single sound types. These scripts seem to have taken shape over the centuries from ancient Egyptian hieroglyphs. The ideograms had names attached, names gradually came to the fore for representation, and then the syllables beginning with the first consonant of the syllable. Phoenician represented consonants in syllables, but the Greeks introduced signs for vowels and adapted the script to their language (Crystal: 2010: 212). The Romans took over the Greek script and adapted it, as did others. Cyrillic and Glagolithic are other descendant scripts. In each case the individual signs for sounds are technically arbitrary; their value is in becoming accepted as representing sounds and then being used systematically. Different languages have different sounds and need different alphabets. New signs are invented and others dropped. For example, Italian does not use the letter J and replaces it with GI, as in *giustizia* for justice.

The study of writing systems is fascinating and takes one deep into the historical development of writing and language (historical linguistics and philology). However, what information can we take as regards application to modern multilingual law? Essentially, each script provides a foundation for the construction of legal texts using writing. The form of the script, its appearance and the conventions used with respect to writing it, such as the spacing of letters, handwriting or print, capital letters or lower case, commas and other forms of punctuation, orthography, spelling and so on, are all basic ingredients for writing and reading texts, as they all convey information and therefore meaning. For example, a full stop indicates the end of a unit of meaning (semantic unit). Commas, semicolons and brackets also serve to chop up text into units of meaning. Smaller units can assist in translating multilingual legal texts. These are all part of graphology, the study of systems of symbols devised to communicate language in written form (Crystal 2010: 204).

We turn next to reflect on some of the branches of linguistics, bearing in mind that when reference is made to the sounds of language (oral usage), we must also have regard to the conventions that apply to represent those sounds in the written script. And so it is with legal language. In a multilingual context there may be a shared script or different scripts, and the relationships between the scripts and their layout and contents need to be thought about with care. For an example of practical application, one could refer to multilingual drafting guidance such as the EU Interinstitutional Style Guide (2015) in 24 languages and 3 scripts: Roman (or Latin),[10] Greek and Cyrillic for the Bulgarian language.

Linguistics: searching for what is useful

We will now take a rapid canter through the fields of linguistics, looking for elements to retain for the concept of multilingual law. Since it is a huge topic, what is the best way of progressing? We are looking for a method by which to organise the information. Two approaches come to mind: first, one can adopt a sequence of headings along the lines proposed by Aitchison (2003: 8). This takes the form of a series of concentric circles. At the centre is phonetics, then going outwards are: phonology, syntax, semantics and pragmatics. The outermost ring is of hybrid fields comprising linguistics and other disciplines: sociolinguistics (sociology), anthropological linguistics (anthropology), philosophical linguistics (philosophy), stylistics (literature), computational linguistics (artificial intelligence), applied linguistics (languages) and psycholinguistics (psychology). To these lists we could perhaps add morphology, as well as comparative linguistics and historical linguistics. And what about translation and related fields of activity such as terminology, lexicology, vocabulary and grammar?

A second approach draws on the distinction by Ferdinand de Saussure (2005) between language, *langue* and *parole*. Applying that approach, we can start with topics relating to language in general and then proceed to languages and everyday general and specialist usage. The only difficulty is that the topics cross boundaries between each other, and we need to bear in mind oral and written language differences, not to mention other forms of communication such as sign language. So, having searched for an organising principle, what follows will be subjective but nonetheless guided by the two approaches indicated. The outer ring of hybrid topics will not be discussed, as it would require enquiring into the related disciplines. The exceptions are applied linguistics and legal linguistics. Attention is restricted to human communication, as law is a product of human activity. We will start with biology and the mechanics of sound production.

Biology of speech production

The biology of speech production is connected to breathing, lungs, throat, mouth, lips, larynx (which controls the flow of air), vocal chords (which vibrate) and nose (which provides a resonating chamber). We need not dwell on them further. We take them for granted until something goes wrong, and then we are studying medical language.

Language and the brain

Language is connected to the brain, its structure, its processes and the way it organises information and handles communications (Crystal 2010: 268–273). As a large and developing field for research, there seems no particular need for knowledge of it for a study of the concept of multilingual law in itself. However, there may well be issues deriving from studying legal language in multilingual and multicultural settings that is of interest for linguistic researchers and which in turn might be of practical value. Related fields of study are *cognitive linguistics*,[11] which places a focus on the relation between language and mind, and *neurolinguistics*, which looks at the neurological processes underlying the development and use of language (Ahlsén 2006). It is proposed to background these fields.

Phonetics

Phonetics is the study of the sounds that humans produce to make speech, or as linguists phrase it, the study of 'human speech sounds' (Aitchison 2003: 8).[12] 'The power source of our speech sounds is the flow of air from our lungs' (Poole 1999: 41). The flow of air is manipulated as it passes through the throat and head. The vocal chords, velum, palate, alveolar ridge, teeth, lips and tongue all play a role in producing different sounds. Sounds created when the vocal chords are closed are 'voiced', and when they are open the sounds are 'unvoiced'. Examples are [v] and [f] (Poole 1999: 42–43).

Consonants are determined by voicing, the place of articulation and the manner of articulation. The places of articulation are identified as bilabial, labiodental, dental, alveolar, palatal, velar and glottal, and the manner of articulation with respect to these can be plosive, fricative, nasal, liquid or semi-vowel (Poole 1999: 44). These give the sounds of English with which one is familiar from the alphabet. However, not all languages use the same sounds and there are languages which include sounds unknown to English, for example the clicks in some African languages such as Zulu and San.[13] Linguists have developed the International Phonetic Alphabet (IPA) for the purpose of having a notational standard for the phonetic representation of all languages.[14] There are different branches of phonetics, for example with respect to oral language: 'articulatory phonetics' (the study of how speech sounds are made or 'articulated', 'acoustic phonetics' (the physical properties of speech as sound waves 'in the air') and 'auditory (or perceptual) phonetics' (the perception, via the ear, of speech sounds). A further field is 'forensic phonetics', which 'has applications in legal cases involving speaker identification and the analysis of recorded utterances' (Yule 2014: 27).

It is important to be aware of phonetics and the IPA as they are of practical assistance with respect to language for pronunciation and learning languages. The IPA is a tool for reading texts in unfamiliar scripts, but it tends to be for specialists. For laypersons the process of transliterating a foreign script into the signs familiar from their own language may be sufficient. *Pinyin* serves this purpose for Chinese, as does *romaji* for Japanese, by reproducing the sounds of each language in Roman script. However, where, as in those languages, nuances of meaning are conveyed primarily through the script, transliteration has limitations for language learning. In addition, native speakers tend not to use it. For the present purpose, accordingly, we retain awareness of phonetics but most of the time do not need to refer to it explicitly. It forms part of the background foundations of language systems, linked to scripts. Similarly, we note transliteration, but leave it aside.

Phonology

While phonetics 'is concerned with the production of sounds which can serve as speech sounds in a language', phonology 'studies sounds in the context of languages and other speech varieties. It is concerned with which sounds a language uses and how it arranges them. It is concerned with the contribution of sounds to the task of communication' (Poole 1999: 55). Linguists and lawyers are interested in sounds when attached to meaning, and they are interested in dissecting words to ascertain meaning from the parts. Phonetics identifies all the different units of sound that exist in languages, but phonology studies the sounds in connection with individual languages to see the range and patterns (Dobrovolsky and Katamba 1997; Crystal 2010: 168–176). From there one can compare the sounds inherent to different languages. This in turn leads to identifying the combinations of sounds that are permitted or not permitted in each language according to the 'phonological rules' of the language. That information is important when new words and terms are being created, as they should normally conform to the permitted sound combinations of the language. In turn, the sounds become connected to meaning.

98 *Language*

Phonologists have methods for identifying the basic units of sound in a language and in finding out how they are patterned; what combinations are allowed, what are not, and what happens when individual sounds in words are changed in a word. In the latter case, is a new word formed with a new meaning, or does it remain the same word but pronounced or spelled differently, such as the difference between 'organise' and 'organize', where /s/ is replaced by /z/.[15] However, if we replaced other letters by something else, we would probably get a nonsense word, one that was 'not permitted'. Differences between British and American spelling of words have regard to phonological rules in this respect. Another example is 'colour' and 'color'. They are variants of the same language, English, with the same meaning. The basic unit in phonology is the phoneme, which is 'a sound or group of sounds that is functionally distinctive in a language system', and phonemes are tested by seeing 'whether substituting one segment for another can produce a different word', such as the words *sue* and *zoo* (Poole 1999: 57).

In oral language, if the /s/ in *sue* is modified by changing how the sound is articulated, it produces sounds like /z/ or like /sh/, and these sounds give different words like *zoo* and *shoe*. In English, these written words have different spellings attached, but the sound of the vowel is similar for both. With the word 'organise' we can change the letter 's' to the letter 'z' without changing either sound of meaning as it is a matter of spelling convention. The position of sounds within a word can also make a difference, whether they are at the beginning, in the middle or at the end of a word.[16] The sounds, combinations and patterns for each language differ.

The field of phonology is an essential part of language study and therefore a foundation element of multilingual law. Law uses language as its principal tool and, like any craft activity that uses tools, most of the time one can use them without reflecting on how they have been made. But occasions arise when one needs to know. An important part of multilingual law is to create new words and terms, or adapt old ones to new uses, often in the context of translation from one language to another. In such a context, knowledge of the phonological rules takes on significance. With new words, after reflecting on the sounds, one needs to reflect on the written form to attach to them – unless the language is Chinese, in which case it is possible that the written character may be settled first. Learning languages involves learning the phonological rules of a language and by extension how words are formed in it. When foreign words are incorporated, borrowed or adapted to a language, the question arises as to whether they are adapted to the phonological system of the language or taken over in the original form of the source language. However, we are sliding from individual sounds towards the ways in which words are constructed, which brings us to morphology.

Morphology

With phonology one is looking at the basic sounds that are used in different languages and ways in which they may or may not be brought together. Morphology takes this a step further by including meanings attached to sounds and their combinations. The basic unit of examination for this seems to be the word, a unit of meaning with a beginning and an end, even if only a single vowel as with /a/. Morphology involves looking at the way in which words are made up or constituted. The example of the Swahili word *nitakupenda* (I will you love) is given by Yule (2014: 66). A single word in Swahili, translated by several words in English, it can be analysed for the elements that create the meaning: *ni* (I), *-ta* (will), *-ku* (you), *-penda* (love) (Yule 2014: 66). Every word in a language can be analysed to see how it is constructed and whether it can be broken down into smaller elements of meaning. For example, *translate* has the elements *trans* and *-late*. To know the meaning hidden in these elements one needs to know Latin, as the word derives from it. In French we have *traduire* (*tra* and *-duire*) containing a different Latin verb. In German, the idea of carrying or leading over inherent in the Latin meaning of the terms is conveyed by *übersetzen*. Each word here has two parts: *-late*, *-duire*, *-setzen*) and the prefix: *trans-*, *tra-*, *über-*. Only in the German word can the two parts stand as individual words.

Linguists have devised specialist terms to use when analysing words in this way. The concept of *morpheme* represents the 'minimal functional element of a word' Poole (1999: 75). As well as sound, it includes semantic and/or grammatical function. Elements that can stand by themselves as individual words are called 'roots' and elements that cannot stand by themselves are 'affixes'. They are also called, respectively, 'free morphemes' and 'bound morphemes'. Analysing languages in this way leads to the identification of all the prefixes which come before a root, all the suffixes which come after a root, and also infixes which come inside. Languages create meanings through word-building in different ways: some add meanings within a single word by adding prefixes, infixes and suffixes (agglutinating languages such as Finnish and Turkish), others tend to use separate words to convey meanings (isolating languages such as English), and others are somewhere in between (inflecting languages such as French) (Poole 1999: 74). Sometimes a root can exist by itself, as in *kingdom*, where the root is *king* and the affix *-dom*. Sometimes it cannot, as with *translate* and *traduire*, but the German word *übersetzen* has two roots – *über* (over, above) and *setzen* (to place, put).

Morphology is important for studying new languages and devising a written script for them. It is part of learning a new language, though more usually referred to under the more general heading of 'grammar' as opposed to 'vocabulary': the latter being lists of words and expressions and the former the rules about how they are combined to indicate relationships. Morphology is an important part of translation: analysing words to uncover the elements and meanings embedded in them. Morphology is also part of legal analysis: analysing words as part of the task of interpretation to determine precise meanings and relationships to other terms. For example, the phrase *multilingual law* was initially analysed (though not using such terms) as two words. *Law* is a 'root' or 'free morpheme'. The word *multilingual* stands by itself as a unit of meaning but also contains two elements that convey the sense of many and of relating to language.

Morphology enables one to make an analysis of the forms that words take. It enables one to see the variations and the ways in which words are made by adding alternative prefixes and suffixes to roots. For example, with *king* we have *kingdom*, *kingship*, *kingly*, and so on, but we do not (yet – for languages can change) have -ness, -ise. There is also the question of why the different forms exist and the internal rules that determine the way that relationships between nouns are indicated (declension of nouns), or verbs are conjugated in terms of person, number, tense, mood, and so on, which all form part of traditional grammar. These questions come into operation when words are used as tools to create meanings and to communicate messages. Language is linear because sounds produced come one after the other. Words relate to each other, but when speaking sentences, the speaker also anticipates later words by adjusting earlier words to them, just as in writing. Law is not quite so linear, as lawyers make references in legal texts to other legal texts and to parts of the same text which come earlier or later in the text, so that things tend to look more like a network.

However, we are starting to look at the operational practice of language, what Saussure referred to as *parole*, and which is covered by pragmatics and the study of actual discourse, like driving a car in the metaphor used earlier. For the present we are still examining the pieces. We have noted basic sounds, their combination into elements containing meanings and their assembly into words. The next step is to reflect on words strung together to make sentences.

Syntax

Whereas morphology is concerned with the 'internal composition of a word', syntax is concerned with 'combinations of words' (Poole 1999: 83). One frequent device for showing the relationship of one word to another is word order. We can see this with the example given by Aitchison (2003: 69) of two sentences containing the same words where it is word order that determines meaning: *The large spider frightened Aunt Matilda*; *Aunt Matilda frightened the large spider*. In some languages relationships are indicated by affixes to a root, and that makes word order more flexible. But subtle nuances of emphasis can also be created in that context through word order.

Linguists analyse sentences and divide them into their parts of speech to see how they are constructed. They identify 'noun phrases' and 'verb phrases', and within each of these categories there are elements such as nouns and verbs, and so on, familiar from traditional grammar. They create 'tree diagrams' to reveal these elements in sentences hierarchically. In that way 'a basic sentence type at the top branches downwards in ever-increasing complexity' (Aitchison 2003: 71–72).[17] Another way of expressing this is to say that sentences are analysed into parts of speech referred to as 'word classes' (Poole 1999: 84) – nouns, verbs, prepositions, adjectives, adverbs, conjunctions, and so on – but also combinations of these – noun phrases, verb phrases, preposition phrases (Aitchison 2003: 72–76) – as well as larger parts of speech – subject, verb, object – which can be in a different order in different languages.[18] This method is followed by translators, who must first understand how a source language text is constructed in its form before analysing the sentence for meanings, which may include cultural references, styles of speech, metaphors and other subtle devices. Working with multilingual legal texts involves making such analyses of sentences 'horizontally' across language versions to see how they align in form and in the meanings generated.

Linguists also study the rules in each language regarding what may be changed in a sentence and in what way, with what effects, and what cannot be changed. This is the 'engine room' of a language, as it concerns the rules of assembly to create meanings and communicate. From it emerge 'phrase structure rules', which are 'rules which govern the structure of utterances' and how sentences are constructed. 'Such rules allow for the generation of grammatical sentences in a language; they constitute a generative grammar for that language' (Poole 1999: 86). Native speakers learn these rules intuitively and second-language learners learn them through conscious study. In a sense one can think of grammar as the correct way of speaking and using words, whatever may be meant by 'correct'. There is an overlap here between syntax and grammar.

From the point of view of multilingual law, syntax is another foundation topic. Legal texts are drafted in the light of syntactic rules and they are interpreted according to them, taking into account any departures from correct usage. Translators analyse source texts and create target texts having regard to syntactic analysis. Long and complex sentences need particularly careful analysis to ensure that all the elements and nuances have been identified. For legal texts, and the purposes of law, it is necessary to standardise and make uniform the rules of syntax so that everyone is brought to interpret the same utterances in the same way and be subject to the law on an equal basis. The rules of syntax, thus standardised, become reference points for creating and interpreting meaning. Multilingual legal systems build on those rules for each language, but they also adapt them to the multilingual context. Perhaps one language is slightly adjusted to fit in with the syntactic rules of another. Perhaps words are pluralised or inflected in particular ways for the purposes of a multilingual context,[19] or for a specialist technical context. Sometimes departures from standard syntax occurs inadvertently, as where texts are drafted by non-native speakers of a language.[20] Knowledge of syntax creates awareness, and that in turn allows one to decide when adjustments are possible and when they are not. It also provides a reference point for determining 'correct' usage and the construction of meaning. As with the other disciplines, there is more to say, but we must leave it at that.

Grammar

For many persons an enquiry into how words are made up and arranged into sentences makes them think of grammar: the study of the categories of words as nouns, verbs, adjectives, prepositions, and the ways in which words are adjusted with suffixes or prefixes to convey information about relationships, such as who does what to whom (subject, verb, object, indirect object). Languages vary in the ways they convey such information and each time it all needs to be learned by heart. Grammar is often thought of as being the counterpart of vocabulary, which usually comprises long lists of words and their genders that also have to be learned by heart. So grammar seems fundamental. Yet there are introductory books on linguistics that do not mention grammar in their index (for example Poole 1999). This seems to be because what is commonly referred to as grammar is subsumed into phonology, syntax and semantics. 'Together they constitute the grammar of a language' (Aitchison 2003: 9). Perhaps one should include morphology within this scope.

It seems that what comprises 'grammar' has shifted over time in its meaning and scope of application. Having origins in ancient India and Greece in relation to the art of writing, the term has carried on through the centuries and has become linked to prescriptive ways to organise and standardise the ways in which language is used, especially written language. Grammar books set out rules to codify and standardise the ways in which a particular language is used, advocating 'correct' usage and disapproving 'incorrect' usage. The terms 'codify' and 'standardise' remind us of legal activity and law-making. Books on grammar lay the foundations for legal language and promote the alignment of creating meanings, or knowledge, and their understanding through reading and interpretation as a shared set of rules and values within a language community. Although generally written by private individuals, when taken over and followed by the community at large and used in legal texts, they become validated through usage and custom.

Many grammar books of European languages in the past looked to Latin and ancient Greek as ideal role models and took their grammars as the basis for making grammars for later languages, such as English. However, each language has its own forms of speech, and linguists decided to study these from the point of view of describing their actual usage, rather than prescribing what it ought to be.[21] The fields of phonology, morphology, syntax and semantics are in this respect more oriented towards actual practice, and that has shifted the way in which grammar is considered. Yet the prescriptive side remains important, as when using a language a person feels that there is usage which is correct and usage that is incorrect. Learners of foreign languages are constantly having their errors pointed out, which can be discouraging if carried to excess.

Linguists have developed the concept of grammar in a range of ways. Crystal (2010: 92) lists six types of grammar: descriptive grammar, pedagogical grammar, prescriptive grammar, reference grammar, theoretical grammar and traditional grammar. Grammar is also thought of in mathematical ways. There are branches of grammatical enquiry with names such as 'generative grammar' and 'transformational grammar' which developed particularly from the work of the American linguist Noam Chomsky (Crystal 2010: 101, 433). Yule defines generative grammar as 'a set of rules defining the possible sentences in a language' (Yule 2014: 291). These rules generate the possible forms of sentences. These branches of study are linked to a search for systems of rules that indicate the combinations of basic elements that would result in well-formed sentences. They are also linked to showing 'how a person constructs a knowledge system out of everyday experience' (Crystal 2010: 433).

Linguists search for underlying patterns in language use and whether these can be explained or described using mathematical language and formulations. In turn, this provides a basis leading on to mechanisation of language through the use of computers, whether to analyse language, or to create or generate language applications, such as text creation or translation. Specialised fields of linguistics such as 'generative grammar' and 'transformational grammar' have been developed. For most purposes, there is no need to be aware of such fields for the purposes of multilingual law and they are not dwelt on here; they are complicated theoretical fields that do not impinge directly on consciousness in daily practice. However, things are changing with computerisation and the generation, reading and translation of language texts by machine.[22] The user of software does not need to know and understand the inner workings and technology, but the programmers and technicians must, and as such they form part of the essential back-up support team necessary for computerised modern multilingual systems. Further, one can imagine that if, or when, robotisation of language develops autonomy, the machines may be programmed to alter the substance of languages themselves, and perhaps even develop new robotic languages. Indeed, insofar as machines are able to 'communicate' between each other, that is already the case and there is 'machine language' created by humans. So thinking about grammar has far-reaching implications. As regards multilingual law and legal texts, it is the beating heart, for it does not just describe language use, it also prescribes correct usage. But what does that all mean? It brings us to semantics.

Semantics

The branch of linguistics that addresses the question of meaning is 'semantics'. With phonetics, phonology, morphology, syntax and grammar, one is to some extent looking at the formal dimensions of language: the different sounds, their written representation through signs accepted as conventional, the patterns of organising the sounds and signs, and so on. All of this activity, however, serves a purpose and that is to convey information and knowledge, through messages as an act of communication, using a code of signs with significations or meanings attached. A simple physical system might use semaphore or Morse: one identifies the sign and looks up a code book to read the information conveyed by the sign, and that is its 'meaning'. With language, the sounds and written signs convey meaning; words convey meanings, and so do sentences and larger units of text, or discourse. For users of a language, whether speaker or listener (utterer or recipient), writer or reader, what matters most is the information or knowledge conveyed. What is it? Is it clear or confused? Is more than one meaning being conveyed, and if so, what and how is it being done? In this context each language constitutes a code, a particular form of language within the overall domain of language. To understand a communication we must understand the language code, just as to write it we must know the code, but that is just the starting point, the *sine qua non*, for uttering and receiving messages.

It helps to remind oneself of the distinction drawn by Ferdinand de Saussure (2005) between 'language', '*langue*' and '*parole*'. We started with aspects of the first with phonetics and moved towards the second with phonology, morphology, syntax and grammar. With semantics we move on towards the third. Meanings are created in everyday use, and this is represented by '*parole*'. In every utterance all three levels are present, whether the context be language used for general (LGP) or special purposes (LSP), including legal language and multilingual legal language. However, the multilingual legal context juxtaposes utterances in more than one language code. It introduces an element of comparison and the question of meaning takes on an added layer of subtlety, because the units that are analysed for meaning are not just single-code texts, though they are the foundation, but also bundles of single-language-code texts treated as units for analysis as to meanings. To understand what that implies, we need to progress slowly: first, to continue identifying linguistic methods for constructing meanings to convey information and knowledge; second, to see how these are adapted to special language such as legal language; third, to see how the multilingual dimension is handled. However, one area that is not going to be covered concerns the features of individual language codes. No exposition of French, German, Spanish, and so on is presented here. The present text makes use of standard English code signs. If it is translated, it will use the code signs of the relevant language, and take examples from that language. In a multilingual context, the meanings would then come from examining all the language versions; that is how EU texts, which are written in up to 24 languages, are handled.

O'Grady (1997: 268) gives a definition of semantics as being 'the study of meaning in human language' and notes that 'some work in this complicated area of linguistic analysis presupposes knowledge in other disciplines (particularly logic, mathematics and philosophy). He addresses four major topics, broadly summarised as: the nature of meaning, the conceptual system underlying meaning, interpreting sentences through analysing syntactic structure, and the role of other factors. There is a range of concepts used in evaluating the meanings of words and sentences. As regards words, these include synonymy, antonymy, polysemy and homophony (1997: 269–271). As regards sentences, there are paraphrase, entailment, contradiction, connotation, denotation, extension and intension, componential analysis, meaning and concepts (1997: 271–276). Reviewing these topics leads to the view that 'meaning must be something that exists in the mind rather than the world and that it must be more abstract than pictures and that there is more to it than just features' (1997: 275).

What is a concept? How are concepts structured, extended and interrelated? O'Grady explains that 'underlying the use of words and sentences to express meaning in human language is a conceptual system capable of organizing and classifying every imaginable aspect of our experience, from inner feelings and perceptions, to cultural and social phenomena, to the physical world that surrounds us' (O'Grady 1997: 276). Concepts can be 'fuzzy' or imprecise, and there can be gradations within them. Thus with the concept of 'bird', some species are felt to be better examples of birds than others, for example robins and magpies rather than ostriches and penguins (1997: 277). Further, concepts expressed through language 'are not isolated from each other. Rather they make up a giant network, with many interconnections and associations among the various subparts' (1997: 278). An example of this is 'metaphor', the understanding of one concept in terms of another. It seems that different linguistic communities do not have different conceptual systems (1997: 279), but languages differ from each other in how they express concepts. This involves lexicalisation, which is 'the process whereby concepts are encoded in the words of a language' (1997: 280). Different languages encode concepts differently. For example, for the verb 'to be' in English we have '*être*' in French and two verbs '*ser*' and '*estar*' in Spanish.

Meanings are conveyed by individual words and phrases, but also by sentences. 'The meaning of a sentence is determined by the meaning of its component parts and the manner in which they are arranged in syntactic structure' (O'Grady 1997: 284). This is referred to as the 'principle of compositionality'. However, there are other factors. O'Grady (1997: 295) says that:

> other necessary information comes from pragmatics, which includes the speaker's and addressee's background attitudes and beliefs, their understanding of the context in which a sentence is uttered, and their knowledge of how language can be used to inform, to persuade, to mislead, and so forth.

These issues lead on to the analysis of discourse where the 'properties of other utterances in the same speech event (the discourse)[23] are also crucial to understanding a sentence' (1997: 298). Pronouns, such as 'he', 'she' and 'it', are examples of this – as is the word 'this' in the present sentence. In order for conversation and discourse to function, linguists have identified 'rules'. Of these the main one is the 'co-operative principle',[24] namely to 'make your contribution appropriate to the conversation' (1997: 300). In support of this principle, maxims or guidelines have been devised: of relation (be relevant), of quality (be true), of quantity (give the appropriate amount of information), of manner (avoid ambiguity and obscurity and be brief and orderly) (1997: 300). But like other rules, these may be observed, disregarded or deliberately flouted.

In his two-volume study of semantics Allan observes that in giving an account of linguistic meaning, both speaker and hearer 'are taken to be model persons, and not any actual, real life speaker and hearer' and they are both ascribed the 'sort of capabilities and judgment attributed to the "reasonable man" in the law' (Allan 1986: vol. I, 2). Such an approach is necessary to set up a system of reference points within which variations and specific features are set. Lawyers, however, are habitually anticipating the 'unreasonable man' and intentions to be uncooperative and to seek alternative readings in their favour. It is this reality that drives legal language towards extremes of technicality and density in meanings. On the other hand, one could say that legal texts are written on the basis that the ultimate readers in terms of meaning are the 'reasonable persons' who have the power and authority to compel 'unreasonable persons' to obey the law, which is one of the functions of judge and court. Multilingual law comes within these parameters, but how far are the analytical features of semantics (or any branch of linguistics) as a discipline similar for all languages? One can explore through translation and analysis of utterances.

From the foregoing selection it is evident that semantics is of fundamental significance to language, legal language and multilingual legal language. It is present in every legal text in each language, though the incidents vary. It is also present in the remaining topics to be canvassed in this chapter, and we will return to it again in later chapters when one of the questions asked (Chapter 9) is whether there is a difference between linguistic meaning and legal meaning. In translation, the question of meaning arises with every word and sentence. The translator must make a semantic analysis of a source text (as well as a formal analysis) and think how best to reproduce the meanings in a target language. We will come to translation shortly (Chapter 10), but first there are issues to explore relating to words as vocabulary, lexicology or terminology, and to enlarge slightly on the notions of pragmatics and discourse analysis. Linguistics is a palace full of many chambers. We have opened a few doors and peered inside. The practitioner of law and language is mainly concerned with *parole* within a *langue*. In that connection it seems necessary to include some everyday issues that touch on pragmatics, discourse analysis, stylistics, register, rhetorics and genre. They are all directly relevant to legal language, creating and interpreting legal texts, and by extension multilingual texts. We will then close this chapter with a mention of historical linguistics, an example of an ancient law still in force, a mention of comparative linguistics and hybrid fields where linguistics merges into other disciplines, such as law. That brings us to legal-linguistics, legilinguistics and the language of law. It is a specialist field and is treated separately in Chapter 7. The linguistic framework of law, legal language and multilingual law should by now be becoming clearer.

However, we are now shifting position away from a theoretical structural viewpoint and towards that of specialist user and participant where language provides tools to achieve particular communication objectives. With that thought, we can ask about the words which represent the meanings we use.

Vocabulary

Vocabulary is broadly thought of as the words that go to make up a language, and learners of foreign languages see this as the counterpart of grammar. The online Oxford Dictionaries[25] provides several definitions of the word 'vocabulary': the 'body of words used in a particular language', the 'words used in a particular subject or sphere of activity or on a particular occasion', the 'body of words known to an individual person', a 'list of difficult or unfamiliar words with an explanation of their meanings, accompanying a piece of specialist or foreign-language text'. All these definitions have in common the idea of a collection of words. The precise range of knowledge of vocabulary may differ between persons, and also as regards activities, whether it be speaking, listening, reading or writing. One becomes more aware of this when learning a foreign language as one's limitations are immediately apparent.

The larger one's vocabulary, the greater the range of choices that are available for communication, but attention is also needed as regards the vocabulary range of a receiver. Every reader of a foreign-language text is aware of encountering unfamiliar words and expressions. Yet it is not just persons who have vocabulary ranges, but also languages themselves. A language spoken by a forest-dwelling community will develop a different vocabulary range as compared with a community living in an industrial city. This distinction is important for law and legal language, as the ideas and concepts expressed about law in different societies will be conditioned by the vocabulary of words available to the speakers. Learning about law involves learning about the concepts and words used by law. In the case of multilingual law, one can find that the vocabulary range of each language may differ, both in total range and in the precise concepts and ideas conveyed by words. If the gap is large, it may be necessary to create words in the smaller language so as to expand its range to match the vocabulary range of larger languages. Chapter 7 builds on this idea to suggest that one can grade languages according to their vocabulary range for legal purposes. However, the term 'vocabulary' is very broad and general and, being collective, it is not adapted to thinking about individual words. Linguists tend to refer to 'lexemes' and 'lexical items' (Crystal 2010: 108), which are more technical expressions. A 'lexeme' can comprise one word, or several words which taken together convey a meaning (example: *to go bananas*). Lexis is another word for vocabulary; however, it gives rise to the field of 'lexicology', which is 'the study of the form, meaning and behaviour of words'.[26]

Lexicology

Lexicologists study words from a scientific point of view, but there is an active and practical side to the study of words which consists in searching for them, recording them, devising definitions and, in some cases, indicating equivalent words in foreign languages. This is the work of making dictionaries in one language, and also bilingual or multilingual dictionaries. Making dictionaries is called 'lexicography', which is carried out by 'lexicographers'. Their work is vital for any multilingual legal system. As to how one goes about compiling a dictionary, Crystal (2010: 115) provides clues in a list of 'Twenty questions to ask when you buy a dictionary'. Another lexicographical product is the thesaurus, which is a book that lists 'words in groups of synonyms and related concepts'.[27]

There are general dictionaries such as the Oxford English Dictionary and the Chambers Dictionary for the English language, and there are specialised dictionaries, such Stroud's Judicial Dictionary of Words and Phrases (2014) and Black's Law Dictionary for legal language and vocabulary. Each language has its general and specialist dictionaries. Making dictionaries is a skilled activity, but so is using them. Bilingual dictionaries, such as the Collins Robert French Dictionary (2010), are invaluable tools in a multilingual environment, enabling one to look up words in one language to ascertain equivalent words in another language.

For multilingual legal systems dictionary-making is an essential activity, as there is a need to establish a comparable lexical range for each of the languages being used at the same level. It is an ongoing task, as not only is each language developing its vocabulary in its general use, but every time a new law is prepared with new concepts and terms, there is a need for the lexical range to be covered in each language through term creation, and these terms must be recorded and explained. As regards legal lexicography, the principles and methods of dictionary-making is explained in French in the Canadian context by Groffier and Reed (1990). For legal terms in France, Cornu (2014) provides authoritative guidance. For EU specialist terms, Barav and Philips (1993) is a source of information for older terms and concepts. For a comparative perspective on legal lexicography, see Mac Aodha (2014). This is a small sample of reference works available.

Perhaps the largest category of users of dictionaries, apart from learners of a language, is translators, who are converting information in one language code into another language code. However, translators tend not to talk about lexis and lexemes; rather, they refer to 'terms' and their constant concern is with 'terminology'. There is a close connection to lexicology, but the function of terminology is different and needs to be mentioned.

Terminology

The definition of terminology by Oxford Dictionaries[28] is that it is the 'body of terms used with a particular technical application in a subject of study, theory, profession, etc.'. Here the important notion is the linkage to technical fields. With terminology we find ourselves in specialised (special) domains of language use, such as legal language or scientific language. The ideal for terminology is that there should be only one term to convey the meaning of a concept or idea. Scientific notation does this with plants and animals using Latin to confer single names on every type that is known: *Pulsatilla vulgaris*, *Corvus corax*, to mention just two at random. Anyone in the scientific world can immediately know without uncertainty what is being referred to. It is standardisation of language. This concept of unicity also works in the other direction, for if one wishes to refer to the pasque flower or the raven in any language and be certain that one will be understood correctly, one uses the scientific name. Thus there is a scientific method behind terminology that aims at precision in language, seeking to overcome or minimise potential variations that arise between languages and cultures for the purposes of specialist communication. It is thus a key idea in LSP.

Looking at terminology from a multilingual perspective, terminologists draw a distinction between primary term formation and secondary term formation. Broadly, a new term is generally coined (created) in one language. It may arise spontaneously among professionals or it may be created by committees.[29] Its meaning becomes established. However, the term must be translated into other languages and for that purpose a new term may need to be found in each of the relevant languages. This task involves secondary term formation. Terminologists have methods for making primary and secondary terms. We noted the use of Latin for scientific terms as a method for fixing terms to apply for all languages, thus avoiding the need for secondary term formation. However, for fields such as law such a method is rarely possible, as the terms are abstract and more linked to legal systems and cultural contexts. Names may be shared generically, and that may suffice, but the precise implications vary between systems. Secondary terms are created by analysing the source term for its elements and constructing a new term. There are different methods for this, perhaps by constructing a term from native roots or borrowing a foreign term as a loanword. EU multilingual texts in every language provide many examples of loanwords, such as *acquis communautaire*, and term formation, such as the name *euro* for the currency. The detailed methods of terminologists are described and explained among others by Sager (1990), Wright and Budin (1997) and Cabré (1998).[30]

Terminologists list terms in glossaries. These are aimed at specialist users and they are intended to provide information on equivalent terms in different languages, examples of usage and indications as to the degree of reliability and confidence for using the terms. Glossaries are essential tools for translators as they are constructed with a view to the maximum amount of precision and reliability. The main EU glossary IATE (InterActive Terminology for Europe) comprises an electronic database accessible online for external users.[31] It provides information on EU terms in 24 (and more) languages. Terminology is important, because without terms there can be no text on a topic. Each time the European Union enlarges by taking on a new Member State and a new language, one of the preliminary tasks before accession is to adapt its language by creating perhaps hundreds of new terms to express EU concepts that must now be rendered using words in the new language. It is a big task and forms part of the even larger task of translating the many thousands of pages of EU *acquis* into that language.[32] Terminology work forms the 'bread and butter' of translation and underpins multilingual legal systems. It finds its place within the pragmatic working environment and is more of an extension of the work of experts and translators than a theoretical field in its own right, although its methods have been extensively theorised.

Pragmatics

When thinking about vocabulary, lexicography and terminology, we moved away from linguistic theories about language and towards the everyday practitioner's use of language and their needs. We noted how terminology is connected to specialist fields of activity, which implies a context of specialist discourse. We can go further and think about this discourse aspect and the ways in which context plays a role and influences the meanings that are generated. Doing so takes one into pragmatics. This field 'encompasses speech act theory, conversational implicature, talk in interaction and other approaches to language behaviour in philosophy, sociology, linguistics and anthropology' (Mey 2001). Pragmatics builds on the linguistic theories mentioned earlier and adds 'context of the utterance, any pre-existing knowledge about those involved, the inferred intent of the speaker, and other factors' (Shaozhong 2005). This field has a bearing on legal language since there is a special context connected to law and a shared culture among participants, and language is used in special ways.

Discourse analysis

Any utterance, whether oral or written, can be analysed for the ways in which language is used and the meanings created. Discourse analysis is 'an approach that looks at patterns of language across texts as well as the social and cultural contexts in which the texts occur' (Paltridge 2006). It can be seen as an aspect of semantics that goes beyond the study of individual words and sentences and connects with actual usage rather than theoretical ideas. The juxtaposition of sentences and embedding in particular contexts can change meanings. An expression such as 'Take that!' might be an intimation of violence or of a kind gift, depending on context, voice register, intention, and so on. Lawyers are very interested in the connections between utterances, actions and knowledge because they are connected to intention; legal systems draw distinctions between intended and unintended actions and consequences. This is very important in criminal law and actions for damages under civil law. By extension, it is important for multilingual law. Translators need to be aware of possible alternative significations of terms and expressions in context in order to judge which meanings to reproduce in their target language texts. The wider context of a text makes intended meanings clear perhaps, but there are many ways to read and interpret texts.[33] Discourse analysis provides an entry point for such reflections. It includes topics such as style, register and rhetorical strategies used.

Rhetorics

Rhetorics is part of legal language. It is the 'art of persuasion' through language, language style and discourse. Examples are found in political speeches and an advocate's pleadings in presenting arguments and submissions to a public, a judge or a jury to convince them of the validity of some point of view. Legal texts are rhetorical; not just court pleadings, but legislative texts and judgments must also impliedly seek to persuade compliance and observance – in a word, 'acceptance'. They must all be structured and use language to those ends. From a multilingual point of view, each language has its own 'genius', that is to say its own innate ways of expressing information. The art of multilingual drafting is to match and align the genius of each language version of a text into a rhetorical whole and a legal singularity in terms of message. For an introduction to rhetorics, see Reboul (2013) (in French).

Genre

Genre looks at different types of language and types of text and their characteristics. For example, in the context of literature there are thrillers, historical novels, fantasy works, biographies and so on. To obtain an idea of the concept of genre, one can imagine one is in a library searching the shelves for headings, with each one representing a genre. What about legal language and legal texts? They are also highly structured and can be classified into different genres, or categories. We have already raised the concept of genre to categorise legal texts into legislative texts, court texts, legal literature and contracts, and we linked them to sources of law. The concept of genre is thus constantly present when we discuss different types of legal text, their authors, contexts and purposes. Genre theory has been developed in recent years, but there is not space to elaborate here. One dimension of it is ESP (English as special language). For an introduction, see among others Chandler (2000), Dudley-Evans (undated) and Bhatia (2008, 2014). Another dimension is literary theory (Bertens 2008, Ryan 1999). In a multilingual legal system one expects the different language versions of a text to form part of the same genre, but each language imposes its own particular forms and features within that, so that one would look at comparative aspects.

Historical linguistics

Before drawing this chapter to a close, a few broader themes of linguistics may be mentioned which place the fields within a context of time and space and also link up with other disciplines. Language exists in time and space. Ideas change over time; we could probably take any aspect of discourse in any language and find that it is different at different points of time. Spellings change, as do pronunciation, lexical range/vocabulary, the meanings of words, and so on. This is the field of study of historical linguistics (Campbell 2013) and philology, the ways in which languages have changed over time.

Historical linguistics may seem to have little interest for modern multilingual legal systems, but to take that view would be misleading. For example, in United Nations texts in Chinese anecdotal information is that there are differences between the Chinese of the early UN texts compared with the texts made in the second decade of the twenty-first century. This generates questions when it comes to amending or modifying earlier texts. Which style to use? Old or new? Something in between? To give a flavour of the sort of problem faced, we can take an old Scottish law, still in force. We can ask how we might amend it using modern language in English. Such questions take one not only into linguistic analysis but also into legal methods and legal language.[34] The text is in fifteenth-century legal language. The Lawburrows Act 1429 states:

> It is statute ande ordanit that gif ony of the kingis liegis haf ony doute of his life outhir be dede or manance or violent presumpcioun ande he ask souerte of thaim that he doutis the schiref sal tak souerte of the party that the complante is maid apoun sa that the party playntife mak prufe of the dede or of manance or of the violent presumpcioun maid or done till hym.[35]

In a context of multilingual law where there are two or more languages within a legal system and each of them is changing and evolving in its own ways over time, it is convenient here to refer to the internal context of each language as the 'vertical dimension' as it reaches up and down through time, as distinguished from the 'horizontal dimension', which comprises the relationships between and across languages. In a multilingual system of law such as that of the EU, languages become 'bundled' together like strands in computer cables transmitting complex signals. Information passes along each language strand and the system needs it to be aligned for all strands. The messages are shared and influence each other through forming part of a single cultural space. Each language continues to evolve in its own way over time, but within a comparative dimension.

Comparative linguistics

Language varies in different places as well as in different times. Different communities have different speech forms, whether it be pronunciation, vocabulary, grammar, syntax, morphology, and so on. Are the differences ones of local variation, dialect or language? Within languages one is within the vertical dimension, but comparing languages takes one into the horizontal dimension. Languages differ. For monolingual legal systems the differences are primarily a matter of curiosity, but when languages become bound within a system of law, each language acquires a vested interest in the others as co-carriers of the message. Comparisons in methods of writing, form, style, register and meanings take on a vital importance.

Linguistics combined with other fields

From the 'core' areas of phonetics, phonology, morphology, syntax, grammar, semantics, and so on, the study of linguistics widens out into the ways in which language is used in different contexts. We noted pragmatics, discourse analysis, rhetorics and genre in that connection. Linguists make specific connections with other fields of scientific enquiry: in connection with psychology (psycholinguistics), sociology (sociolinguistics), anthropology (anthropological linguistics), philosophy (philosophical linguistics), literature (stylistics, literary criticism), artificial intelligence (computational linguistics), as well as language use in all the specialised walks of life, such as medicine, science and the law. The study of legal language is referred to as legal linguistics, a branch of applied linguistics and of pragmatics, the study of language in action as opposed to theory.

So we could say that the theme and contents of this book lie essentially within the field of applied linguistics, legal linguistics and legal-linguistic pragmatics. However, they also lie within the sphere of legal theory and practice, as we saw in earlier chapters. And that is not all; for we must think about the nature of legal language and reflect on what makes a language code fit to serve as a legal language. We also need to think about how legal texts are constructed to convey meanings and how these meanings are transferred from one language to another through translation. What are the units of meaning? How can we get inside the heads and minds of different persons involved with making or reading texts in different languages? Do they share the same ideas or not? Here, an awareness of semiotics, the study of signs, offers useful insights. This all appears terribly intimidating. It is indeed complex, but if we can pick our way through the different fields that come together in multilingual law, we can see if we can form a general picture of the intersecting elements. That is what is being aimed at with the framework, summarised in the appendices.

Summary

This chapter has made a rapid survey of some principal themes of linguistics, the study of language. The primary aim has been to indicate the extent to which different fields are useful for a knowledge of legal language within multilingual legal systems. To that end it has been necessary to place the themes in a sequence. For this, two ideas were followed: first, that of concentric circles with inner and outer circles; second, the distinction between language, *langue* and *parole*. A range of topics in linguistics have been canvassed. To a greater or lesser extent they are all present in legal language and impact on multilingual law. We turn now to explore a few of these ramifications from the viewpoint of legal language and legal terminology.

Notes

1. For a brief history of linguistics see Crystal 2010.
2. See www.oxforddictionaries.com/definition/english/language.
3. See also World Federation of the Deaf at http://wfdeaf.org/our-work/focus-areas/sign-language.
4. New Zealand Sign Language Act 2006. The legislation gives people the right to use and access New Zealand Sign Language (NZSL) in legal proceedings, including in court.
5. Maps and photographs are examples of non-linguistic documents used for the purposes of law.
6. See International Association of Forensic Linguists. [Online]. Available at: www.iafl.org/forensic.php.
7. See, for example, Comparative Legilinguistics. [Online]. Available at http://legilinguistics.amu.edu.pl/.
8. It reminds one of the children's game of 'Chinese whispers', where a sentence is whispered to one child in a circle, who whispers what is heard to their neighbour, who also passes it on; sentence at input and output are compared.
9. Yen 2010 describes Hong Kong experience in translating English legal texts into Chinese.
10. The terms seem to be used interchangeably.
11. For background, see International Cognitive Linguistics Association (ICLA) (2015). [Online]. Available at: www.cognitivelinguistics.org/en/about-cognitive-linguistics.

12 See also Crystal 2010: 160–167.
13 To hear the sounds, see Zulu & San Click Language. 2010. [Online]. Available at: www.youtube.com/watch?v=MXroTDm55C8.
14 See International Phonetic Alphabet. 2014. [Online]. Available at: www.internationalphoneticalphabet.org/.
15 There are conventions about how to refer to letters and sounds which should be consulted in the specialist literature and are not mentioned here.
16 Arabic marks these differences of position in the script forms (Ager 2015b).
17 For examples, see among others Aitchison (2003: 72–85), Crystal (2010: 98–100), Yule (2014: 94–102).
18 This is one of the defining features of a language: subject, verb object (SVO); verb, subject, object (VSO), etc.
19 For example: 'actions' in English to match '*les actions*' in French in EU texts.
20 International English spoken and written by non-native speakers and writers provides a 'happy hunting ground' for such examples.
21 Crystal (2010) discusses the differences between American and European approaches in this respect; North American languages being very different and unwritten necessitated different methods of investigation.
22 On the use of computers in linguistics, see Lawler and Dry 1998.
23 This could be a written text.
24 Note the blurring between rule and principle. Linguists use language differently from lawyers.
25 Available at: www.oxforddictionaries.com/definition/english/vocabulary.
26 Oxford Dictionaries [Online]. Available at: www.oxforddictionaries.com/definition/english/lexicology.
27 Oxford Dictionaries [Online]. Available at: www.oxforddictionaries.com/definition/english/thesaurus.
28 Oxford Dictionaries [Online]. Available at: www.oxforddictionaries.com/definition/english/terminology.
29 The creation of ISO codes is an example.
30 For EU terminology, see Terminology Coordination at the European Parliament (2013).
31 Available at: http://iate.europa.eu/SearchByQueryLoad.do?method=load.
32 For a language and translation viewpoint on EU accession, see Šarčević (2001).
33 For a history of reading, see Manguel 1996.
34 As case law is built on the act, any modernisation of the language would require a study of all the amending acts and cases, as well as impacts on other branches of law. It is an example of historical multilingualism.
35 It is statute and ordained that if any of the King's lieges has any doubt for his life whether by deed or menace or violent presumption and he ask surety of them that he doubts the sherrif shall take security from the party that the complaint is made against provided the party complaining makes proof of the deed or menace or violent presumption made or done to him.

7 Language(s) for legal purposes

Introduction

At the beginning of this book we identified multilingual law as comprising two elements – law and language – and set about exploring these concepts. We sought to separate the two, although since both involve the use of language, that is not easy. Having canvassed many concepts from theories of law and language, it is time to turn towards synthesising the elements, bringing them together and setting them within a multilingual context. We need to keep in mind two dimensions, which were referred to earlier as the vertical and horizontal dimensions, in order to represent the dimension internal to each language and that between languages. In both dimensions the fundamentals of language are taken as given and attention is placed on the *langue* and *parole* of Ferdinand de Saussure. The horizontal dimension takes us into the relationships, similarities and differences between languages and from there into multilingual drafting, interpretation, translation and the construction of meanings multilingually. Translation is the method for transferring information (knowledge and meaning) from one language to another.

This chapter takes a look at the form of special language (LSP) that comprises legal language. Multilingual law uses legal language, so it needs to be understood to form a full picture. Like everything else connected to the theme of this book, there is much that could be said – too much for the available space. So it is necessary to be selective. This chapter places attention on two broad facets: first, the nature of legal language in general; second, the vocabulary range that is implied in a language as used and recognised as a language of law. The latter topic raises two issues: first, concerning the scope of a language used for carrying legal meanings, and second, the extent to which a legal system confers on it a legal status under its linguistic regime. Given that there are over 7,000 languages, is it possible to tag each of them with an indicator in that respect? A table of classification of use and status is proposed in this chapter, and reproduced in Appendix IV.

The third section of this chapter takes a look at legal language in the multilingual context. That takes us back to Chapters 4 and 5 and the different types of legal order or legal system and their linguistic regimes. We remind ourselves that legal systems are divided into branches and lower-level fields, which broadly match with 'domains' of linguists as providing context with respect to meanings. We will background this dimension in order to focus on structure and method. We also remind ourselves of the legal distinction between substantive law and adjective or procedural law. Substantive law ties in with the branch structure of law, so we will leave it aside, but procedural law provides a structure and methodology for making new legal texts and institutionally conferring meanings in them. We have examples of this with the legislative process and the court or judicial process. We encountered them in Chapter 4 in connection with sources of law as sources of legal texts.

One can place multilingual law within a procedural context. Texts in two or more languages must be produced; how is that to be done? Texts in two or more languages must be interpreted; how is that to be done? For legislative texts, we reflect on drafting strategies, mentioned in Chapter 4, but also on translation scenarios, to be mentioned in Chapter 10. For court procedures, we enter into interpretation and the construction of meaning multilingually, while remembering that judicial texts must also be drafted and created. In order to understand how meaning can be drawn from a bundle of language versions, it helps to clarify what is involved. There is the linguistic analysis which draws on the topics in Chapter 6, but for legal texts we should bear in mind that a legal text is a source that a judge draws on in order to construct the law. If one bears that fact constantly in mind, the methods of multilingual interpretation become clearer. The act of construction is an independent abstract action, set in substantive, procedural and factual contexts.

Legal language

Legal language is specialist (special/specific) language (LSP). What is it that makes language 'legal'? What are the features of legal language? Can any language be used as a legal language? Are some more fitted than others, and if so, what are the principal distinguishing features? These questions become relevant in a multilingual context, especially one where new languages are being added to a legal system. Behind them lies the concept of 'official language'. We met this concept in Chapter 5 in connection with the concept of linguistic regime, rules on language, but now we want to delve deeper and see what that means in practice.

A simple answer to the question just posed is that legal language is language used for the purposes of law. In Chapter 4 we reflected on sources of law and saw how the sources can generate types (genres) of legal texts: legislative, judicial, administrative, and so on. These are clearly legal texts. However, a legal context surrounding a text may also confer on it a capacity of legal text. For example, witness statements presented in court have a legal flavour as they are being used for legal purposes. If documents are medical records or scientific data, perhaps they too can become legal documents. However, they were drafted in a non-legal genre (medical, scientific), so how can they become legal? The answer here is that they are interpreted by lawyers (courts, judges) for the purposes of the law. Meanings may be given to them that are legal meanings and perhaps differ from scientific meanings. We are in a borderline zone between disciplines where the reader selects the category of meanings required, here legal. In effect the nature of a text as legal or not is connected to status, use made of the text and the existence of rules of law concerning it. The purpose and viewpoint of the legal reader is the significant ingredient in this respect, a way of reading and interpreting. Having said that, it is of course the case that there is a range of genres and styles of writing that are typically regarded as being legal. We will retain attention on those.

If we remain with conventional legal language made by lawyers for legal purposes, there are core legal concepts and terms (court, procedure, law, enactment, contract) and concepts and terms from policy branches (family, agriculture, medicine, engineering) which are used to regulate a field of activity. We have met some of these terms already in Chapters 3 and 4 when expounding ideas about law. Concepts and terms can be seen as basic units of meaning (vocabulary, lexicon, terminology) that are linked together using linguistic methods adapted to the particular *langue* and desired *parole*. Here we think of phonology, morphology, syntax, discourse methods, semantics, and so on. If we wish to analyse legal utterances, whether written or oral, we can take each field of linguistics as a source of questions to ask to elicit information. That is what linguistic researchers do.

As law seeks, in theory, to ensure a single instruction on what ought to be done in each particular set of circumstances, it needs to achieve singularity in the meanings generated (semantic singularity) by its texts. It does not always succeed in this objective, which is why it has mechanisms to resolve doubts and ambiguities, in particular through court procedures. Nonetheless, the requirement is ever present and underpins the ways in which legal language is created and read. Unicity of meaning implies using language with precision; that in turn means thinking carefully about possible scenarios that might arise and reflecting on how the text would apply, or be applied (or not) as regards those circumstances. This need generates two opposite directions as regards legal drafting: first, anticipate every possible scenario and write in the rule to be applied in each case; second, write broadly with clear indications of the philosophy and type of solutions sought and confer discretion on the judge to order what is right in individual cases. An example of the former approach can generally be seen in tax law and social security law involving monetary payments, whereas the latter approach is perhaps found more in regulation of administrative and professional activities of a specialist nature where facts may be very complex and new technology is coming all the time. Most legal texts oscillate between these extremes.

Detail or discretion: the linguistic counterpart is density, whether high or low. Connected to that is the genre of the text: legislative, court, contract, and so on. Each genre has its methodology for creating texts through drafting and interpreting them. These vary according to the legal system in question and its conventions. They vary according to the creating institution and its particular tasks. They may vary within an institution according to the particular organ and its functions. They may vary according to the individual personal style of the drafter. To this, one can add the historical dimension: changes in the approach preferred (drafting in plain English, gender-neutral drafting, and so on). Nonetheless, from a legal point of view every legal text must have certain formal features if it is to be treated as a legal act recognised as part of the legal system. For example, there must be an authorised signature. The act needs to be set in a context of time, place, author and the world of facts on which it seeks to operate. Beyond that, the text has a structure, adapted to purpose. For example, EU legislative acts comprise the following: title, date, enacting body, citations, recitals, enacting provisions, annexes. The form of each is laid down in guidance (Interinstitutional Agreement of 22 December 1998, Joint Practical Guide (EU 2013)). Many standard clauses are laid down and ways in which language is to be used is likewise formalised. EU texts serve as examples here, but the same goes for every legal system.

It follows from the foregoing that in order to serve as a language for legal purposes, a language must possess the words, terms and range of vocabulary needed to express all the concepts that a lawmaker wishes to express. For modern systems of law, many languages more than match this need, but others do not. That does not mean they do not give rise to legal language, or rather language with legal implications; it just means they are not equipped to handle the full range of concepts needed by modern industrial society and legal systems. A language that is purely oral does not make written legal texts. A language that has a written form but is only used within families or local societies does not possess sufficient conceptual range to be used for all purposes as a legal language. And yet the law may declare that an oral language or a local language is an official language, recognised by the law. The Constitution of South Africa 1996 provides evidence of that. So there is a distinction to be drawn between legal language and official language. Nonetheless, for a language to serve as a legal language there are certain minimum requirements: rules of grammar are needed on correct speech and writing forms; punctuation needs to be standardised; the lexical range (vocabulary) needs to be classified, with definitions established for the purpose of fixing meanings in dictionaries; glossaries of terms need to be produced for translating into and out of the language, and so on. On a more specialist note, there is a need for setting methods for the fixing of new terminology, whether it be through primary or secondary term formation. These are all issues which arise within the context of a discussion on official languages. We are once again within the vertical language dimension.

Official languages

Thinking about legal language places attention on the dimension of *parole*, the way in which language is used. However, that must be placed within a context of the language code that is being used. Language acquires meaning because it is codified, whereby meanings are attached to the elements being strung linearly.[1] The concept of language code places us within Saussurean *langue*. It is the code system which is declared by law in a legal text such as a constitution to be an, or the, official language of a legal system. If there is no qualification, an official language is a language recognised for use by official bodies and organs in their documents and communications, whether written or oral. On the one hand there is the question as to what falls within the scope of the language in question, and on the other hand there is the question as to who may or must, or perhaps may not, use the language so recognised. We are brought back to Chapter 5 and the discussion on linguistic regime with languages being used in national, international and supranational legal orders, as well as languages recognised for regional, local or more specific uses.

In order to serve the purposes of law and administration, a language needs to be organised and made suitable for the job. Technical matters need technical description; whether it be for tax-raising or repression of crime, one must be clear and precise about what is involved. Drafters must know what and how to draft, and judges and users must know what conventions are being used so that they can fully understand the intended meanings in legislation. What are the ways in which official language is organised? In terms of oral language, there is perhaps a preferred accent, preferred choice of vocabulary and particular ways of speaking, such as register. For written language, one needs a similar set of standards, overlapping with oral language, for example as regards register and terms, but going to other matters such as the sign system for the alphabet. It helps if words are spelled in standardised ways and put together and assembled in standardised ways, as this all assists in the precise communication of subtle meaning and information. To these ends, grammar books, which have a long antiquity, spelling books, dictionaries and thesauruses have been developed. They are an integral feature of an official language.

Language(s) for legal purposes 117

A language may be the sole authorised language for use in official documents and discourse, or it may share official space with one or more other language codes in the public sphere. It is usually written down according to a single set of sign systems, such as an alphabet, but there may be alternative scripts as with Serbo-Croat in the former Yugoslavia (Roman and Cyrillic alphabets mutually aligned on each other). If a language coexists with other official languages in the same legal system, then it logically must share features with them, such as legal concepts, vocabulary and legal terminology. That arises because it is the same system of law which is expressed in different language codes, so each code must express the same system linguistically. Yet the script forms, alphabets, grammar, syntax and spelling of the languages may be totally different. Take the example of Hong Kong where Chinese and English coexist as official languages, but the languages and sign systems are far apart. While different in many respects, both languages must surely seek to convey similar ideas and represent shared cultural values in Hong Kong. That must especially be the case for language devoted to law and administration, where rules are intended to be the same for all citizens regardless of race, colour, ethnic group or religion. So we can see how the fact of being a legal language in a multilingual legal system binds the languages together within the system in a close symbiotic relationship. They become alternative vehicles for expressing a message. This leads to words, expressions, sentences and indeed whole blocks of text being treated as equivalent across the languages. It is a form of inter-language standardisation. The relationship is created, and the legal-linguistic forms and terminology are driven, by the function of being official languages.

When legal texts are interpreted, depending on the rules of the system, courts may be called on to consider the different language versions, and their rulings derive from them all and may be binding in respect of all of them. But if there are slight divergences in literal meaning between language versions, a ruling based on one language version may imply a legal meaning that is not exactly reflected in the wording of another language version, so that a discrepancy emerges (see *Case C-265/03 Simutenkov*; Robertson 2012b). That can make it look as if there is an error in the text of a language version, which logically should be rectified. Where there are errors in texts, or where an interpretation is given that departs from the strict wording of a particular language version of a text, we can see limitations in a purely linguistic reading of a legal text on the face of its wording alone. This is an important issue for multilingual law and one that is difficult for an 'innocent reader' of a given language version to detect without expert legal-linguistic advice, because it means that the legal meaning of the text is different from the ostensible linguistic meaning of their language version. That is contrary to the basic legal principle that the citizen should be able to know the law; but in a multilingual legal system the citizen is perhaps required to pay attention to all language versions. This implies not only reading all language versions of acts, but also the case law interpreting them.[2] That is why reliance on a single language version is insufficient.

We can now turn to consider the horizontal dimension between official languages. The relationship between languages in a multilingual system, like other relationships, may be complex and involve power relations, with some languages being 'bigger', 'stronger' or 'more powerful' because they are spoken by the majority of the population, or by an economically stronger group. There is a historical dimension here too; have all the languages always been official languages, or have some acquired that status only recently? Has one language developed 'in the shadow' of another one and taken over ideas, terms and concepts from it? These questions bring us to reflect more closely on the nature of multilingual legal language in specific contexts and the ways in which languages have an influence on each other, especially when bound together as official languages of the same legal system. We noted this relationship in the drafting context in Chapter 4 and it occurs again in the context of translation in Chapter 10.

We can turn to reflect on the range of relationships between official languages. The simplest way of doing that is to make a table setting out the range of possible variations and then use the table for studying the permutations and variations. There are implications for terminology and this will assist in thinking about what needs to change when a language becomes an official language or acquires a new legal role. That in turn leads on to language planning, which in fact underpins any multilingual system of law.

Classifying languages by use and status

When new things arise, new words are needed and it is useful to have methods for making them. Words are always being generated spontaneously within a language community by its members. Some remain and others do not; some become part of the language of the community and are recorded in dictionaries, while others remain local, family or individual. In a multilingual context words and terms used in a source language text may not exist in a target language, and vice versa. Left to themselves, the languages do not match up in the information that can be expressed. This may not be an issue for a monolingual system, but in a multilingual legal system it becomes a problem. Concepts must be expressed in all the languages and there needs to be alignment between them to achieve the same legal effects. The solution lies within the field of terminology. Terms must be created where they do not already exist, as mentioned in Chapter 6. On another front, it may be found desirable to align the syntax of language versions, adjusting here and there, so as to bring them closer together. A smaller language that regularly serves as a target language to a larger language may do most of this adjustment. On the other hand, a lingua franca, such as English at present, that is widely used by non-native speakers in international contexts is subject to pressures to accommodate the concepts and syntax of other languages. These problems can be alleviated by shortening sentence lengths, and adhering to more standardised formulations, all of which facilitates translation. Careful use of punctuation also helps to organise information and clarify intended meanings.

Any language may acquire the status of 'official language'; it is simply a question of declaring it 'official' in a legislative or judicial act, preferably supported by indications as to the range of use and application. The Constitution of South Africa 1996 declares 11 languages as official, but what are the precise implications? We must enter into the details of the legislative texts and the pragmatic environment in order to find out. In the UK, Welsh has been made an official language by the Welsh Language Acts of 1967 and 1993 for limited purposes, and there is official recognition of Scots Gaelic by the Gaelic Language (Scotland) Act 2005. To find out the implications of official status in each case one needs to study the terms of each enacting document, but this is only the starting point as each language, once made official, needs supporting arrangements. There are conceptual implications of making a language official for the first time. What legal texts, if any, must exist in it? Which laws? Which court cases? Parliamentary proceedings? How are they produced? The quick method is through translation, but do these translations acquire the same status as the originals? What if there are divergences? What is the relationship between the languages in such a situation? What about textbooks? What about terminology across all the fields of legal and governmental activity? Must they all be covered (which implies matching terminology for each)? Does a minority language (for that is usually what it is) have official status for the whole territory or just part? Can it be used in the courts of law anywhere or only in a restricted area? What about language training for lawyers, judges, government officials? Is interpretation required for oral proceedings? There are many questions to answer and extensive implications attach to official status for a language. These all form part of multilingual law, and they all involve language policy and language planning. They are all implicit in the concept of official language and are covered in Appendix VIII.

It is also possible for languages to be proscribed, prohibited from being used and their use subject to punishment, as happened in Scotland with the Gaelic language after the 1745 rebellion. This, too, is part of linguistic regime, as discussed in Chapter 5. There are implications for legal language, because depending on the degree of recognition, or rejection, of a language, the terminology, orthography and syntactic styles will be more or less highly regulated. Beyond that there are questions that may be asked: what are the features of a language that make it serviceable as a legal language? Are there different types of legal language? What is the impact for a multilingual legal system in which languages receive different degrees of recognition?

A first step in addressing such questions is to develop some criteria and see if one can arrange them into patterns, rather like the models in Chapter 2 and Appendix II. Can one do something similar here? If one takes a criterion of extent of use and combines it with official status and extent of recognition as a language of law, one has several variables that could be brought together. A possible classification system could be in the form of a scale with lower range of use as a language of law at the bottom and higher range of use at the top. Official recognition and legal status could be fitted to the scale, although the latter is more variable as a factor, since any language can be given official recognition by law for any particular set of purposes regardless of its size. Official status is an indicator, but it is the reality backing up the status that is significant, since a language may be unable in practice to sustain the burden placed on it if the support mechanisms are not in place. In its data on world languages Ethnologue uses a 13-level scale from 0 to 10 with subdivisions that allow for subtle distinctions. The scale is labelled EGIDS (Expanded Graded Intergenerational Disruption Scale). It combines two types of information: first, 'an estimate of the overall development versus endangerment of the language' and second, 'a categorization of the Official Recognition given to a language within the country'. Further, 'each higher number on the scale represent[s] a greater level of disruption to the intergenerational transmission of the language.'[3] The levels are: 0-international, 1-national, 2-provincial, 3-wider communication, 4-educational, 5-developing, 6a-vigorous, 6b-threatened, 7-shifting, 8a-moribund, 8b-nearly extinct, 9-dormant, 10-extinct (Lewis *et al.* 2015).

The Ethnologue scale is invaluable but it goes beyond the present purposes. It is broader as it includes use of a language for education and places attention on the degree of endangerment. For the present purpose, however, we are in an essentially legal context and are interested in the terminological range of a language and its degree of adaptation as a legal language. The question takes on practical significance in a context where a lesser-used or minority language is given a higher level of official recognition, or where it changes its formal status through becoming an official language of an international or supranational organisation. When a language takes on additional functions there are significant implications, as, for example, a new burden of terminology creation arises in view of the need to be able to express concepts that have not previously been part of its lexical range. In view of these considerations, it is useful to be able to place each and every language on a scale that is adapted to the specifically legal context. It could also have two dimensions: first, the practical question of range of actual use, and second, the legal question of the extent of formal status. We would expect most of the time that these two dimensions would run in tandem, but as already observed, that need not be the case.

One of the purposes of a scale linked to legal status and use is to facilitate making comparisons within and between multilingual systems. How do languages within a multilingual legal system match up? How equivalent are they for the purposes of expressing the same legal concepts, ideas and messages? This is the horizontal dimension to language. First, one checks the broad status on a scale of levels, then one moves to focus on details of terminology, and each of the different topics raised in Chapter 6. When reflecting on the legal dimension to multilingual law in Chapters 3 and 4, we identified different legal orders, different types of legal system and different internal arrangements within legal systems. These need to be taken into account in a scale of levels oriented towards terminology. That in turn leads to embracing the concept of state and different types of state. So the scale takes on the form of a legal-linguistic classification of languages. In that respect it differs from the scale in Ethnologue. It has a different purpose.

There are questions about what constitutes the lowest level and what the highest level, and also about languages which have a different status within different legal systems, or which have changed their status in time (the historical dimension). Some languages are used only in the home and family, others more widely. Some are recognised for official use at the local or regional level, some at national and some at international level. The same language may be used informally in one country while being an official language in another. For example, at the time of writing Russian is not an official language in certain Baltic countries, but many people speak and use it in those countries as their first language. Breton is an ancient language which is still spoken in Brittany. It is currently not formally recognised as an official language, but it is used for education.[4] It is a language that, like others, has been declining for a long time. Ethnologue classifies it at level 7-shifting.[5]

Making a language an official language is one way of stemming the process of language death, since it stimulates investment in the language and creates conditions for its survival. The European Charter for Regional or Minority Languages 1992 addresses the problem of smaller languages facing extinction. It contains provisions which are connected with the degree of use of a language and sets out detailed steps and methods for raising a minority language to a higher level of use and effectiveness. The Charter is an important source of guidance for language-planning in respect of minority languages and implicitly reinforces the notion that one can classify languages according to their general level of use. Building on all the foregoing ideas, here is a possible classification of languages based on use and status for legal purposes. It is reproduced in full in Appendix IV. Suggestions are added for a possible candidate for each status.

Language(s) for legal purposes 121

Table of classification of languages by use and status

Level 0 – dead language: totally lost, no speakers, no users, no documents; no hard evidence of its existence but a belief that it existed.
Level 1 – dead language: evidence of it exists in written or graphic form but these remain undeciphered.
Level 2 – dead language: exists in written or graphic form; script deciphered and read.
Level 3 – living language: oral only; family and local use; not standardised; dialect forms predominate; no official recognition.*
Level 4 – living language: oral and written; family, local and informal use; not standardised in either oral or written form; no official recognition.*
Level 5 – living language: oral and written; family, local and informal purposes; standardisation of written form (perhaps informally or formally in another place); no official recognition.*
Level 6 – living language: oral and written; standardised as regards grammar, orthography, etc.; partial official recognition by law for limited purposes or areas on the state territory.
Level 7 – living language: oral and written; standardised as regards grammar, orthography, etc.; full recognition by law for all purposes on the state territory.
Level 8 – living language: oral and written; standardised as regards grammar, orthography, etc.; full recognition by law for all purposes on the territory of one or more states; used at international level for the purposes of international legal transactions.**
Level 9 – living language: oral and written; standardised as regards grammar, orthography, etc.; full recognition for all purposes on the territory of one or more states; used at the international level for the purposes of international legal transactions; used also at supranational level as part of an integrated supranational legal structure.

* Variant: official recognition.
** Any language may be used for an international transaction, but here the emphasis is on general and widespread practice.

The classification aims to be complete from lowest to highest level, but is nonetheless open to questions, and the demarcation lines are not entirely clear-cut. The main purpose is as a starting point for enquiry. The standpoint of reference is from location within a specific legal system at a specific point of time. It seems necessary to include dead languages in order to aim for completeness and to provide a baseline. If one can place a language on the scale, one can immediately convey an approximate idea of where it now stands in relative terms with respect to its lexical range as a legal language. If one links its position to the guidance in the European Charter for Regional or Minority Languages 1992, one has a ready-made set of objectives for a raise in status. This is significant where a minority language is being recognised by law as an official language for the first time, since there is a lot of groundwork to be done and considerable organisation and contacts to be made within the community of speakers. We can use this classification system to explore legal languages and different types of legal language.

The classification system covers dead languages. Some of these used to be legal languages, if one thinks of ancient Egyptian, ancient Greek or classical Latin. Some of these retain an influence through terms and expressions in legal language and remain alive in a modern form, as with Latin. The classification makes distinctions for 'unofficial' languages, and here the idea is to focus on the extent of use. The idea is linked implicitly to terminology; a local language probably has a restricted vocabulary/terminology/lexical range. Raising the status of a language implies extending this range. That can involve a lot of work, as new words must be created for new concepts to be expressed in the language. The language is 'stretched' and grows. This same process occurs when a language becomes used as a national language, as it must have words for 'everything'. At the international level, a language may be used for limited purposes. Any language can be used at the international level, except that it must be capable of being written down in acts. In the early days of European colonialism, when treaties were made with indigenous peoples, who may or may not have understood their full implications, a language version may have been made in the local language. For example, in New Zealand the Treaty of Waitangi of 1840 was written in English and immediately translated into Maori, which had a few decades earlier acquired a written form.[6] Maori is now an official language of New Zealand. The fact that a language is used at the international level does not automatically imply it has a higher status elsewhere, but with modern states it is usually the case that a state language is employed in international texts, so that in most cases it does have full official status, hence placing international usage at a higher level. However, international use implies adaptation through contact with other languages as well as the development of genres in the international legal order that differ from those of the national legal order.

The highest level is given as the supranational level; this is because the language is 'locked' into a multilingual environment where it must match all the other languages at all the requisite levels. It must have the most extensive specialised terminology and be capable of rendering concepts that are rendered in the other languages in the multilingual system.[7] The classic example is the European Union, with its large range of specialised terminology. When a new state accedes to the EU and brings a new official language, there is a large preliminary exercise in creating terms in the new EU language for EU concepts and translating the hundreds of thousands of pages of official EU texts known as the *acquis* before the date of accession, which takes years of intensive work.

The classification scale proposed above can be 'tweaked' here and there in various ways by introducing emotional factors, such as 'attitude' towards the language. Is it actively supported or discouraged or subject to repression, or simply ignored? This could be an indicator of whether it is 'on the way up' or 'on the way down'. For this purpose one could introduce three attitude markers: 'positive', 'neutral', 'negative'.

A language may have one status in one country and an entirely different one in another. Russian has already been mentioned in that connection, with respect to certain Baltic countries – Estonia, Latvia and Lithuania were formerly part of the USSR. Some languages are 'shared' by different countries. Thus English is an official language in Commonwealth countries and the USA; French is an official language in France, Belgium, Luxembourg and countries in Africa and elsewhere. German is an official language in Austria and Germany and in Southern Tyrol in Italy. The situation is similar with Mandarin, Portuguese and Spanish, all major world languages. In each case there are (or may be) differences in terminology and concepts as well as local variations in spelling, pronunciation, syntax and so on. What happens when a legal text is made between countries using the same language? In an international context it is a matter of negotiation. Some language agreements between countries have been mentioned in Chapter 5 in this connection. The perspective of the proposed classification is from inside a specific legal system, so the precise status of a language can vary according to which system is under enquiry.

Which of the language-levels in the classification system are relevant to multilingual law? In principle, a language comes within the legal scope where it receives official recognition as a language of the law. Languages at Level 6 and upwards come within that scope. A Level 6 language can only be part of a multilingual system, since its scope is partial. A Level 7 language may form part of a mono- or multilingual system, bearing in mind whether the system is unitary or federal. A Level 8 language operates in a multilingual legal context internationally. A Level 9 language adds to that the more intense supranational level. Languages may be Level 7, 8 or 9 for some systems, and lower for others. The criterion is the context of the system. This status links in with terminological range and the extent to which the language is bound up horizontally with other languages and mutual influences.

A Level 5 language is identified as not receiving official recognition and so it and all lower levels of language would be excluded from this study as not being languages of the law. However, the law may decide to confer recognition on them. In that situation one expects support arrangements to match the status change, and here the European Charter for Regional or Minority Languages 1992 is relevant. In addition, since people do speak unofficial languages and use them in various activities, the legal system has to accommodate them in some way, even if only by arranging for interpretation of oral evidence given by a witness in a court of law or translating written materials from time to time.[8] The situation is not much different from that of a monolingual country where a foreigner is required to give evidence in a lawsuit.

The above approach might imply an absence of law in non-literate societies, but that is not the case. In such societies law is not written down and remains oral. The structure of oral societies differs from those regulated by a modern system of written law, for example in technology. The application of law in non-literate societies tends to be linked to custom and oral traditions. There are many instances of countries which must manage an interface between Western-style law and indigenous customary law and language (Australia, New Zealand, Nigeria, etc.). It is another facet of multilingual law that must be included within the picture. South Africa has given express legal recognition to a range of indigenous minority languages and made them official languages in its Constitution. One can ask how all the languages are integrated into the whole system and how the lexical and conceptual ranges are aligned.

Perhaps one of the most useful issues behind the classification system concerns 'terminology' and the range of domains of terminology that can be implied from it. The lower down the scale of living languages (excluding dead languages), the more restricted the terminology/vocabulary range is likely to be, and probably the higher the degree of local variation in local patois. This is an issue for specialised language used in the numerous fields of activity of modern life. It is why the raising of the level of small languages is so difficult, as so many words may need to be invented through secondary term formation. There is also the question of deciding on words, spelling and styles from competing dialects to construct a standardised language. Lastly, we can observe that while we have been reflecting on the status and levels of use of languages, we have implicitly been reflecting on language policy and language planning. The classification system can also be seen as a tool to that end.

Language policy

Language arises spontaneously, but when used for the purposes of law as an official language it tends to become planned. The speech sounds, phonology, manner of pronunciation and so on become formalised. The sign system in the form of alphabet or ideograms becomes fixed. The same issues arise with punctuation.[9] Dictionaries of words with definitions are established, and so on. These things can be undertaken by the state, by officially recognised bodies such as the Académie française or by private individuals whose work is adopted and followed by society at large and endorsed through use by legal institutions, as is largely the case with English. Spelling reforms and writing reforms are part of language policy and language planning. Another aspect is where lesser-used languages receive official recognition. We noted the examples of Welsh and Gaelic in the UK. Likewise, banning a language, or letting it die, forms part of language policy, as does simply paying it no attention.

Summary

This chapter has taken a look at some aspects of language as special legal language (LSP). It has noted some features of legal language and explored the concept of official language from the point of view of practical implications. It has proposed a table of classification of languages for legal purposes and used that system to explore different sets of circumstances that can arise. Linking the system to the objectives and guidance set out in the European Charter for Regional or Minority Languages 1992 provides a step towards language planning and language policy, which is a matter for each society to decide according to its own needs and circumstances.

The perspectives adopted within this chapter have mainly stayed within the vertical dimension referred to earlier, looking at the situation within a language within a particular legal framework. The horizontal dimension is implicit, arising from relationships between languages in legal systems. If we are going to enter into the horizontal dimension, we could take a look at comparative law. This, however, would mainly take us into substantive law and concepts, which have up to now been backgrounded, in order to place attention on structures and methods. On the other hand, we could study comparative linguistics. Here we run the risk of becoming engrossed with phonology, morphology and syntax as compared between languages. Both sides are important for multilingual law. The pragmatic activity that mediates both fields is translation, converting text from the source language into the target language, in the process encountering all the legal and linguistic issues that can arise and finding solutions to them. The important element here is meaning (semantics) – identifying it and reproducing it.

It helps to develop a clearer idea about the comparative dimension, the differences between languages and the ways in which speakers think, see the world and interpret information. It is not possible to develop these ideas very far here, but we can open the door towards cultural mental variation by reflecting on signs and ways of thinking about them. Ferdinand de Saussure talked about the 'viewpoint creating the object'. He was a founder of the field of the study of signs, semiotics, and taught linguistics. Another founder was Charles Sanders Peirce. His theories of the sign provide an entry point into analysing terminology, concepts and meanings across languages. Semiotic ideas can help one to enter the translation and terminology environment and they illustrate the sort of questions that translators face and must resolve. An understanding of semiotics helps one to reflect on multilingual law at the micro-level of words, phrases and cultural nuances, where everything becomes relative. Each participant retains his or her individual identity and ways of seeing the world, but they come alongside the identities and viewpoints of speakers of other languages and of other cultures. Chapter 8 makes a brief introduction to semiotics, with an emphasis on Saussure and Peirce. Chapter 9 then reflects on implications for meaning, terms and texts, and Chapter 10 takes us into translation, where the ideas expressed up to now take on a more concrete form through the need to make hard choices in the words and terms to be used.

Notes

1 Even 'nonsense' carries meaning.
2 EU legislative acts are routinely corrected through a corrigendum procedure involving consultation and publication in the Official Journal.
3 Available at: www.ethnologue.com/about/language-status.
4 See for example: www.ac-rennes.fr/jahia/Jahia/accueil/pid/3070.
5 See www.ethnologue.com/language/bre.
6 See www.nzhistory.net.nz/culture/maori-language-week.
7 An official language in a multilingual system of national law is similarly 'locked' into the other languages of the system.
8 In that connection the existence of EULITA should be mentioned. This is a network to enhance access to justice multilingually. See www.eulita.eu/.
9 On English punctuation see, for example, Truss (2005).

Part IV
Signs

8 Law and language as signs

Introduction

In Chapter 1 it was suggested that one could study multilingual law from two different points of focus: law and language. Up until now we have been following that track, reflecting on dimensions of law and then of language with an eye to setting up a conceptual framework in respect of multilingual law. Now, however, it is proposed to introduce a new topic of enquiry: semiotics, the study of signs. This needs explanation. The answer lies in the idea, from foundation thinker for semiotics Ferdinand de Saussure,[1] that we can think about words and language as being signs that convey information, and there are practical benefits from doing that. For a study of multilingual law, we can use the concept of signs culturally to 'get inside' words in different languages, so as to make comparisons, draw conclusions and derive meanings. That is useful for drafters, who must think carefully about which words to use, for translators who transfer meanings and information from one language to another, and for lawyers and others who are searching for the appropriate meanings to give to legal texts so as to give them their due effects.

The concepts of semiotics are, as in other fields, not always easy to grasp as they tend to be highly abstract and diffuse. They give the impression of saying what one already knows, since all our senses function through detecting signs and giving meanings: the ears hear noises, the eyes see sights, the nose smells scents, the fingers touch rocks, and so on. Each sensory perception involves a mental process of attributing a cause to the sign perceived. Science studies signs, plants and animals detect signs (perhaps chemical or physical ones), and so on. Semiotics has blossomed out to cover an extensive range of disciplines that include: biosemiotics, semiotic anthropology, cognitive semiotics, computational semiotics, film semiotics, music semiology, social semiotics, visual semiotics and semiotics of law. This diversity makes the subject difficult to apprehend. That said, Chandler (2007) provides an accessible introduction which points to the wide range of domains, including literary theory, in which semiotic ideas have been applied. No attempt is made here to give an overview of the full scope of semiotics; the aim is simply to outline some approaches which appear of particular use for a study of multilingual law. This chapter gives a short introduction to two theories of the sign and explores their application to multilingual law.

Sign as comprising two elements

A foundation text for the study of signs, and eminently readable, is the *Cours de linguistique générale*[2] (Saussure 2005), a compilation of the lectures on linguistics by

Ferdinand de Saussure drawn up by his students after his premature demise and first published in 1916. Among other things he explored the nature of words. He noted that words were in competition with each other; each occupied a certain space of its own and sought to occupy a space not occupied by other words. But, as one knows, there are words which overlap and occupy the same space as synonyms (different words with the same meaning). These can be found in a thesaurus, for example, but often one finds subtle nuances of difference and associations, whether it be in degree of politeness (money: *cash*, *lolly*, *dosh*), alternatively referred to as 'register' (high: formal, polite, respectful; medium: on the same level; low: informal, casual), or whether it be of origins, since a language such as English has words drawn from Anglo-Saxon, Danish, French, Latin and Greek, and loanwords from many tongues, and sometimes they overlap (*defenestrate: throw out the window*). Poets and novelists thrive on these and create new words all the time.

De Saussure thought of each word as being linked not to a 'thing' but to a 'concept' and as representing it using language. The combination of concept and an 'acoustic image' formed a 'linguistic sign' (Saussure 2005: 98–99). There are synonyms for 'concept', such as 'idea'. They may link to physical objects and things or to abstract notions that are purely mental. The words 'object', 'concept' and 'idea' are not identical in meaning, but there is an area of space that they have in common, because they are what is being represented by a word. Saussure gave a name in French to the concept element of the sign: '*signifié*' (signified) and also to the word (acoustic image) used to refer to it: '*signifiant*' (signifier). The combination of the 'signified' with the 'signifier' formed a 'sign', a combined unit unique to each combination. So here we see two elements: a thing, or rather a concept (or it could be an action, a doing of something, a verb or a concept of something) and a word to refer to it, so that when one person (utterer) mentions the signifier, another person (receiver) immediately thinks of the concept referred to (signified).

Thus if an utterer says: *I have an apple*, the receiver knows what the utter has. If we transfer this to a multilingual context, we can translate the sentence into French as *J'ai une pomme* or into German as *Ich habe einen Apfel*. This all appears nice and simple. So let's start to complicate matters and move towards multilingual legal reality. We can start by taking each word in each language and thinking of it as one element of a sign. What is the counterpart? Do the signs match up in each language? If the utterer is holding the apple, the receiver can see it and identify the physical object. There is fully shared mutual understanding, since language is backed up by physical presence. However, supposing the utterer left the apple at home and is speaking in the street; the apple is not physically present. It exists, but here it is being imagined by the utterer and by the receiver. The apple has become a purely mental object, an object in the mind, which can be called a 'semiotic object' to distinguish it from the physical object. So the sign is a combination of semiotic object and the word to refer to it. Now when the utterer says *I have an apple*, the receiver cannot check the physical object but relies on the value of the sign to construct meaning. Each word is a 'sign', but the whole sentence can also be seen as a sign. It is a unit of meaning. Supposing the receiver comes from a remote tribe of people who have never seen an apple, or who have things called 'apples' which are quite different; in this case the information does not pass correctly as an act of communication. There is a misunderstanding, though neither side may be aware of it at the time. This is not a theoretical issue but the everyday reality in a multilingual, multicultural environment, and we can replace the word apple with a multitude of less or more complicated objects, concepts and ideas. How does one cope with such diversity in a legal system? That is what we are exploring. The answers seem to hinge on the concept of meaning and how it is created and interpreted. How does sign theory assist here?

Thinking in terms of signs can help us ask pertinent questions and search for answers. It does not solve problems, but provides an armoury of conceptual tools to help us think about any given problem. Ferdinand de Saussure argued for a science that studies the life of signs and called it '*sémiologie*' (semiology) from the Greek word for sign (Saussure 2005: 33). This gave the origin to the term 'semiotics'. He coined the terms '*signifié*' and '*signifiant*' and considered the two aspects to combine into a '*signe*' or sign. He also noted that this sign came into being, or was created, by the way in which it was examined: *le point de vue crée l'objet* (the viewpoint creates the object). Semiotics is the study of signs in this sense.

We can note the importance of viewpoint. It is not by chance that this book refers so frequently to viewpoints; the debt is readily acknowledged. However, we should remember also that there is a viewer with a mind and culture, and perhaps extend our image of the sign to include these aspects also. In a multicultural, multilingual context the role of mind and culture may loom very large, so that the mental image of the apparently same 'signified' and 'signifier' may in fact be very different. We need to be able to take this dimension into account in our theorising. We need to explore it, and we can take an example. We referred to 'apple' before; let us take another familiar foodstuff: 'cheese'. If we understand 'simple' examples, it facilitates coping with more complex mind-bending abstract legal concepts that are to be expressed in, say, 24 languages as in the EU.

Ask people from different countries what they imagine in their minds as being 'cheese' and some quite different items may emerge: cheese from cow milk, goat milk, sheep milk, buffalo milk, camel milk. They are all produced from 'milk' from mammalian animals, but strictly speaking not only is the 'milk' in each case not identical, neither is the cheese. Furthermore, cheeses can be prepared in many different ways from the same type of milk,[3] so there is yet more variation in meaning behind the term 'cheese'. Thus, when an utterer says *I have cheese*, what image does a receiver retain? What meaning is attached to the word 'cheese'? One has a general idea that it relates to a preparation derived from milk of some animal, but beyond that the notion is vague. In everyday usage the gap in information is filled by knowledge shared by utterer and receiver; maybe there is only one type of cheese around, so it must be that. However, this knowledge is cultural information that is not necessarily encoded in the sentence. Where utterer and receiver share the same language and also the same culture and concept, the information may pass accurately; but where they do not, then one should be prepared for surprises.

In a monolingual homogenous society a statement such as the above may be clear and precise enough, but in a multilingual, multicultural context it is not. The mental image of the utterer may differ greatly from the mental image constructed by a receiver, who may in fact have a confused blurry blank in their mind, or an image of something quite different. Can we still refer to 'milk' and 'cheese', or must we qualify each type by referring to cow milk, goat milk, sheep milk and do the same for each type of cheese? If the utterance is in a legal text regulating cheese production, the answer must almost certainly be yes, and that is why one finds terms such as 'sheepmeat' and 'goatmeat' in EU texts translated from French ('*viande ovine*' and '*viande caprine*').

If we have an object in front of us, we can see and feel it; but if we are talking in the abstract, the object is not physically present. It is in our minds as a mental image (semiotic cheese or meat) and an abstraction. This abstract dimension is important for law, and by extension for multilingual law. When a lawyer writes a legal text about cheese, let us say, the phenomenon is in his/her mind. He/she imagines 'cheese' and uses that mental image. A person reading the text reads the word 'cheese' and forms a mental image; the question is how far that mental image matches the one in the mind of the drafter. The legal ideal is for a complete matching to achieve accurate information transfer. However, if the drafter comes from a culture where cheese is made only from milk from cows and the reader comes from a culture where cheese is made from milk from sheep or goats, there is clearly a divergence in mental imagery. The drafter's problem is to make the reader understand what is referred to; the reader's problem is to figure out what the drafter meant to refer to – two viewpoints, related but in opposition. The burden is on the drafter to make the precise intended meaning clear in the text. This is assisted through the use of definitions for terms that may generate uncertainty.

Sign as comprising three elements

The insights of Ferdinand de Saussure, built on, and developed and deepened by a huge literature,[4] relate specifically to language and linguistics, and by extension to legal language. However, from our example of 'cheese' made of 'milk' from different animals in different cultures, there is a dimension that seems difficult to reach coming from a purely 'binary' approach to the sign. We can have the same 'sign' apparently being attached to different things, although we can answer that the signified 'cheese' here is at a high generic level. But there is another dimension and that is that words can have different meanings attached to them (polysemy), so that we can be unsure which concept is covered by our 'sign'. There seems to be a gap somewhere. In particular, it seems difficult to get a handle on the range of associations that we have in our mind in relation to particular words and objects, especially with respect to abstract semiotic objects. Legal concepts are essentially abstract concepts, which means they are mental constructions and therefore 'semiotic' by nature.

Legal systems differ and have different concepts. Legal words and terms take their meaning from the context of the legal system, and the particular branch in it. The same words can have different meanings across systems. For example, the term 'domicile' exists in English and French law, but the incidents are subtly different.[5] Languages are structured differently and 'chop up reality' in different ways. The spaces occupied by words in different languages do not necessarily match up exactly. A study of words as signs shows that what seems to be the same thing can in reality be quite different in different languages. We need to go further here. For that reason it is proposed to turn attention to another semiotician: Charles Sanders Peirce (pronounced 'Purse'),[6] an American scientist and philosopher in the late nineteenth/early twentieth centuries who among many other things studied logic and 'phenomenology'. His research led him to develop theories about the sign; he saw signs as comprising three elements. These can be adapted as tools to assist in analysing multilingual terminology and contexts.

Peirce put forward the view that a sign comprises three elements to which he gave names the *object* (the thing), the *representamen* (the word or symbol representing it) and the *interpretant* (the connection between the other two) (Merrell 2001: 28). When all three elements come together, we have a 'sign', and if any element is modified, we have a different sign. This concept of the sign is not specifically linked to language but is conceived as applying to phenomena more widely.[7] This concept of the sign seems perhaps rather abstract, but it introduces a third element, the *interpretant*, that was missing from the binary approach discussed earlier. 'It is, roughly speaking and sufficient for our purpose, close to what we would usually take as the sign's meaning' (Merrell 2001: 28). The *interpretant* introduces the individualised cultural dimension that nuances the scope of the other two elements. It is a third element that can be used for the purpose of examining variations in cultural or individual associations affecting an *object* or a *representamen*. This is important for a multilingual, multicultural environment as it facilitates comparisons between signs, which in turn is important as a method for checking the quality of translations between language versions of legal texts. We will proceed slowly as the ideas are not easy to grasp, especially for persons unfamiliar with translation and multilingualism. Perhaps the simplest way into the subject is to let our imagination loose and start from an age-old habit of searching for meaning from signs of nature.

Imagine one is in the countryside and one sees a flock of birds circling around in the air. They have found a nice air current and they are enjoying themselves, rising ever higher – an event that happens quite often. Or there is an eclipse of the moon or the sun – again, natural and regular events. Now imagine a priest of a religion who wants to find an answer for a problem posed; he searches for clues, or signs, that will help him find an answer; he scrutinises the sky for a message from (the) God(s); he sees the birds circling overhead and sees them as messengers carrying information; he interprets them as a sign representing something according to his religious and cultural precepts, let us assume. This example can be regarded as an exercise in superstition, or not, but the point here is that we have certain ingredients present: some 'thing' or event (phenomenon), an observer, the mind of the observer interpreting the 'thing' as a 'sign' conveying information or message, decoding the information and interpreting it to obtain meaning, and then acting, or not, on the information obtained. Let us suppose that a priest from another religion is also present; does he interpret the signs in the same way? Maybe, but perhaps not.

The value of the 'sign' is not perceived by the birds themselves,[8] but is perceived by the viewer who 'creates the object', which is here the 'message'; the actions of the birds represent this message and the meaning is derived from both by the viewer. Yet, in order for the viewer to draw conclusions, there must be some previous expectations or knowledge in their mind. This can be viewed as a mental cultural dimension and it seems difficult for the sign to exist without the presence of the mind to view, interpret and give meaning. A viewer from a different culture witnessing the same phenomena may make a very different interpretation. This example may seem far-removed from law and language, but let us replace the birds by a legal sentence and replace our viewers by two persons who come from different legal systems that share the same language. Or we can replace the legal text with a multilingual legal act written in 24 languages and our two viewers become 24 viewers, each reading a different language version of it. Do they arrive at the same understanding?

The Piercian approach enables us to explore the multilingual, multicultural context of divergences and differences. The approach is useful for thinking about abstract concepts and words used to refer to them, because we are made aware of the way in which the 'sign' is constructed, and it forces us to think carefully about what exactly an *object*

134 *Signs*

actually is, how it is interpreted and the precise nature of the label used to refer to it. We are thus able to come inside the 'sign' and explore the implications of modifying any of the elements of it. What if we change the *representamen* (word) for an *object* (concept)? What if we change the *object*? What if we substitute different associations via the *interpretant*? We become more aware of polysemy, or that there are different cultural associations with objects and words. This is important for translation as it means identifying what is important in a source text and thinking how best to convey information (and which information if there are several cultural layers implicit) in a target language text. It means reflecting on the cultural ideas hidden behind a source language word or sentence and those behind a target language word or sentence. What are the expectations of readers of each language version? How can these be brought closer together through drafting or translation of the text?

We are anticipating Chapter 10 here with respect to translation, but we can imagine three environments for legal translation: first, a court needs information about a legal text in a foreign language; second, an international convention is to be implemented in the national law of a signatory state; third, a multilingual act must be drawn up within a legal system. If one compares the elements of the sign between source and target languages in each of these three scenarios, one can consider that in a multilingual legal system the individual objects or concepts should largely be the same, since it is the same system with the same legal culture and the same message. The language versions are serving the same ends and seek to express the same legal concepts. The words are in different languages, so the *representamens* are different, but the names of legal concepts could be seen as alternative labels for the same objects shared across the system. Applying this to the EU system, 'regulation' (English) should be the same as '*règlement*' (French) and '*Verordnung*' (German), and so on across all 24 languages. The associations connected to the *interpretant* should also be close to identical.[9] Compare that scenario with translation of legal concepts between unrelated legal systems in different languages: the *objects* differ, the *interpretants* differ and, of course, the *representamens* differ. So how can one translate legal concepts across different legal systems? Impossible, surely, but a daily occurrence. The Piercian theory of the sign opens doors to such reflections.

The mental dimension to signs

Neither the binary nor the tripartite sign theory in themselves refers explicitly to the mind as a formal part of the concept of the sign, but following Saussure, the mind of the viewer determines the object and so determines what the sign is. The birds circling in the air were just flying (let us say), but the viewing mind gave this action particular meaning. Language is mere sound if there is no receiver who can interpret it and give it meaning. Words on paper are mere marks if there is no one who can read them. If there is no mind, there is no word, no language and, it can be argued, no 'sign'. On this view a 'sign' is a mental construct and it is on that level that it is something that represents or stands for something else. The viewer constructs the message from the signs generated in his/her mind.

The mind is an integral part of semiotics and creates the sign, but it also creates the context and decides which elements should be connected to others in patterns, and it creates and gives meaning to images it creates. Lawyers do that when creating and interpreting legal texts. Intertextuality is a mental construction of associations and not something which 'exists' in the external factual world; likewise with all the other phenomena about law and language discussed in earlier chapters. So we come to the point that we see law and legal texts as essentially mental products; when we look at law, we look at representations from our collective mind transmitted over generations. What lies beyond? We cannot go beyond our minds, it seems. Each mind is bathed in 'culture' in the form of past experience, education, shared assumptions and views about the world. Every time we draft a legal act, or interpret it, we bring that culture into action. In the multilingual environment each language represents a culture and way of thinking. Multilingual law adapts to that reality and serves it.

Semiosis: creating new signs

Semiosis is the process of creating new signs. While words are signs, so are sentences, chapters, books and legal texts. How do legal acts arise? One can again adapt Peirce's ideas as they help understand the process of law-making. He makes use of the concepts of *firstness*, *secondness* and *thirdness* (Cobley 2010: 217, 316–317, 343–345). Broadly, we can take this as an idea of how things start to happen, and how signs start to happen; for example, how legislative texts come to be created. Put simply, there is a background situation and some event occurs, such as a disaster, or a new technological development, or a circumstance (firstness). This generates a reaction, an opposition, or a feeling that something needs to be done in response (secondness) and the response takes the shape, among other possibilities, of a legislative act to regulate the matter, avoid a repeat of a disaster, accommodate the new technology, adapt to the situation, or whatever (thirdness). Legal language in written form thus takes place in thirdness. On this view, secondness is the domain of feeling and emotion and the desire for action and change using, among others, legal methods. This sequence again provides a basis for reflecting on the range of factors that arise at each stage. Court cases and case law can also be seen as involving semiosis, as there is a prior circumstance, a reaction or opposition and a consequence that involves legal language and procedural stages in which texts are produced, perhaps multilingual ones. Semiosis is an ongoing process of change; a court judgment may be a starting point, firstness, for new laws or new court cases.

Objectifying the subjective

Everything can be thought of in terms of 'signs' conveying meaning, and signs can take every form and shape imaginable: visual as in pictures or texts, aural as in music and speech, tactile as in the feel of paper or a cactus, olfactory as in the smell of a rose or of a prison cell. Yet other signs are in the mind and imagined: the signs created by language, novels, literature and law. It is with these 'imagined' signs that we are interested as regards multilingual law, since legal concepts are abstract and therefore essentially mental. All law has been 'imagined' and brought into existence to influence behaviour. The advantage of thinking about phenomena in terms of signs is that we can step outside the relationship between phenomenon and viewer/interpreter and attempt an 'objective' viewpoint. The relationship between a viewer and a sign is first person: I see, I think, I feel, I hear. Here there is no objective truth; all is subjective as the meanings are created by the minds of persons. But by thinking in terms of signs, we have a way to handle subjective information in an impartial third person way without making value judgements on it. This is important in a multilingual, multicultural environment that strives for equality among all. We can say that viewer A perceives sign X in such and such a way, whereas viewer B perceives it in another way. But we must remember that this 'impartial third person' approach is itself semiotic and implies a viewer; we too, as external impartial observer, are a viewer and interpreter of signs. It seems there is no escape.

Semiotic sensitivity is important for multilingual law because in a multilingual legal system individuals speak different languages and construct reality using 'their' language. Phenomena are thought about using different words and terms. If we then proceed to analyse each language to identify its various elements and components, we soon note that there are differences not only in the words used to refer to phenomena (vocabulary), but there are also differences in individual components of grammar: variations in genders of nouns, tenses of verbs, prepositions, adjectives, articles, and so on. When we dig yet deeper, we find that phenomena which at first seemed to be the same may turn out to be different, as we saw with 'cheese'. This is especially so for legal concepts where the precise boundaries of meanings of terms vary from system to system. Linguistics is part of semiotics, since language comprises signs. Such signs have been analysed and classified in ways touched on in Chapter 6 when reflecting on linguistics. For legal language and legal texts one needs a large range of words to express many concepts. Lawyers organise these into patterns or branches of law.

It was noted earlier in this chapter how words occupy space; they can relate to different objects and there can be overlap between words. In the case of general language this is unavoidable and perhaps not a problem, but with specialised language it becomes important to limit the overlaps between words. Lawyers, for example, need specific words with specific meanings and preferably only one meaning attached to a word; but then a word becomes a 'term'. Terms aim to be monosemic (one meaning); one can think of scientific nomenclature which attributes a unique name to plants and animals. The work is taxonomic as it indicates relationships through naming, describing and classifying. In industry and commerce it has become necessary to standardise and fix the names attached to things; for international trade and setting international standards it becomes necessary to fix names and introduce equivalence between terms in different languages. This can be done by making semiotic analyses to establish equivalence. This field of activity goes by the name of 'terminology' and it is an integral part of translation work. It relies on semiotic analysis and is closely tied in to the problem of meaning, which is the subject of Chapter 9.

Summary

This chapter has taken a step sideways and examined some ideas taken from semiotics concerning the nature of the sign. Two theories have been put forward: a binary concept of the sign and a tripartite concept of the sign. The field of semiotics extends much more widely, but the aim here has been to explore a way of analysing meaning in legal texts, both in how they are created by a drafter and how they are read and constructed by a reader. It is a matter of shared culture with shared knowledge of the signs used to encode texts and the inferences and associations between them. Taking a semiotic approach serves to enhance one's awareness of the possibilities for misunderstanding within a multilingual and multicultural environment where the cultural assumptions may not be shared. The next chapter will take these ideas further and explore the difference between semiotic, linguistic and legal meaning.

Notes

1 The origins in fact are much older, since the study of signs is ancient and forms part of the history of philosophy.
2 Course in General Linguistics. English version [Online]. Available at: http://home.wlu.edu/~levys/courses/anth252f2006/saussure.pdf.
3 One must merely visit a modern supermarket to see that for oneself.
4 See the bibliography list in Saussure (2005).
5 For translation the terms would be equivalents, but in each language version they would acquire the meaning of the particular language-text context and so could diverge in implications. This scenario occurs when terms move between legal orders and legal systems within the same language.
6 For background information see, among others, Deledalle (1978); Chandler 2007); Cobley (2001: 233–234, 2010: 282–283); Merrell (2001: 28–39); www.iep.utm.edu/peircebi/ and www.peirce.org/.
7 Peirce also identified signs as being iconic, indexical or symbolic (Cobley 2010: 242, 243, 338–339).
8 They perceive other signs. Birds also are observers of their environment: zoosemiotics.
9 The door opens to enquire whether there are any subtle differences arising in different language contexts in what seems ostensibly to be the same.

Part V
Meaning

9 Texts, terms and meanings

Introduction

The purpose of this chapter is to attempt to draw some threads together and form a picture addressing a difficult issue, the problem of meaning from a practitioner, rather than a theoretical, perspective. How is legal meaning created, how is it transmitted across languages, how is it read, interpreted and applied in a multilingual environment? We are in the field of communication and so one could take on board theories of communication, of which there are many.[1] However, we will limit ourselves to a few issues which are perhaps useful from the standpoint of setting up a framework for enquiry.

The first thing is to think about places where meaning arises in legal language. While there is oral legal language, it is principally in legal texts. These are 'sites of engagement', or of 'legal action' as legal tasks are performed by them as 'performative utterances'. The texts as sites of engagement influence the form and contents of the message, the communication, and the meanings given and extracted. From this starting point it is proposed to consider meaning from three perspectives: semiotic, linguistic and legal. The reason for this choice is that while law uses language to communicate information, it also uses other channels for its purposes. These other channels can be revealed by adopting a broad semiotic stance and thinking in terms of signs connected to law. However, semiotic meaning goes beyond legal phenomena and takes one into realms of science and other fields. One of these is linguistics. Law uses language as a principal tool of communication, so it creates linguistic meanings (semantics). We can ask whether there is a difference between linguistic and legal meaning. These issues are relevant to multilingual law, if it means there are domains covered by law that are independent of language, since logically they also lie outside multilingualism. So legal meaning may be different from linguistic meaning.

In Chapter 8 it was said how the viewpoint creates the object. We can adapt this dictum by suggesting that it is the question in the mind of an author or reader that determines what is being sought and the nature of the information obtained. Science asks questions; so do lawyers. A legal text can be analysed from different points of view. One expression of that is to ask whether individual words, terms, sentences and articles are primarily legal matters or policy matters, what are the intended action and effects, and what about the language used to express everything. These four viewpoints are briefly canvassed. Lastly, a brief mention of the role of terminology is added, in preparation for Chapter 10 on translation.

Sites of engagement

Linguists talk about texts as 'sites of engagement'. These are typically the situations or documents where language is manifest. It is a picturesque description as it implies a 'battle' or 'operation', a place where things happen, perhaps a contest between the creator of a text (utterer) and a reader (receiver). The centre of this contest is 'meaning' and the information that is conveyed. What information did the utterer intend to convey? What information did the receiver (choose) to understand? Are there alternative ways to read a given text? Meaning is created by an utterer in a context of time and place by means of a support of some nature. How does the support selected influence the message and meaning? How do these factors impinge on a reader?

In most cases of legal language, and by extension multilingual language, the site of engagement is likely to be a written text, but the concept goes wider. Oral speech provides a 'site of engagement', though more fleeting. Yet why restrict the notion of 'site of engagement' to language? In Chapter 8 we saw that information and meaning is created through signs of all kinds, and a lot depends on what one is searching for by adopting a particular viewpoint. The linguistic concept of site of engagement can perhaps be linked here to the semiotic idea of the sign. Engagement feels more active and a sign feels more static and passive, but both can be involved. Legal texts are both sites of engagement and signs, and they have a purpose of bringing about some change or effects, or of recording a set of circumstances. In that sense they are sites of action, and different actions take place with respect to them: drafting, translating, interpreting, implementing.

Legal texts are closely connected with legal rules and provide sources for rules and law, as seen in Chapter 4. Legislative texts create rules. Court texts interpret the meaning of legislative texts and past cases, and in so doing frequently lay down a new rule, one connected with the facts of the case. We saw in Chapter 3 that there is a close relationship between rules and facts. Linguists think of rules as conditional statements: if X facts exist, then Y rule comes into operation. Legal texts are constructed around facts, as well as around rules. So perhaps one can also think of facts in terms of being 'sites of engagement' for meaning. Here the meaning is not necessarily linguistic, as it may be acts and behaviour, or a factual reality that is in evidence. A motorist runs over a pedestrian. What can one infer? Perhaps the motorist was drunk and fell asleep. Perhaps the pedestrian was drunk and walked in front of the car. In law, facts can speak: *res ipsa loquitur* (the facts speak for themselves). No additional evidence is required as to meaning. Facts can be seen as a sign, as a 'site of engagement'; they speak and convey information. Legal rules apply to the information thus conveyed.

In this situation, 'facts' communicate directly, but as we saw from Chapter 8 on signs, it is the human mind that gives them meaning, interprets them and draws conclusions. In effect the legal dictum *res ipsa loquitur* means that the court makes its own interpretation from the facts, and there is thought to be no uncertainty. Where facts are 'read' directly, this may take a non-linguistic form, but it is expressed or referred to using language. In a multilingual system there may be a need for a multiplicity of languages. Are the facts seen in the same way in each language, or in each legal culture represented by the particular language?[2]

Sites of linguistic engagement take different physical forms. Apart from the physical medium (clay tablet, papyrus, vellum, paper, CD-ROM or electronic website to mention a few) there is the way in which information is patterned on it as a text, in terms of print materials, font type, and so on. Then there is the type of text, or genre, linked to author, function, content, purpose, style, and so on. There is a multilingual dimension here, for in a multilingual system one would expect the formal appearance and presentation to be as nearly identical as possible in each language version, so that there emerges from the pages of all language versions a shared common and transcendent identity. This is evident from the language versions of all EU texts and goes under the term of the 'synoptic' approach (EU 2015: 45).

In legal utterances, the site of engagement as a written legal text, or an oral statement of some form, has an impact on the choice of words, the way they are linked together, the rhetorical purpose of the act, the form and structure, and the contents. From all of these factors, the site of engagement thus has an influence on the meanings created or to be understood and interpreted. If a text is a formal legal act with an authorised signature, it is treated as creating rules that are binding and the text is read with that idea in mind; it implies obligations and compliance in how one acts. Yet if the same words are written by a person with no authority, then the text may be the same linguistically, but no one pays any attention to it and it carries no weight. The status of the site of engagement is thus highly significant. This is linked to rules and is a legal matter. The way in which it is looked at is also relevant, because as a sign a text can provide information not only on rules contained in it, but also about the culture in which the text is embedded, for example its technology or ethical standpoint. We can tease out differences between semiotic, linguistic and legal meanings in sites of engagement.

Semiotic meaning

The concept of semiotic meaning allows us to think about anything that can generate meaning in any way, since 'everything' is connected to signs in the mind. Semiotic meaning is connected to the concept of signs and we saw in Chapter 8 that signs arise everywhere. Peirce identified signs as being iconic, indexical or symbolic (Cobley 2010: 242, 243, 338–339). In each case the sign is perceived as standing for something else, or representing it in some way, and semiotic meaning is linked to this mental connection. A meaning drawn from a weather vane is the direction it points as indicating where the wind is coming from (indexical). A meaning drawn from a map points to landscape features of an area (indexical). The map uses symbols to convey its information and meanings, and these can only be fully understood by reference to the table attached to the map (symbolic). A model car represents the real life-size thing and perhaps a way of life (iconic).[3] The letters of an alphabet are symbolic. In themselves they have no meaning and are just squiggles, but through habit and custom meanings are conferred on the squiggles, which become units for constructing ever more complex sets of meanings, as in language.[4] When thought about closely, these classifications tend to merge into each other as a map is both indexical, pointing to landscape forms, but is also iconic when reflecting a state of geographical knowledge. Drawing meaning from the features of physical things is not in itself a linguistic activity. It becomes linguistic when we communicate what we learn through language and our utterance becomes a site of engagement.

There are signs that are of particular relevance to language, and by extension to law and multilingual law. Letters of an alphabet and scripts are signs. They represent sounds and ideas and are semiotic. They are symbols and icons insofar as they stand for particular sounds, but they point towards particular cultures. Initially letters are arbitrary, but once endowed with representational meaning, they are assembled in structured ways to create meanings which relate to content and encode the message communicated. There is form and there is content or substance; lawyers talk about 'formal' aspects and 'subject matter'. For multilingual legal acts there is a difference between the formal aspects and the subject matter in each language version of a text, as each version follows the methods laid down for its language version. Within a multilingual legal system there is alignment of formal aspects as well as subject matter, because each language version flows from the same source and is intended to convey the same message, albeit in a different language. Thus the physical appearance of the language versions is aligned so that they all look as similar as possible. This shared identity carries meaning: an idea of 'oneness' and unity within linguistic diversity. A different approach would constitute a sign conveying a different meaning and would perhaps imply that the texts should not be interpreted as intending to carry the same message, even where the words are the same, as there would be a tacit message of difference that could imply difference in intention psychologically. Form influences content. We are on the edge of, or beyond, language at this point.

Lawyers use linguistic signs, as well as signs from facts, to construct mental images and pictures of relationships and connections. If this ... then that ... and if that ... then something else ... and so on – an infinite string of conditionality that is linked to facts, circumstances and people. Law is human-centred. The images created centre around people and how they are to act in an endless variety of circumstances. Ideas are created as concepts. They are given form in words and shaped in meaning in relation to other words. They occupy conceptual space and have boundaries. Lawyers argue over the boundaries; indeed, a function of court cases is to identify conceptual sign boundaries through argumentation between lawyers. The 'pictures' created by legal concepts in the mind are perhaps not 'static' images like a painting of a landscape, but 'dynamic' images of action and power. A 'right' is a concept that confers power to claim and possess and displace others. 'Liability' implies submission to the power of others. Law is a language of power. One sees these dimensions when thinking semiotically in terms of signs and the meanings they convey, and we can explore the ways in which lawyers construct meaning through language, linked to facts and people. This is all relevant to multilingual law. Perhaps we can summarise semiotic meaning as depending on the eye of the viewer and what they are searching for. Anything can be taken as a sign, and it reaches wider than language or law.

Linguistic meaning

The branch of linguistics linked to meaning is semantics, and for a full discussion of it one should turn to the literature on it. The door was opened in Chapter 6 and we can push it a little wider. From a pragmatic viewpoint one can emphasise the communication function of language and that it involves an act of communication from utterer to receiver. That provides the dichotomy of creating the text on the one hand and reading and interpreting it on the other. A purely linguistic viewer of a legal text can be seen as an 'outsider' and generally not a subject matter legal expert, although familiarity develops knowledge of the issues handled. For them, the focus is on how a text uses language rather than on its particular legal effects, as these require specialist knowledge and cannot always be predicted in the way they apply to particular sets of facts. That said, such issues also form part of semantics, with an emphasis on the interaction between texts (intertextuality), as does the way other, non-linguistic factors impact on the meaning taken from legal texts, which draws one into specialised areas such as discourse analysis, sociolinguistics and legal-linguistics. This brings us back to Chapter 6.

Using legal terminology, linguistic meaning is linked to the 'literal meaning' of words and sentences. The meanings of words are ascertained from dictionaries. The meanings applied may be ordinary meanings or technical meanings, preferably with definitions attached. The text is studied within itself and in conjunction with other texts referred to by it. How does one place semantic ideas in a multilingual context? One examines the semantic dimension for each language 'internally' and then makes links between them 'externally' or 'horizontally' across and between languages. That gives two dimensions to explore, and this view is matched by reality in a multilingual legal system such as the EU, where each language version must be coherent and consistent as regards the terminology used in past and present texts in the same and in other related domains.

At the same time all language versions of a text need to be aligned on the same message. That implies comparing the semantics of different languages and placing them side by side in parallel and making comparisons. Are the semantics of all 24 languages of the European Union the same? It seems very unlikely. Is what is true for a text in English also true for Bulgarian? That hinges on the question being asked, the way the text is being viewed as a sign and the information being sought. Where the answer is 'yes', there is a shared cultural approach, but where the answer is 'no', there are variations which have a potential impact on meaning. With linguistic meanings one remains attached to the semantic contexts of language in texts.

Legal meaning

Lawyers draw widely to construct legal meaning, that is to say to 'construct the law'. They draw widely in drafting legal acts and they draw widely in interpreting and giving them legal effects, as widely as they find necessary to resolve a legal problem and provide convincing justifications. They identify facts, circumstances, persons, places, events and times and draw inferences from them. This is the world of fact on which legal rules are intended to operate. It includes language, but is in essence not specifically linguistic.

On the other hand there are legal utterances: written texts and oral utterances. These are expressed in language and are amenable to linguistic analysis and semantics. However, assumptions linguists may make to establish a picture of linguistic meaning do not necessarily all apply to legal language. Lawyers pay attention to the reasonable, but also to the unreasonable; to cooperation, but also to non-cooperation extending to outright opposition and hostility. For every assumption based on semantics, a lawyer will anticipate an exception or the opposite. These factors modulate legal language and influence the construction of legal meaning. There are, of course, linguistic signs that are of particular relevance to law, and by extension to multilingual law, for example the letters of an alphabet, writing scripts and the features of each language code. Drawing legal meaning from the features of physical things is not in itself a linguistic activity. It becomes linguistic when we communicate what we learn and our utterance becomes a site of engagement.

Legal meaning has regard to semiotic meanings and linguistic meanings, but it adapts and uses them for its own ends. Perhaps we can adapt the semiotic approach to think about legal meaning from three approaches: first, meanings drawn from events, occurrences and states of being (facts); second, legal meanings that are purely abstract and in the mind (semiotic objects) as legal concepts, which are brought into relationship with each other and facts so as to generate mental pictures and images; third, legal meanings drawn from utterances, whether oral or written. This last approach involves first drawing a linguistic meaning from a given utterance and then placing it alongside other utterances, as well as behaviour and facts, so as to make comparisons between them. But the legal meaning is linked to purpose. A problem has arisen, and a question has been asked: what are the legal effects, what is the correct behaviour, who has the 'right' interpretation of the law on such and such a matter? Legal meaning is constructed out of a web of interconnecting factors. This makes it more complicated than individual representational meaning or linguistic meaning from individual utterances. It means it is possible for a text to be declared to have 'no meaning'. In linguistic terms that is nonsense, but it means a text carries no weight in law. This situation arises where a legal act is declared void or is nullified by a court.

On the other hand, one can use the idea of 'representation' to obtain information, as lawyers do to draw inferences from facts. Behaviour points to intentions; being present in a person's house at night with house-breaking tools points to an intention to burgle, for example. Holding a smoking gun points to having fired it. There is the expression: 'caught red-handed.' Yet the 'facts' may be given a wrong meaning. The extraction of meaning can be fraught with uncertainties as different readings are possible. It can be a problem to know which are the correct legal rules to apply to certain behaviour. The law deals with uncertainty by having concepts such as 'beyond reasonable doubt' and 'on the balance of probabilities'. Legal meanings and the value of signs are constructed accordingly.

From there, one thinks about how legal meanings are created through drafting and how they are read and constructed through interpretation. There is a multilingual dimension to both processes. On the one hand there are the methods by which legal texts are produced in several languages; this leads to the subject of translation, and in particular legal translation. It also leads to discussion on drafting by non-native speakers in their second or third language, which is a frequent occurrence for international and supranational EU texts. The signs intended by the drafters may have origins in a mother tongue and may not always accurately reflect the conventional sign system of the language of the text. Does the reader opt for the mother-tongue conventions presented in calque form or the conventions of the ostensible sign system?

When analysing legal texts in terms of their drafting and content, it can be useful to think about the text from different angles, as they elicit different information. This is a refinement of the dimension of legal meaning taken as a whole. One takes individual elements, whether fact, text, concept, rule or effects, and one subjects each to a particular form of enquiry, a standpoint that asks particular types of question in order to obtain and elucidate certain types of information; the question defines the information and meanings sought and obtained. In essence, that is perhaps a key element of legal meaning.

Four viewpoints: law, language, policy and action

Four individual viewpoints, which have a direct bearing on legal texts with respect to the ways they create legal meanings and have already been mentioned, are the viewpoints of law, language, policy and action within a text. Each viewpoint yields information from a text. It is a tool for checking and revising draft texts, as well as for interpreting them. Legal texts serve a purpose; they cost time and effort to bring into being and there must be a pragmatic reason being served. That leads to the legal effects, or what is here called 'action'. For every part of a text, including the whole text and several related texts taken together, one can ask what action they effect. What is their purpose or object? This idea is linked to intention: what effects are intended? A drafter or reviser of a text constantly checks for the effects in the meaning of each part of a text against the results desired by the client. The criterion of effects and action is a tool for comparing different texts, especially texts in different languages. Linguistic and legal meanings in the texts can be compared to see if they are the same. For legal translation, if the action and effects between source language and target language are the same, or close enough, that can be seen as one test of efficiency.

Effects in a legal text always take place within the context of a branch of law, which we can also refer to as a 'policy field', since it is also a field of political action and choices. It creates both a legal and a linguistic domain in which words and terms take on their precise meanings through relationships to other words and terms. The policy criterion asks about the branch of law and how the individual text fits conceptually into that branch. It also looks at its overall purpose and objectives. This ties in with language in respect of the terms selected and whether they are used in the same way as in the rest of the policy field. To check that, the text is compared with other texts and their terms in the same policy domain to see if they are used in the same way or differently; different terms may imply a different meaning. In multilingual texts one needs to examine other language versions to see if they use different terms or the same ones in a similar way. It is possible for terms to be the same in one language in different texts and different in other language versions and still be functionally accurate. However, one needs to be aware that by virtue of being placed in a legal text, for 'construction' by lawyers as to legal effects there may be a subtle shift in meaning from the same terms used in non-legal contexts.

The law viewpoint places attention on legal aspects: the place of the text in the hierarchy of legal texts, the power to make the act and the effects sought. There is linkage with other legal texts in the policy field and within the system as a whole. There are linguistic implications in respect of choice of terms to use, and whether something needs to be mentioned expressly or is understood as already arising by operation of law. The fact that something is not mentioned in a text does not mean that there is no law on the issue, nor that nothing is intended, as rules elsewhere in the field or system may apply to the issue, although not expressly mentioned in that particular text. This is something recitals in a legal act might mention, for example to alert an 'innocent' or unwary reader. In a civil law system, principles of law come into operation to influence meaning, and texts may be treated as meaningless, or void, if they are defective in form or breach a fundamental principle of law. In a common law system, principles of law also apply with similar implications, but there is the background set of judge-made law that is assumed and a legislative text, for example, may just focus on ways in which those background rules are changed. Without knowledge of the background common law, it may be difficult to fully understand the significance of a legislative text. International and EU supranational texts, however, need to minimise such assumptions as they are multilingual and multicultural, and readers in different systems do not necessarily share the basic background assumptions one finds in national systems of law. The law criterion also covers the structure of the act and the way it is put together in its form. In this respect it overlaps with the language view.

The language view covers everything in a text in the sense that the text is in language, but one can use it to draw attention to things such as format, structure and layout of the act, as well as punctuation, syntax and choice of terms used, and their aptness to express the concepts. Behind language lies intention and multilingual texts are assumed to have the same intention expressed in different languages. This unity of intention can be a criterion for comparing multilingual versions of a legal act. Of course, there may be an express intention to make different provisions in different language versions, which means that distinctions are expressly built in via language versions. This is not good practice, as intended divergences should be reflected in all languages. They are more likely to arise inadvertently, usually in the form of unidentified errors. In that event, when noticed, they become the subject of a formal correction or 'corrigendum' procedure.[5]

Role of terminology

Any discussion about meaning in a legal context very quickly comes to a focus on individual words and expressions. What is a 'person'? What is the difference between 'physical person' and 'legal person'? What is 'legal personality'? 'Can an animal have legal personality? Language is made up of words and we have noted in Chapter 6 some of the ways in which linguists analyse words, as to how they are formed and how they are placed together in sequences to make sentences and larger units. Words are collected, studied and listed, and their meanings are set out through definitions in dictionaries. This is lexicology, the gathering of the words that are used in everyday life by the community and specialist groups. Lexicographers 'collect' words and 'lexicography' is the activity of finding, compiling, analysing and describing words. They are used in legal texts as in other texts.

The terminology viewpoint is slightly different. There is overlap with lexicology, but the starting point is different as it is more concerned with how terms are created (primary term formation) in a language, how they are linked to specific objects or concepts, and how new terms are created across and between languages (secondary term formation). So it is perhaps a more active and 'invasive' function as regards individual words than lexicology. There is a close connection between terminology and translation. Many translators are terminologists. They search for terms in other languages to match source language terms. To do so, they use dictionaries, but also glossaries that list term-equivalents, and they also study previous texts (corpora) to find previous uses of terms. They record examples of uses of terms embedded in contexts of subject domain, genre, and so on, in databases such as the EU database IATE. To assist translators, they provide indications as to the source of terms and an assessment of reliability, so that the user is aware whether it is safe to use or needs special care and attention. Where complicated new terms are being created in a language, committees of language specialists may come together to settle on possible term equivalents. Consulting experts in the field form part of this activity.

For terminology work, it is useful to think about terms as signs. Semiotic analysis underpins term analysis. One can ask a range of questions to elucidate the contexts and range of possible meanings of terms and their equivalents in other languages. For example, if one thinks about words or terms in their contexts and their possible meanings, one can ask about the sign in the source language. What is the term/word (*signifier/ representamen*)? What is the concept (*signified/semiotic object*)? What is the *interpretant*? In each case the sign can be seen as the sum of the three elements. Where one of them varies, there is a different sign. The concept of sign is abstract as a unit, but it leads on to asking further questions. Are there different possible semiotic *objects* for the *representamen*? Are there different possible *interpretants*? What is the central core signification of the term? Where are its boundaries? What are the fuzzy areas and the overlaps with other terms? In that way, an analysis is made of a source language term and the search goes on for an equivalent target language term. Perhaps there is no doubt and the answer is ready to hand, which is the case most of the time. Perhaps there is an order 'from on high' to use certain terms. Perhaps there is no clear single term, or there is a range of possible terms. Which to select? How is the language being changed or extended? Will an 'innocent' reader understand as intended? Should one seek for the term to be specially defined in the text for all languages, so as to make clear the precise intended meaning for the term in the text in hand? What happens if there are disagreements over terminology? There are many questions; answers come in specific contexts after careful reflection and analysis, consultation and negotiation. This is the world of multilingual translation and revision, and it revolves around terminology.

Summary

This chapter has taken a practitioner view on certain aspects involving meaning. It mentioned the text as site of engagement and reflected on some differences between semiotic, linguistic and legal meanings, while recognising that all meanings involve signs. Four viewpoints were presented as aids for asking questions about legal texts and analysing them. Lastly, the role of terminology was briefly evoked. It prepared the way for turning attention to the role of translation in multilingual law, which is perhaps its centrepiece.

Notes

1 On communication theories, see among others: http://communicationtheory.org/list-of-theories/ and www.afirstlook.com/edition_9/theory_list.
2 A culture that prohibits alcohol, restricts it, tolerates or encourages it, for example, may see the motorist/pedestrian scenario differently; but that is also because of other rules in the system.
3 The model *denotes* the car and *connotes* the way of life – two forms of representation; the interpretant suggests which is intended or read.
4 Other meanings also attach to symbols; see Cobley (2010: 338–339).
5 For examples of corrigenda in EU acts, see copies of the Official Journal of the EU.

Part VI
Translation and revision

10 Viewpoints of translation

Introduction

This chapter shifts the focus from a 'vertical' internal dimension that looks at law and language through the eyes of a single language, in this case English, and moves towards a 'horizontal' across-languages dimension that places languages side by side and compares similarities and differences between them, aware that each language is used in many different specialist contexts and may be used for more than one legal system. How far does, or can, a language march 'in step' with others in terms of meanings, messages and information communicated? How far can information be transferred and reproduced between languages in an identical way? Is it possible, and if not what is lost in the process? Is 'pure' legal translation theoretically possible? Is translation more in the nature of a pragmatic exercise, and if so, what role does theory play? How do translation method and theory impact on multilingual law? These are some questions that are touched on, but not necessarily answered in this chapter, as they go very wide. We find ourselves once again in a field where there is a large and extensive literature, though much of it is in languages other than English.[1] To study and understand translation, including the translation of legal texts, there is no substitute for doing it. Translate this chapter or this book into any other language and you will be faced with dilemmas and uncertainties discussed in the abstract. Translation theories acquire their full meanings.

This chapter is selective in the topics raised. Earlier chapters have made frequent reference to translation issues. It is desirable to avoid repetition, but it is necessary to present the translation role within multilingual systems of law. There are different specialised viewpoints on translation depending on the type of text to be translated, as well as the language combinations involved, which are connected to degrees of proximity of language families and culture. Thus, strategies are different in translating between Chinese and English as opposed to between French and Italian. The former are distant in script and syntax, whereas the latter are extremely close. With the former, the sense has to be identified and reformulated using different types of sign system, morphology and syntax in accordance with the methods of the language. With the latter, the alphabet system is the same, though Italian does not use the letter 'j', and literal replacement of words in the same sequence and often in almost the same form is frequently possible, though there are traps for the unwary, in particular 'false friends' (Boch 2009) and subtle syntax variations. False friends (*faux amis*) are 'pairs of words in two languages that look similar, but differ in meaning'.[2] French terms such as *actuel*, *éventuel* and *sensible* are examples of this for English readers.

Different strands and approaches run historically through translation practice, in particular whether to make 'literal' word-for-word translations, or whether to translate the 'spirit' or 'idea' in a text.[3] Legal translation prefers the former where possible, but with an eye to the effects. Multilingual systems of law are driven to create matching terminology and to create standardised equivalent sentences and paragraphs to that end. One sees that clearly with EU legislative texts and in the guidance given in the Joint Practical Guide (EU 2013) in the different language versions, in particular with regular repetition of recitals relating to 'proportionality' and 'subsidiarity'. A culture of legal drafting tends to extend to all language versions and translation becomes part of the wider legal text creation process, with consequential rigidification in form, style and content. Thus, EU drafting guidelines and manuals are drawn up to apply to all EU languages and are binding on drafters of source texts and translators from them.

For this chapter it is proposed to start with a broad approach, focusing on some translation viewpoints and the nature of translation in general, but attention will then move towards legal translation. No attempt is made to expound theories of legal translation as detailed information is readily to hand from Šarčević (1997), among others. Instead, the purpose is to invoke a range of practical scenarios where legal texts have to be translated and invite reflection on the types of strategy and approaches that might be relevant to coping with the situation. What are the questions that need to be posed? How do they define the reality and the form of the text to be produced? In a word, what is needed in each scenario and for each text? We start with some viewpoints.

Translation viewpoints

There is a paradox in drawing attention to translation, since a tradition exists that translation is something which should be 'invisible' and not perceived by readers (Venuti 1995). The ideas and words are those of the original author and the genius of creativity lies with them. The translator 'merely' 'mechanistically' reproduces the information in another language. It can be, and is, done by machines, as anyone can see by going onto the Internet and searching for the button to 'translate'. On this (contested) view, the translator should preferably be anonymous as well as invisible. It is only the author and his or her message that are placed before the reader. It is their ideas and their responsibility which are engaged for what they say. If their message is controversial or unpopular, translator anonymity provides a form of protection for the translator, perhaps.[4] However, this mechanistic view ignores the creativity and imagination that lie behind each translation. Even with machine translation there is a huge invisible knowledge of languages, linguistics and computer science hidden in the background.[5]

For the reader of a translated text, there is an expectation of equivalence to the original source text. The reader expects to obtain the same information from a translation as from the original; in a word, they become interchangeable. For most purposes there is no need for the reader to enquire further into the background. The translation is acceptable if it expresses the information in the source text faithfully and in a good linguistic style.

Nonetheless, by placing in the background the translator, his or her work and skill and the fact of the text being a translation from an original in another language, a reader may be led unwittingly into error and may to a certain extent be 'deceived'. Most of the time this is without consequence, and the reader gains immensely from the work of the translator,[6] since the alternative is to master the source language. Sometimes, however, it is important to know that a text is a translation, especially with specialist texts such as legal ones. To counter possible misunderstandings by readers and often to explain unfamiliar concepts or phenomena referred to in a text, it is current practice for a translator to present a note at the start of a work to draw attention to various issues. Thus we find a note at the start of The New English Bible (1970) for both the Old and New Testaments.[7] This is also the case with translations of historical literature, such as the works of the ancient Greek and Latin authors (for an example, see Grant 1973). Translator explanations are useful with respect to texts which relate to cultures very different from that of the target readers of the translation. In our modern world we have become used to technology, mass markets, travel and consumerism, and there are city-dwellers who are unaware that milk comes from cows, let alone other details of rural life, or perhaps of nature more generally. Texts such as those of ancient Greece, Rome and China portray different ways of life with different technology and cultural references. However, it is not just with ancient texts that explanations may be needed, for the same issues arise with modern texts translated across diverse cultures. Within a legal context, it may be important, for example, for an English reader to be aware that the concept of domicile carries subtly different implications in different legal systems, or that 'person' may have different significations depending on whether the word appears in a civil code or a commercial code, as well as whether the person is a physical being or a corporate abstract concept.

What strategy should a translator follow to convey to the reader unfamiliar ranges of meanings and cultural references within a text? We can change the references from ancient cultures to ones of modern literary texts, poetry, advertising, labelling on packaging, product instructions, advertising, as well as specialist texts such as are found in science, medicine and law. Are notes and supplementary information necessary? More frequently the question is: are they allowed? In most cases they are not. The translator must take the words of the source language text and create words in a target language text that within themselves reproduce the required information in the source text. One cultural context is reproduced in the language of another cultural context. The translator tasks and viewpoints concentrate on the strategies and methods for achieving this objective. What then is translation?

What is translation?

It seems self-evident, but at its simplest translation consists in writing a text in a language code that aims to reproduce information written in another language code, usually following the same sequence of ideas and structure. The usual idea is that a reader can obtain the same information regardless of whichever language version is read. Translation consists in inserting words in sentences on pages. This is the action of doing. The task is to select appropriate words and place them in an appropriate sequence in a target language so as to convey the meanings of the original source language text, and to do this as faithfully and elegantly as can be managed. The translation reads as if it had originally been written in the target language.

However, translation can also be seen as a process, involving a series of steps from a start to a finish. It resembles a production process: raw materials of source text, support tools and translator lead to the output of a new text in the target language. In a multilingual system different language combinations are worked on, which may be done sequentially or at the same time. In the EU context target language versions tend to be produced in parallel, with centralised coordination. Adding a new language means adding another language unit to the process and enlarging the scope of coordination. Adopting a viewpoint of process opens up the possibility to reflect on the different steps in the target language text-production process, on what information is needed at each stage, and on different ways of tackling tasks. For example, translation can be segmented into two phases: first, the act of producing a draft; second, the act of checking and revising the draft and turning it into a final product. Translators undertake both phases as a matter of routine, but for specialist legal texts the revision phase may include revision by legal specialists (lawyer-linguists) in order to ensure the text aligns with the legal system and legal terminology. Legal-linguistic revision can be extended to embrace the whole finalisation process in respect of draft legislative texts in the official languages, which undergo amendments in the parliamentary process to ensure the final texts are complete and aligned in all language versions. That is the case in EU legislative institutions (Robertson 2010, Šarčević and Robertson 2013). Revision is treated separately in Chapter 11.

The 'simplest' translation model is to draw up a text in one language as the 'source' language and make a version of it in another language as the 'target' language to express the same message. In the case of oral translation, oral interpretation, the utterance is spoken rather than written and the interpreter speaks the target language version as soon as possible after the source language has been uttered by the speaker. This task involves skills in simultaneously hearing and receiving, decoding and recoding, and speaking the target language for the listeners. It requires an extensive knowledge of vocabulary as well as of relevant background cultures. It also requires the translator always to keep abreast of developments in the fields in order to master the terminology. In formal conferences interpreters may sit in special cabins and speak into microphones, and what they say is heard through earphones worn by their listeners. Interpreters are assisted by good speakers, who are aware that interpretation is necessary, speak slowly, use short sentences and give interpreters in advance a copy of any written texts they intend to refer to or quote from.[8] That said, the emphasis in this chapter is placed on written texts and written translation, where the element of immediacy is (most of the time) less pressing.

A typical situation with written translation is that a text has been produced, perhaps made public, and now other language versions are required. The translator works with the source text to produce a new text in the language desired. In doing so, he or she follows every twist and turn in the thoughts and text of the author; it is the closest one can come to being in the actual place of the author and thinking their thoughts from 'inside', including embracing their emotional burden in the case of literature of a sad or tragic nature. The source text is fixed and immutable. There are invariably problems, difficulties and uncertainties. The translator interprets and chooses how to convey information into the target language pragmatically, adopting various strategies that can be presented in terms of theories of translation: interpretation theory, action theory, skopos theory, game theory, polysysteme theory (Guidère 2010: 69–77). Particular questions and problems that arise include: meaning, equivalence, faithfulness, modes (adaptation through suppressing, adding, substituting, explaining, compensating), types of translation, units of translation, and so on (Guidère 2010: 79–104).

Legal texts use terms and adopt styles that are specific to the source language system and context. Are notes and explanations allowed? Is it necessary to follow the source language syntax absolutely? New laws frequently adopt new concepts and terms to express them. Sometimes old words are used in new ways. Sometimes new terms are invented. Sometimes there are definitions attached and often not. For target language translators the question arises as to whether existing terms may also be adapted, or whether new terms must be created, and if so how, as a matter of term creation. Is it permitted to insert descriptions or explanations of source terms that are difficult to understand? Must the syntax be followed absolutely? What happens if a source language syntax is impossible to reproduce in the target language version – for example, very dense and long sentences, with several subordinate clauses, such as occur in German, particularly in legal German? They may be difficult or impossible to reproduce in exactly the same format in, say, English, French or Italian (and vice versa). Does one attempt to follow the complex structure in each detail in a way that is faithful but must appear unnatural in the target language, or does one extract the elements and reconstruct them, retaining all the elements and placing them in a sequence adapted to the target language? The latter implies translating the ideas rather than the individual word sequence.

Here is an example taken from a preliminary reference from the German *Bundesfinanzhof* (federal tax court) to the EU Court of Justice. The question was a single sentence in German, translated and published in EU languages[9] in a notice in the EU Official Journal C 184/5 of 23 June 2012:[10]

> Ist Art. 13 Abs. 1, Abs. 2 Buchst. a der VO Nr. 1408/71 dahin auszulegen, dass er der Gewährung von (Differenz-) Kindergeld durch einen Wohnmitgliedstaat in den Fällen entgegensteht, in denen ein Kindergeldberechtigter – ebenso wie der andere Elternteil – in der Schweiz als Grenzgänger einer nichtselbständigen Beschäftigung nachgeht und dort Familienleistungen für seine im Wohnmitgliedstaat lebenden Kinder bezieht, die geringer sind als das im Wohnmitgliedstaat vorgesehene Kindergeld?

Here is the French version:

> L'article 13, paragraphes 1, et 2, sous a), du règlement no 1408/71 doit-il être interprété en ce sens qu'il s'oppose à l'octroi d'allocations familiales (différentielles) par l'État membre du domicile dans les cas où une personne ayant droit aux allocations familiales allemandes exerce (de même que l'autre parent) une activité salariée en Suisse en tant que frontalier et où elle y perçoit, du chef de ses enfants vivant dans l'État membre de résidence, des prestations familiales d'un montant inférieur à celui des allocations familiales qui sont prévues dans l'État membre de résidence?

Here is the English version:

> Are Article 13(1) and Article 13(2)(a) of Regulation No. 1408/71(1) to be interpreted as precluding the granting of (differential) child benefit by a Member State of residence, in cases where a person entitled to child benefit – like the other parent – is a cross-border commuter employed in Switzerland and draws family benefits there in respect of his children living in the Member State of residence which are lower than the child benefit provided for in the Member State of residence?

We can note the way the sentence has been configured elegantly in each language while retaining the elements, each of which is vital for the message, and occasionally adding an interpretation element, such as in French where the word '*allemandes*' has been inserted after '*allocations familiales*'. The formal structure of a single sentence with question mark has to be complied with.

158 *Translation and revision*

How does one cope with cultural divides between readerships of source and target language texts? Inserting clarifications in the translation, as with the French insertion, is one way. Another is to insert a description, or explanation, of a foreign term, as was given above in connection with the *Bundesfinanzhof*. However, in legislative texts such glosses tend to be avoided as they create divergences between language versions. Each text speaks from a common source as a single multilingual voice, and they are not translations but co-texts of equal force and validity, according to the basic theory. So terminology and language become forced into a legal 'straightjacket'. To this, one can add the question, where a language is widely used, as with English, which form of the language does one opt for in the texts? Who is the imagined readership?

Translators frequently encounter source texts that contain terms which can be reproduced in their target language texts with equivalent terms as a matter of language, but the precise meanings attached to the terms are different between source and target cultures. Earlier in this book we discussed cheeses and how many different types there are. The translator has to think whether to adjust the wording in subtle ways to mark such differences; for example, Bulgarian cheese is sometimes translated as 'yellow cheese' What is that? Well, at least the reader is alerted to the fact that it is something special. Translators are mediators, standing between languages, but also between the cultures represented by the languages. They can seek ways to alert a reader to cultural issues, but they are limited by the words in the text. It is a chain that prevents excursiveness into explanations. Words and terms are to be reproduced by other words and terms. In terms of room for manoeuvre, it is like dancing on the head of a pin.

Let us change the question and ask: why translate? What is the purpose, the aim, the need? The answer, whether it be for oral language or written language, is invariably the same. An 'utterance' is expressed in a language code that someone does not understand. They are unable to access or decode the information conveyed by it. Language knowledge tends to be pretty black and white, in the sense that an unfamiliar language is a total block to comprehension. Any information as to contents is better than none, provided it does not mislead; a poor translation at least conveys some information. However, as an act of communication, the fact that little or no linguistic information as such is received may not matter as the surrounding context, gestures and other non-linguistic signals may suffice to indicate the probable meaning of an utterance. Shopping in foreign countries frequently takes this form. On the other hand, there may be no need for translation. If only native speakers are the intended audience of a magazine, there is no need to translate. Alternatively, there may be a need, but it does not justify the cost and effort involved, or no one is prepared to pay the price tag. So we can say that translation takes place when there is a need, a request, someone able to undertake it and someone able to pay the price (unless it is for free, or by machine). But what does the client actually need? What will the text be used for? These are also criteria that must be considered.

The act of translation is both simple and complicated – simple and quick to perform by an experienced translator, but difficult to explain in terms of how it is done, at least if one seeks to explain the cognitive processes. It involves considerable education and training, as mentioned in Chapter 13, covering knowledge of source and target languages and their attached general and specialist cultures. In the case of legal translation, it involves knowledge of the legal systems of source and target languages, so that the full implications of terms are understood for the finer nuances. It involves research, since unfamiliar terms must be carefully analysed as part of the search for equivalent terms. It is here that a semiotic approach can assist. If one analyses a source term to identify the *signified/object* and *interpretant* behind a *signifier/representamen* indicated by the word on the source language page, one searches for the sign. Then one takes that sign and searches for the object in the target language, seeking for as close a match as possible. One is aware that terms tend to have a central focus of meaning (perhaps several) and around that is a more general fuzzier circle of application, and one makes one's choices. In legal texts, these choices tend to become standardised through repetition, and sometimes they become fixed because a court has made a ruling on them as term equivalents. Legal translation offers much less scope for variation and personal intuition than other forms of translation. Errors take on particular significance, as they may have legal consequences through changing the effects between language versions. Legal translation steers towards a search for accuracy in detail while endeavouring to retain elegance and naturalness in the specialist speech forms of the target language, so that it reads as if originally drafted in that language.

In the case of legal texts of a legislative nature, the translator moves towards the role of legal drafter, faced with similar problems, except that they are bound by the wording of the source language text to be translated. They anticipate readings and adjust terminology in anticipation, keeping in mind the effects to be achieved. They follow the structure, layout and path set by the source language drafter. They work with words and terms as tools, and are tied by those chosen by the source language drafter. They search for equivalent terms, but they cannot go beyond the source text in what it provides. As with the source language drafter, legal meaning in a judicial sense escapes them, and they can only seek to steer and influence; the legal meanings will ultimately be constructed by judges in court cases.

The target language words and terms, and the translation as a whole, can be examined from the point of view of effects. Are the effects the same as for the source language text? Will readers of each language version react in similar ways, and act in the ways being sought? Different approaches can achieve the same effects. Diversity in style and approach is part of translation, including to some extent in legal translation. Occasionally this can be a source of uncertainties.

For example, EU texts were originally drafted mainly in French. English was a translation language and EU English can be seen in terms of a calque of French. Translation variations periodically arose. Later, English became a drafting language and so a source language for translation. Translation variations in terms were noticed by translators who wondered whether different terms were involved. Checking the versions in the original four EC languages helps to clarify doubts. The underlying message is that there is sometimes an element of 'fuzziness' in texts. This fuzziness extends more widely because the process of international negotiation implies negotiation and achieving consensus through compromises. Different systems have different approaches and a text may need to embrace them all. Language and terms become adapted to that end and ambiguity and fuzziness enter the scene. It is possible for sentences, on careful analysis as to meaning, to have none – a curious experience, as the sense is of black emptiness. A literal approach of word-for-word translation provides a solution. The role of translator is to produce matching signs, but not necessarily to indicate what they mean.

Variation in translations forms an inherent part of translation. It is not an exact science; there is a subjective personal element. Even machine translation is a product of humans with their preferences when programming. How much does variation matter? Let us take one example, which incidentally serves to place us within an EU 24-language and Court of Justice context. It also touches on the question of what is a unit of meaning or

160 *Translation and revision*

term. Regulation No. 1 determining the languages to be used by the European Economic Community, as amended, sets out the EU language regime. Article 7 concerns the language rules for the EU Court of Justice. The text is a single combined text in all the languages listed in 'protocol' order set out in the EUR-Lex database:

BG: Езиковият режим на процедурата на Съда на Европейските общности се определя в неговия процедурен правилник.
ES: [11] El régimen lingüístico del procedimiento del Tribunal de Justicia se determinará en el reglamento de procedimiento de éste.
CS: Užívání jazyků v řízení před Soudním dvorem stanoví jeho jednací řád.
DA: Den sproglige ordning for sagerne ved Domstolen fastlægges i dennes procesreglement.
DE: Die Sprachenfrage für das Verfahren des Gerichtshofes wird in dessen Verfahrensordnung geregelt.
ET: Euroopa Kohtu menetlustes kasutatavad keeled määratakse kindlaks Euroopa Kohtu töökorraga.
EL: Το γλωσσικο καθεστως της διαδικασιας του Δικαστηριου καθοριζεται στον κανονισμο διαδικασιας του.
EN: The languages to be used in the proceedings of the Court of Justice shall be laid down in its rules of procedure.
FR: Le régime linguistique de la procédure de la Cour de Justice est déterminé dans le règlement de procédure de celle-ci.
GA: (No version.)
HR: Jezici koji se koriste u postupcima Suda određeni su u njegovom poslovniku.
IT: Il regime linguistico della procedura della Corte di Giustizia è determinato nel Regolamento di procedura della medesima.
LV: Tiesas tiesvedībā izmantojamās valodas nosaka Tiesas reglamentā.
LT: Kalbos, vartojamos Teisingumo Teismo nagrinėjamose bylose, nurodomos Teismo darbo tvarkos taisyklėse.
HU: A Bíróság saját eljárási szabályzatában állapítja meg, hogy eljárásai során mely nyelveket alkalmazza.
MT: Il-lingwi li għandhom jintużaw fil-proċeduri tal-Qorti tal-Ġustizzja għandhom ikunu stabbiliti fir-regoli ta' proċedura tagħha.
NL: Het taalgebruik bij de procesvoering van het Hof van Justitie wordt geregeld in het Reglement voor de procesvoering van het Hof.
PL: System językowy postępowania przed Trybunałem Sprawiedliwości jest określony w jego regulaminie.
PT: O regime linguístico dos processos no Tribunal de Justiça será fixado no regulamento processual deste Tribunal.
RO: Regimul lingvistic al procedurii Curții de Justiție se stabilește prin regulamentul de procedură al acesteia.
SK: Používanie jazykov v konaní pred Súdnym dvorom sa upraví v rokovacom poriadku Súdneho dvora.
SL: Jeziki, ki se uporabljajo v postopkih Sodišča, so določeni v njegovem poslovniku.
FI: Yhteisön tuomioistuimen oikeudenkäyntimenettelyssä käytettäviä kieliä koskevat järjestelyt vahvistetaan tuomioistuimen työjärjestyksessä.
SV: I fråga om förfaranden vid domstolen skall språkanvändningen regleras i domstolens rättegångsregler.

The Regulation was originally published in four languages: Dutch, French, German and Italian. The others are subsequent translations made at the time of accessions, but all versions are authentic and equivalent in accordance with EU law. If we look carefully, we see different approaches to the (French) source concept of *'le régime linguistique'* (linguistic regime). Thus we find: 'languages to be used' (English), *'die Sprachenfrage'* (German) (the question of languages),[12] *System językowy* (Polish) (the language system), *'Het taalgebruik'* (Dutch) (the use of language),[13] and so on. Thus for the same object we have at least the following variations: *linguistic regime, languages to be used, question of languages, language system.* If we take individual words, there is a clear divergence. On the other hand, if we take the whole sentence, these seem to have the same effects. We can also take these expressions as units of meaning as terms, and here again they would seem to be equivalent.

Does the variation matter? This is a question translators and revisers ask themselves ceaselessly. If the terms are analysed as signs, does each *signifier/representamen* refer to the same or different *signified/objects*? What about the *interpretant*? Within a unified system of legal concepts, the *signified/objects* should be aligned, indeed the same, as they stem from the same single source. But are they? Is theory matched by reality? How does the reader construct the meaning of the various terms? The linguistic meaning, in a literal sense of the words employed, is different in the language versions, but the overall concept expressed appears to be the same and one could say that the 'legal meanings', or 'meanings in law', are the same in each text. Can the equivalent expressions be challenged so that one 'goes inside' them and the units of meaning become smaller? If so, the singularity of the message is removed and the texts acquire different meanings and diverge. This technique is a legal method used to 'break' a text.

Such issues lead to questions of power: who decides on interpretation and how much control do they have over meanings? In the case of Article 7, meaning is under the control of one body, the EU Court of Justice (let us say, to keep matters simple). That Court has final say on meanings in EU law, and in this case it makes its own rules of procedure (we again simplify reality), so it has control over the implementation of the meanings in Article 7, including over the term in question. Should it be forced to make a choice on one or other language version, as frequently happens, then the Court would follow its usual methods of interpretation to arrive at whatever result is appropriate.[14] One can obtain an idea of where the legal translator stands within this overall set of arrangements and the significance of their work.

From a translation viewpoint, drawing on the foregoing example, we can see how there is no single and absolute approach to translating. Different paths can lead to the same results. What matters is that having decided on a particular approach, one remains consistent throughout. So, use the same words for the same concepts in each text and across texts in the same branch or policy. A translator of a later legislative text becomes bound by the decisions made in earlier ones. The terminology in a high-ranking text must be followed in lower-ranking ones. Technical terms, once established, must be used. In this way stability, precision and term-equivalence is built up in all languages in a multilingual system through translation. The scope for variation becomes extremely narrow as each part of a sentence in language A needs to be in alignment with the equivalent parts in languages B,C, D and so on. There is pressure towards a convergence of meaning between language versions, and it can be checked by making a semiotic analysis of each term in each language, and making comparisons using concepts discussed in Chapter 8. Linguistic meanings are brought as closely as possible together to generate the same legal meanings. That can lead to regulating the use of terms in a legal-like way, such as using the EU concept of 'codification' to embrace the English concept of 'consolidation', or providing for declensions in different languages of the EU currency unit – the euro – in singular and plural.[15] Texts are structured into larger and smaller units of meaning through punctuation: full stops for sentences, semicolons and commas for clauses, as well as the legal devices of numbered articles, paragraphs, points, indents, and so on. Punctuation facilitates multilingual texts as it segments information into blocks. Blocks of text may become standardised and treated as equivalent units of meaning, as is the case with standardised EU recitals (subsidiarity, proportionality) (Joint Practical Guide (EU 2013)) or articles dealing with delegated decision-making by committees, referred to by the EU multilingualised term 'comitology'. Legal language is specialist language; EU language is a variety of language for all of the languages and in each case it differs from national language (Robertson 2012a, Mollin 2006). New concepts are needed and new terms are created for them, and reproduced in all languages.[16]

Translation as a process

Translation can be seen in terms of a process, or a series of steps. These include: understanding the source text, deconstructing its elements to access deeper meanings, identifying terminology difficulties, devising a strategy for creating the target text, visualising the concepts (*signified/semiotic objects*) created by the words (*signifiers/representamens*) in the source text and their implications (*interpretant*), reproducing them in the language forms of the target language while following source syntax as closely as possible, then checking, revising, comparing source and target texts as to meaning, equivalence and effects, consulting other language versions, undertaking research and consulting experts and specialist terminologists in cases of doubt or uncertainty.

Checking for equivalence in effects may be linked to individual terms, to a clause, a sentence, or higher levels of units such as a text as a whole. In literature or poetry meanings may function at several levels and the translator's task shifts to accommodate those different levels, seeking to reproduce them in ways which may even lead to radical departures from a source text; here proverbs come to mind,[17] or maybe it is punning that is important, which makes translating Shakespeare rather interesting. Such literary forms of translation do not generally apply to legal translation, which is predominantly literal, aiming for closest parallelism in term and structure between languages, with as much elegance as possible. Yet legal texts may be ambiguous. International and supranational legal texts contain wording that results from 'political compromise' and is frequently open to alternative readings, or designed to have no real meaning. This method enables a text to be adopted and signed and the overall benefit is significant, but the text nonetheless presents a challenge for translators as some languages, notably inflected languages such as German and Slavic languages, mark relationships precisely and may be obliged to make an interpretation. If different languages make different interpretations, not only linguistic but also legal, meanings may diverge. A user may be obliged to go to court for clarification, leading perhaps to an interpretation that applies one of the approaches (but after intensive review and discussion in a legal forum with different viewpoints presented), so that language versions following other interpretations become literally incorrect and liable to lead an 'innocent' reader into error. Drafters, translators and revisers bear such scenarios in mind ceaselessly. Legal texts in criminal law carry implications of fines and imprisonment as well. In the end it is the courts who decide.

Translation does not occur in a vacuum. There is always a context, even if it is just an instruction exercise in a language school or college. It forms part of a larger set of arrangements. There is always a reason for undertaking a translation and usually some purpose or objective to be achieved. It may be literature or advertising, film subtitles, a business contract, a court judgment or a legislative act. Depending on what category, or genre, the work to be translated falls within, the product will be expected to take a certain shape and appearance and to be written in certain ways. Each type of translation poses different sets of issues and problems. With Bible translation from original texts in Hebrew, Aramaic or Greek, one may not always be sure about the precise meaning of an ancient word or one may make choices which are subsequently revised in the light of new information or developments.[18] For advertisements, a straight translation of a slogan that works in language A may sound silly, rude or ineffective in language B, so a different slogan is devised. One of the pleasures in a country such as Belgium is spotting differences in adverts in French and Flemish, and similarly with film titles.

For legal translation in a multilingual environment such as the EU, it is convenient to think of it as a form of industrial production. Modern translators work in 'text factories'. The raw materials are source legal texts and these must be worked on, transformed and processed into a new product: the translated legal text. This is subjected to 'quality control' by revisers and experts to ensure it is fit for service. It is then dispatched for the client to see and use. It goes off into the wide world to be read, interpreted and acted on, taking on a life and identity of its own. Not a romantic vision perhaps, but by thinking in industrial terms one can envisage operations that occur at each step. One can identify knowledge and tools needed at each stage of production and one can consider how each stage might be undertaken more efficiently. Translation is a skilled activity that costs time and money, which is a principal argument against multilingual legal systems and against engaging in translation. Modern technology, however, is moving strongly in the direction of 'reducing costs' of translation and multilingualism through mechanisation of the process. Translation is probably more widespread nowadays than ever before, and it is for that reason that the field of translation studies (Munday 2012) and translator training (Robinson 1997) has emerged as an important field of activity.

Let us revisit the translation process, this time stepping back from the translation act to think about the organisational context and the steps involved. We can imagine a scenario: Client X has made a text in language A and wants a version of it in language B. He contacts the translator's organisation, or the translator directly, with a request. So a legal contract is entered into, covering the product to be delivered, price, delivery time and any other incidental details. The translator takes on the work, plans the time schedule, studies the source text for potential problems and difficulties, checks terminology and decides on the translation strategy. Perhaps the client has specified particular needs and requirements, such as to observe a specific range of terminology or to write for an American rather than British readership. The translator makes terminology researches and consults experts for specialist information so as to obtain a good picture of the text's message. Then the creative part happens and the translator generates the target text in a first draft. This is checked, reread, revised, adjusted and polished. Individual points are checked with experts as necessary. The text is now ready and a final version produced, which is sent off to the client.

In an organisation such as the EU the translators are employees paid a wage rather than paid for piecework, and they are organised in translation departments according to language of their mother tongue. An in-house translation service permits the build-up of technical specialist knowledge and high levels of quality, together with the development of specialised terminology databases and systems adapted to the specific needs of the organisation. Legal translation is also undertaken by freelance translators.

Seven scenarios for legal translation

We turn now to reflect on some scenarios where translation of legal texts[19] may arise. This helps us to visualise the sort of problems faced and factors that influence translation strategies. The aim is always to produce a translation that is fit for service, as a quality text, but precisely what is needed to achieve that end may vary subtly according to the specific context. Placing translation in a pragmatic context also enables theoretical issues to find a place for exploration in practical application. It is not possible to explore all possible scenarios, but a few examples linked primarily to a public law context should set the tone and show some patterns.

One of the first questions to ask concerning a legal text to be translated (source language text) concerns its status and the future status of the translation to be produced (target language text). Is the source language text a formal part of the legal system in which the translator works, and is the target language text also to be a formal part of that same legal system? Do both texts have legal effects? Will they become treated as equal and interchangeable? That is a key question for a multilingual context. In a monolingual legal system the answer is unlikely to be affirmative, since the legal system by definition functions in a single official language. So there is no general need for translation. Nonetheless, even monolingual legal systems have a need for translation where there is a foreign element, and that brings us to the first scenario.

First scenario

We can imagine a monolingual legal context, where there is a court case involving foreign elements. On the one hand, there may be a witness who can only give evidence in a foreign language and requires an oral interpreter.[20] On the other hand, there may be foreign-language documents as evidence that the court orders to be translated by a certified or sworn translator.[21] In both cases it is important for the court to be able to fully grasp all the information and assess its significance. That means understanding the foreign-language context. The information is for the purposes of the court case, as information, and attention is addressed to that end. In this context, the text is likely to relate to a foreign legal system and facts occurring abroad, and a question will arise as to how to handle terms and concepts that do not exist in the legal system of the enquiring court. The translator bears in mind that the reader may be unfamiliar with the concepts and reflects on strategies that, while adhering to the wording, best bring out the meanings of the foreign terms and concepts. The source text nonetheless remains the document of reference. The translation is an aid to the court in constructing its image of the foreign law or circumstances.

This scenario can arise in any legal system. The text to be translated forms part of a foreign system and its value and meanings are located within the foreign context. The function of the translation is so that the court and parties can access the meaning and fully understand the implications; in semiotic terms, fully understand the value of the signs in terms of *signified/object* and *interpretant*. The translation task is to construct new *signifiers/representamens* while seeking to keep the other elements of the sign as unchanged as possible. The court needs to understand the significance of the text within its original context. In practical terms, this may imply a need for notes and explanations (if permitted) by a translator, or inserting source language terms alongside proposed translations, where there is no clear and precise equivalence in concepts between source and target language. However, in the case of formal documents and certificates no such additions are generally allowed.

Second scenario

A second scenario for legal translation may be in a context of law reform where a researcher needs to find out how other legal systems have solved particular problems in some branch or domain of legal activity and policy-making. The foreign laws may need to be translated into the language of the place where the information is required ('the local language') to find this out. One can place the need for translation within a context of different types of legal text, whether laws, court documents and judgments, contracts, and so on. The primary focus is on identifying the significance of the source terms in their context. The text is for information only and explanatory notes and comments may assist. A variant may be where a client needs a working copy of a contract written in a foreign language. In countries such as Japan it has become routine to translate laws into English and other languages so as to help foreign businessmen.[22]

Third scenario

A third scenario is where a monolingual state through its agents and officials participates in an international conference to prepare international legal texts and there is a need to translate working papers into a foreign language for the purposes of the negotiations. The working papers may in the alternative be written directly in the foreign language of negotiation, but that requires a high level of knowledge on the part of the drafter. This situation arises all the time in the EU supranational law context where international negotiations constitute the daily routine.

In these first three scenarios, one can ask who is undertaking the translation work. It can be undertaken by a state's agents and officials, by lawyers or private individuals, or contract translators; alternatively, the tasks may be assigned to an international organisation to undertake as part of its overall activities. The choice is essentially pragmatic, but there are implications for quality and term equivalence stemming from the degree of control and uniformity that can be established in each case. Transferring translation tasks to specialised organisations or agencies takes a load off the national authorities and facilitates the adopting of cross-language methods and approaches. It works towards a shared cultural identity multilingually, but there may also be some loss of individual influence.

In the EU supranational context, each EU institution employs its own translators for all official languages[23] and there is a separate Translation Centre[24] that services EU bodies and agencies that do not have their own translation facilities. On the other hand, when a new state is negotiating to become a member of the EU, it must arrange for its own translations of the EU texts initially, subject to checking and revision by EU legal-linguistic revisers. After accession, EU institutions arrange translation of EU texts. The difficulty with translating in the early stages before accession is that it takes time to build up knowledge and experience and to settle the terminology. There is a corrigendum procedure, but it is best used sparingly. An anecdotal opinion is that it takes perhaps ten years for terminology to become fully stabilised after accession.

Fourth scenario

A fourth scenario is where there is a legal text in a foreign language but the translation is intended to be used for official purposes in the local legal system and have effects. So it is not purely for information. For example, an international convention is drawn up in language A as sole authentic language and needs to be translated into language B so that it can be integrated into the legal system of language B. An official translation is required.[25] The status of this translation will depend first on any rules agreed and set out in the convention as regards translations, and second on the rules of the destination legal system. To make the status of a text as translation clear, it may have the words 'translation' inserted at the start of it. That means it does not carry the official legal meaning, but it may nonetheless serve as a foundation point for drafting laws in the legal system of language B. The problem with such texts is that the convention probably introduces new concepts, or uses existing concepts in new specialised ways, that are not yet known in the legal system of language B. So the translation into language B may seek to steer a path between the language of the convention and the existing language of its national legal system in the knowledge that domestic lawyers will probably tend to read the text from their domestic viewpoint and knowledge, which may lead to effects not intended by the drafters of the convention in language A. This reminds us of Chapter 8 and the semiotic viewpoints, which can be used to analyse such situations.

Fifth scenario

The fifth scenario builds on the fourth, but goes a step further. It represents a 'watershed' in the sense that it marks a difference between translating a source language legal text that is *external* to the target language legal system for the purposes of the target language system, as opposed to a source language legal text that is *internal* to a legal system and translated into a target language within the *same* system. The fifth scenario brings us inside the internal environment of a multilingual legal system. Each language version is subject to the rules of the *same* system on how it is to be drafted, and the construction of meanings in texts becomes shared. The translator is not entitled to translate solely in the way that seems best to him or her, but must take account of official guides, manuals, styles and instructions on terms to be used and standard expressions. In a word, the translation task becomes codified, more rigid, and takes on features of legal drafting.

Many implications arise from this. One is terminology. It becomes necessary to ensure that terms exist in each language for the shared concepts of the system – alignment of *signified/object* and the *interpretant* but using different *signifiers/representamens* according to each language. For citizens, the language versions are interchangeable. Each is authentic. Term creation is important for each of the languages, and it needs to be aligned across the languages. That in turn places an emphasis on quality terminological support and efficient glossaries and databases to assist in drafting and translation. Standardisation is enhanced and that in turn leads to the benefits of mechanisation.

Computerisation and computer-assisted tools (CAT) are important in that respect. The fifth scenario assumes that the source text is finalised *before* translation. The sixth scenario adds a nuance of difference.

Sixth scenario

The sixth scenario is similar to the fifth, insofar as it envisages translation of legal texts within the same legal system, but it assumes that translation takes place on *draft* versions of a base-language text in a multilingual legal system. It assumes that there is input from all languages into the base version and each other. This scenario shifts the scope from 'pure' translation of a finished text into a situation where the translator (and reviser, see Chapter 11) shift imperceptibly towards taking part in co-drafting of multilingual texts. Insofar as the texts involved are specialist legal, it becomes desirable for the translator, or the reviser, to have legal knowledge and skills. This scenario reflects EU legislative practice (Morgan 1982, Gallas 1999, Robertson 2013). However, EU legislative acts can reflect more than one scenario at the same time, insofar as they need to function in different legal contexts: first, as EU acts within the EU legal order; second, as acts impacting on national legal systems; third, in some cases as acts impacting on the international legal order. They are thus at a nodal point in a matrix of legal discourse contexts. This has implications for terminology and the construction of meanings (Robertson 2012b). In the background to the sixth scenario there is frequently the need for national authorities to adapt national law to the EU acts through 'transposition', typically of directives. This is not exactly translation, but it involves transferring information from the EU legal order to the national legal system for the purpose of creating new texts that implement the EU objectives in the language forms and styles of each individual national system of law using the discourse methods of that system (*parole*). Terms become ambiguous when they cross the EU/national law system boundary: is meaning linked to the EU context or the national context? It may be necessary to make things clear through definitions. Transposition involves a form of intra-lingual translation. The 'hybrid' function of EU legal texts needing to function in different contexts and languages, combined with discourse divergences, is one of the sources of difficulty in their comprehension. Another is that the texts address economic issues and use economic language. The differences are structural. The semiotic view discussed in Chapter 8 assists in understanding the dynamics.

Seventh scenario

The seventh scenario shifts away from translation and towards drafting and revision. It assumes that each language version is drawn up and drafted separately from the start and then the versions are compared and mutually adjusted between each other to arrive at a combined joint integrated result for all languages. Terms are fully shared in *interpretant* and *signified/object* and only the *signifiers/representamens* differ. It is an ideal of equality between languages. One thinks of Canadian federal law-making as the model in this connection (Levert 1995). With more than two languages the approach becomes more complicated. The EU system has certain features of the seventh scenario, insofar as language versions are compared and aligned early on and prior literature in terms of reports and preparatory materials by EU institutions is generally available in all languages.

168 *Translation and revision*

There are other scenarios involving legal language and legal translation, in particular in the context of court documents and contracts, but the foregoing provides an indication in respect of some of the issues that arise for consideration. Each text presents its own set of issues.

Summary

This chapter has taken a look at translation. The aim has been not to give an exposition of translation theory, as there is a an excellent supply of guidance in existence, but to illustrate some themes from translation that arise in legal translation and give a flavour of contexts and reflections. The presentation has been pragmatic and has drawn heavily on EU legal-linguistic practice. Such details of translation as attention to grammar, syntax, parts of speech and the finer details of the process have been taken for granted as linguistic knowledge, for it is assumed that the translator has a complete grasp of the vocabulary, grammar and syntax of the source and target languages. Elements from the translation context are included in the framework in Appendix VIII. Lastly, early on in this chapter it was said that a distinction would be drawn between translation and revision. This chapter has looked at translation, so we turn next to revision.

Notes

1 On translation and translation theory, see among others (in English and French): Tytler (1907), Mounin (1963/2008), Picken (1989), Ballard (1992), Ladmiral (1994/2010), Newmark (1995), Robinson (1997), Šarčević (1997, 2001, 2009, 2015), Truffaut (1997), Munday (2012), Venuti (1995), Ost (2009), Sočanac *et al.* (2009), Guidère (2010), Bellos (2011), Oustinoff (2011a, 2011b), Albi *et al.* (2013), Cheng *et al.* (2014).
2 Commission (2012); see also European Commission, Claire's Clear Writing Tips.
3 For a history of translation including this dichotomy, see among others Ballard (1992) and Venuti (1995).
4 Translators have indeed been persecuted and murdered for their work: William Tyndale 1536.
5 This chapter does not address machine translation. It is touched on in Chapter 12 in the context of tools.
6 Our scientific and philosophical ideas have been transmitted through translation.
7 The Bible has served, and still does, as a source of law, as does the Koran.
8 For information on interpretation scenarios and skills in an EU context (all languages), see European Commission Interpretation (SCIC) website: http://ec.europa.eu/dgs/scic/.
9 Not in Irish or Croatian.
10 An answer has not been published as at the time of writing.
11 Castilian.
12 Alternatively: the 'languages question'.
13 Alternatively: 'language use' or 'use of languages'.
14 Summarised in the Opinion of Advocate General Stix-Hackl in Case C265/03: *Reference for a preliminary ruling from the Audencia Nacional: Igor Simutenkov v Ministerio de Educación y Cultura, Real Federación Española de Fútbol*. European Court Reports 2005 p. I02579.
15 For English, whether the plural is 'euro' or 'euros'; both are to be found.
16 For some statistics on EU Commission translation in 2014 see: http://ec.europa.eu/dgs/translation/whoweare/translation_figures_en.pdf.
17 Call a spade a spade: *appeler un chat un chat*. For more differences between English and French, see www.english-for-techies.net/mainstream%20vocabulary/proverbs.htm.

Viewpoints of translation 169

18 An example here is with the Biblical text where Moses came down from the mountain with 'horns', subsequently revised to 'shining' or 'radiant' face: Exodus 34:29. For an explanation see Yerushatenu (2012)
19 On legal translation see in particular Šarčević (1997).
20 See EULITA at www.eulita.eu/.
21 See www.iti.org.uk/about-industry/certification-sworn and www.listlanguage.com/translation-organizations.html.
22 See, for example, the Ministry of Justice, Japan website: www.japaneselawtranslation.go.jp/?re=02.
23 On the EU translation environment, see among others the Commission DG website http://ec.europa.eu/dgs/translation/index_en.htm; European Parliament website at www.europarl.europa.eu/the-secretary-general/en/organisation/directorategenerals/translation.html; Council of the European Union (2011).
24 http://cdt.europa.eu/EN/Pages/Homepage.aspx.
25 Council of Europe treaties and conventions are translated into languages other than English and French. The translations can be accessed from the Council of Europe website at www.coe.int/en/web/conventions/translations.

11 Revision

Introduction

This short chapter starts from the proposition that there is an existing source-drafted or translated text and reflects on issues that attract attention. It considers the reviser viewpoint and reviser role and the specialised function of the legal-linguistic reviser.

Revision viewpoint

Translators review, revise and check their draft translations before making them final as a matter of routine. That is part of the task of translation. However, it is also quite usual to submit a translated text to another person to look over, a person who is more distant from the text and may spot points overlooked by the translator. Four eyes are more efficient than two, as they say. Different approaches on this matter are possible: an experienced translator asks an inexperienced one to read over texts as part of their training, as well as to spot inadvertent errors. A less experienced translator has their translations checked by an experienced translator and reviser to correct errors, ensure quality and as part of their training. Or a specialist text translated by a non-specialist is checked over by an expert in the field to ensure accuracy of specialist terminology and that the discourse style (*parole*) reflects expert use in the field in question. EU linguistic revisers are experienced translators familiar with the range of text genres, habitual expressions and terminology traps, as well as the needs of the users. They bring their experience to bear when checking draft translations with source texts. Perhaps no interventions by a reviser are necessary; the target language draft is accurate in terminology and follows the meanings of the source language well, with good style and punctuation, and reads as if originally written in the source language. On the other hand, there are often points to be made, sometimes a lot of points. When it is a case of material errors, intervention is required to correct them, but when it comes to finer issues of style and selection of alternative possible terminology, how far should a reviser intervene in a text before them? When should they intervene? Is one sure that the proposed alternatives are necessarily more appropriate? Where they differ, whose style should prevail: that of the translator or that of the reviser?[1]

The revision viewpoint is subtly different from the initial translation viewpoint. Let us try and draw a distinction between the viewpoint of the translator who makes a draft and that of the reviser who comes after to check and correct, while recognising that frequently this is one and the same person. Perhaps one can imagine that the translator pays attention to the author, their message and the way they say it, whereas the reviser pays attention to the readership, the end-uses and the intertextual environment, which forms part of quality control.[2] The translator has his/her culture and methods and so does the reviser. They may read and interpret the information in the source language text in the same way or differently; they may create meanings in the same way or differently; each has their preferred style and set of expressions. They may match up, or not.

The reviser can look at the target language text as a whole, checking it from different viewpoints, such as those of law, language, policy and action, discussed earlier. They will ask questions of the target language text, compare with the source language, review the answers that emerge, discuss these with the translator, as well as with experts, check and research individual problem terms, and so on. The objective is to achieve a quality product that is fit for service.

The reviser viewpoint is encompassed within the translator role, but drawing a distinction serves to draw attention to issues of detail and quality. Its defining function is essentially negative: searching for faults, errors and infelicities in order to correct them. Texts are read not for the interest of their contents but to check whether the information in source language versions are appropriately reproduced in target language versions in terms of form, structure, layout and content in the appropriate discourse style, with correct punctuation and orthography, bearing in mind the purpose of the text. Revisers may have to read through and process large quantities of text in this way and a lot of time may be spent on resolving individual details. If the translator is 'invisible', the reviser is even more so.

Revision

Many considerations which apply to the primary translation task apply equally to revision. The texts worked on are the same, as are the context and constraints. What is the difference between the two viewpoints? Indeed is there any real difference? The initial translator has the closest relationship to the author and fidelity to the author's thinking and message. He or she concentrates on the individual trees in the metaphorical wood. The reviser comes afterwards and has a more distant relationship, looking at the text as a whole, the wood rather than the trees. The reviser is perhaps closer to the audience and can be considered as the first 'innocent' reader, looking to the use and function of the text and the way it fits in within other texts of that genre and readership needs and expectations. Yet the reviser is generally not so much 'innocent' as a skilled expert reader who is checking every detail for errors, infelicities and possible misreadings and divergences between source and target language texts. It is a curious role, as it leads to specialised ways of reading, like editors and proofreaders, who perform a similar function in looking for faults. If they perform their work well, like the translator, the text reads well and subsequent readers are unaware that any work has been performed. It is hoped that the final reader can read the text for pleasure, education and learning and concentrate on the message.

The role of revision tends to be glossed over in translation studies, but in multilingual legal systems it is an important role as it serves to ensure alignment of multiple language versions of texts and that they are of the required quality. With the advent of machine-assisted translation (see Chapter 12) the role of translator itself is perceptibly shifting towards that of reviser of an automatically generated target language text. To this one can perhaps add that in multilingual contexts where texts are drafted by non-native speakers, as is the case in international organisations such as the EU, the translators perform a function as proofreaders of draft source language texts as well. They become expert linguistic advisers. So what are the sort of things that need to be looked at?

If we recall Chapter 6 on linguistics, a number of topics were listed and their relevance to multilingual law was briefly canvassed. If we wish a short answer as to what falls within the scope of revision, we could start by including most of the topics listed in that chapter, at least in so far as written language is concerned. The concept of revision of oral utterances has not been widely developed. This would seem to be more a case of a dialogue between those present in which the precise meanings intended are clarified through discussion. One can imagine that taking place in a courtroom where an interpreter is asked to clarify points by a judge, for example. With the written text, on the other hand, the reviser might start with the translation and read it like an original in that language, searching for grammatical, punctuation and syntax errors as a proofreader, and then checking with the source text for consistency. On the other hand, a reviser may take the source text and the translation and read them side by side, checking for consistency of each part. So long as things match, everything is fine; but when in the eyes of the reviser they do not match, then the discrepancy becomes a problem to research and resolve.

Typically, it is terminology that raises the most difficult questions: which term is appropriate? Part of the problem is that no suitable term may exist in the target language, or a concept may be very difficult to understand, or sometimes alternative terms are possible and it is difficult to know which is the most suitable. Sometimes there is conflict in opinion between different persons having an interest in the text. Alternative formulations are possible; we saw an example in Chapter 10 in relation to Article 7 of Regulation No. 1. Perhaps the translator has chosen term A and the reviser prefers term B. The question arises whether the reviser should necessarily replace term A with term B. Perhaps; but once this is done, the whole text must be checked so that in every place where term A appears it is replaced by term B, otherwise the text has both terms, which can create confusion as a specialist reader will assume that different meanings are intended. The golden rule is: same term for same concept. This objective extends to embrace other texts on the same theme in the field as a matter of intertextuality.

A wider aspect of term variation is style variation. Translators are individuals, as are revisers, and each has their own style. How far should a reviser impose their style on a translated work? If the primary translation is consistent and 'works' as a text, what is the benefit from changing it? There may be good reasons, but the old adage 'if it ain't broke, don't fix it' is always lurking in the background. On the other hand, a client or expert may insist on certain terms and phrases, and if these are viable as term equivalents, that is another factor that must be included. In legal texts there is usually a background of specialist expert language and terminology which has to be respected, as well as formal guidance and instructions. Terminological research may be needed, using semiotic techniques, to arrive at solutions.

There are many genres of written text, and there are just as many genres of translation and revision, since all are related. The precise task and scope in revision will be adapted to genre and text. Thus the needs for advertising and product promotion differ from those of scientific language. With the former, totally different formulae may be appropriate, but with scientific writing, close adherence to the wording of the source is important. Both types of writing are specialist, and that brings one into the domain of language for special purposes (LSP). Medical, scientific and technological writing is specialist, and so is legal writing. Legal translation is a specialist activity, and so is the revision of draft translated legal texts, in particular when those texts are draft laws and are intended to bring about legal effects and consequences.

With legal texts, bearing in mind the scenarios outlined in Chapter 10, the translator and reviser move closer to the role of legal drafter and become subject to the controls and constraints of legal drafters. In practice, while primary translators may not have formal legal training and experience, it has become increasingly accepted that where specialised legal texts of a court or of a law-making nature are involved, revision will be by a trained lawyer with linguistic knowledge. These are legal-linguistic experts and they are commonly referred to as 'lawyer-linguists' or 'jurist-linguists' from the French *'juriste linguiste'*. The role is not to give legal advice on substantive matters, but primarily to check draft translated legal texts and ensure they fulfil the criteria of quality and being fit for service. The EU institutions employ lawyer-linguists as legal translators and revisers of court texts in the Court of Justice of the European Union and as legal-linguistic revisers of draft legislative texts in the European Parliament, Council, Commission and European Central Bank (Šarčević and Robertson 2013). We can take a look at the role of legal-linguistic revision, drawing on the EU legislative context.

Legal-linguistic revision

The lawyer-linguist performs a specialist role within an organisation that generates legal texts. While all legal texts when drafted need to be checked and revised, including in single-language systems, the concept of legal-linguistic revision is inherently multilingual: draft legal texts in different languages need to be checked against each other, compared, and made to converge and align with each other so as to convey the 'same' information and lead to the 'same' effects. That can be done by experts for all languages sitting down to read and compare each version and adjust them all together (Morgan 1982). That is feasible if all participants understand each language version, which implies a relatively small number of people. However, where many languages are involved, such as 24 in the EU at the time of writing, methods need to be different as it is not possible for everyone to know so many languages in sufficient detail, and it takes too long to read them all out individually. It is easier to select one version as a model, revise it as a final version and use it as the model with which all other languages are aligned, working as a team, in close contact, and meeting regularly with the subject matter experts familiar with the purpose and intentions of the draft text. In EU institutions, for example, legal-linguistic experts for each language check their draft texts against a source language model. On the one hand, they seek interventions in the model to correct errors and clarify meaning so as to assist with their particular language version, and on the other hand they all align their language versions together on the source language model. The individual language versions are then made ready for final adoption, signature and publication (Morgan 1982; Gallas 1999; Robertson 2010, 2013; Šarčević and Robertson 2013). A drafting and revision checklist for multilingual acts is set out in Appendix V for indicative purposes. It is based on EU acts and can be adapted as appropriate. Each organisation makes its own arrangements according to its needs.

174 *Translation and revision*

Summary

This short chapter has taken a look at the role of revision as a part of the translation process, has presented a reviser point of view and has suggested a range of revision tasks. It has placed emphasis on specialist legal-linguistic revision in an EU context. An indicative reviser's checklist for EU multilingual legislative texts is set out in Appendix V.

Notes

1 The reviser is assumed to be fully competent in all respects; where that may not be the case, see Martin (2012).
2 On quality, see among others: Pastor (2006), European Commission (2009), Council of the European Union (2011), Vuorinen (2011), Beaven (2014), Translation Centre for the Bodies of the European Union (2015). See also ISO quality standards, in particular ISO 9000.

Part VII
Back-up, support and training

12 Tools and technology

Introduction

Up until now attention has been directed at the tasks, activities, theories and contexts that form part of multilingual law. In the operational world of professional practice these shape the documents that are drafted, translated, revised and interpreted. However, for a professional these do not cover the whole picture. The newcomer is placed in an office in front of a computer and expected to perform. Yet performing means not only understanding the product or service to be delivered, it also means knowing the operational environment and the tools and technology that increasingly shape and influence the content of working life. All of this knowledge is acquired through prior education, vocational training, on-the-job experience, advice from colleagues and in-house and self training. This chapter takes a brief look at technology.[1] It does not form part of the concept of multilingual law as such, but it has become an essential component in the life of actors in the field of multilingual law.

To that end there will be a brief survey of some of the specialist roles in multilingual legal practice, and an indication as to some of the types of computer tools that are available and some of the uses that these are put to. The list is primarily indicative, with a few names mentioned by way of example. Each legal system has its own computer databases and programmes and they cannot all be mentioned here. It is sufficient here to be aware that such tools exist, so that one can search out for those which are of most relevance for the task in hand. As hitherto, an emphasis is placed on the EU context as the information is readily accessible in many languages through the Internet.

Technology viewpoint

Looking at things from a technology viewpoint means essentially paying attention to machines, what they can do and how they work. It is a philosophy of mechanisation. Machines can undertake repetitive tasks faster than humans; they may be expensive to buy, but they can work non-stop. That may reduce unit costs. Law and language are fields that are difficult to mechanise, but here too machines have made their entry to assist with specialised tasks. One of the factors of mechanisation is the involvement of persons devoted to maintenance of the machines. The legal and linguistic professionals know about their disciplines, but are probably not able to construct or repair their machines, or even know how they actually work. Thus dependency is created and mechanisation introduces new forms of collaboration between specialists. The management dimension becomes more significant.

Broadly, one can distinguish two categories of machine – analogue and digital – to take account of pre-and post-computer technology. For lawyers and linguists whose work is primarily mental, the former category leads one to think of such items as pens, paper, manuals and style guides, paper dictionaries of words, glossaries of terms, books of legislation, case reports, and such like. Typewriters and dictaphones, with an accompanying secretary, have in many cases become a thing of the past, but not everywhere. The contemporary age is of computers and information technology. Professionals are expected to be experts in using these machines and the relevant software programs, and to do the typing directly themselves. Many translators become expert in creating their own software. The secretary becomes a specialist in layout and formatting of different language versions. Computerised 'word processing' has become standard, using one of the proprietary brands. So have electronic messaging, emails and document transmission. It is possible to work simultaneously on a text in different parts of the world. There is no limit to the number of recipients of texts sent electronically. These are major benefits for multilingualism internationally.

Computer tools have proved their worth and are now essential tools for multilingual law. They offer many opportunities which have by no means been exhausted in their scope. A memory of past work and solutions, whether of drafting or translation, can be retained and incorporated for reuse each time the same issue arises. Standard texts and formulations can be created for all language versions in a multilingual environment and used systematically each time they are needed. They provide a means for reducing costs, speeding up and rendering ever more complex multilingual environments readily feasible. Yet the human beings in the system should not be overlooked or undervalued. Many lawyers and translators work very fast and with precision without machines, and the machine does not replace their cultural knowledge and intuitive skills. Machines break down and can be expensive to repair or replace, and they require a support team. Humans can spot errors. While machines can be programmed to detect errors, the human element always remains, whether as initiators of texts, authors, revisers, production managers or end-user/consumers. Adding more languages increases the task of coordination and places more pressure on negotiating and obtaining consensus among more participants, but from the point of view of language, it is like adding more production units in parallel to already existing modules. Databases can be extended. More recipients can be included in a distribution list for texts to be translated.

Tools and aids for specialists

We can take a quick tour through some of the types of tool available to different professionals. This list is indicative only. Each legal system has its own range of specialised tools, and they are being adapted all the time to specific tasks and needs.

Lawyers

Lawyers need to know the law, draft documents, plead in court, write opinions and decisions, advise clients and much more. They are assisted by styles, guides and precedents they develop for their own use, as well as by information made available by professional, public and private bodies. They need access to the texts of laws and case reports, as well as books expounding the law. They use manuals of styles and precedents for drafting, and computer-assisted drafting software.

Lawyers are aided in their activities by copies of laws and court cases, with lists and indexes of these arranged to facilitate researches. There are academic legal text books on most subject areas that expound, explain and give guidance. These are updated regularly, as law changes fast with the arrival of new laws and court decisions. Originally on paper, these sources of information have in many cases been computerised and are accessible through the Internet, often by subscription. UK laws, for example, can be accessed directly online[2] and UK court reports are available.[3] EU treaties and legislation can be accessed via the official website of the European Union[4] and EUR-Lex,[5] and reports of the Court of Justice of the European Union can be directly accessed via its website.[6] These are in addition to the paper versions of EU legislation published in the Official Journal of the European Union and European Court Reports. Private commercial websites also exist.

When it comes to drawing up legal texts, whether contracts or legislation, there are examples of past texts to follow as precedents and styles. There are also manuals and guides that set out standard paragraphs, words, expressions and layouts that appear regularly according to the type, or genre, of the act. Again, originally in paper, these have become computerised and electronic models are created for everyday use. In many cases these styles and precedents are not in the public domain but owned privately by their originators and users. Thus they cannot be accessed, and are in any case subject to copyright and authorship rules. In that respect the possibility to draw on EU sources is useful for the purposes of illustration and accessibility. Thus, for example, guidance on EU legislative drafting can be obtained from the Council's Manual of Precedents (2002), which is available on line (though not the latest version in use), as can other guidance on making EU laws such as the Interinstitutional Agreement of 22 December 1998 and the Joint Practical Guide (EU 2013). There is also general multilingual drafting guidance in the Interinstitutional Style Guide (EU 2015) in 24 languages for writing EU documents, also available online.[7]

A third type of tool is a computerised drafting tool where text is generated and formatted according to the type of act. There can be cues and reminders to assist a drafter to insert particular clauses. For a multilingual context, there can be linkages to other languages and the automatic generation of multilingual texts through machine-assisted translation. It becomes possible to generate text in more than one language, starting from any given language. The EU uses a multilingual system going under the name of Legiswrite.

Linguists, translators and revisers

Linguists study language in all its forms and work with it in many specific ways. They are the analysts of language and different languages. They compile lists of words and expressions used in a language (lexicology). They analyse and describe newly 'discovered' languages and devise written scripts for them. They study primarily the topics mentioned in Chapter 6. They use computer programs to assist them, for example to analyse the frequency with which words appear in texts. An example of such software is WordSmith Tools. These applications go beyond the everyday scope of multilingual law with which we are concerned here and where the emphasis is mainly on producing legal texts and interpreting them.

Linguists working with programmers have developed machine tools for translation. Machine translation generates a target language text by processing a source language text mechanically. It analyses and generates a target text based on the data inserted into the program. The quality of the product depends on the degree of development of the program. An example of this type of software is Systran.

An alternative form of automatically generated translation text derives from inserting translated texts into a computer program that 'memorises' them alongside the source texts used to create them. This is the 'translation memory' approach. Units of text are set up as equivalent. An example of this type of software is SDL Trados. The program searches its database for past texts that match the new source language text to be translated and generates a new target language text based on it. Translator memory programs retain the 'memory' of past blocks of translated text and compare new source texts against previous texts to generate new target language text. Translators use such programs routinely. However, one must ensure that it is the final revised and approved form of a text that is inserted into the memory and not earlier draft versions of it. If a target language text is subsequently revised by a reviser or a committee of experts, it must be the revised version that is entered into the memory; otherwise it will always be the unrevised form that is generated each time and will require correction yet again by a reviser.

Computer tools are of particular use when it comes to handling large volumes of information. For example, linguists analyse texts, often groups of texts, as a 'corpus' for the types of word used and occurrences of particular words such as 'shall', to see their frequency and make comparisons with other texts. In that way linguistic styles can be compared between different systems or cultures. This is one application of Wordsmith Tools. The resulting information can be relevant for teaching and training translators and drafters, as it allows one to explore language styles, registers and technical details.

A third type of tool for translators, as well as revisers, connects with the need to check and research terminology. Which words or terms are the most apt as equivalents between languages? Recourse can be had to dictionaries, whether monolingual or bilingual, and whether in paper or electronic form. In many cases these have been digitalised and placed on the web. Reference has been made to Oxford Dictionaries online word definitions in earlier chapters. Glossaries are more specialised terminology sources (see Chapter 6), and these too have moved from paper to digital format. Terminology databases provide a method to develop lists of terms adapted to one's own organisational and text context. The best-known EU terminology database is IATE (InterActive Terminology for Europe), which exists in an in-house form and in an external form available publicly on the Internet.[8]

With dictionaries and terminology databases there is a link to the work of other professionals. Lexicographers produce the dictionaries used by translators, as well as lawyers, and anyone seeking information on a word or its equivalent in another language in a bilingual dictionary. Terminologists produce glossaries used by translators. It is quite frequent for translators to work as terminologists, to research terms, update the databases and assist translator colleagues with problem terms and expressions.

A fourth category of tool consists in sources and texts that are referred to in a source language text and must also be referred to in the target language text. In a multilingual system, such as the EU, the target language changes the source references and quotations from source language format to the equivalent ones in target language format where they exist. So titles of a text cited are changed, say, from English in a source language text into French in a French target language text, and into German in a German target language text, and so on. That implies that the sources exist in each of the languages in parallel. The same approach applies to quotations. Thus where an EU act in English cites another EU act in English and quotes from it, the French translation cites the French title of the act and quotes from the French version of the text. In each case the texts must be accessed and passages identified and reproduced accurately. Databases, such as EUR-Lex for EU legal materials, are invaluable for undertaking such tasks. EUR-Lex provides a method to check terminology, as one can search a term in language A, identify its exact location and then switch to language B to find the same location in the text in context. This is useful for spotting neologisms such as *flexicurity* or *gender mainstreaming*, and especially for terms which may not yet have been entered into the databases but have already been used in an earlier text.

Fifth, and most important, translators need to know the subtle details and cultural associations behind texts and terms in source and target language. This is perhaps not a 'tool' as such, but it points to other types of tool as sources of information. It goes without saying that translators must know the languages in question, which means access to information on grammar, vocabulary, spelling, syntax, and so on, as they apply to each language. Information about 'false friends' is important; these are terms and expressions across languages that look the same or similar, but have different meanings. For such matters the terminology database may provide information, but if not, then the Internet can play a significant role here as it provides an increasing variety of search, information and translation tools. However, such sources need to be used with caution, and it is for that reason that terminologists insert a reliability rating alongside terms proposed in their databases. *Caveat traductor.*

Sixth, on a more specialised level linked to working methods of text production, there are databases such as EURAMIS,[9] a system that is 'is used to store and retrieve translation memories, i.e. segments from original documents with their translation and a set of metadata that includes the translator's login identification'.[10] One can also think of the workflow programs devised to record and track the flow of work at each stage of a document's progress from inception to dispatch. Modern word processing programs have many features that are useful in multilingual revision work, for example being able to see source and target texts side by side, using 'track-changes' and 'comments' functions, or 'document comparisons' so as to be able to follow text changes and compare apparently identical documents to locate potential divergences, which is useful when many versions of a text are floating around and one has lost track of which is which. These tools are all useful for team-working on an electronic text, and where a language version serves as the source for other language versions that need to be aligned on it and adjusted to each change made throughout the drafting process. However, spellcheck functions must be treated with care, because there are different conventions on spelling for languages in different legal systems and one must be sure the right convention is being applied (UK or American English, for example), and it must be applied consistently.

These observations are made from a 24-language viewpoint, such as the EU. It is probably the biggest producer of multilingual texts in the largest range of languages, and it is constantly developing its technological instruments. The European Commission DG Translation website is a useful source of information in that respect.[11] One particular area of programming that is important specifically for multilingualism concerns the ability to produce texts in every script and every alphabet in upper and lower cases, reproducing all the diacritical signs of each language, in all the possible variations. Each language needs its dedicated keyboards and software, but EU legal texts frequently have individual 'multilingual pages' and technical annexes in which text in all languages appear in all language versions. Examples of this are the signature formulae in international agreements, and lists of names and addresses of national ministries listed in annexes to legislative acts. These are reproduced in all language versions, so the software used for each language must be compatible with the software for all the other languages, which requires special programming skills.

Different scripts have letters that appear the same but represent different sounds or phonemes. For example, upper case 'P' in Roman script is different from 'P' in Cyrillic script used by Bulgarian (which is equivalent to letter R in Roman script). If the wrong code is used for the letter, surprises can happen when an upper case is changed to a lower case letter, or vice versa. Hidden out of sight behind a modern multilingual legal system, especially one as complex as that of the EU, there is a lot of technical expertise – not obvious but essential. Naturally, one needs to know how to use the plethora of tools and aids available. That is a matter of training and education and this has to be continuous.

Lawyer-linguists

For lawyer-linguists, whether as translators or revisers of legal texts, the tools used by lawyers and those used by translators potentially come into play depending on their role and particular problems encountered. This depends on whether the task is undertaken while texts are still in evolution or once they have become stabilised and nearly final. In the latter case, there may be no advantage in using the drafting or translation memory tools, and simply working on the draft final text using word processing technology with its searching, tracking, revising and comparing functions may be sufficient. On the other hand, a function that checks and alerts for specific term equivalences inserted in advance might be useful, as might functions that link up things like titles in different language versions, and so on. There is always scope to think up further refinements, if one has the time.

Summary

This brief chapter has taken a look at some of the tools and aids that form part of the 'baggage' of practitioners of multilingual law. Only a few items have been mentioned and everyone creates their own list, adapted to their needs and specific context. Different specialists require different tools. Some items for lawyers, linguists, translators and revisers have been touched on, taking the EU context by way of example. Other systems have different requirements. Appendix VIII includes a section on such matters.

We turn next to another dimension of multilingual law, one which underpins the purpose of this book. It concerns the training and education of future and current practitioners in multilingual law. This is another big topic, but the presentation is again very restricted, since it is ancillary to the theme of multilingual law. How topics are to be allocated and how much time is spent on each of them in education and training is a matter for the curriculum, and that is out of bounds here as the emphasis is on the practice and theory of law and language in a multilingual environment. Nonetheless, a few words are needed in order to include some questions in the framework in Appendix VIII.

Notes

1. Mention of products is subject to copyright and trade mark restrictions. Products are named as generic examples and no opinion is expressed beyond that.
2. Available at: www.legislation.gov.uk/.
3. See for example www.judiciary.gov.uk/judgments/.
4. See http://europa.eu.
5. Available at: http://eur-lex.europa.eu/.
6. See http://curia.europa.eu/.
7. Available at: http://publications.europa.eu/code/en/en-000100.htm.
8. Available at: http://iate.europa.eu/SearchByQueryLoad.do?method=load.
9. For information on EU Commission computer-assisted translation tools, see Vuorinen (2011).
10. Available at: http://ec.europa.eu/dpo-register/details.htm?id=35647.
11. Available at: http://ec.europa.eu/dgs/translation/index_en.htm.

13 Education and training

Introduction

Just as the concept of multilingual law from a practitioner view should embrace tools and technology, so also should the importance of education and training not be overlooked. One can have an excellent system of multilingual law on paper, but if there is no one trained to make it work, nothing will happen. In the preceding chapters we have been thinking about different activities and contexts that taken together underpin the concept of multilingual law. We have glimpsed the range and variety of specialist activity that is involved. So a few words on education and training will not come amiss here.

It seems self-evident that for each professional involved, whether lawyer or linguist, administrator or expert, a deep and extensive education is the first foundation. It is an education in which instruction in languages features prominently. On top of that comes specialised vocational training to equip the professional for the particular tasks to be performed. There are many issues that are specific to the multilingual context that are connected to the topics of the previous chapters. In that respect this book can be seen as a training manual, a handbook and an introduction to those fields, and to multilingual legal work generally. It is hoped it can also serve as an ongoing source of reference and ideas. This chapter is short and its purpose is simply to draw attention to a number of training areas and invite reflection.

Appendix VII sets out a range of background training questions on law and legal language.

Training viewpoint

From the point of view of training with respect to multilingual law, we can think in terms of legal skills, language skills, translation skills, terminology skills and legal-linguistic skills, as well as administration and diplomatic skills for the negotiation processes. These are foundation areas. Typically, lawyers place attention on the study of laws and case reports, but the language side of multilingual law is also important: styles of language in use and how meanings are created in multilingual systems – a branch of legal linguistics. To those we can add knowledge and skills connected to computers and information technology. Lastly we should mention research skills, for an important dimension to the study of multilingual law should be to extend scientific knowledge about specialist language as a part of applied linguistics and legal-linguistics. Researchers study language as it occurs as a phenomenon. Their insights are important for practitioners, but it is equally important that practitioners explain to researchers their methods and reasons for the linguistic choices they make. To encourage this process of collaboration Appendix VI entitled 'Making a Presentation or Writing a Paper on Multilingual Legal Language' proposes guidance to practitioners to encourage them to take a first step, time permitting, towards making a legal-linguistic research paper.

Within each of the broad categories of professional skill lie subdomains, for example legal skills in drafting of legislative texts or private commercial contracts. The environment for the exercise of these skills may be one of national law, international law or supranational EU law. Further, it may be within a branch of civil law or criminal law, private law or public law, and specialised according to the particular branch or activity therein. For each area in a multilingual context there is a drafting dimension, but there is also translation, interpretation and terminology, as well as the tools, aids and technology to be learned.

Language skills are an important part of the picture. High levels of knowledge of source and target languages, and other languages, are required. It is not sufficient just to have knowledge of general language, as knowledge of specialised legal concepts, terminology and syntax is also necessary, according to the particular domain. Terminology looms large in specialised fields and there is a need to be familiar with the technology and databases that assist in translation and term extraction. Lastly, cultural dimensions behind each language need to be understood in order to be able to ensure a minimum basis for mutual comprehension that is the foundation for building multilingual legal systems.

What sort of training is needed and how does one proceed? These are practical questions and they find their answers in terms of the identity of the students and the tasks they will be expected to undertake. Are they lawyers requiring language skills? If so, then the emphasis is placed on languages and linguistic methods, such as linguistic analysis, translation and terminology. Are they linguists seeking legal knowledge and skills? Then the focus is on law, legal concepts and legal method. The earlier chapters of this book cover themes for both strands to explore concepts necessary to handle multilingual law.

Characteristically, training is for an end, a purpose, and there is generally a professional activity in mind, whether it be lawyer, interpreter, translator, legal-linguistic reviser, and so on. For such posts there are requirements and necessary qualifications, an interview and perhaps a competition, as is traditionally the case for posts to be an EU official.[1] These qualifications and requirements set the levels of knowledge to be achieved and the training is organised so as to enable the student to meet the level and succeed. For EU-related posts requiring the passing of a competition, a careful study of the notice of competition or invitation to apply is necessary and careful preparation in anticipation of the requirements and the tasks to be performed is essential.

While it is desirable to know information, it is equally desirable to know where to find it and also how to use what has been found. Having a broad picture of the whole field helps in solving problems and organising the information at one's disposal. For example, 'nominal clusters' or 'verb phrases': how do these fit into legal drafting or multilingual text interpretation? What significance do 'density' and 'cohesion' have for multilingual legal texts? What does 'intertextuality' amount to in practice? To assist in reflecting on topics raised in this book, Appendix VII poses a set of training questions on law and legal language. They build on but also extend the ideas and concepts raised in the chapters.

Specialist knowledge and skills

There is little more to add here of a generic nature. To go further means entering a specific training context: the students, their background, their needs and interests, the amount of time available, methods of communication, language(s) of communication, and so on. For training in multilingual law we can note some of the types of skills involved.

Legal skills

Legal skills are those of the lawyer: legal knowledge of relevant systems, knowing how to undertake legal analysis, knowing where to find the law; drafting skills, adapted to type of text; advocacy skills, adapted to type of court case; judicial skills for lawyers who become judges; lawyer/client skills (and accountancy skills) for those in private or commercial practice. Also included is an awareness of the legal culture and unwritten cultural codes of conduct and ways of thinking that abound everywhere.

Language skills

Everyone requires language skills. It is just that in a multilingual context these skills are of central importance to the field of activity and are much more developed, insofar as they appertain to more than one language. While mother-tongue skills are learned early on in the education system, second and third (and more) languages tend to be learned later on, sometimes late in life. The skills cover among others: spelling, grammar and syntax; vocabulary and terminology; using dictionaries, glossaries and thesauruses; drafting; interpreting; speaking; listening. Broad cultural knowledge is also important for each of the languages involved.

Translation skills

Translation skills cover language skills, but also specialist skills. For legal translation they include knowing: the source language and culture; the source language legal system, terms, concepts and culture; the target language and culture; the target language legal system and terms, concepts and culture. They also require awareness of international and supranational law and their concepts and the way in which legal rules handle system boundaries. They also include knowing how to find legal and non-legal information and handle terminology, being aware of the ways in which terms take on different meanings in different contexts. Good style and techniques are learned though practice.

Terminology skills

It is useful to learn how terminologists work, what they do and how they do it. This increases sensitivity to nuances and the way words shift meaning in context. However, it also serves as an introduction to the products of terminologists: glossaries and databases and individual terms. By understanding how these are produced, they can be used more efficiently and, importantly, one learns how to propose new terms and expressions for insertion into them, thereby enlarging the language as well as the databases for all users. This is of particular relevance for 'smaller' languages that are building up their vocabulary range. The ways in which new terms are created is also useful information, as is developing sensitivity when existing terms are used in new or unusual contexts and when it is necessary to create new terms from scratch, whether through borrowing, constructing from indigenous roots, or otherwise. An introduction to semiotics can be included under the heading of terminology, as terminology work is heavily semiotic by nature.

Information technology skills

The range of tools and aids mentioned in Chapter 12 form part of professional life and would also be included in a training programme, in particular with respect to legal and translator tools. Linguistic tools of language researchers used for analysing texts and utterances are probably too specialised for general purposes, but that depends on the task in hand.

Legal-linguistic revision skills

We can assimilate 'revision' skills to those of translators, but mark out the activity of legal-linguistic revision by the legally trained lawyer or lawyer-linguist engaged in legal translation, multilingual drafting or revision. Here the essential skill base is legal, plus language, plus translation skills. There is an emphasis on legal texts and on legal drafting across languages. Within the multilingual context, there is likely to be a team approach and the cultural dimension and ability to work in a multicultural environment are important.

Research skills

Research takes many forms. There is the immediate and *ad hoc* research of terms and concepts for a translation, or legal research comparing concepts and systems for methods and solutions as part of comparative law. There is linguistic research into the way language is used, whether through density, length of sentences, use of nominal or verb phrases, or analysing the frequency of occurrence of particular words, such as the English 'shall'. The research may be limited to a single language and perhaps cover different legal systems using the same language, or it may relate to several languages, seeing how the same concepts are rendered, how the same effects are achieved, typical translation strategies for types of phrase or sentence, and so on. This type of work is relevant to the implementation of international or supranational texts in national legal systems and comparing the results.

A subjective impression is that most published legal-language research seems to take place in a monolingual context, except for comparative law, and there seems to be a general lack of research into multilingual legal language, except in a context of translation, terminology and secondary term formation, where it is a constant activity. Perhaps it is seen primarily as part of translation studies. It is certainly the case that if one is not exposed to multilingual law and multilingual texts, it is difficult to make researches into those fields. Further, to pursue such research, a knowledge of languages is essential, as well as sufficient linguistic theory for the purposes. Nonetheless, the view offered here is that there is a need for more multilingual research and that this need is strengthened first by the trend towards globalisation, and second by the dwindling and dying of smaller languages. In the first context there is increasing use of major languages such as English by non-native speakers as second language and lingua franca. In the second context there is an urgent need to find ways of maintaining weaker and dying languages at a sustainable level, which can only be done effectively by ensuring them a degree of recognition and support.

The EU multilingual legal system operating in 24 languages provides excellent opportunities for many types of legal-linguistic research, because virtually everything can be accessed through the Internet free of charge in the official languages. When a new state accedes to the EU, extensive research is required in order to prepare for its accession. As well as the necessary political, economic and legal adaptations, part of the work involves linguistic research, notably on concepts and terminology, to prepare the way for translation and the creation of EU legal texts in the new language. The existing *acquis* must be translated, and that involves many thousands of pages of text and the creation of hundreds of new terms – quite a daunting task. In addition, new teams of specialists must be trained in preparation for taking on the everyday work of supporting the language in the future.

Specialist literatures

We come now to one of the reasons for writing this book. Multilingual law is a realm for specialists, yet there is no 'overview' of the field and the specialist literatures in each domain are largely inaccessible to specialists in other domains. First, there is little wider awareness of what exists. Second, there is little wider awareness of where or how to find and access it. Third, there is widespread unfamiliarity with the concepts, approaches, aims and ambitions of the literature. Fourth, it takes time to read and assimilate it. Fifth, it is frequently not evident what use can be made of the information for one's own specialisation. The barriers are real and it is only through attempting summaries and syntheses that they can be lowered and overcome. It is with that idea in mind that the concept of a framework to analyse multilingual law has been devised and separate treatment given to many discrete topics which come into contact within the concept. How can we find ways to make accessible and bring to a wider audience the vast extent of research findings that have already been undertaken and which have a message for the everyday practice of multilingual law?

The solution offered here has been to organise the threads in such a way that they come together as elements of a larger picture. The umbrella concept is 'multilingual law'. This is the unifying concept. It is a term and a sign. Thus everything is placed within a semiotic context. This approach opens the door to placing any information alongside any other information to see what emerges. It is neutral and relatively objective, but nonetheless remains subjective in view of the mental element believed to be inherent in the approach of viewpoints. The key principal is not to argue that any viewpoint is 'right' or 'wrong', but just that there are different ways of looking at the same information and making choices. Here is one point of view and here are others. Yet regardless of the viewpoint, one can draw attention to a range of matters that require attention when thinking about, studying, analysing and seeking to understand multilingual law in its diverse forms. The framework provides an organising tool and the next step is to use it, test it and adapt it in the light of experience. For that, however, we must draw a pause and assign the task to another place. Each system in its language environment needs to be thought about separately and individually. If the appendices at the end of this book can serve as such a starting point for enquiry, and if they can assist in training and research, then their purpose is served.

Summary

This short chapter has served to draw attention to the need for education and vocational training of the professionals who are to carry on the tasks involved in maintaining a multilingual legal system. Attention has also been drawn to the existence of a wide diversity of specialist literature that needs to be made more accessible to practitioners in multilingual law, so that they can benefit from the findings. There is a need for intermediaries between the practitioner and academic worlds, who must be capable of transmitting information in each direction. The framework concept in this book aims to serve these purposes and the appendices have been inserted to be used, tested, developed and adapted in the light of experience. In the next chapter we will turn attention to an outline of the elements of the proposed framework. It takes the form of appendices, but the principle expression is in Appendix VIII.

Note

1 See http://europa.eu/epso/apply/jobs/index_en.htm.

Part VIII
Framework, models and applications

14 Framework for analysis and understanding

Introduction

This chapter introduces the appendices at the end of this book. Each one has been mentioned in the course of the chapters. Each has a purpose and is intended as a technical summary of specialist issues. Links to the chapters are indicated in the notes at the end of each appendix. The first seven appendices are thematic, by which is meant that they are restricted to a particular dimension. The framework that is the objective of this book is set out in Appendix VIII. It aims at a coverage of the whole range of topics raised. It has been drawn up so as to incorporate the preceding annexes within it by reference, but it aims at a structured overview of multilingual law, subject to certain limitations mentioned in this chapter in connection with it.

How can the appendices be used? This question is addressed in the latter part of this chapter. The appendices can be seen as containing points that can be turned into questions to ask, so as to elicit information about any given system, organisation or text under investigation. It is a form of legal-linguistic profiling. The appendices aim at making legal-linguistic profiles though such questions and this information may help in clarifying the drafting, translation, interpretation and terminological contexts. Many of the ideas in this book have been tested in presentations and articles published and included in the bibliography. The approach is rooted in practitioner experience as lawyer and linguist over many years. Each appendix is conceptual, experimental and offered on the basis that it reflects 'work in progress', to be revised and adapted in the light of experience.

Yet perhaps one should ask why the framework takes the shape of appendices? Are there alternative ways to summarise the information? The concept of framework somehow implies making a set of reference points, creating a structure within which to organise information. In the course of preparing this book, each appendix emerged spontaneously as providing a practical method to condense a lot of information: easier to see at a glance and saving much ink. Some, like Appendix I, have too much implied content to be able to produce in full and have been left open; others have been developed in more detail. As they emerged, the appendices started to look like an internal network with links between them: meta-law and language pointers to a larger picture. Each appendix takes the form of lists as a shorthand summary. Each topic could be elucidated further at length, but how long would that take? Each item thus becomes an entry point for exploration. Each is a sign and a doorway to further information.

The underlying message is probably that one needs to pay attention to a variety of levels simultaneously. The daily work of a practitioner is at the 'microscopic' level, but one needs to be able to see how the task in hand fits within a progression of widening and broadening spheres of activity until one arises at the overarching concept and entry point: the concept of 'multilingual law'. If one can see the patterns at each level, then one is in a position to identify any field requiring attention and work downwards or upwards to the requisite level of detail in order to tackle whatever issue is at hand. The appendices are designed to assist in such an approach, since they are in essence pragmatic. The focus is on the 'what?', sometimes on the 'how?' or the 'which?', but rarely on the 'when?' or the 'where?'. Likewise 'who?' does not figure prominently and nor does 'why?'. Nonetheless, these latter are also questions to ask. By attaching the 'wh-?' questions to each entry in each appendix, the power of the appendix can be multiplied as a research tool. The abstract lists of theory become practical tools of enquiry as questions to ask in respect of a system under inquiry. So through the appendices, this book takes on the form of a technical manual. Perhaps a disclaimer of lack of responsibility for defects encountered should be entered at this stage.

States, languages and official languages (Appendix I)

Chapter 1 reflected among other things on the extent of multilingualism in the legal systems around the world. The question was raised as to how many countries have multilingual legal systems and it was suggested that one could make an analysis taking information *inter alia* from United Nations, as well as national, sources. The task is too big to envisage here, but the appendix has been inserted as a token to mark the potential utility of making such a table as part of a study of multilingual law. If the information is linked to the other appendices, one could build up a range of complex legal-linguistic models for the world's systems of law. The viewpoint in Appendix I is on states and state-created organisations, but the range could be extended. One is aware of the significance and role of multinational corporations and their legal-linguistic dimensions. They follow different patterns and have been placed in the background for the purposes of this book, but one could use the concepts in the appendices to make legal-linguistic profiles of them also.

Legal-linguistic models (Appendix II)

Appendix II contains a list of types of multilingual legal arrangement, seen as legal-linguistic models based on the concepts of 'legal order' and 'legal system', discussed in Chapter 3. However, the range has been extended to include other variants relating to business or religious organisations, as a token recognition of their importance and as a point of departure for research. Appendix II has been structured in terms of models, with variants being proposed in terms of status or level within the scheme, together with the number of official languages. That generates a set of law/language matrices as alternatives for each model. The appendix has been kept simple conceptually. Non-official languages could be added in each case to extend its scope.

Searching for rules, practice and guidance on language(s), drafting and interpretation (Appendix III)

Appendix III addresses the situation that unless one has extensive legal knowledge and training, one may have little idea where to find certain types of legal information. The appendix is oriented to searching for rules on language and languages, and where to look for them. A set of suggested places to look is proposed. It is not exhaustive, but merely indicative. Each of them can be seen as a source for a 'corpus' of texts for linguistic study. Equivalent texts from equivalent sources in different systems may be studied on a comparative basis.

Classifying languages by use and status (Appendix IV)

Appendix IV is directed at the status of languages. It sets out a method for classifying languages according to the extent of their use and status in terms of whether or not they are officially recognised for use in a legal system or legal order. It differs from the Ethnologue classification, as the function envisaged is essentially legal. The aim is to provide not only an approximate tool for comparisons, but also a pointer to the probable terminological range of a language, on the view that it increases up the scale. Becoming a 'universal' legal language implies being able to cover any policy domain in legal discourse and having the terminology to do so. The appendix can be used to explore different scenarios and combinations. Appendix IV links to the European Charter for Regional or Minority Languages and the guidance from it that can assist in language policy and language planning for smaller languages.

Drafting and revision checklist for multilingual acts (Appendix V)

Appendix V proposes a checklist for an EU legislative context. It is included to demonstrate a range of specific matters that have to be addressed in multilingual drafting and legal-linguistic revision. Some issues are valid for all types of legal text such as checking that the official guidance is followed, but others are context-specific and variable. In so far as a given operational environment is different, the detailed entries fall to be changed and adapted. In that respect the appendix is for illustration. It reflects an approach of looking at legal texts from different viewpoints: legal, linguistic, policy and action. It is part of quality control.

Making a presentation or writing a paper on multilingual legal language (Appendix VI)

More research is needed into multilingual legal language in different fields and languages. Many practitioners lack time and knowledge to undertake legal-linguistic research work. For those who find the time and energy and do not have access to expert guidance, Appendix VI is intended to provide some ideas as to how to start. It is subject to expert academic guidance in each case.

Training questions on law and legal language (Appendix VII)

Appendix VII sets out a range of questions about law and legal language. While very general, they may provide some ideas for practical teaching and training in multilingual law and language. The list can readily be extended. There are not necessarily any 'right' answers, just different points of view. The appendix can be extended by translating the questions into any language (representing a system or culture) and comparing the answers. Or one can pose the questions from the perspectives of different legal systems that use (say) English as their legal language and see if the answers match.

196 Framework, models and applications

Framework for analysis and understanding (Appendix VIII)

Appendix VIII delivers what this book promises: a framework for understanding and analysis. There is no suggestion that law and language should be thought about in particular ways in a moral or ethical sense. The framework comprises a list of topics that have a relationship to law and language and, in particular, multilingual law. The term 'framework' may not be the best, but it conveys the idea of a patterning and organising of information in a structured way. Appendix VIII represents the heart of the book, and its culmination. The elements are drawn from the preceding chapters and they are listed in summary form. Each topic is a point of entry, a window or doorway to further exploration, for example through asking questions – what? why? who? when? where? which? and how? – in the context of specific systems and situations. The topics are an *aide-mémoire* for selecting questions to ask.

Appendix VIII is structured in parts which are arranged so as to move focus from general questions relating to the legal system towards particular details. The sequence of headings reflects the concept of viewpoints in the order: legal, linguistic, terminological, individual text, interpretation and meaning, and translation, followed by tools, aids and technology, education and training. The topics are linked to functional activities, but they can be recombined in any sequence wished. While a semiotic view underpins the whole framework, it has not been felt necessary to make this explicit.

Appendix VIII closes with three broad topics relating to links with other systems and contexts, particular problems and solutions and research. These are short open-ended entries inserted with an eye to ongoing studies into multilingual legal systems and sharing information on the most practical methods for handling the numerous questions and problems that arise. They are left open as a stimulus to additional reflection within specific contexts. As the approach of the appendix is generic, some parts clearly do not apply to all systems of law, so it is a case of identifying what is relevant and excluding what is not. In that sense, one can think of the appendix as being like a questionnaire and use it to create legal-linguistic profiles of systems or organisations. We will now comment on the individual parts.

Part A: General legal context and procedures

Part A places the study within a legal context and draws attention to the overall type of system and its rules governing languages. It is the macro-context in which the details find their place. Part A proposes an outline of general organisation in terms of the main institutions that are in place for law-making, notably legislative, judicial, executive and administrative. That said, the main emphasis is on the first two.

Part A also keeps in mind the 'private' side of law, where persons make use of the law to enter into private contracts and agreements. This is connected to the concept of contract law. Within national legal contexts the multilingual implications are likely to be limited or even zero where contracts are drawn up solely in one language, and there is no need for translation. However, as contracts are important multilingually in international law, a reference to them needs to be maintained. To that one can add that there are international organisations that are not governmental which also function in a variety of languages. While not strictly speaking law-making bodies, they frequently play an important role in law-making and constitute an important part of the international scene. Similar considerations apply to multinational businesses. They are not directly addressed in the framework, but these methods can also be applied to them. Part A links to Appendices I and II.

Part B: Types of legal text

Part B remains within a legal perspective and shifts a step towards detail. One remains in an organisational context, but the centre of attention is the type of text as an aspect of genre. Attention is placed on three kinds of text: legislative, judicial/court and contracts/agreements. That said, it has been found useful to draw attention to contexts where there is no text in a formal sense. This may seem odd, but the purpose is to provide space for customs, practices and habits where particular approaches are followed, perhaps because seemingly self-evident and never challenged. If everybody knows only the same language in a community, it is unlikely that there will be a need for a specific rule on the subject of language. We can draw attention to this reality and ask whether it is a matter of habit and convenience, or stronger, amounting to a custom-based rule.

Part B is also concerned with organisation, identifying roles and institutions and bodies which fulfil them, as well as methods and procedures used to produce legal texts. The aim is an overview, so it covers languages used, types of text, the role of translation and the end-uses of texts produced. It gives a picture of the operational context in which multilingual legal texts are produced and used.

Part C: Linguistic regime and language(s)

After establishing the broad legal context, the focus shifts to linguistic issues. The idea in Part C is again to start from a broad overall context and gradually shift focus to increasingly specific topics, so relationships between the macro and micro levels become more evident. There is overlap with earlier topics from the legal view, which is to be expected, but from a starting point in language. It provides a form of check, since if the information derived from the legal view and the linguistic view is complementary, that reinforces their validity; whereas if a different result emerges, there is something requiring attention. Taking that approach, the first area of attention concerns the broad linguistic background of the people and society to whom a system or order applies. The focus is geographical, in terms of an area of territory, rather than legal, but it enables an impression to be formed as to the 'linguistic efficiency' of a system in terms of the coverage of a population. It can be extended to include bilinguals, trilinguals and second-language speakers as appropriate.

The next topic is to classify the languages used on the territory, using the table in Appendix IV. Here the languages are sorted into categories. Those which lie below Level 6 in the table fall outwith the scope since they are not formally languages of the law, but that does not mean that the legal system ignores them completely; for example, interpretation of oral evidence in a court case may be needed. Should it be desired to raise the status of a language to Level 6 or higher, then Appendix VIII, in conjunction with the other appendices, provides material for reflection, taken with the guidance in the European Charter for Regional or Minority Languages, and other sources.

We next move into technical legal domains within linguistic topics. First, the linguistic regime falls to be made specific: number of official languages, classification status, features of each language in terms of terminology range, standardisation, use in other legal systems, and so on. It should be noted that there is an implicit linkage to legal order and type of model, since if it is in international law or supranational law, the terminology and standardisation levels will be at the highest levels. The problems come at transition stages, when a language shifts to a higher level of classification and must be adapted. For example, when a new state accedes to the European Union and brings an additional language, that language moves to a higher classification status and requires to be adapted to the new context. Thus the items listed are not absolute, but relative to the context being considered.

The remaining items in Part C are connected to specific contexts in which legal texts are created: legislative, court, contracts, and so on. Space is left for other types of legal text. The focus of the framework is targeted on the first three genres, but there are other specialised forms and these can be analysed linguistically in similar ways. It will be noted that there are two headings for courts. One takes account of the internal organisation linguistically of the court; the other takes account of the languages of procedure of court cases and the languages of court judgments and judicial decisions, as there may be variation. The framework introduces different categories according to the numbers of languages: one, two, three or more in which legal texts are created.

As regards the preparatory phases of texts, in particular legislative texts, eight phases are identified. The reason for this is to make it possible to identify the stages where different languages may be used for text production. For example, in a given system there may be only one language that is used for policy discussions, but the final text may be produced in several languages, through translation. These questions allow more refined questions of method to be assessed and provide a starting point for analysing different contexts.

Part D: Terminology issues

Part D shifts the point of view to terminology. Languages are identified and the terminological picture of each of them clarified by thinking about their terminological range and domains. Are all domains covered? Are there weaknesses or gaps and if so how are these filled? Is there terminological coherence and consistency? These issues arise especially for languages which are at a lower level in the classification table and where they are being developed and expanded towards a higher level.

The framework is not all-embracing from a terminologist's point of view, but draws attention to certain matters such as methods for creating new terms. Frequently these arise spontaneously in a language in the everyday discourse of society; lexicologists collect the words, analyse them for meanings through examples of usage and record them in dictionaries. Terminologists study them, insert them in glossaries, analyse concepts and search for or create terms in other languages. There are entries to draw attention to glossaries, dictionaries, term banks and databases, terminology bodies, international organisations, ISO standards, and so on.

Part E: Text Issues

Part E places attention on text issues. There is a difference from Part B. There the emphasis is on type of text, or genre, whereas in Part E we enter into the text itself. First, there is the language(s) of the particular text. Second, we identify its type or genre, whether legal or non-legal. A third topic inserted concerns essentially the legal culture or type of system. As each text exists in a context, and legal texts in a legal context, one needs to ask questions about that context. In direct terms there is the internal organisation, structure and linkage of words, terms and concepts within a system, but each legal system tends to exist within a higher level, broader and more diffuse environment. Legal systems are 'system bound', but there are families of system, such as common law systems and civil law systems. Identifying this 'family' level assists in term analysis and in comparisons with other systems, and there are subdivisions within each family as well. Thus civil law has variants in French law, German law and Scandinavian legal systems.

Starting with type of text (legislative, judicial, contract), the genre of a text can be further refined into the branch or policy area (domain) of which it forms part. Within these criteria, one can become more specific in terms of the type of legislative text, court text or contract out of a range of possibilities. We enter the practical world of law and the terrain of style guides and manuals of precedents.

The remaining topics under Part E list further questions that can be asked in connection with individual texts. Comparisons can be made across languages in respect of texts. However, it is when one compares style guides, manuals of precedents, names of acts, drafting guidance and the detailed nuts and bolts of text preparation and interpretation between and across languages that one is confronted with the detailed implications of multilingualism and the multilingual legal context. It means analysing the legal and linguistic (and other) implications and making choices. Sometimes what counts is not so much the particular choice of solution but devising a method by which to arrive at the choice, and doing so in an impartial and methodical way.[1] By having a series of questions that can be asked, the processes can be assisted, since attention is drawn to them and an opportunity given to weigh the relative value.

Part E includes the topic of meaning in the context of text creation, because drafters create meaning through language and text and need to reflect carefully on the meanings, and actions, intended. Four viewpoints in that connection are included: action, policy, law and language.

Part F: Meaning, interpretation and reading

In the preceding parts of Appendix VIII, the emphasis is rather from the side of the whole system and text creation. But multilingual legal texts are made to be used and applied, so the user and reader viewpoints count. In a multilingual system the user is confronted by different language versions and must decide which to use. For a speaker of one language, the choice is self-evident: it is the language version they can read. For a speaker of several languages, the choice is wider. The monoglot understands one language version; the legal environment becomes monolingual. The polyglot can compare language versions, and the task of drafter, translator and reviser is to optimise the 'identicalness' of meaning between language versions so that legal certainty and predictability is maintained, regardless of the language version of the legal text consulted. Thus equivalence of treatment and legal equality as citizens are maintained regardless of language. That is the theory and the aim of multilingual law in a democratic society. It requires constant effort and attention.

Part F suggests some items that appear relevant from the viewpoint of the reader and for ascertaining meaning. It helps to have an overview. However, it is recalled that the interpretation or 'construction' of legal meaning may be based on 'intention', alongside non-linguistic matters such as behaviour as an indicator, or sign, of intention. Intention looks beyond language to actions and behaviour, so to that extent we step outside language, multilingualism and the context of this study.

200 *Framework, models and applications*

Part G: Translation issues

Part G deals with issues of translation. It is only at this late stage that we come to translation. That may seem odd, since translation lies at the heart of multilingual activity. Yet, if one recalls the discussion in Chapter 10 on the transfer of meaning across languages, one is reminded that in order to translate, a translator must have a good knowledge about as much as possible relating to the source text and its environment of creation, and the environment in which the target text is being created and the possible effects that it may entail. The translator is like the Greek hero Atlas, who held the world on his shoulders; the translator is not holding the physical mass of the world, but is holding in his or her head two worlds: the world as imagined in the source language and the world as imagined in the target language. So, before translating, one has to have knowledge of these two 'conceptual worlds', and that is why translation comes towards the end of the framework, after the mental images of the conceptual worlds have been stimulated.

In Part G a few topics are proposed as a starting point. Translation is an *ad hoc* activity. There are theories and approaches, but legal translation is perhaps ultimately driven by non-theoretical issues. What counts for legal texts are the effects, behaviour and intentions, and these go beyond language. The language of target text is aligned on source text and takes into account these non-linguistic factors.

Part H: Databases, Tools and Technology

Part H focuses on the technology side of multilingual law and the preparation of multilingual texts. There are legal tools and linguistic tools and aids. There are aids for drafting and for translation and terminology. The background is of traditional tools based on paper and ink – analogue tools – but it is the modern computer-based digital tools which offer most assistance for multilingual law and legal systems. They facilitate and enhance, while at the same time complicating life through their degree of detail and the need to know and understand each piece of software – what it can do, what it cannot, its tricks and traps – and hope that there is no crash or power failure. The systems are wonderful so long as they work; and when they stop working, so does everyone.

Part I: Education and training

Part I draws attention to education and training. Experts in multilingual law need training in law, languages and linguistics, as well as in terminology and translation.

Part J: Links with other systems

The function of Part J is to draw attention to the network, or matrix, of links and connections between legal systems and orders and language. None of them exist in isolation.

Part K: Particular problems and solutions

Part K is intended as a place for noting special 'bugbears' or items that create special difficulties, and the solutions found. The *ad hoc* nature of text production and translation, combined with an environment driven by costs and production needs, can obscure the value of preserving a memory of what has been done, problems and solutions. The development of style guides and manuals of precedents is of great assistance in that respect, but one also needs more discursive information. This book has been created with such considerations in mind. It is a first version, and like all first versions it is eminently perfectible. Time, and the reader, will tell how.

Part L: Research

Part L refers to research. This book is a piece of research, conceptual in its orientation, and its function is to contribute towards a better understanding of multilingual law and thereby enhance the rule of law and the ability of citizens to exercise their human rights, as well as undertake their obligations, through being able to do so in a language they understand. The Framework can be used to analyse legal systems and make legal-linguistic profiles along a standardised model, which is helpful for making comparisons.

Part M: *Miscellaneous*

Part M serves the purpose of a catch-all entry for anything overlooked. One should not expect anything else from the canny lawyer – there is always something that has been overlooked. This entry is for such items, and later on they can be inserted into the Framework, which can be further developed. The Framework is a semiotic act and part of the process of semiosis. The cycle of semiosis means that there is creation, interpretation and action, and these lead to further extension through another act of creation. In that respect the next step is to consider how to apply the information in the appendices to real-life situations.

The appendices as tools of enquiry

If space permitted, we should now proceed to analyse individual systems of law. We would expand Appendix I and use the information obtained to develop Appendix II. We would take each model and list individual systems and organisations. We would become aware that there would be a need to make comments, add qualifications and adaptations, as systems are complex and have incidental details that vary. In preparing this book, the idea of expanding Appendix II into a classification of existing systems was explored, but it rapidly took on the shape of an exploding nebula. Accordingly, it seems preferable to proceed on the basis of one system at a time.

Summary

This chapter has introduced the appendices and explored how they could be used as a tool of analysis and understanding. It represents work in progress.

Note

1 Such as the order in which to list countries or languages.

15 Multilingual law

Introduction

In Chapter 1 we set out to make a legal-linguistic analysis of the concept of multilingual law. We started with a linguistic observation about the term comprising two dimensions: law and language. We used that observation to make an enquiry about law and legal language seen from the viewpoint of law, and then made an analogous enquiry about legal language from the perspective of language. We extracted ideas and concepts, and used them to produce lists of topics organised in what seemed useful ways, capable of being used as starting points to analyse and construct deeper levels of implication of the concept of multilingual law. We labelled this exercise a 'framework for enquiry and analysis'.

As we progressed along the path of enquiry, ever more viewpoints emerged and we entered into ever-larger circles of complexity. Each of those could be taken as a focus of attention for some particular problem at hand. That led to broadening the scope to think of law and language in terms of signs conveying meanings, and this approach provided assistance for reflecting on terminology, translation and revision of multilingual legal texts. For completeness from a practical point of view, it was felt desirable also to make mention of some of the factors that fill the daily lives of practitioners and enable them to function, such as the supporting roles of tools, aids and technology, and the vital need to educate and train. What began small became increasingly large, complex and difficult to handle. Indeed, this hyper-complexity has been a formidable obstacle in writing this book, incomplete as it is.

To tackle the complexities, we sought to simplify and have recourse to models to make it easier to navigate through the information. However, while models are fine for theory, law is above all pragmatic and linked and adapted to everyday experience and reality. So methods are needed that go beyond theory to find ways to apply, and test, in operational reality. The framework put forward in Appendix VIII and the preceding appendices all serve that end, but they all stand at the threshold of application. Like the swimmer at the edge of the pool, the next step is to dive in and get wet. But which pool to choose? Up to now we have been describing generalities and variants on themes relating to multilingual law, but to move forward, we pick a system, dive in and immerse ourselves in its details. In so doing, however, we depart from the conceptual level of multilingual law. We focus on and analyse specific details of the selected system. We risk losing our way, or becoming engrossed in details. Yet, if we keep in mind the framework and the ideas set out in the appendices, we can use them as a guide and orientation to make a legal-linguistic profile of the system we have chosen to study. Further, we can use them to study organisations and institutions that exist within and as part of wider systems. This book has reached its conclusion and it remains to draw together a few threads and put forward a few observations that seem to permeate the field of study.

The aim throughout has been to draw a broad picture of the many dimensions to multilingual law within a unifying structure, but it has not been possible to explore everything. Thus, for example, the political dimension has been deliberately avoided. Each community has its own political environment, it is always complex and the issues are always deep and embedded in history and perceptions. The aim here has been to focus on questions of method and technique, and in so doing to enhance awareness of the range of alternative approaches and some of the implications. Likewise, there has been little discussion of policy fields. Those areas mentioned, such as contract law, have been mentioned because they themselves form an integral part of multilingual law. An organisation such as the European Union exists because states entered into contracts to bring it into being, and its continued existence is equally based on contract. In addition, no attempt has been made to give a full, detailed description of any particular multilingual legal system. EU experience has been heavily drawn on, as the sources of information are readily accessible in many languages in equivalent form. Less attention has been paid to other multilingual legal systems than they merit, and most have received no attention at all; similarly with languages. This has been difficult to avoid, but it has also not been felt necessary to try and cover everything. Apart from the volume of information involved, the idea behind this book was to find a means to identify and place in a pattern the different branches of activity that come together within a multilingual legal system, with a focus on practical matters. That implies a conceptual approach, threading a path illustrated by examples where possible.

Within these restrictions, we have covered a lot of ground and identified many aspects that form part of the picture of the complex reality of multilingual law. We have found that multilingualism is widespread and probably represents the norm rather than the exception. Even the 'purest' monolingual system of law is not unaffected by multilingual considerations; every system of law is subject to foreign influences, even if it is only a foreigner appearing in court as witness or accused, or documents drawn up in a foreign language. There is 'no escape' from this reality. So, ultimately the concept of multilingual law plays a part in all legal systems and they might all be analysed using the ideas and concepts in the appendices.

Matrices of law(s), language(s) and culture(s)

With that thought, we can shift ground to change emphasis. Up to now we have been 'deconstructing' and analysing legal systems for their legal and linguistic parts through a semiotic lens. However, it is now time to think about the 'construction' side of mutilingual law and to reflect on it from a different perspective, perhaps a more wholistic one. How does it all 'hang together'? What is the big picture? We have used the concept of 'framework' to analyse systems, but like the parts of an engine in a motor car, they need to be fitted together in the right way for the machine to work. There is a relationship between each of the individual parts, and between them and the whole. In this connection, the concept of 'matrix' comes to mind: the idea that multilingual law comprises a web of interrelated actions and activities that, taken together, comprise a 'whole'. These create relationships and bring fact, law and language together.

The concept of matrix is abstract, but there are effects in space and time, and things are in a state of constant flux and change, as with a living organism. Viewed this way, we can reflect on different strands and ways in which these mutually influence each other, and the whole. For example, one can think of legal systems as concentrations or clusters of connections between different specialist fields of knowledge. This is not a legal or linguistic way of thinking about law, but it perhaps helps us to be aware of the variety of influences at work. In this book the emphasis has been on law and language, but both of these fields are 'applied' fields, as they serve the needs of society at large. They bear witness to influences of politics, economics and culture at large which have been formalised, or 'hardened', and made specific (potentially 'fossilised') in linear threads of coded signs that constitute legal utterances. If a legal system is multilingual, this is also as a result of such influences at work.

Following the way we analysed the concept of multilingual law, we can first take matrices of law. Each legal system is composed of many of them: for example, the different branches of law and the ways in which they relate together when they become juxtaposed together in the infinite variety of ways that life throws up. Then there are the relationships between national legal systems, as systems with boundaries and linking points between them (or not), as well as between the legal orders. For example, a person of nationality A, who has exceeded their right of residence in state B, drives a car registered in state C while in state B and has an accident with a person from state D driving a car registered in state E bearing false number plates. Suppose there is a criminal law prosecution, a civil law action for damages, or an administrative enquiry about rights of residence and false number plates? One can explore legal implications, bodies of law, applicable rules, and so on. This example may seem fanciful, but real life throws up much more complicated situations. The work of the lawyer is to work through the matrices, analyse, structure and classify the legal relationships using language, and to draw conclusions for possible implications.

As regards the matrices of language, we have seen in earlier chapters two dimensions: that within a language, and that between languages within a system. Multilingual legal systems express themselves in two or more languages, but even within one and the same language, different forms of language exist. Further, we have seen how language is analysed into oral and written forms, types of sounds and scripts, strung together to create meanings interpreted by a hearer or reader. Words and terms take their meanings from context and each legal order and legal system comprises a context, so there can be considerable variation. The USA and the UK are said to be 'two countries separated by a common language'. Legal systems frequently use words for concepts that appear to be the same, but turn out on close inspection to be different: for example, the concept of 'domicile' between English and French law. Context and interpretation in the light of other terms in a system determine the meaning of terms, and we become aware of the way in which each legal term exists in a sort of multidimensional matrix: first, the legal context as legal order, legal system, specific branch and detailed part of the branch of law; second, the dimension related to the linguistic context, in terms of part of speech, role in the text, grammatical configuration as noun, verb, adjective, subject or object, active or passive voice, and so on.

Within the multilingual context we think how words and terms in languages are tied to equivalent words in other languages. Do they express the same concept, as perhaps where they are all part of the same system of law which aims at the same effects in each language version? Or are there hidden differences, whether intended or unintended, that require monitoring? There are no general answers; only specific individualised answers closely connected to facts and circumstances can be given, and it is for this reason that legal interpretation of legal texts can be a complex issue.

All the foregoing matrices may be subsumed into matrices of culture, for that can embrace everything. The topic of culture has not been raised specifically, but it has been present throughout the study. The choice of multilingualism in law is a cultural choice, as well as political and legal. Multilingual law is multicultural. The mere fact of there being more than one language present within a society or territory implies different words for things, different concepts and different ideas. Each language sets forth and expresses a view of the world, reflects the experiences, history and geography of the speech community, and encodes this linguistically. Even within a single small territory, speakers of language A may have a different view of the world from speakers of language B. It may be one of inequality, whether higher or lower, or it may be one of cultural competition for scarce resources. The mere fact of having a multilingual legal system does not resolve difficult issues, but it does recognise the right of each speech community to be able to express its views and to share in the cultural life of the society using its own language, reflecting its identity. Thus there is a mechanism for handling and debating cultural differences openly and finding solutions and compromises for shared problems. That seems preferable to the alternatives; for denying the weak also harms the strong.

One last factor to mention here is time. We move through time; so do law, language and culture. There is constant change and the historic dimension is also present in multilingual law. Time is also part of the matrix.

Themes and patterns

Terminology

Before drawing to a close, let us briefly recall some of the themes and patterns that have emerged. The constant themes have been law, language, translation, interpretation and terminology. Yet, if one is to emphasise anything, it should perhaps be terminology, because it tends to be overlooked and is less well understood generally. Legal concepts are technical and have fairly precise meanings, and these are expressed through terms of commensurate precision. The task of analysing terms in a source language and searching for term equivalents in target languages is a constant feature of multilingual legal work, complemented by the return flow from target back to source to check alignment. The terminological range of a language, its lexicological range and its vocabulary are indicators of its use and status, as discussed in Chapter 7 and Appendix IV. When changes are made to raise a language to a 'higher' or wider usage, as where it is made an official language for the first time, or becomes an international or supranational language, there are significant terminological implications that require to be addressed in good time.

Context

Throughout any narrative on multilingual law and the meanings of words and terms, the constant refrain is that of 'context'. Everything seems to depend on the context and the particular factors in operation. One searches for the links between the individual term being investigated, the law being drafted, the text being translated and the system as a whole. For the practitioner, how does one construct a message in different languages to convey the same information? How does one ensure that texts are translated 'correctly' and convey the 'right' information? How far is context culturally determined and how far is it 'objective' or 'scientific'? To this, one can add the identity of the target audience, the purpose of the text and the level of precision in the information required.

Technology

Another important theme is the role of technology. Computers and information technology have brought about changes in everyday life for everyone. Mechanisation of the professions is underway. It is enhanced by standardisation in texts and procedures. Legal texts tend to use many standard formulae where meanings become fixed through discussion, analysis and judicial ruling, and this seems set to continue. The tools will become ever more sophisticated; translation programmes will become better, and no doubt new aids for drafting and revising legislative texts will be devised. There are implications for professionals: pressures to produce more in less time, but also an enhanced need for training in the equipment and technology in operation. Perhaps the precise nature of the tasks will change as a result. For example, as translation tools become better, so the role of translator shifts towards that of reviser. Perhaps it may also give a misleading impression of objectivity to term equivalence.

From the viewpoint of multilingualism and multilingual law generally, technology provides benefits. It facilitates the use of more languages and is capable of providing material support for lesser-used languages; a few people can investigate topics and make their findings available worldwide through the Internet, thereby saving everyone else hours of time in the same research. With the aid of technology and skilled professionals, there seems to be essentially no upper limit to the number of languages in which a legal system can decide to function. Other factors come into play to place limits on this: politics, demography, coordination, economics, and so on. The European Union has 24 official languages at the time of writing; this figure could increase further if there are more accessions of states. Even so, as a result of the Agreement on the European Economic Area,[1] many EU texts are already regularly translated into two further additional non-EU languages: Icelandic and Norwegian. A good use of technology is to prepare terminology databases. However, it is also possible that computerisation and standardisation may lead to rigidification.

Size of a language

Another issue that should be mentioned touches on the size of a language; this can be seen in terms of numbers of speakers, or the economic importance of the language. It has not been highlighted in this book, except in Chapter 7 and Appendix IV concerning use and status. The larger and stronger a language within a territory, the more likely it is to be an official language. Such languages generally have resources brought to their support. However, the situation of languages that do not have official status tends to be more preoccupying. These are lesser-used and minority languages. They have fewer speakers, smaller terminology ranges and often little or no resources to support them. Many are facing extinction. What attitude does one take as regards them? What is the value of a language, or the culture and identity attached to it? What is actually lost when a language dies? How many resources should be put into building up or preserving a smaller language? It would be a big task to create a full description and terminology database, but what about education, training and actual use? These are issues for language planners and the speech communities themselves, and are not dwelt on here. It is hoped that some of the ideas set out in this book may provide some assistance and encouragement in the tasks they face. The European Charter for Regional or Minority Languages and accompanying literature provides a source of guidance in this respect.

Boundaries in law and language

One of the inherent themes that seems to be particularly difficult to grasp concerns the existence of linguistic boundaries within multilingual law. People are familiar with legal boundaries, as when one crosses the border from France to Germany and knows that it is German law that now applies. Similarly, they are aware that there is a change of language from French to German. These boundaries are clearly defined, but other boundaries are not so clearly defined. In the case of legal language, we can have a language like French, German or English which is used in different countries, as well as in different legal orders. What are the implications for a language and for individual terms and expressions where usage is in a different country or a different legal order? Boundaries are present, but the dividing lines and the way terms are affected is not always evident. This is the domain of specialists. Multilingualism means crossing these boundaries, moving from one 'pool' to another. What happens in this process of jumping from one to the other? How does it take place? What are the mental processes? What role does 'fuzziness' play in all this? What about blurring or widening the scope of terms to encompass different cultural approaches? We find ourselves at the point of interface between drafting and interpretation – the eternal conflict over meanings.

Pros and cons of multilingual law

What, then, are the advantages and disadvantages of multilingual legal systems? It is not the subject of this book, but the question lies in the background. The main disadvantage is that they cost money to run. They are more expensive as there is a need for translators, interpreters, terminologists, sophisticated computer systems and extensive education and training. There is a greater need for coordination as there are more participants. On the other hand, one can argue that multilingualism in law offers choice, greater personal freedom and equality, and respect for human rights. Perhaps it enhances justice and fairness in society and also stability, economic prosperity and wealth creation. There are costs attached to monolingualism also, though these may not necessarily be evident (Hoppe 2015).

Another argument against multilingualism is that if everyone is taught to speak the same language, they can communicate directly and easily, and the community is more homogeneous and stronger. The costs of production and commercialisation of goods and services are lower, and so the economy is more efficient. Again, this view has its strengths, and it is certainly desirable for there to be a shared language for the whole community, but that does not mean that lesser-used languages should be killed off. Many 'monolingual' communities are actually bilingual, having a local dialect and the national speech form. That is the case, for example, in parts of Scotland. The question should rather be how much recognition should be given to lesser languages. On the other hand, where a state is formed from different linguistic groups, as in Belgium, Canada and Switzerland (to name three out of many), multilingualism comes as the *sine qua non* for the existence of the state. Other countries, such as the USA, have large linguistic diversity and have used official monolingualism of English as a factor for integration. This book has been written on the assumption that multilingualism is broadly a 'good thing' and that it is desirable to understand it better.

Multilingualism implies respect

Behind any fully functioning system of multilingual law lies a hidden ingredient: respect for the other and respect for differences. A multilingual legal system not only allows differences, but also expressly builds on them and is adapted to them. That is its strength. It leads to commitment and support from the wider community, because each can derive some benefit from it. The fact of respect for the other leads to a readiness to search for shared solutions. This enhances law-making and the legislative process, and leads to the necessary linguistic and translation support for the system to function. It also goes towards meeting ideas about equality in all forms and touches on natural law and ideas about justice.

Problems and solutions

Can one answer a question about typical problems and solutions in multilingual law? Perhaps the most typical problem is the one that has not been thought about beforehand and how to work out the least bad way of resolving it. Frequently, this is a terminology dilemma. Beyond that, there is the ever-present pressure to produce more in less time, with fewer people and at less cost; but that is not restricted to multilingual law. More specifically to the present theme, one can attach importance to two areas: methods for producing multilingual legislation and methods for deciding cases. With the former, one has a choice of approaches. First, one can make a law in one language and then translate it into one or more other languages. Here, two variations are possible: (a) the source text is fixed and cannot be changed, so that the target language version must adapt to it in term and syntax; (b) the source text remains in draft and is adjusted to accommodate the target language(s). Second, legislative texts are negotiated using a source language (which may change), and other languages are created at the same time in parallel to it and can influence the draft source language version throughout the process of creation (EU method). A third approach is to construct separate language versions of texts in parallel from separate initial instructions and then weave them together through a process of revision. Yet whatever the approach, the problems are likely to be similar: what action is sought? What is the policy intention? What legal texts apply? How should the text be constructed? Which concepts are relevant and which terms apply to them? How should terms be matched up across languages?

On the other hand, with court cases the language of the case is linked to the parties, and the language rules applying will determine the languages involved and the need for translation. Most of the problems lie within the legal sphere of conducting the court case, gathering evidence, deploying arguments, and so on. On the translation side, there is the problem that the range of possible source languages may be very wide. For example, in the EU context it is possible for cases to be raised before the Court of Justice of the European Union in a wide range of languages; translation is required into the other languages. There are many possible language combinations for translation, and one solution is to review what needs to be translated into which languages and to use certain languages as 'pivot', or 'relay', languages, for onward translation into others.

Specialist knowledge, training and education

Throughout this book the specialised nature of legal language, and by extension of multilingual legal language, has been emphasised. It is a problem for the uninitiated. In every field one is concerned about questions of training and education, making sure the next generation can learn the tools of the trade and carry on the work. No doubt things are becoming ever more complex in line with the technological evolution of our societies. New branches of law develop, as do new organisations for making law and more specialised concepts, and in an international environment such as the European Union, more languages are being added. There is more to know, so more to learn. That places a premium on education and training. In general, it is best if a person can come fully formed to the role. In the case of EU permanent staff, capability is tested by rigorous entry competitions. A new candidate soon adapts to the tasks and the ongoing in-house training ensures constant updating. Training in languages and updates in law are also desirable. Language training enlarges horizons and awareness of different cultural viewpoints, which assists in overall quality in multilingual law. Finding methods to render specialist literatures more widely available and helping people to understand them would be useful.

Areas for study and research

This book has stopped short of entering into a study of individual multilingual legal systems, but there are areas for study and research. In many cases there exist excellent legal descriptions and analyses of systems. However, there are also systems where that seems not to be the case, or rather they have not been researched from a legal-linguistic perspective. Appendix I proposes an outline for a list of countries and their basic language arrangements. The appendix could be developed into a long list, and it could be linked to the framework, converted into a questionnaire and sent off to every country or international organisation to enquire how they manage their legal-linguistic affairs. With computerisation and a good database, perhaps one might even be in a position to handle the potentially vast amount of data. Yet what would such information tell one, and would the information be useful? These are questions to ponder before embarking on such a project.

If one believes that individuals are entitled to know their rights and obligations in a language they understand, and if one believes that every citizen has a right to participate in society in a language with which they feel comfortable, then there is an argument that the way forward is through a multilingual approach to law, and on that view the more information that is widely available about multilingual law and how legal systems are managed in different countries and organisations, then so much the better for our modern globalised life. The human world is changing; it faces unprecedented problems (and opportunities) of a global nature, and the only way forward is through debate, dialogue and shared problem-solving. That means communicating across languages and legal systems. It is the multicultural matrix of multilingual law.

Conclusion

It is time to close this study of multilingual law and the search for a framework for analysis and understanding. The issues are complex. A set of views and opinions have been given which are based on the author's experience working with law and language in monolingual and multilingual contexts, backed up by extensive reflection and study. The views offered are entirely personal. An interest in the linguistic side of law was triggered many years ago by discovering how Scottish legislation had suddenly changed in 1707 from being written in the centuries-old language of Lowland Scots to being written in contemporary English. How was it possible for a legal system to accommodate such changes? How also was it possible that at the same time lawyers had used Latin for a long time in parallel? And what about the ancient languages of Gaelic and Pictish, in place before those newcomers arrived? How does this all work out? That is the fascination of multilingual law.

Note

1 Available at: www.efta.int/eea.

Appendix I
States, languages and official languages

State	Spoken/written languages	Official languages	Legal sources	Notes
Name of state	(a) total number (b) name of each (c) level of each per Appendix IV	(a) number (b) name of each (c) level of each per Appendix IV	(a) type of system per Appendix II (b) legal texts on language regime and languages	Sources of information and literature

Comments:

1. For background, see Chapters 2 and 14.
2. The table serves as a token outline to assemble diverse information in one location.
3. Information on states, languages and official languages is available inter alia from national authorities, the national constitutions, the United Nations website (www.un.org/en/index.html), the Ethnologue website (www.ethnologue.com/).
4. See Appendix III on searching for rules, practice and guidance on language(s), drafting and interpretation.
5. The table can be adapted to cover international and supranational organisations, as well as commercial and other bodies.

Appendix II
Legal-linguistic models

Part I: Legal orders and systems

(i) National

Model A: national unitary legal system

(a) National level (N) – number of national official languages: N1, N2, N3, N4, etc.
(b) Local level (L) – number of local official languages: L1, L2, L3, etc.
(c) Special cases of language recognition (S): S1, S2, S3, etc.

Model B: national federal legal system

(a) Federal level (F) – number of federal official languages: F1, F2, F3, etc.
(b) Province level (P) – number of province official languages: P1, P2, P3, etc.
(c) Local level (L) – number of local official languages: L1, L2, L3, etc.
(d) Special cases of language recognition (S): S1, S2, S3, etc.

Model C: national hybrid legal system

(a) National level (N) – number of national official languages: N1, N2, N3, etc.
(b) Subnational level (SN) – number of official languages in the main component parts of the state: SN1, SN2, SN3, etc.
(b) Local level (L) – number of local official languages: L1, L2, L3, etc.
(c) Special cases of language recognition (S): S1, S2, S3 etc.

(ii) International

Model D: international law agreements and contracts (IL)

Number of languages used: IL1, IL2, IL3, etc. (see comment 4).

(iii) Supranational

Model E: supranational law (SPL)

Number of official languages: SPL1, SPL2, SPL3, etc. (see comment 5).

Part II: Particular organisations and entities

(i) National

Model F

Incorporated and unincorporated bodies, companies, organisations, etc.: number of languages, identified according to national, local or special status use in Models A to C.

(ii) International

Model G

International law organisations created by international agreement: number of official languages, identified according to Model D; distinguishing between official languages and internal working languages.

Model H

Non-governmental organisations, including companies, religious organisations and entities whose activities spread across legal systems and languages: number of official languages, identified according to Models A to D; distinguishing between official languages, internal working languages and languages for the conduct of activities locally.

(iii) Supranational

Model I

Supranational law organisations created by international agreement: number of official languages identified according to Model E; distinguishing between official languages and internal working languages.

Part III: Miscellaneous

Model J: other

Does not fit with any of the above. For example, dependent territories and entities that are not clearly defined.

Comments:

1. For background, see Chapters 2, 3 and 14.
2. This Appendix indicates a range of law/language combinations and organises them into headings as 'models'. The labels A, B, C etc. are for convenience and have no intrinsic value.
3. A separate model is proposed for each type of 'legal' variant in terms of legal order, type of legal system, and type of context in which law, or rules in the

broadest sense arise, as well as different types of organisation and the language combinations.
4. Concerning Model D, intrinsically international law as a legal order has no language regime and any and all languages are available for use, so there is no specific model for international law itself. Model D covers practice and agreements that do not create organisations.
5. Concerning Model E, supranational law is created through international agreements but is seen as a different legal order. Here the model is seen in terms of the system as a whole, while Model I places the focus on institutions.
6. The primary focus in this Appendix is on the language arrangements created by law and governing state-created entities, but the range can be extended to include non-state private and commercial entities acting in an international context. This is relevant to extending legal-linguistic research into those domains.
7. Each model type proposes variants in terms of numbers of languages. Individual systems and organisations can accordingly be allocated to a model and language variant and given a coded reference, such as 'Model A, N2' for Ireland. An important purpose here is to enhance awareness of multilingualism and raise the visibility of lesser-used languages by bringing them up to the same level as the mainly used languages through allocation of such a coding. Unofficial languages are not specifically catered for here, but could be included in a model by marking as 'unofficial' (U), and suggesting the level according to Appendix IV.
8. Unitary national systems may be structured according to a variety of levels; here two levels are retained, referred to as national (N) and local (L) to cover any localised arrangements at or below national level. National federal models are more complex in terms of potential variation as there is the federal level and province level, as well as local variations. Model B proposes three levels of language variation. However, in addition there are cases where individual languages have a special status for a limited area or group[1] and this possibility is recognised through the concept of 'special case' (S). It can be extended to the international and supranational models, as appropriate.
9. Model C is a general category for systems that do not precisely fit Models A or B (the UK is an example). The viewpoint of this Appendix is that of the whole system, but individual parts may be foregrounded. To cater for language variations at a level between the national and the local, where it is incorrect to refer to 'province', the general label 'sub-national' is proposed.
10. This Appendix links in with the other Appendices, in particular Appendices I, III, IV and VIII.

Note

1 See, for example, Ethnograph [Online]. Available at: www.ethnologue.com/.

Appendix III
Searching for rules, practice and guidance on language(s), drafting and interpretation

Part I: National law systems[1]

Searching for rules on language(s)

A. Legislative texts

(a) constitution
(b) codes
(c) primary laws
(d) secondary and lower-level laws
(e) ministerial or executive bodies' laws, rules, regulations, decrees, orders
(f) administrative circulars and notices
(g) province or local laws, regulations, bye-laws
(h) official gazettes in which laws are published
(i) lists of legislation
(j) official guidance[2]

B. Courts and case law

(a) national, province and local court and tribunal reports
(b) legal journals reporting and discussing cases
(c) lists of case reports
(d) rules on jurisdiction or competences of courts
(e) organisation of courts, language qualifications of judges and staff, internal working languages
(f) rules of court

C. Other sources of information

(a) textbooks[3]
(b) legal journals and articles
(c) comparative law journals, books and treatises
(d) professional persons: librarians, lawyers, law societies, embassies, etc.
(e) the Internet
(f) histories of the legal system
(g) custom, practice and what is done, why and how
(h) Ethnologue website: www.ethnologue.com/

216 *Appendix III Guidance for drafting and interpretation*

(i) *European Judicial Atlas in Civil Matters*, which contains names and addresses of all courts in the EU Member States competent in civil and commercial matters and geographical areas in which they have jurisdiction

(j) *Judicial Systems in Member States*, which contains information on EU Member State legal systems

D. What to search for

(a) rules on languages, at different levels in the legal system (national, province, local, particular groups or localities)
(b) rules on languages/language use laid down for/by courts for internal organisation
(c) rules of court on language(s) for the conduct of cases
(d) administrative practice in organisations regarding language rules and use
(e) customary practice regarding language(s)
(f) special arrangements or local practices and exceptions
(g) rules and practice on translation and oral interpretation

E. Legal drafting and language use

Searching for rules, practice and guidance on drafting legal texts

(a) legislative drafting manuals, guidance, circulars, notes[4]
(b) administrative guidance on (multilingual) drafting
(c) articles, journals and books on legal language and drafting[5]
(d) judicial observations in case law on drafting, styles and methods
(e) guidance on drafting court pleadings
(f) guidance on drafting (multilingual) judicial and other court documents
(g) guidance on drafting contracts and other legal acts (specialised types)
(h) examples of each type of text as precedents to follow
(i) guidance on plain legal language in a multilingual context
(j) guidance on gender-free drafting in a multilingual context
(k) guidance on multilingual national law drafting by different institutions
(l) background legislative procedures and context information

F. Legal interpretation

Searching for rules, practice and guidance on interpretation of legal texts

(a) legislative drafting manuals, guidance, circulars and information on methods
(b) articles, journals and books on legal language and interpretation
(c) judicial observations on interpretation of different types of act, case and text
(d) guidance and advice on multilingual interpretation
(e) legal text books on methods of interpretation

Appendix III Guidance for drafting and interpretation 217

Part II: International law and organisations

Searching for rules on language(s)

A. Foundation and other texts

(a) treaties, conventions and agreements creating an organisation
(b) legislative, administrative and other texts made by an organisation
(c) secondary-level and implementing texts
(d) internal texts on language(s) made by an organisation
(e) treaties, conventions and agreements on languages and language use
(f) background texts on international relations[6]
(g) international agreements touching on language and language use in different sectors or activities

B. Courts and case law

(a) court reports of international and specialised courts and tribunals
(b) court reports of national courts and tribunals touching on international law
(c) legal journals on court reports
(d) reports involving an organisation and its activities
(e) rules on jurisdiction or competences of courts
(f) organisation of courts, language qualifications of judges and staff, internal working languages
(g) rules of court

C. Other sources of information

(a) index of treaties: United Nations Treaty Series Online Collection[7]
(b) national lists of treaties and agreements
(c) official gazettes in which agreements are published
(d) annual reports and statistics by organisations on their activities
(e) administrative practice in organisations regarding language rules and use
(f) information on custom and practice: official languages, working languages, etc.
(g) customary practice regarding language(s)
(h) special arrangements or local practices and exceptions
(i) languages of texts produced
(j) text books
(k) legal journals and articles
(l) professional persons: librarians, lawyers, law societies, embassies, etc.
(m) the Internet
(n) histories

218 *Appendix III Guidance for drafting and interpretation*

D. What to search for

(a) rules on languages (authentic/official languages)
(b) individual provisions in treaties, agreements, etc., on authentic languages of the text in question and rules on languages
(c) rules on languages/language for internal organisation of courts
(d) rules on language knowledge requirements
(e) rules on languages for conduct of cases
(f) administrative practice in organisations regarding language use
(g) customary practice regarding language(s)
(h) rules and practice on translation and oral interpretation
(i) tasks conferred on the organisation as relating to language(s)
(j) special arrangements or local practices and exceptions

E. Legal drafting and language use

Searching for rules, practice and guidance on drafting of legal texts

(a) treaty drafting manuals, guidance, circulars, notes
(b) organisation manuals, drafting guidance, circulars and notes
(c) articles, journals and books on legal language and drafting
(d) judicial observations in case law on treaty and agreement drafting and meanings
(e) guidance on drafting international court pleadings
(f) guidance on drafting judicial and other international court documents
(g) guidance on drafting contracts and other legal acts (specialised types)
(h) guidance on multilingual international legal drafting
(i) examples of each type of text as precedents to follow

F. Legal interpretation

Searching for rules, practice and guidance on interpretation of legal texts

(a) drafting manuals, guidance, circulars, notes, information on practice
(b) articles, journals and books on legal language and interpretation
(c) judicial interpretations and observations on methods to interpret types of act
(d) guidance and advice on multilingual interpretation

Part III: Supranational law and organisations

(See Part II and adapt as appropriate)
   The following is drawn from EU law and serves as an example. It is indicative and not exhaustive. The precise details and information are not elaborated.

Searching for rules on language(s)

A. Foundation and other texts

(a) EU treaties: TEU, TFEU and preceding treaties, TEAEC (EURATOM Treaty), Accession Treaties, etc.
(b) Regulation No. 1 of 15 April 1958 determining the languages to be used by the European Economic Community and Regulation No. 1 of 15 April 1958

Appendix III Guidance for drafting and interpretation 219

determining the languages to be used by the European Atomic Energy Community (24 official languages)
(c) acts setting up EU institutions and agencies and providing for their activities and internal organisation
(d) internal regulations and rules of procedure of the institutions, agencies and other bodies

B. Courts and case law

(a) case reports of the Court of Justice of the European Union[8]
(b) case reports of Member State national courts where questions of EU law arise
(c) Common Market Law Reports, European Court Reports
(d) Protocol (No. 3) on the Statute of the Court of Justice of the European Union[9]
(e) Rules of Procedure of the Court of Justice of the European Union[10]
(f) Court of Justice of the European Union: guidelines for lawyers[11]

C. Other sources of information

(a) Official Journal of the European Union[12] and the supplement dedicated to public procurement (TED)[13]
(b) the Internet and websites, for example http://europa.eu; http://eur-lex.europa.eu/homepage.html
(c) Community Research and Development Information Service (CORDIS)[14]
(d) EU law and publications website[15]
(e) textbooks and journals
(f) national sources of legal information
(g) professional persons: librarians, lawyers, law societies, embassies, etc.

D. What to search for

(a) rules on languages (authentic/official languages) for EU law, institutions and agencies and their activities
(b) rules of procedure of EU Court of Justice on languages of cases
(c) internal court, institution and agency rules regarding language use
(d) rules on language knowledge requirements for posts
(e) administrative practice in organisations regarding language use
(f) customary practice regarding language(s)
(g) individual provisions in treaties, agreements, etc., on languages
(h) rules and practice on translation and oral interpretation
(i) special arrangements or local practices and exceptions

E. Legal drafting and language use

Searching for rules, practice and guidance on drafting legal texts

(a) Manual of Precedents for Acts Established within the Council of the European Union 2002[16]
(b) Interinstitutional Style Guide (EU 2015)[17]
(c) Joint Practical Guide (second edition, EU 2013)[18]
(d) European Commission Manual on Legislative Drafting (1997)[19]

Appendix III Guidance for drafting and interpretation

(e) European Commission translation and drafting resources for each of the 24 EU languages[20]
(f) guidance on drafting from national law systems, for adaptation
(g) guidance on drafting from international law, for adaptation
(h) case law of EU Court of Justice[21]
(i) European Parliament Legislative Observatory (OEIL)[22]
(j) N-LEX. A common gateway to national law[23]
(k) EUR-Lex. Access to European Union Law[24]
(l) Interparliamentary EU Information Exchange (IPEX)[25]
(m) IATE Interactive Terminology for Europe[26]

F. Legal interpretation

Searching for rules, practice and guidance on interpreting legal texts

(a) drafting manuals, guidance, circulars, notes: information on practice
(b) articles, journals and books on legal language and interpretation
(c) judicial interpretations and observations on methods to interpret different types of act
(d) guidance and advice on multilingual interpretation

Comments:

1. For background see Chapters 4 and 14.
2. The purpose of this Appendix is to suggest places to search for information on linguistic regime, languages and language use. It is not exhaustive and is merely indicative. It can be applied to searches on other topics.
3. Searches should be made in different languages.
4. Materials are frequently monolingual and there may be no cross-language referencing. EU official texts, however, are generally published in all official languages.

Notes

1. Separate searches at national, federal, province, region, local levels as appropriate.
2. See, for example, guidance on Swiss federal drafting with four languages in Swiss Confederation. Federal Chancellery (2015).
3. For example, with respect to research on English law, see Holborn (2001).
4. See, for example, Office of the Scottish Parliamentary Counsel (2006) and sources listed therein, Commonwealth Association of Legislative Counsel: an annotated catalogue of publications. [Online]. Available at: www.opc.gov.au/calc/docs/CALCCatalogue_Feb2011.pdf; Uniform Law Conference of Canada. [Online]. Available at: www.ulcc.ca/en/uniform-acts-en-gb-1/546-drafting-conventions/66-drafting-conventions-act.
5. See, for example, Wilson (2007).
6. For example, Vienna Convention on the Law of Treaties 1969 (authentic texts: English, French, Chinese, Russian and Spanish); Vienna Convention on Diplomatic Relations 1961.
7. Available at: https://treaties.un.org/pages/UNTSOnline.aspx?id=1.
8. Available at: http://curia.europa.eu/en/content/juris/.
9. Available at: http://curia.europa.eu/jcms/upload/docs/application/pdf/2008-09/statut_2008-09-25_17-29-58_783.pdf.

Appendix III Guidance for drafting and interpretation

10 Available at: http://curia.europa.eu/jcms/upload/docs/application/pdf/2012-10/rp_en.pdf.
11 See, for example, guidance in Altalex.eu. *European Court of Justice: Guidelines for Lawyers*. [Online]. Available at: http://www.altalex.eu/content/european-court-justice-guidelines-lawyers.
12 Available at: http://eur-lex.europa.eu/oj/direct-access.html.
13 Available at: http://ted.europa.eu/TED/main/HomePage.do.
14 Available at: http://cordis.europa.eu/.
15 Available at: http://publications.europa.eu/en/web/about-us/who-we-are.
16 Available at: http://bookshop.europa.eu/en/manual-of-precedents-for-acts-established-within-the-council-of-the-european-union-pbQC4101381/ [not the latest version in use].
17 Available at: http://publications.europa.eu/code/en/en-000100.htm.
18 Available at: http://eur-lex.europa.eu/content/pdf/techleg/joint-practical-guide-2013-en.pdf.
19 Available at: http://ec.europa.eu/smart-regulation/better_regulation/documents/legis_draft_comm_en.pdf.
20 Available at: http://ec.europa.eu/translation/index_en.htm.
21 See http://eur-lex.europa.eu/collection/eu-law/eu-case-law.html and http://curia.europa.eu/juris/recherche.jsf?cid=492573.
22 Available at: www.europarl.europa.eu/oeil/home/home.do.
23 Available at: http://eur-lex.europa.eu/n-lex/index_en.htm.
24 Available at: http://eur-lex.europa.eu/homepage.html.
25 Available at: www.europarl.europa.eu/webnp/webdav/users/jribot/public/IPEX_leaflet_EN.pdf.
26 Available at: http://iate.europa.eu/SearchByQueryLoad.do?method=load.

Appendix IV
Classifying languages by use and status

Level 0 – dead language: totally lost, no speakers, no users, no documents; no hard evidence of its existence but a belief that it existed.

Level 1 – dead language: evidence of it exists in written or graphic form but these remain undeciphered.

Level 2 – dead language: exists in written or graphic form; scripts deciphered and read.

Level 3 – living language: oral only; family and local use; not standardised; dialect forms predominate; no official recognition.*

Level 4 – living language: oral and written; family, local and informal use; not standardised in either oral or written form; no official recognition.*

Level 5 – living language: oral and written; family, local and informal purposes; standardisation of written form (perhaps informally or formally in another place); no official recognition.*

Level 6 – living language: oral and written; standardised as regards grammar, orthography, etc.; partial official recognition by law for limited purposes or areas on the state territory.

Level 7 – living language: oral and written; standardised as regards grammar, orthography, etc.; full recognition by law for all purposes on the state territory.

Level 8 – living language: oral and written; standardised as regards grammar, orthography, etc.; full recognition by law for all purposes on the territory of one or more states; used at international level for the purposes of international legal transactions.**

Level 9 – living language: oral and written; standardised as regards grammar, orthography, etc.; full recognition for all purposes on the territory of one or more states; used at the international level for the purposes of international legal transactions; used also at supranational level as part of an integrated supranational legal structure.

   *   Variant: official recognition.
   ** Any language may be used for an international transaction, but here the emphasis is on general and widespread practice.

Comments:
1. For background see Chapters 7 and 14.
2. The purpose of this Appendix is to identify different degrees of use and levels of legal status for languages and to provide a shorthand reference to their probable terminology/vocabulary range. By nature of being abstract and the subject of rules,

Appendix IV Classifying languages by use and status 223

legal status of whichever kind can be conferred on a language independent of the precise extent of its use. A mainly oral language may be a national language.[1] However, that does not necessarily mean it is in use as a language of law and administration. In general, use and legal status tend to go together. This Appendix makes certain assumptions, on the basis that individual divergences will be signalled.

3. Ethnologue[2] uses a classification system (EGIDS: Expanded Graded Intergenerational Disruption Scale) for language use and status. The table here is supplementary in so far as it is aimed specifically at legal systems, legal contexts, legal terminology and legal language.
4. Each language may be viewed in general terms as a language per se, or within a specific legal context. For example, a language may be officially recognised in state A for all purposes but not recognised in state B even though there are native speakers in state B. The classification given would depend on the legal system of enquiry rather than the language as a whole, but with a marker to signal the widest use/status elsewhere as an indicator of terminological range.
5. The scale of levels proposed in the table need modification for various realities. Examples include the following:
    (a) an oral and unwritten language receives official recognition. It is set at Level 3 but marked as 'official';
    (b) a Level 4–6 language is used for an international agreement. It is set at the basic level but marked as 'international use';
    (c) a language is Level 6, 7, 8 or 9 in state A but is not recognised in state B even though there are native speakers in state B.[3] Where the context is that of state B, the level linked to non-recognition can be marked by the higher level in brackets plus an indication as to the relevant state for it. Other variations can be marked in similar ways.
6. The health of a language is linked to *attitude*, which could be the attitude of the speech community or of officialdom, since the survival of a language depends on whether the speakers *want* to continue using it and whether the authorities support it, repress it or pay no attention to it. Individual languages could also be tagged with this information (positive: <, neutral =, negative >). This information is especially addressed to lesser-used languages that are near extinction.
7. Some distinctions may appear arbitrary, for example that between Levels 8 and 9. However, from the point of view of specialised legal terminology there is a difference, because a Level 9 language must embrace the full specialised terminology at the highest level and engage semantically in term equivalence with other languages in the supranational context. A Level 8 language may be used for international texts and yet not embrace the full range of specialised terminology across all fields of activity. The role model here is that of EU specialised terminology for Level 9.
8. The table is approximate and intended as a quick guide for terminology range. This Appendix links to the other Appendices, in particular Appendix I, II and VIII.

Notes

1 For examples, see the languages in the Constitution of the Republic of South Africa 1996.
2 Available at: www.ethnologue.com/about/language-status.
3 An example is Russian in certain Baltic countries.

Appendix V
Drafting and revision checklist for multilingual acts

Part I: Revising a source/base language (SL) draft text

Points to check:

A. Formal aspects of the instrument (act)

(a) conformity with drafting guidance, manuals of precedents or previous styles of acts as regards formal layout and structure of the draft act
(b) conformity with legal base in treaty or powers in authorising act(s)
(c) conformity with enacting institution's internal rules of procedure for such acts
(d) purpose of act: new provisions, amending existing acts, codifying and replacing previous acts? Special instructions on method respected?

B. Contents of a legislative act

1. *Title*

(a) conformity with drafting guidance, manuals of precedents, and past styles for the type of act in question
(b) does the title reflect the contents of the act and in particular the opening articles?

2. *Citations*

(a) appropriate legal base(s) or authorising provisions, cited correctly according to guidance
(b) each citation consistent with regard to authorising provisions on substance, consultations, procedure, etc.
(c) titles of other acts referred to correctly cited
(d) footnotes all correct in reference and wording
(e) obligatory consultations cited and optional consultations referred to in accordance with guidance
(f) applicable legislative procedure mentioned according to guidance
(g) citations listed in the conventional order according to guidance or precedents.

3. *Recitals*

(a) formal aspects (numbering, layout, etc.) in accordance with guidance
(b) overall structure, consistency, clarity, sense, sequence of ideas match those of enacting provisions/articles) of the act

(c) linguistic aspects: grammar, syntax, clarity, ambiguity, etc., in accordance with guidance
(d) terminology, terms to use or avoid, standard sentences or paragraphs to be followed, in accordance with guidance
(e) footnotes for acts, court reports, etc., inserted and correctly worded
(f) consistency between recitals and articles
(g) verbs of command avoided in recitals and reserved for articles (should versus shall)
(h) translation implications considered, addressing among others the following points:
  (i) avoiding sentences too long and complicated
  (ii) avoiding words and expressions that cause problems for other languages
  (iii) avoiding ambiguity (multiple qualifiers/adjectives, heavy use of pronouns)
  (iv) ensuring use of gender-neutral language, where possible
  (v) being aware of implications of idiosyncratic national terms, concepts and language styles
(i) standard recitals inserted according to the subject matter of the act, checked against corresponding articles in the act.

4. *Enacting provisions/articles/operative part*

(a) formal aspects (hierarchy of parts of the act, numbering, layout, etc.) in accordance with guidance
(b) overall structure, consistency, clarity, sense, sequence of ideas match those of the recitals
(c) numbering of articles, paragraphs and points correct and internal cross-references to them match up
(d) legal aspects: contents of enacting provisions in accordance with authorising acts and the legal system as a whole
(e) policy aspects: the act is consistent with other acts in the policy field, and the policy elements of the act are internally consistent
(f) action aspects: is it clear to the reader in each provision what is to be done and the action intended?
(g) linguistic aspects: grammar, syntax, spelling, clarity, ambiguity, etc.
(h) conformity with guidance and manuals of precedents (Manual of Precedents, Interinstitutional Guidelines, Joint Practical Guide, Interinstitutional Style Guide, etc.)
(i) footnotes correctly cited and worded
(j) consistency between recitals and articles
(k) translation problems: sentences too long or too complicated; words and expressions causing problems; ambiguity; idiosyncratic national terms and concepts
(l) publication arrangements (institution's rules of procedure; need for separate article?)
(m) committee procedures (comitology): which procedure? Correct standard wording?
(n) text is purely an amending act: no autonomous provisions?
(o) definitions: necessary, accurate and not containing normative wording (with a verb)?

5. *Annexes*

Points to check:

(a) which provision in articles refers to the annex; is the annex introduced in an article?
(b) formal layout of the annex is clear and makes sense; follows guidance?

226 *Appendix V Drafting and revision checklist*

(c) consistency with articles, in particular with terminology used
(d) overall structure, consistency, clarity, sense and sequence of ideas
(e) linguistic aspects: grammar, syntax, spelling, clarity, ambiguity, etc.
(f) possible translation problems?

6. *Whole text*

General check on pagination, margins, font type and size, spelling, punctuation, numbers, etc. in accordance with standard instructions. (NB concept of the 'multilingual page' adapted to fit all language versions synoptically.)

Part II: Revising a target language (TL) text to align it on a source/base version

The role of the target language reviser is to take the source language version and align the target language version on it in every nuance.

(a) has the SL reviser made any errors? Notify.
(b) check TL version for same points as in Part I
(c) compare whole TL version against the SL version in terms of structure, layout, numbering, references, etc.
(d) terms and expressions in TL version match SL as equivalents throughout?
(e) consistency in terminology with past texts in the field and other texts in the same domain?
(f) creation of new terms?
(g) how the TL fits within the legal culture of the text and the legal-linguistic culture of reception, readership, transposition?
(h) degree of room for manoeuvre on issues with respect to the SL?

Comments:

1. For background see Chapters 4, 11 and 14.
2. This Appendix addresses legislative acts and is based on the EU legal-linguistic method. It is indicative and intended to be adapted as appropriate. The EU legal environment is one of constant updating and development, and past styles and methods are regularly adjusted to keep pace.
3. The viewpoints of law, policy, action and language are incorporated in this Appendix.
4. Multilingual language versions are cross-checked horizontally where possible.

Appendix VI
Making a presentation or writing a paper on multilingual legal language

This Appendix is directed towards practitioners venturing to make a research presentation or write a paper for the first time on a multilingual legal or legal translation theme and who do not (yet) benefit from any expert advice and guidance.

Introduction

For a practitioner detached from an academic environment and support, making a research presentation or writing an article on the theme of multilingual legal language can be daunting. This Appendix sets out some provisional guidance so that you can get started and obtain access to expert guidance.

Let us assume you are asked to make a presentation, or submit a paper, on a legal-linguistic theme to a group of specialists, or to a journal; alternatively, you have identified a topic that has not been dealt with before and merits being presented on or recorded in the literature.

Presentations

Conferences and seminars are typically a place of presentation and source of papers and articles on legal-linguistic and translation themes. They are good places to start as there is an invitation and a theme, and the process of participation is set out step by step, usually starting with submission of a summary in the form of an abstract, followed by oral presentation and attendance at the conference/seminar, after payment of the attendance fee. The abstract is generally written before starting to write the actual paper/presentation; it sketches out a plan and the organisers indicate whether it is accepted or not. If accepted, you can proceed further, taking into account whatever comments may have been received. Questions can be put to the organisers as you have by now established contact.

Presenting papers at conferences and seminars is a good method of learning, as individual contributions are presented orally before persons who are themselves making presentations (and equally anxious); there is feedback from the conference and frequently ideas, suggestions and support. You are not alone; friends and contacts in your field of interest will be there. All this provides confidence to proceed further and possibly points to a destination for a paper. Frequently, contributors are asked to convert their presentations into a written paper for publication. This is a good method of approach; the academic community needs access to information about what is happening in the field, which is in the knowledge of the practitioner, and they assist the practitioner in making this available in efficient ways. The academic community are able to use the information in their teaching of students and in their researches, and that in turn feeds into their teaching and the level of knowledge of new recruits to the professions.

As regards formal details, the organisers indicate the length of time available for each speaker and relevant technical information. If the presentation is to be converted into a written paper, and if not already in the form of a paper, the editors will also indicate the length of text sought and give guidance on technical matters such as type of font, methods of citing and referencing other works, and so on. Since you have heard other contributions, you will know the overall context and can judge how your own text might fit in. Advice and guidance is generally available should you encounter problems.

Research papers

Writing a paper from scratch in a void is more complicated. Perhaps you have an idea drawn from your own experience and you would like to develop it and commit it to an article for publication. You have no prior experience and it is not possible to take part in seminars or conferences for whatever reason.

The first remark here is one of encouragement. The task is not easy. It takes time, but in the end is worth the effort. Others have trod the path before. Decide how much time you can afford to set aside and for how long. This will set the limits on what is possible. Most often the work is undertaken in personal time and at personal cost, so motivation is important. Here are some initial questions to ask yourself: Why write the paper? Who do you want to read it and why? Where will it be published? What journal? What is their market and readership? What length of article do they usually print? What style? What presentation? Information can be obtained by reading the publications and visiting the website of possible publishers.

For many, the language of writing is self-evident, but for others that is not the case. Which language should you choose and why? Could you write in your first language? Could your draft be translated into another language? Could your draft in a foreign language be proofread by a native speaker?

It is useful to start by setting out your initial thoughts as and when they occur to you and to note them down; they will come quick or slow, depending on when the 'butterfly of inspiration lands on your shoulder' and for how long it stays there. The next stage is to pause to reflect and shape the ideas, so as to give them structure, purpose and direction. Perhaps there is a set of texts that are being analysed in some way; that is usually the case for linguistic articles. This is the 'corpus', and it needs to be defined and identified. On the other hand, it may be that the corpus is represented by a whole multilingual legal system and you are identifying strands, tendencies and typical features, drawing on a range of texts for illustration and examples. Perhaps you wish to make comparisons with other legal systems, their linguistic features, terminology or translation issues.

Each paper is a journey of exploration. One starts with an idea, wish, goal or aim and then one starts to explore. One finds things and then one wants to say what one has found. This is a difficult task, especially if you are writing in a foreign language. If so, you should not worry too much about linguistic errors; you need to find a native speaker who can proofread your work and help to correct them. Your ideas will evolve, change and take different shapes, and you should not be afraid of that.

It is difficult to write an article in the void as there are no parameters and one 'gets lost' and loses direction. However, when one knows the readership, the length expected, the general theme and the purpose, things become easier as one has limits and these limits help very much. The clearer the overall structure, the easier it becomes to fill in the details, as the structure becomes a framework.

You need to think about the following matters in particular:

(a) The title, structure and different parts of the article. The title sets the theme. It attracts the reader, and the publisher who must sell the journal. The title must be clear, simple and focused. It must convey what the paper is about. It makes a promise; the paper delivers.
(b) Can you summarise the purpose of the paper in one sentence? This assists in the narrative of the paper and its consistency. Sometimes there is a tendency to want to cover too many diverse topics. Perhaps each merits a separate treatment?
(c) Why should someone read it? Does it contain new information? Does it say things not already known?

These are tough questions, but are faced by everyone. Once you learn the technique, you will be able to write well on many things. The first paper is the hardest (maybe). Structure is important as it is the skeleton on which the narrative hangs – you are telling a 'story' and must keep the reader's attention. That means the ideas must flow simply, logically and in progression from a start, to a development to a conclusion.[1] Perhaps start by setting the context. Give the agenda, so the reader knows in advance what sort of journey to expect; he/she is ready for the sequence and the ideas come steadily. Review the headings and for each of them write down a series of keywords to represent the ideas. Do that for the whole text. Now study it and see how the ideas flow.

For a paper the following may be expected:

(a) title;
(b) abstract in 100 words (or sometimes 300);
(c) keywords: these help researchers find your paper;
(d) text:
  (i) introduction to define and describe the field of study, set the scene and list the topics to be explored; perhaps also a summary of the conclusion;
  (ii) topic A: information, data, etc.;
  (iii) topics B, C, etc.;
  (iv) discussion;
  (v) conclusion;
  (vi) references of works consulted, etc. It is important that assertions, statements, etc., be supported by primary sources such as laws, cases, original texts (best) or secondary sources (books, journals, etc.). All references are indicated and listed together, usually at the end, according to the publisher's preferred methods of citation. By this stage you will be in contact with a possible publisher and will be receiving advice on these technical aspects.

A reader needs to be able to see the progression of the argument in a single straightforward narrative. Simplify the range of ideas, so that they follow in a line and avoid adding other topics into the text, as this gives an impression of randomness. The language style should be clear and concise.

In multilingual legal-linguistic researches, you can find yourself tackling a very large and complex subject. It can help to make an overview: make a 'mindmap' of the subject and identify different elements. Brainstorm and do not worry where it leads. Record ideas for possible use later. Chop off a part that can be handled in, say, 7,000 words, which is a normal length for a paper for publication in a journal. Limiting the scope makes things easier. You can tackle another topic in another paper and gradually build up a complex work in stages.

Lastly, reflect, discuss, consult, take your time. Do not try to do everything. Take one topic at a time and things will come. Clarify and simplify. Remember that information is best received in little drops; small doses of information are easier to adapt to than big doses. But drop by drop, you will arrive where you want to be.

Once a draft text has been prepared, if not already done (strongly advised), you need to think in terms of a publisher and their requirements. Check possible publishers and their terms and conditions. In particular, check their advice for writers and contributors, which says what they want and how they want it. Check whether the publication, if electronic, will be 'open access'. Check on copyright ownership. Check whether there is a fee to be paid by the author on publication. Check whether authorisation is needed for quotations and that you have been careful to avoid plagiarism.

Conclusion

Let the text rest, so as to create distance. Come back to it as a critical reviser and reader. Check everything and polish and improve. Consult, seek advice and submit. Be ready to accept constructive advice and criticisms and to adapt. Now launch ... and good luck.

Comments:

1. For background see Chapters 13 and 14.
2. This Appendix is subject to specialist guidance received.

Note

1 Note that special format, style, content and methodology are generally prescribed for professional academic work and are not addressed here. Specialist guidance must be sought.

Appendix VII
Training questions on law and legal language

1. **Law in general**
   (a) What is law?
   (b) What does law do?
   (c) What are the theories of law?
   (d) How do you know when you are dealing with law?
   (e) What are the types of law?
   (f) Where do you find law?
   (g) What do you do with law?
   (h) Who makes law?
   (i) How is law made?
   (j) Why is law made?
   (k) Where is it made?
   (l) When is it made?
   (m) Why does one need law?
   (n) What happens if one pays no attention to it?
   (o) Law is so complex, how can one know it all? Does this matter?
   (p) What happens if one breaks it?
   (q) How does law cease to exist?
   (r) What is the difference between law and justice?

2. **Law as a system**
   (a) What do we mean when talking about a legal system?
   (b) What is a system?
   (c) What types of legal system are there?
   (d) What are the contents of a legal system?
   (e) How do the parts of a legal system relate to each other, and why?
   (f) What goes to make up a legal system?
   (g) What makes a legal system multilingual?
   (h) In a multilingual legal system what is the relationship between the languages?

3. **Law as a legal order**
   (a) Why are national, international and supranational law considered as different legal orders?

232 *Appendix VII Training questions*

(b) What is a legal order?
(c) How many legal orders could there be?
(d) What is the difference between a legal order and a legal system?
(e) Can one imagine other types of legal order?
(f) How do legal orders relate to each other?

4. **Legal language**

(a) What is meant by 'legal language'?
(b) What makes legal language different from other forms of language?
(c) Is legal language concrete or abstract?
(d) Are legal terms concrete or abstract?
(e) How do legal terms acquire their meaning?
(f) Are legal terms fixed and constant or can they change?
(g) How are legal terms created?
(h) Who decides what legal terms mean, and how?
(i) How can one analyse legal terms?
(j) Which is more important: written language or unwritten language? Why?
(k) Does law use other signs?
(l) How does one translate legal concepts into another language?

5. **Legal texts**

(a) What is the difference between 'the law' and 'a law'?
(b) What is a legal text?
(c) What are the types of legal text?
(d) What do the different types of legal texts do?
(e) Why are they made?
(f) How are they made?
(g) How are legal texts 'unmade'?
(h) What happens once they are made?
(i) What happens if there is doubt or uncertainty?
(j) What happens if they are ignored?
(k) Are private contracts made by legal texts?
(l) Who signs a contract?
(m) Are laws made by legal texts?
(n) Are court judgments made by legal text?
(o) Are arbitration decisions legal texts?
(p) What is a multilingual legal text?
(q) How can multilingual legal texts be made to 'align' on each other?
(r) What is meant by 'alignment'?

6. **Legislative process**

(a) What is the difference between a legal instrument and a legal act?
(b) What is a legislative act?
(c) How do legislative acts start?
(d) Who decides what goes into them?

(e) How are they made?
(f) Who is involved in making them?
(g) Who drafts them?
(h) How are they drafted?
(i) Who checks them?
(j) Who can change or amend a draft legislative act?
(k) What does parliament do?
(l) Who signs legislative acts?
(m) What happens when they have been signed?
(n) Where can one find legislative acts?
(o) Where are legislative acts published?
(p) When do legislative acts come into force?
(q) What is meant by 'coming into force'?
(r) How do legislative acts come into force?
(s) What is the difference between 'come into force', 'commence', 'take effect' and 'apply'?
(t) To whom does a legislative act apply?
(u) What is the difference between a legislative act and an administrative decision or an administrative circular?
(v) In a legislative act, what is the purpose of the title, citations, recitals, articles (*UK sections*), and annexes?
(w) What is the difference between a law and a treaty?
(x) What is the difference between 'treaty', 'convention', 'agreement', 'concordat', 'protocol', 'exchange of letters'?

7. Judicial process

(a) Who ensures that the law is observed?
(b) Who uses legal texts?
(c) Who reads legal texts?
(d) Who interprets legal texts?
(e) What is the difference between reading and interpreting?
(f) What is meant by 'constructing the law'?
(g) Who can order compensation or punishment for non-compliance?
(h) What are courts?
(i) What is the difference between a court and a tribunal?
(j) What are judges?
(k) What is the function of a judge?
(l) What is the purpose of courts?
(m) How do courts function?
(n) Who takes part in a court case?
(o) What is court procedure?
(p) What are rules of court?
(q) Who makes rules of court?
(r) What is the difference between 'having rights' and 'enforcing rights'?
(s) What is the difference between 'rights' and 'obligations'?
(t) What is the difference between 'powers' and 'liabilities'?
(u) What stages might a court case go through, and why?

(v) How does a court know what are the facts and who is right?
(w) What is the difference between 'evidence' and 'proof'?
(x) What is the difference between 'facts' and 'law'?
(y) How does a court case end?
(z) How does a judge decide on a case?
(za) How is a judgment structured?
(zb) Who pays for a court case?
(zc) What are expenses?
(zd) What are appeals?
(ze) What different types of court case can there be?
(zf) What different types of judicial decision can there be?
(zg) How does a court case differ from 'arbitration' or 'mediation'?
(zh) What is an 'amicable settlement'?
(zi) What problems does one encounter in translating court texts?

8. Legal reasoning

(a) What methods of reasoning do lawyers use?
(b) How do lawyers think?
(c) How do lawyers analyse problems?
(d) What sort of solutions do lawyers come up with?
(e) What sort of words and expressions do lawyers use?
(f) How do legal reasoning and analysis differ in different legal systems, legal orders, legal cultures and languages?
(g) What translation problems arise in connection with legal reasoning?

9. Legal terminology

(a) What is terminology?
(b) What is legal terminology?
(c) What is the difference between 'terminology' and 'lexicology'?
(d) Is there a difference between 'term' and 'word'?
(e) Where does one find legal terminology?
(f) What does one do if there is no term in one's language for a concept?
(g) How does one make new terms?
(h) How can one know if terms in different languages are equivalent?
(i) When do terms in different languages have the same meanings?
(j) When do legal terms in different languages have the same meanings?
(k) Is there a way of testing for equivalence or sameness in meanings across languages?

10. Legal language

(a) What are some 'genres' of legal language?
(b) What is meant by 'genre'?
(c) What are the features of legal language that make it a genre?
(d) What features indicate different genres in legal texts?

(e) How do oral and written legal language differ?
(f) What is the difference between: 'must', 'ought', 'shall', 'should', 'can', 'could', 'may', 'might', 'is/are', 'is to/are to', 'shall not', 'may not', 'cannot', 'could not', 'should not', and which are used in legal texts, in which parts of such texts, and for what purposes?
(g) What is the difference between: 'however', 'notwithstanding', 'without prejudice to', 'subject to', 'whereas'?

11. Tools and aids

(a) What technological aids are used by lawyers, linguists, translators, terminologists and legal-linguistic revisers?
(b) What are the strengths and weaknesses of each tool?
(c) What other aids might be useful?

12. Skills and knowledge

What skills and knowledge are required by lawyers, linguists, translators and legal-linguistic revisers in relation to multilingual law?

13. Research

(a) What topics would benefit from research?
(b) How might one go about undertaking such research?
(c) What corpus would one work with?
(d) What is a 'corpus'?
(e) What information would one look for?
(f) What methods would one use?
(g) How reliable might the information be?
(h) Who could provide assistance?
(i) Where might the research findings be presented or published?

Comments:

1. For background see Chapters 13 and 14.
2. The questions are structured to tie in with 'wh-?' questions in discourse analysis (see Chapter 6).
3. There are many issues that arise in multilingual law that are difficult to address in a single monograph because they are subtle, highly specific and closely tied into individual texts that require knowledge of law, languages, the policy domain and the results intended. Frequently, there are no 'right answers' and it is a question of searching for a balance, or a 'least worst' solution, as an optimum, plus making a risk assessment. In that context the emphasis needs to be on awareness and an open mind to ask questions of the text and the problem addressed. This Appendix aims at the space between a formal exposition and operational reality by enhancing awareness as to the ranges of variables to be taken into account.

4. There are not always 'correct' answers to the questions and different responses may arise depending on the legal system or the language of enquiry; indeed, the questions may be extended in scope by translating into a language of choice (itself an exercise) and reposing them in that language.
5. The cultural orientation of the questions is English language as it is a significant source language (lingua franca) for multilingual legal texts, but the legal orientation is hybrid EU and UK.

Appendix VIII
Framework for analysis and understanding

Summary

Part A: General legal context and procedures
Part B: Types of legal text
Part C: Linguistic regime and language(s)
Part D: Terminology issues
Part E: Text issues
Part F: Meaning, interpretation and reading of texts
Part G: Translation issues
Part H: Technology, tools and aids
Part I: Education and training
Part J: Links with other systems
Part K. Particular problems and solutions
Part L: Research
Part M: Miscellaneous

Part A: General legal context and procedures

1. General description of the legal order/system[1]
   (a) country, state, territorial or political unit
   (b) name of legal system/legal order
   (c) type of system and number of languages
   (d) territory covered
   (e) persons covered[2]
   (f) domains, branches, fields of law involved
   (g) purpose of the system
   (h) legal family.
2. Legal order and type of system, according to level[3]
   (a) National system:
      (i) unitary system at:
         (A) national level
         (B) intermediate level
         (C) local level
      (ii) federal system at:
         (A) federal level
         (B) province/region level
         (C) local level

238 *Appendix VIII Framework for analysis/understanding*

        (iii) mixed/hybrid/other type of national system at:
- (A) national level
- (B) intermediate level
- (C) local level

  (b) International law context:
- (i) international agreement[4]
- (ii) custom or practice
- (iii) international organisation, of whatever type
- (iv) other

  (c) Supranational organisation:
- (i) EU
- (ii) Other.

3. Laws on language(s)[5]
   - (a) total number of official languages and the status of each[6]
   - (b) languages spoken throughout whole territory
   - (c) languages used in individual parts of the territory (region, province, local)
   - (d) languages applying to individual persons, groups or particular communities
   - (e) legislative texts governing each language at each level (national, federal, province, local)
   - (f) judicial rulings, court cases on each language
   - (g) custom and practice as regards each language at each level
   - (h) administrative practice as regards each language at each level
   - (i) languages used for contracts, agreements, etc.
   - (j) arrangements for bringing together and aligning language versions of laws, and judicial rulings and interpretations of them.

4. Organisation, institutions and procedures
   - (a) main bodies of the legal system/order
   - (b) tasks, functions and products of each institution/body
   - (c) organisation of each institution/body
   - (d) languages used internally in each institution/body
   - (e) types of (legal) text produced
   - (f) languages of the texts produced
   - (g) procedures for making legal texts (draft, translate, co-draft, etc.)
   - (h) role of translation
   - (i) uses of the legal texts (e.g. directly, or to create other legal texts through transposition)
   - (j) users of the legal texts produced.

Part B: Types of legal text[7]

1. Legislative texts
   - (a) legislating body/bodies
   - (b) level of text:
     - (i) constitutional
     - (ii) primary
     - (iii) secondary
     - (iv) tertiary
     - (v) other

Appendix VIII Framework for analysis/understanding 239

- (c) languages of the texts
- (d) working languages of the legislating institution
- (e) role of translation
- (f) stages of preparation:
    - (i) policy formation
    - (ii) instructions for drafting
    - (iii) drafting of the text
    - (iv) structure and form of the text[8]
    - (v) scrutiny and amendment of the text
    - (vi) final stages: completion, signature, formal adoption of the text of the law
    - (vii) entry into force
    - (viii) publication.
2. Judicial and court/tribunal texts
    - (a) court/tribunal name
    - (b) jurisdiction and level in system
    - (c) organisation of the court
    - (d) language(s) of the texts
    - (e) working languages of the court/tribunal
    - (f) role of translation in the court/tribunal
    - (g) procedural stages for cases:
        - (i) background circumstances and facts
        - (ii) court procedures (written/oral) prior to hearing/trial
        - (iii) written pleadings by parties (application, defence, etc.)
        - (iv) oral stages/procedures
        - (v) hearing of evidence and arguments
        - (vi) judgment/verdict/decision
        - (vii) appeal procedures (repeat the above)
        - (viii) enforcement of judgment/decision.
3. Contracts and agreements
    - (a) parties
    - (b) language(s) of the text(s)
    - (c) law applicable (for legal context and meaning)
    - (d) working languages of the parties
    - (e) role of translation for negotiations, preparatory documents and text(s)
    - (f) type of contract (genre):
        - (i) private agreement
        - (ii) commercial agreement
        - (iii) public law contract
        - (iv) international agreement
        - (v) other
    - (g) subject matter (for domain context and meaning)
    - (h) negotiation arrangements
    - (i) structure and form of text(s)[9]
    - (j) dispute resolution (court, tribunal, arbitration, mediation: who determines meaning?)
    - (k) enforcement.

4. Law creation through custom
   (a) evidence and facts for/against existence of custom/practice
   (b) documents establishing a custom (legislative, judicial, contract) and their language
   (c) language(s) used in the custom or practice.

Part C: Linguistic regime and language(s)[10]

1. General linguistic environment
   (a) languages and dialects spoken
   (b) languages and dialects written
   (c) classification status of each language/dialect.
2. Linguistic regime
   (a) number of official languages
   (b) name of each official language
   (c) non-official languages used on territory and numbers of speakers
   (d) for each official language:
       (i) status
       (ii) terminology range[11]
       (iii) script(s) used and its/their characteristics
       (iv) degree of standardisation of vocabulary, grammar, spelling, syntax, etc.
       (v) dialects and variations
       (vi) use in other legal systems and classification status within each of them
       (vii) similarities and differences in the language as compared with its use in other systems
       (viii) sources and materials (dictionaries, grammars, terminology databases, etc.)
       (ix) comparisons with other languages used in the same system (grammar, syntax, spelling, lexicology, terminology, linguistic and cultural proximity)
       (x) other aspects of the general linguistic profile.
3. Linguistic regime in legislative context[12]
   (a) legal texts regulating use of languages for legislation
   (b) number of languages for legislative texts
   (c) which language(s) used for each stage in legislative processes
   (d) internal working languages of the legislative bodies for:
       (i) debates
       (ii) amendments to draft legislative texts
       (iii) preparatory and working documents
       (iv) other.
4. Languages used for legislative drafting
   (a) monolingual system: one language
   (b) two-language system:
       (i) source text drafted in language A only and translated into language B afterwards when A final (little or no influence from B on A):
           (A) source language A always the same
           (B) source language varies between A and B
           (C) language versions A and B published jointly or separately?
       (ii) source text drafted in language A, but influences from language B; translated into language B while A still in draft; published jointly or separately?

Appendix VIII Framework for analysis/understanding 241

      (iii) source text drafted in both languages A and B at the same time; each influences and adapts to the other language; publication as single bilingual act

      (iv) other arrangement

  (c) three-language system:

      (i) source text always drafted in language A only and translated into languages B and C once A is final (little or no influence from B or C on A)

          (A) source language A always the same

          (B) source language varies between A, B and C

          (C) language versions A, B and C are published jointly or separately?

      (ii) source text always drafted in language A, but influences from languages B and C; translated into languages B and C while A still in draft; published together

      (iii) source text varies between language A, B or C and the others follow, with each influencing the other two; publication joint or separate?

      (iv) source text drafted in languages A, B and C at the same time; each influences and adapts to the other languages; published jointly as single act or separately in parallel?

      (v) other arrangement

  (d) four languages

      (i) source text drafted in language A only and translated into the other languages afterwards; little or no influence from them on A

          (A) source language always the same

          (B) source language varies

      (ii) source text drafted in language A, but influences from other languages while A still in draft; published jointly or separately?

      (iii) source text drafted in some of the languages together; with influences from the other languages

      (iv) source text drafted in all of the languages together; each influences and adapts to the other language versions; published jointly or in parallel?

      (v) other arrangement

  (e) five or more official languages: see foregoing permutations and adapt.

5. Linguistic regime in court/tribunal context

  (a) legal texts regulating use of languages within the legal system generally

  (b) legal texts regulating use of languages in court cases

  (c) authorised languages for court and judicial texts

  (d) rules on choice of language of the case and procedure

  (e) rules on languages for parties and interveners' submissions in the procedure

  (f) internal working language(s) of the court(s)

  (g) arrangements for oral interpretation:

      (i) hearings

      (ii) witnesses

  (h) arrangements for translation:

      (i) court documents

      (ii) documentary evidence

      (iii) judgments and decisions

  (i) status of each language version of judgment or court document (authentic source or translation?)

242 Appendix VIII Framework for analysis/understanding

     (j)   language(s) of court reports
     (k) language(s) of publications, official notices, information, etc., about cases
     (l)   practical translation arrangements for court texts[13]
     (m) other points.
6. Contracts, agreements, etc.
     (a)   legal texts regulating use of languages within the legal system generally
     (b)   legal texts regulating use of languages in contracts
     (c)   languages for the contract, agreement, etc.
     (d)   language(s) of negotiation
     (e)   language(s) of drafting of the text
     (f)   authentic language version(s) of the text
     (g)   translation of the text and status of the translation(s):
         (i)   informal for information
         (ii) official translation(s); not authentic
         (iii) official translation(s); authentic and equivalent source(s)
     (h)   contracts in a multilingual context:[14]
         (i)   one-language system
         (ii) two-language system:
         (iii) three-language system
         (iv) four languages or more.
7. Custom and practice
     (a)   in the absence of formal legal rules on languages, what custom or practice prevails?
     (b)   have practices been informally/formally recognised as custom?
     (c)   where legal rules exist, what are the gaps and interstices requiring 'completion' through practice/usage/custom?
     (d)   what 'habits' apply as regards language use?

Part D: Terminology issues[15]

1. General issues
     (a)   name of legal system/order and key features of legal context and text context from Parts A and B
     (b)   name of language and linguistic information from Part C
     (c)   classification level of the language[16]
     (d)   lexical/terminological range of the language by domain:
         (i)   domains of national law covered/not covered
         (ii) domains of international law covered/not covered
         (iii) domains of supranational law covered/not covered
     (e)   glossaries, dictionaries, term banks, databases etc.
     (f)   methods for new term creation:
         (i)   foreign loanword
         (ii) new word from native language roots
         (iii) new word formed in same way as foreign word (calque)
         (iv) other
     (g)   terminology bodies and organisations
     (h)   use of ISO standards
     (i)   degree of standardisation of terms in system
     (j)   languages shared across legal systems/orders horizontally:

Appendix VIII Framework for analysis/understanding 243

      (i)   same terms in same language in different legal system:
          (A) how similar or different are the legal systems?
          (B) how close are the terms shared between them as to meanings?
      (ii) same terms in different language in different legal system:
          (A) how similar or different are the legal systems?
          (B) how close are the terms shared between them as to meanings?

2. Individual terms compared across languages (term equivalence)
   (a) core meanings match?
   (b) penumbral meanings overlap sufficiently?
   (c) effects of using the terms: same results (*effet utile*)
   (d) have the terms become linked as equivalent through constant practice or judicial interpretation?
   (e) do the texts define the terms as equivalent in meaning?
   (f) are all the language versions within the same or a different legal system/order?
   (g) standardised terms and expressions declared as equivalent?
   (h) semiotic analysis (Peirce) of terms across languages for match:
       (i) same object?
       (ii) same *interpretant*?
       (iii) same *representamen* (usually different between languages)?
   (i) place of terms within terminology trees, etc.
   (j) legal terms; scientific terms; other technical terms
   (k) general language terms
   (l) terms set out in higher-ranking texts to be followed consistently.

Part E: Text issues[17]

1. Language(s) of the text.[18]
2. Type of text (genre)[19]
   (a) legal or non-legal
   (b) legal system/legal order of which the text forms part[20]
   (c) type of text:
       (i) legislative
       (ii) judicial
       (iii) court-related
       (iv) contract, agreement
       (v) unilateral (e.g. will)
       (vi) other
   (d) status of the text in the legal system/order:
       (i) high
       (ii) medium
       (iii) low
   (e) body/bodies making the text
   (f) policy field, domain
   (g) particular category and style of text.
3. Length and complexity of text, paragraphs, sentences; lexical density.
4. Structure, layout and organisation of the text.
5. Standard clauses for the type of legal text.
6. Linguistic issues.[21]

244 *Appendix VIII Framework for analysis/understanding*

7. Register and style.
8. Applicable drafting guidance.
9. Terminology: general or specialised language.
10. Intertextuality: link to other texts as regards terms and references:
    (a) links to other laws in same system/order
    (b) links to other legal systems/orders; texts and terminology
    (c) links to case law in same system/order
    (d) links to other texts and sources.
11. Cultural issues having an influence on the text, in its drafting and interpretation.
12. Meaning in context:
    (a) specific action intended
    (b) policy field
    (c) legal context
    (d) linguistic context.
13. Controlling meaning in reading and interpretation (drafting style and techniques).
14. Coherence and consistency of text with other texts in same genre.
15. Purpose of the text:
    (a) direct application and use
    (b) transposition into another system (e.g. supranational EU text).
16. Checklist for drafting and revision.[22]

Part F: Meaning, interpretation and reading of texts

1. One-language perspective:
   (a) overall context drawn from all headings in this Appendix
   (b) linguistic approaches:
       (i) dictionary meaning of words
       (ii) grammar rules
       (iii) syntax rules
       (iv) definitions of meanings
       (v) references from other texts (intertextuality)
       (vi) related texts (intertextuality)
       (vii) other
   (c) legal approaches:
       (i) all linguistic approaches[23]
       (ii) ordinary meanings
       (iii) exception: narrow interpretation
       (iv) overriding principle of law affecting permitted actions, affecting meaning
       (v) logic of the context; impossibility of outcome
       (vi) obvious error
       (vii) common sense, general knowledge, science
       (viii) public policy exclusions
       (ix) intention of drafter, legislator, parties
       (x) judicial precedents and case law
       (xi) principles of justice and equity
       (xii) coherence and consistency with the legal system internally
       (xiii) avoidance of nonsensical, illogical, or otherwise undesirable results.
2. Multilingual perspective
   (a) single language perspective, as per point 1, for each language version

Appendix VIII Framework for analysis/understanding 245

- (b) degree of divergence as to meaning between language versions in respect of each aspect of meaning
- (c) practical effects of each part of each language version (same/different)[24]
- (d) majority view of language versions as to meaning
- (e) original language of drafting (source)
- (f) clearest expression as to meaning
- (g) intention of drafters from prior papers (if allowed as aid to construction of meaning)
- (h) interpretation that leads to 'most equitable' result
- (i) interpretation that furthers the aims of the drafter
- (j) existence of material errors in language versions
- (k) interpretation that enhances the 'efficiency' or 'goals' of the legal system/order (teleological).

3. Semiotic analysis in support of legal and linguistic methods of analysis: *left open for the application of different semiotic methods and approaches.*

Part G: Translation issues

1. Role of, and arrangements for, interpretation of oral utterances.
2. Role and arrangements for translation of written utterances.
3. Organisational arrangements for translation:
    - (a) in-house translation
    - (b) outsourcing to freelance translation
    - (c) translation into mother tongue
    - (d) translation out of mother tongue to language 2 (or 3 etc.)
    - (e) translation to and from relay languages
4. Individual texts
    - (a) source language(s)
    - (b) target language(s)
    - (c) source of request for translation
    - (d) purpose and intended use of target language version(s)
        - (i) evidence in a court case (e.g. foreign law or documents)
        - (ii) general background information only
        - (iii) official information (e.g. notice)
        - (iv) official use: target text(s) status of 'translation'; not authentic
        - (v) official use: source and targets are authentic texts with same legal status as source of law
    - (e) other.
5. General legal context and legal text context.[25]
6. Linguistic issues[26] (for source and target languages).
7. Terminology issues.[27]
8. Text issues[28] (to compare source and target versions).
9. Meaning, interpretation and reading issues for each language version.
10. Databases, tools, aids[29]
    - (a) term banks, glossaries, databases
    - (b) machine-assisted drafting in one or more languages
    - (c) machine-assisted translation
    - (d) machine-assisted revision.
11. Education and training.[30]

Part H: Technology, tools and aids

1. Legal databases for legislation, court reports, literature, etc.
2. Drafting tools and aids:
    (a) computer drafting tools
    (b) manuals and guides.
3. Terminology databases, glossaries, terminographic tools.
4. Dictionaries, thesauruses, lexicographic tools.
5. Translation tools and aids.
    (a) machine translation
    (b) machine-assisted translation (translation memory programs)
    (c) terminology glossaries and aids (general and specialised)
    (d) dictionaries: monolingual, bilingual, multilingual
    (e) manuals and guides
    (f) the Internet
    (g) computers, spelling and syntax-checkers, etc.
6. Revision tools
    (a) translator tools and aids
    (b) legal tools and aids
    (c) document comparison, highlighting, notes and comments, etc.
    (d) standardised terminology-checking
    (e) manuals and guides.
7. Other tools and aids.

Part I: Education and training[31]

General and specialised arrangements, training, etc., as regards law, each language, translation, terminology, computer skills and databases, including the following.

1. Legal skills
    (a) knowing the law
    (b) knowing where to find the law
    (c) drafting legal texts
    (d) advocacy skills
    (e) judicial skills
    (f) lawyer/client skills
    (g) unwritten cultural codes.
2. Language skills
    (a) spelling, grammar, syntax
    (b) terminology and vocabulary
    (c) using dictionaries, glossaries and thesauruses
    (d) drafting
    (e) interpreting
    (f) speaking
    (g) listening
    (h) technical reading and writing.
3. Translation skills:
    (a) knowing source language

- (b) knowing source language culture
- (c) knowing source language law, legal terms, concepts and culture
- (d) knowing target language
- (e) knowing target language culture
- (f) knowing target language law, legal terms, concepts and culture
- (g) knowing how to find information in each language
- (h) knowing how to handle terminology in each language
- (i) being aware of the multilingual matrix between systems and orders, domains and contexts
- (j) developing good writing technique in style and register
- (k) understanding target audience, needs and levels of knowledge, culture and expectations.
4. Terminology skills
    - (a) knowing how to analyse terms
    - (b) knowing the databases and how to use them
    - (c) knowing how to create new terms
    - (d) knowing how to create glossaries, databases and terminology entries.
5. Legal-linguistic revision skills
    - (a) understanding all the points in this Appendix and the other Appendices
    - (b) knowing how to apply the knowledge to draft and revise legal texts in one, two or more language versions
    - (c) having translation skills and experience, understanding client, purpose, implications, terminology, etc.
    - (d) revision skills.[32]

Part J: Links with other systems

1. Identify relationships to other legal orders, legal systems, contexts and texts.
2. System choices: choice of law, choice of language, choice of court, choice of genre, choice of terminology, etc.
3. Transfer of information across systems: transposition from/into another legal order or system.
4. Intra-linguistic relations: same language, different systems, etc.

Part K: Particular problems and solutions[33]

1. Which issues constantly recur?
2. What solutions are followed?
3. Where have solutions been stored for future use?
4. Who has been informed about the solutions and where to find them?
5. What issues have not been solved (so far) and why not? For example:
    - (a) legal (substantive, procedural, conceptual)
    - (b) linguistic
    - (c) terminology
    - (d) translation
    - (e) revision
    - (f) technology
    - (g) other.

248 *Appendix VIII Framework for analysis/understanding*

Part L: Research[34]

1. What research has been undertaken in respect of each Part of this Appendix?
2. What domains covered by this Appendix have not been researched, and why?
3. What is required to undertake research in those domains?
4. What would be the benefits from making research into particular domains covered by this Appendix?

Part M: Miscellaneous

Any matter not covered in the foregoing.

Comments:

1. For background see Chapter 14.
2. The preceding Appendices form part of this Appendix and are to be read with it.
3. This Appendix proposes a general framework for legal-linguistic analysis of legal orders, legal systems, organisations, texts, etc. It comprises a series of parts following the sequence of the chapters. Each entry is to be seen as a prompt or question that invites reflection on a point. This Appendix is intended as a technical working tool to be adapted to individual contexts. It is also intended as a research and training tool.
4. This Appendix performs a descriptive function insofar as it offers a structured legal-linguistic outline, but it also performs a predictive function insofar as it is possible to anticipate certain consequences that may arise when a given legal-linguistic context is changed, for example through the addition of a new official language.
5. This Appendix is structured to function at all levels, from macro to micro, whether it be a system, organisation or specific text. Each part represents a different focus of attention.
6. The scope of the Appendix can be extended for each entry by means of 'wh?' questions: what, who, why, where, when, which, and how?
7. The range of entries is not exhaustive, and the form of presentation is not uniform.
8. The Appendices are all intended to be adapted in the light of experience.

Notes

1 Link to Appendices I and II.
2 This Appendix can be applied to organisations, whether governmental, business, religious or other, with adaptations according to context.
3 Link to Appendix II.
4 Any type of agreement.
5 Link to Appendices I, II and IV.
6 See Appendix II.
7 Select as appropriate.
8 See Part E.
9 See Part E.
10 This Part relates to the system or specific context in question and links to Appendix IV.
11 See Part D.
12 See Part B.

Appendix VIII Framework for analysis/understanding 249

13 See Point 4 of this Part and Part G.
14 See Part C and adapt as appropriate.
15 For each language.
16 See Appendix IV.
17 For each individual text.
18 See Part C.
19 See Part B.
20 See Part A.
21 See Part C.
22 Link to Appendix V.
23 See Part C.
24 Semiotic analysis; see Chapter 8.
25 See Parts A and B.
26 See Part C.
27 See Part D.
28 See Part E.
29 See Part H.
30 See Part I.
31 Link to Appendix VII.
32 Link to Appendix V and adapt as appropriate.
33 Apply 'wh?' questions to extend the scope of this Part.
34 Link to Appendix VI.

Bibliography

The websites cited in this bibliography and all notes were operational as at 29 February 2016.

Books, articles and other documents

The Aboriginal Justice Implementation Commission. 1999. *Report of the Aboriginal Justice Inquiry of Manitoba. The Justice System and Aboriginal Peoples.* Chapter 2: Aboriginal Concepts of Justice. [Online]. Available at: www.ajic.mb.ca/volumel/chapter2.html.

Ager, Simon. 2015a. *Japanese Kanji.* Omniglot. [Online]. Available at: www.omniglot.com/writing/japanese_kanji.htm.

Ager, Simon. 2015b. Omniglot. [Online]. Available at: www.omniglot.com.

Ager, Simon. 2015c. International Phonetic Alphabet (IPA). [Online]. Available at: www.omniglot.com/writing/ipa.htm.

Ahlsén, Elisabeth. 2006. *Introduction to Neurolinguistics.* Amsterdam: John Benjamins Publishing Company.

Aitchison, Jean. 2003. *Linguistics.* Teach Yourself. London: Hodder Education.

Akehurst, Michael and Malanczuk, Peter. 1997. *Akehurst's Modern Introduction to International Law.* London: Routledge.

Albi, Anabel Borja and Prieto Ramos, Fernando (eds). 2013. *Legal Translation in Context. Professional Issues and Prospects. New Trends in Translation Studies Vol. 4*. Oxford, Bern, Berlin, Brussels, Frankfurt am Main, New York, Vienna: Peter Lang.

Allan, Keith. 1986. *Linguistic Meaning.* 2 vols. London and New York. Routledge & Kegan Paul.

Altalex.eu. *European Court of Justice: Guidelines for Lawyers.* [Online]. Available at: http://www.altalex.eu/content/european-court-justice-guidelines-lawyers.

Alvarez, A. 2001. Justifying Genocide: The Role of Professionals in Legitimizing Mass Killing. *IDEA* 6(1) 20 December. [Online]. Available at: www.ideajournal.com/articles.php?sup=10.

Archer, Clive. 2015. *International Organizations.* 4th edn. London: Routledge.

Asher, R. E. and Moseley, C. (eds). 2007. *Atlas of the World's Languages.* 2nd edn. London and New York: Routledge, Taylor & Francis.

Ballard, Michel. 1992. *De Ciceron à Benjamin. Traducteurs, traductions, réflexions.* Lille: Presses universitaires de Lille.

Balmford, C. 2015. *Plain Language: Beyond a 'Movement'. Repositioning Clear Communication in the Minds of Decision-Makers.* Plainlanguage.gov. [Online]. Available at: www.plainlanguage.gov/whatisPL/definitions/balmford.cfm.

Barav, Ami and Philips, Christian (eds). 1993. *Dictionnaire juridique des Communautés européennes.* Paris: Presses universitaires de France.

Barber, Charles, Beal, Joan C., Shaw, Philip A. 2012. *The English Language. A Historical Introduction.* 2nd edn. Cambridge: Cambridge University Press.

Barr, Alan, Dalgleish, Andrew, Stevens, Hugh, Biggar, John. 2009. *Drafting Wills in Scotland.* 2nd edn. Haywards Heath: Tottel.

Beaven, John. 2014. *Quality Assurance in a Large Translation Organisation: The Experience of the Council of the EU*. Brussels: General Secretariat of the Council of the EU. [Online]. Available at: http://stl.recherche.univ-lille3.fr/colloques/20132014/Beaven_2014.pdf.

Bellos, David. 2011. *Is that a Fish in your Ear? Translation and the Meaning of Everything*. London: Penguin.

Benjamin, A. and Templin, J. D. 2003. *Four Strategies to Think Like a Lawyer*. Lawnerds.com. [Online]. Available at: www.lawnerds.com/guide/mind.html.

Bennion, Francis A. R. 1990. *Bennion on Statute Law*. London: Longman. [Online]. Available at: www.francisbennion.com/book/statutelaw.htm.

Bennion, Francis A. R. 2001 and 2009. *Understanding Common Law Legislation: Drafting and Interpretation*. Oxford: Oxford University Press.

Bennion, Francis A. R. and Jones, Oliver. 2013. *Bennion on Statutory Interpretation*. 6th edn. London: LexisNexis Butterworths.

Bertens H. 2008. *Literary Theory: The Basics*. 2nd edn. London and New York: Taylor & Francis. Available at http://www.sciencedirect.com/science/journal/08894906/27/2.

Bhatia, Vijay. 2008. Genre Analysis, ESP and Professional Practice. *English for Specific Purposes*. 27(2), 161–174.

Bhatia, Vijay. 2014. *Worlds of Written Discourse*. London, New Delhi, New York, Sydney: Bloomsbury.

Biblica. 2013. *How Many Different Languages Has the Bible Been Translated Into?* [Online]. Available at: www.biblica.com/en-us/bible/bible-faqs/how-many-different-languages-has-the-bible-been-translated-into/.

Black's Law Dictionary. The Law Dictionary [Online]. Available at: thelawdictionary.org/.

Boch, Raoul. 2009. *Dizionario dei falsi amici di francese. Les faux amis aux aguets*. Bologna Zanichelli.

Bonvini, Emilio, Busuttil, Joëlle, Peyraube, Alain (eds). 2011. *Dictionnaire des Langues*. Paris: Quadrige/PUF

Bowman, G. 2005. *The Art of Legislative Drafting*. [Online]. Available at: http://webarchive.nationalarchives.gov.uk/+/http:/www.cabinetoffice.gov.uk/media/190031/dale.pdf.

Bragg, M. 2003. *The Adventure of English. The Biography of a Language*. London: Hodder and Stoughton.

Braudo, Serge. 2015. *Dictionnaire du droit privé français*. [Online]. Available at: www.dictionnaire-juridique.com/.

Broadie, A. 2000. *Why Scottish Philosophy Matters*. Edinburgh: The Saltire Society.

Brownlie, Ian (ed.). 1985. *Basic Documents in International Law*. 3rd edn. Oxford: Clarendon.

Brownlie, Ian. 1990. *Principles of Public International Law*. 4th ed. Oxford: Oxford University Press.

Bugarski, Ranko and Hawkesworth, Celia (eds). 1992. *Language Planning in Yugoslavia*. Bloomington: Slavica Publishers.

Cabré, M. Teresa. 1998. *Terminology. Theory, Methods and Applications*. Amsterdam/Philadelphia: John Benjamins Publishing Company.

Calman, Ross. 2013. *Māori education – mātauranga – Education in traditional Māori society*. Te Ara – the Encyclopedia of New Zealand, updated 20 June 2013. [Online]. Available at: www.TeAra.govt.nz/en/maori-education-matauranga/page-1.

Campbell, Lyle. 2013. *Historical Linguistics. An Introduction*. 3rd edn. Edinburgh: Edinburgh University Press.

Chalmers, Damian, Davies, Gareth, Monti, Giorgio. 2014. *European Union Law*. 3rd edn. Cambridge: Cambridge University Press.

Chandler, Daniel. 2000. *An Introduction to Genre Theory*. [Online]. Available at: http://visual-memory.co.uk/daniel/Documents/intgenre/chandler_genre_theory.pdf.

Chandler, Daniel. 2007. *Semiotics: The Basics*. 2nd edn. London: Routledge. [Online]. Available at: https://analepsis.files.wordpress.com/2011/08/69249454-chandler-semiotics.pdf.

Cheng, Le, Sin, King Kui, Wagner, Anne (eds). 2014. *The Ashgate Handbook of Legal Translation*. Farnham, Burlington: Ashgate.

Cobley, Paul (ed.). 2001. *The Routledge Companion to Semiotics and Linguistics*. London and New York: Routledge.

Cobley, Paul (ed.) 2010. *The Routledge Companion to Semiotics*. London and New York: Routledge.

Collins Robert French Dictionary. 2010. 9th edn. London and Glasgow: Collins.

COMEST/UNESCO. 2005. *The Precautionary Principle*. [Online]. Available at: http://unesdoc.unesco.org/images/0013/001395/139578e.pdf.

Commission Manual on Legislative Drafting. Available at: http://ec.europa.eu/smart-regulation/better_regulation/documents/legis_draft_comm_en.pdf.

Commonwealth Association of Legislative Counsel An Annotated Catalogue of Publications. [Online]. Available at: www.opc.gov.au/calc/docs/CALCCatalogue_Feb2011.pdf.

Communication Theory. List of Theories. [Online]. Available at: http://communicationtheory.org/list-of-theories/.

Conseil d'État. 2008. *Principes de technique législative. Guide de rédaction des textes législatifs et réglementaires*. [Online]. Available at: www.raadvst-consetat.be/?lang=fr&page=technique_legislative.

Cooper, Andrew F., Heine, Jorge, Thakur, Ramesh (eds). 2013. *The Oxford Handbook of Modern Diplomacy*. Oxford: Oxford University Press.

Cornu, Gérard. 2014. *Vocabulaire juridique*. 10th edn. Paris: Presses universitaires de France.

Council of Europe/ERICarts. 2015. *Compendium of Cultural Policies and Trends in Europe*. 16th edn. ISSN 2222–7334. [Online]. Available at: www.culturalpolicies.net/web/index.php.

Council of the European Union. 2002. *Manual of Precedents for Acts Established within the Council of the European Union*. Brussels: General Secretariat of the Council. [Online]. Available at: http://bookshop.europa.eu/en/manual-of-precedents-for-acts-established-within-the-council-of-the-european-union-pbQC4101381/.

Council of the European Union. 2011. *Quality Assurance at the Council's Translation Department*. Brussels: General Secretariat of the Council Directorate-General A – Personnel and Administration, Directorate 3 – Translation and Document Production. [Online]. Available at: www.consilium.europa.eu/uedocs/cmsUpload/Quality_assurance_EN.pdf.

Courts and Tribunals Judiciary. 2015. *Magistrates*. [Online]. Available at: www.judiciary.gov.uk/about-the-judiciary/who-are-the-judiciary/judicial-roles/magistrates/.

Craig Barker, J. 2004. *Mechanisms to Create and Support Conventions, Treaties, and other Responses. The Binding Nature of International Law* [Online]. Available at: www.eolss.net/eolsssamplechapters/c14/e1-44-01/E1-44-01-TXT.aspx#3.

Crawford, James. 2012. *Brownlie's Principles of Public International Law*. Oxford: Oxford University Press.

Crawford, James. 2015. *Language Loyalties. Historical Roots of U.S. Language Policy*. [Online]. Available at: www.languagepolicy.net/archives/LLPT1.htm.

Crystal, David. 1980. *Linguistics*. Harmondsworth: Penguin Books.

Crystal, David. 2003. *English as a Global Language*. 2nd edn. Cambridge: Cambridge University Press.

Crystal, David. 2010. *The Cambridge Encyclopedia of Language*. 3rd edn. Cambridge: Cambridge University Press.

Crystal, David. 2014. *Language Death*. Cambridge: Cambridge University Press.

Curzon, L. B. 1993. *Dictionary of Law*. London: Pitman.

Dalby, Andrew. 2004. *Dictionary of Languages: The Definitive Reference to more than 400 Languages*. London: A and C Black.

Dale, Sir W. (ed.). 1986. *British and French Statutory Drafting. The Proceedings of the Franco-British Conference of 7 and 8 April 1986*. London: Institute of Advanced Legal Studies, University of London.

Daniels, Peter T. and Bright, William. 1996. *The World's Writing Systems*. Oxford: Oxford University Press.

Bibliography 253

Deledalle, Gérard. 1978. *Charles S. Peirce. Écrits sur le signe*. Paris: Seuil.

d'Entrèves, A. P. 1970. *Natural Law*. London: Hutchinson.

Derlén, Mattias. 2009. *Multilingual Interpretation of European Union Law*. Alphen aan den Rijn: Kluwer.

Dobrovolsky, Michael and Katamba, Francis. 1997. Phonology: the Function and Patterning of Sounds. In William O'Grady, Michael Dobrovolsky, Francis Katamba (eds), *Contemporary Linguistics: An Introduction*, 591–624. London and New York: Longman.

Dobrovolsky, Michael and O'Grady, William. 1997. Writing and Language. In William O'Grady, Michael Dobrovolsky, Francis Katamba, (eds), *Contemporary Linguistics: An Introduction*, 591–624. London and New York: Longman.

Domenichelli, L. 1999. *Constitution et Régime linguistique en Belgique et au Canada*. Brussels: Bruylant

Du Cann, Richard. 1993. *The Art of the Advocate*. London: Penguin.

Dudley-Evans, Tony (undated). *Genre Analysis: A Key to a Theory of ESP?* [Online]. Available at: www.aelfe.org/documents/text2-Dudley.pdf.

Enright, M. 2009. *Irish Language in the Courts, South and North*. Human Rights in Ireland. [Online]. Available at: http://humanrights.ie/co nstitution-of-ireland/irish-language-in-the-courts-south-and-north/.

European Commission. 1997. *Manual on Legislative Drafting*. [Online]. Available at: http://ec.europa.eu/smart-regulation/better_regulation/documents/legis_draft_comm_en.pdf.

European Commission. 2009. *Programme for Quality Management in Translation. 22 Quality Actions*. Brussels: European Commission. Directorate-General for Translation. [Online]. Available at: http://ec.europa.eu/dgs/translation/publications/studies/quality_management_translation_en.pdf.

European Commission. 2012. How to Write Clearly. [Online]. Available on download at: http://bookshop.europa.eu/en/how-to-write-clearly-pbHC3212148/.

European Commission. 2015. *European Judicial Atlas in Civil Matters*. [Online]. Available at: http://ec.europa.eu/justice_home/judicialatlascivil/html/cc_information_en.htm.

European Commission. Claire's Clear Writing Tips. [Online]. Available at: http://ec.europa.eu/translation/documents/clear_writing_tips_en.pdf.

European Commission. Translation and Drafting Resources. Translating EU texts made easier – links to resources. [Online]. Available at: http://ec.europa.eu/translation/index_en.htm.

European Union. 2010. *Practical Handbook on European Private International Law*. [Online]. Available at: http://ec.europa.eu/justice/civil/files/practical_handbook_eu_international_law_en.pdf.

European Union. 2013. Joint Practical Guide of the European Parliament, the Council and the Commission for persons involved in the drafting of European Union legislation. 2nd edn. [Online]. Available at: http://eur-lex.europa.eu/content/pdf/techleg/joint-practical-guide-2013-en.pdf.

European Union. 2015. Interinstitutional Style Guide. Luxembourg: Publications Office of the European Union. [Online]. Available at: http://publications.europa.eu/code/en/en-000100.htm.

Evans, M. D. 2011. *Blackstone's International Law Documents*. 10th edn. Oxford: Oxford University Press.

Eversheds. 2011. *Legal Drafting in English*. London: Eversheds. [Online]. Available at: www.eversheds.com/documents/Legal-drafting-in-English.pdf.

Feltham, R. G. 2012. *Diplomatic Handbook*. 8th edn. Leiden and Boston, MA: Martinus Nijhoff.

Ferrara, M. and Gaglioti, A. R. 2012. *A Mathematical Model for the Quantitative Analysis of Law. Putting Legal Values into Numbers*. [Online]. Available at: www.wseas.us/e-library/conferences/2012/CambridgeUSA/MATHCC/MATHCC-31.pdf.

Fish, The Honourable Justice Mr M. J.,. 2012. *The Art of the Advocate: From Cicero to Erskine to Martin. The Honourable Charles L. Dubin Lecture on Advocacy*. Osgoode Hall, 4 October 2012. [Online]. Available at: www.advocates.ca/assets/files/pdf/Dubin%20Lecture%20FINAL%20webversion.pdf.

Fitzgerald, P. J. 1966. *Salmond on Jurisprudence*. 12th edn. London: Sweet and Maxwell.

Friedrich, C. J. 1963. *The Philosophy of Law in Historical Perspective*. 2nd edn. Chicago and London: University of Chicago Press.

Frydman, B. 2011 *Le Sens des Lois: Histoire de l'interprétation et de la raison juridique*. 2nd edn. Brussels: Bruylant. Paris: L.G.D.J.

Gallas, Tito. 1999. Coredazione e Traduzione Giuridica nella Legislazione Multilingue, in Particolare Quella Comunitaria. *Quaderni di Libri e riviste d'Italia, la Traduzione, Saggi e documenti*. 43(IV) 135–147.

Gibbons, John (ed.). 1994. *Language and the Law*. Harlow: Longman.

Gilder, A. 2009. *Le français administratif. Écrire pour être lu*. Paris: Éditions Glyphe.

Glenn, H. P. 1974. The Local Law of Alsace-Lorraine: A Half Century of Survival. *The International and Comparative Law Quarterly*. 23(4) October, 769–790.

Gloag, W. M. and Henderson, R. C. 1995. *The Law of Scotland*. 10th edn. (edited by W. A Wilson, A. D. M. Forte, Rt Hon. Lord Rodger of Earlsferry, A. Paton, L. Dunlop, P. Hood, A. R. W. Young. Edinburgh: W. Green/Sweet and Maxwell.

Gloag, W. M., Henderson, R. C. 2012. *The Law of Scotland*. 13th edn. (edited by Hector L. MacQueen, The Rt. Hon. Lord Eassie, Douglas Bain, David Cabrelli, Gordon Cameron, D. L. Carey-Miller, Malcolm M. Combe, W. C. H. Ervine, Nicholas Grier, David Irvine, Simone Lamont-Black, Catherine Ng, David Nichols, Roderick Paisley, Morag Wise. Edinburgh: W. Green/Sweet and Maxwell.

Goodrich, Peter. 1990. *Languages of Law: From Logics of Memory to Nomadic Masks*. London: Weidenfeld and Nicolson.

Grant, Michael (ed.). 1973. *Greek Literature in Translation*. Harmondsworth: Pelican.

Greenberg, M. L. 2014. *The Writing on the Wall: The Russian Orthographic Reform of 1917–1918*. [Online]. Available at: http://russiasgreatwar.org/media/culture/orthography.shtml.

Greenberg, Robert. 1998. *The Politics of Language Reform in the Yugoslav Successor States*. [Online]. Available at: www.wilsoncenter.org/publication/159-the-politics-language-reform-the-yugoslav-successor-states.

Groffier, Ethel and Reed, David. 1990. *La Lexicographie juridique. Principes et méthodes*. Cowansville: Les Editions Yvon Blais Inc.

Guidère, Mathieu. 2010. *Introduction à la traductologie. Penser la traduction: hier, aujourd'hui, demain*. 2nd edn. Brussels: De Boeck.

Harris, J. W. 1997. *Legal Philosophies*. 2nd edn. London, Edinburgh, Dublin: Butterworths.

Hart, Herbert L. A. 1997. *The Concept of Law*. 2nd edn. Oxford, New York: Oxford University Press (3rd edn: 2012).

Hartley, Trevor C. 1994. *The Foundations of European Community Law*. 3rd edn. Oxford: Clarendon Press.

Hartley, Trevor C. 2014. *The Foundations of European Union Law*. 8th edn. Oxford: Oxford University Press.

Heffer, Chris, Rock, Frances, Conley, John. 2013. *Textual Travels in the Law*. Oxford: Oxford University Press.

Herrin, Judith. 2008. *Byzantium: The Surprising Life of a Medieval Empire*. London: Penguin Books.

History of Language Rights in New Brunswick. [Online]. Available at: www.legal-info-legale.nb.ca/en/publications/you_and_your_rights/History_of_Language_Rights_ENG.pdf.

Holborn, Guy. 2001. *Butterworths Legal Research Guide*. 2nd edn. London, Edinburgh: Butterworths.

Hoppe, D. 2015. *Le Coût du monolinguism. Quand la pluralité des langues recule dans les organisations internationales*. Le Monde diplomatique. May 2015: 9.

Huang, A. 2009. *Aboriginal Languages in Canada*. [Online]. Available at: http://indigenousfoundations.arts.ubc.ca/home/culture/languages.html.

International Organization for Standardization. 2015. Language codes – ISO 639. [Online]. Available at: www.iso.org/iso/home/standards/language_codes.htm.

International Organization for Standardization. 2015. ISO 9000. [Online]. Available at: www.iso.org/iso/iso_9000.
Internet Encyclopedia of Philosophy (IEP). *Charles Sanders Peirce (1839–1914)*. [Online]. Available at: www.iep.utm.edu/peircebi/.
The Irish Times. 21 February 2015. Experts say constitutional changes should look at subtlety of Irish translation. Call for co-drafting of laws in English and Irish to avoid differences of interpretation. [Online]. Available at: www.irishtimes.com/news/politics/experts-say-constitutional-changes-should-look-at-subtlety-of-irish-translation-1.2111749.
James, Philip S. 1989. *Introduction to English Law*. 12th edn. London: Butterworths.
James, Philip S., Shears, Peter, Stephenson, Graham. 1996. *James' Introduction to English Law*. 13th edn. London: Butterworths.
Jones, C. 2002. *The English Language in Scotland: An Introduction to Scots*. East Linton: Tuckwell Press.
Kaczorowska, Alina. 2003. *Public International Law*. London: Old Bailey Press.
Kaczorowska, Alina. 2005. *Public International Law*. 3rd edn. London: Old Bailey Press.
Kapteyn, P. J. G. and VerLoren van Themaat, P. 2008. *The Law of the European Union and the European Communities*. 4th edn. Edited by P. J. G. Kapteyn, A. M. McDonnell, K. J. M. Mortelmans, C. W. A. Timmermans, L. A. Geelhoed. Alphen aan den Rijn: Kluwer.
Kelly, J. M. 1992. *A Short History of Western Legal Theory*. Oxford: Clarendon Press.
Kemmer, S. 2009. *The History of English. Spelling and Standardization in English: Historical Overview*. [Online]. Available at: www.ruf.rice.edu/~kemmer/Histengl/spelling.html.
Kimbrough, Paula. 2015. *How Braille Began*. [Online]. Available at: www.brailler.com/braillehx.htm.
Kirby, Peter. 2014. Mapping the Languages of the Roman Empire. [Online]. Available at: http://peterkirby.com/mapping-the-languages-of-the-roman-empire.html.
Ladmiral, Jean-René. 1994/2010. *Traduire: théorèmes pour la traduction*. Paris: Gallimard.
Lancashire, Adrian. 2015. *Portuguese Language Reform Law Goes Global*. [Online]. Available at: www.euronews.com/2015/05/14/portuguese-language-reform-law-goes-global/.
Lawler, John and Dry, Helen Aristar (eds). 1998. *Using Computers in Linguistics. A Practical Guide*. London and New York: Routledge.
Lawson, F. H, Anton, A. E., Neville Brown, L. 1966. 3rd edn. *Amos and Walton's Introduction to French Law*. Oxford: Oxford University Press.
Learn German Online. *The German Spelling Reform*. [Online]. Available at: www.learn-german-online.net/en/learning-german-resources/german-spelling-reform.html.
Levert, Lionel A. 1995. *Bilingual Drafting in Canada. The Loophole*. July. Commonwealth Association of Legislative Counsel. [Online]. Available at: www.opc.gov.au/calc/docs/Loophole/Loophole_Jul95.pdf.
Levert, Lionel A. 2011. *Work Methods and Processes in a Drafting Environment*. [Online]. Available at: www.opc.gov.au/calc/docs/Loophole_papers/Levert_Feb2011.pdf.
Lewis, Geoffrey. 2002. *The Turkish Language Reform: A Catastrophic Success*. Oxford: Oxford University Press.
Lewis, M. Paul, Simons, Gary F., Fennig, Charles D. (eds.). 2015. *Ethnologue: Languages of the World*. 18th edn. Dallas: SIL International. [Online]. Available at: www.ethnologue.com.
Listverse. *Top 10 Most Spoken Languages In The World*. [Online]. Available at: http://listverse.com/2008/06/26/top-10-most-spoken-languages-in-the-world/.
Louis, Jean-Victor. 1980. *The Community Legal Order*. Brussels: Commission of the European Communities.
Mac Aodha, Máirtín (ed.) 2014. *Legal Lexicography: A Comparative Perspective*. Farnham: Ashgate.
McCrum, Robert, MacNeil, Robert, Cran, William. 2011. *The Story of English*. London, Boston, MA: Faber and Faber.
MacCulloch, Diarmaid. 2010. *A History of Christianity*. London: Penguin Books.

McLeod, I. 2011. *Legal Method*. 8th edn. Basingstoke: Palgrave Macmillan.
McLeod, I. 2012. *Legal Theory*. 6th edn. Basingstoke: Palgrave Macmillan.
McLeod, Wilson. 2001. Gaelic in the New Scotland: Politics, Rhetoric and Public Discourse. *Journal on Ethnopolitics and Minority Issues in Europe*. [Online]. Available at: www.ecmi.de/fileadmin/downloads/publications/JEMIE/JEMIE02MacLeod28-11-01.pdf.
Manguel, Alberto. 1996. *A History of Reading*. London: Flamingo.
Martin, Charles. 2012. The Dark Side of Translation Revision. *Translation Journal*. 16(1), January.[Online]. Available at: www.bokorlang.com/journal/59editing.htm.
Mattila, Heikki E. S. 2006. *Comparative Legal Linguistics*. Aldershot: Ashgate.
Mattila, Heikki E. S. 2013. *Comparative Legal Linguistics: Language of Law, Latin and Modern Lingua Francas*. 2nd edn. Farnham: Ashgate.
May, S. 2011 *Language and Minority Rights: Ethnicity, Nationalism and the Politics of Language*. London, New York: Routledge.
Mayer, Felix (ed.). 2001. *Language for Special Purposes: Perspectives for the New Millennium*. 2 vols. Tübingen: Gunter Narr.
Mellinkoff, David. 1963. *The Language of the Law*. Boston, MA: Little, Brown & Co.
Merrell, Floyd. 2001. Charles Sanders Peirce's Concept of the Sign. In Paul Cobley (ed.). *The Routledge Companion to Semiotics and Linguistics*, 28–39. London and New York: Routledge.
Meston, M. C., Sellar, W. D. H., Cooper, T. M. The Rt. Hon. Lord, 1991. *The Scottish Legal Tradition*. 3rd edn. Edinburgh: Saltire Society and Stair Society.
Metz, Helen Chapin. 1995. *Turkey: A Country Study*. Washington DC: GPO for the Library of Congress. [Online]. Available at: http://countrystudies.us/turkey/.
Mey, Jacob L. 2001. *Pragmatics: An Introduction*. 2nd edn. Oxford: Blackwell.
Mikelsone, Gundega. 2013. *The Binding Force of the Case Law of the Court of Justice of the European Union*. [Online]. Available at: www.mruni.eu/upload/iblock/3ef/JUR-13-20-2-06.pdf.
Mills, H. C. 1956. Language Reform in China: Some Recent Developments. *The Journal of Asian Studies*. 15(4) August, 517–540.
Mollin, Sandra. 2006. *Euro-English. Assessing Variety Status*. Tübingen: Gunter Narr Verlag.
Morgan J. F. 1982. Multilingual Legal Drafting in the EEC and the Work of Jurist/Linguists. *Multilingua*. 1(2), 109–117.
Mounin, Georges. *Les problèmes théoriques de la traduction*. 1963/2008. Paris: Gallimard.
Muir Watt, Horatia. 2015. *DROIT – Droit comparé*. Encyclopædia Universalis. [Online]. Available at: www.universalis.fr/encyclopedie/droit-droit-compare/.
Munday, Jeremy. 2012. *Introducing Translation Studies. Theories and Applications*. 3rd edn. London, New York: Routledge.
Nations Online. *Overseas Territories, Dependent Areas, and Disputed Territories*. [Online]. Available at: www.nationsonline.org/oneworld/territories.htm.
The New English Bible. 1970. Oxford: Oxford University Press, Cambridge University Press.
Newmark, Peter. 1995. *Approaches to Translation*. Hemel Hempstead: Phoenix ELT.
Norman, Paul. 2006. *Comparative Law*. New York: Hauser Global Law School Program, New York University School of Law. [Online]. Available at: www.nyulawglobal.org/globalex/Comparative_Law.htm#_Print.
O'Grady, William. 1997. Semantics: The Analysis of Meaning. In O'Grady, William, Dobrovolsky, Michael, Katamba, Francis (eds). *Contemporary Linguistics: An Introduction*, 591–624. London and New York: Longman.
O'Connor, J. D. 1973. *Phonetics*. Harmondsworth: Penguin Books.
Office of the Scottish Parliamentary Counsel. 2006. Plain Language and Legislation. [Online]. Available at: www.gov.scot/resource/doc/93488/0022476.pdf.
O'Grady, William, Dobrovolsky, Michael, Katamba, Francis (eds). 1997. *Contemporary Linguistics: An Introduction*. London and New York: Longman.
Ost, François. 2009. *Traduire. Défense et illustration du multilinguisme*. Paris: Librairie Arthème Fayard.

Ostler, Nicholas. 2005. *Empires of the Word: A Language History of the World.* London: HarperCollins.
Oustinoff, Michaël (ed.). 2011a. *Traduction et mondialisation. Les Essentiels d'Hermès.* Paris: CNRS Éditions.
Oustinoff, Michaël. 2011b. *Traduire et communiquer à l'heure de la mondialisation.* Paris: CNRS Éditions.
Paltridge, Brian. 2006. *Discourse Analysis: An Introduction.* London, New York: Continuum.
Pastor, Gloria Corpas. 2006. *Translation Quality Standards in Europe: An Overview.* Malaga: University of Malaga, Department of Translation and Interpreting. [Online]. Available at: www.uma.es/hum892/publicaciones/corpas_2006b.pdf.
Perell, Paul M. 1987. *Stare Decisis and Techniques of Legal Reasoning and Legal Argument.* [Online]. Available at: http://legalresearch.org/writing-analysis/stare-decisis-techniques/.
Peruginelli, Ginevra. (no date). *Multilingual Legal Information Access: an Overview.* [Online]. Available at: http://webfolder.eurac.edu/EURAC/LexALP_shared/media/Peruginelli.pdf.
Picken, Catriona (ed.) 1989. *The Translator's Handbook.* 2nd edn. London: ASLIB.
Pîrnuță, Oana-Andreea and Arseni, Alina-Adriana. 2011. *Ne Bis in Idem. A Principle of Paramount Importance in the European Union Area of Freedom, Security and Justice.* [Online]. Available at: www.afahc.ro/ro/revista/Nr_1_2011/Articol_Pirnuta_nr1_2011.pdf.
Poole, Stuart C. 1999. *An Introduction to Linguistics.* Basingstoke and New York: Palgrave.
Portal da Língua Portuguesa 2015. *Acordo Ortográfico da Língua Portuguesa de 1990.* [Online]. Available at: www.portaldalinguaportuguesa.org/acordo.php.
Požgaj Hadži, Vesna (ed.). 2013. *Jezik između lingvistike i politike [Language Between Linguistics And Politics].* Belgrade: Biblioteke XX vek.
Premier ministre, Secrétariat général du Gouvernement. 1997. *Circulaire du 30 janvier 1997 relative aux règles d'élaboration, de signature et de publication des textes au Journal officiel et à la mise en œuvre de procédures particulières incombant au Premier ministre.* Paris: Journal officiel de la République française.
Qiyao, Deng. 2009. *The Other Writing of People without a Written Language.* [Online]. Available at: http://iel.cass.cn/english/Detail.asp?newsid=8026.
Reboul, Olivier. 2013. *Introduction à la rhétorique: Théorie et pratique.* Paris: Presses Universitaires de France.
Richards, Paul. H., and Curzon, Leslie. B. 2011. *The Longman Dictionary of Law.* 8th edn. Harlow: Longman.
Ridout, S. 2014. *Complete List of Arabic Speaking Countries 2014.* [Online]. Available at: http://istizada.com/complete-list-of-arabic-speaking-countries-2014/.
Robertson, Colin. 2001. Multilingual Law: A Framework for Understanding. In Felix Mayer (ed.), *Language for Special Purposes: Perspectives for the New Millennium,* Vol. 2, 697–703. Tübingen: Gunter Narr.
Robertson, Colin. 2009. Multilingual Law: What Is It? How Is It Made? How Is It Used and Applied? (with reference to EU practice). In, Lelija Sočanac, Christopher Goddard and Ludger Kremer (eds), *Curriculum, Multilingualism and the Law,* 373–395. Zagreb: Globus.
Robertson, Colin. 2010. Legal-linguistic Revision of EU Legislative Texts. In Maurizio Gotti and Christopher Williams (eds), *Legal Discourse across Languages and Cultures,* 51–73. Bern: Peter Lang.
Robertson, Colin. 2012a. EU Legal English: Common Law, Civil Law or a New Genre? *European Review of Private Law.* 5/6, 1215–1240.
Robertson, Colin. 2012b. The Problem of Meaning in Multilingual EU Legal Texts. *International Journal of Law, Language & Discourse.* 2(1), 1–30. [Online]. Available at: www.ijlld.com/wp-content/uploads/pdf/Free-Journals/IJLLD2-1-2012/ijlld%202.1%20content.pdf.
Robertson, Colin. 2013. *How the European Union Functions in 23 Languages.* SYNAPS. [Online]. Available at: www.nhh.no/Files/Filer/institutter/fsk/Synaps/28-2013/Robertson_28_2013.pdf.

Bibliography

Robinson, Douglas. 1997. *Becoming a Translator. An Accelerated Course*. London and New York: Routledge.
Robinson, O. F., Fergus, T. D, Gordon, W. M. 2000. *European Legal History*. London, Edinburgh, Dublin: Butterworths.
Ronelle, Alexander. 2006. *Bosnian, Croatian, Serbian, a Grammar: With Sociolinguistic Commentary*. Madison: University of Wisconsin press.
Rousseau, Jean-Jacques. 1762. *Du contrat social ou Principes du droit politique*. [Online]. Available at: http://classiques.uqac.ca/classiques/Rousseau_jj/contrat_social/Contrat_social.pdf.
Ryan M. 1999. *Literary Theory: A Practical Introduction*. Massachusetts and Oxford, Blackwell.
Sager, Juan C. 1990. *A Practical Course in Terminology Processing*. Amsterdam/Philadelphia: John Benjamins Publishing Company.
Šarčević, Susan. 1997. *New Approach to Legal Translation*. The Hague, London, Boston, MA: Kluwer.
Šarčević, Susan (ed.) 2001. *Legal Translation. Preparing for Accession to the European Union*. Rijeka: Faculty of Law, University of Rijeka.
Šarčević, Susan (ed.). 2009. *Legal Language in Action: Translation, Terminology, Drafting and Procedural Issues*. Zagreb: Nakladni Zavod Globus.
Šarčević, Susan (ed.). 2015. *Language and Culture in EU Law. Multidisciplinary Perspectives*. Farnham and Burlington: Ashgate.
Šarčević, Susan and Robertson, Colin. 2013. The work of lawyer-linguists in the EU institutions. In Anabel Borja Albi and, Fernando Prieto Ramos (eds), *Legal Translation in Context. Professional Issues and Prospects*, 181–202. Oxford: Peter Lang.
Saussure, Ferdinand de. 2005. *Cours de linguistique générale*. Paris: Payot.
Saussure, Ferdinand de. 2011. *Course in General Linguistics*. Translation by Wade Baskin,. Perry Meisel and Haun Sauss (eds). New York: Columbia University Press.
Shah, Sheena. 2007. German in a Contact Situation: The Case of Namibian German. *eDUSA* 2, 2–20. [Online]. Available at: www.sagv.org.za/edusa/edusa_2-07-2/sha_2007_2.pdf.
Shaozhong, Liu, 2005. *What Is Pragmatics?* [Online]. Available at: www.gxnu.edu.cn/Personal/szliu/definition.html.
Sočanac, Lelija, Goddard, Christopher, Kremer, Ludger (eds). 2009. *Curriculum, Multilingualism and the Law*. Zagreb: Nakladni Zavod Globus.
Society for Anglo-Chinese Understanding (SACU). 2006. *Reforming the Language*. Reprinted from SACU's magazine *China Now 24*, August 1972, p. 10 and *China Now 27*, December 1972, p. 7. [Online]. Available at: www.sacu.org/pinyinissues.html.
Stanford Encyclopedia of Philosophy. 2014. Austin, John. [Online]. Available at: http://plato.stanford.edu/entries/austin-john.
Starke, Joseph G. 1989. *An Introduction to International Law*. 10th edn. London: Butterworths.
Stroud's Judicial Dictionary of Words and Phrases. 2014. 8th edn. London: Sweet & Maxwell.
Sutherland, E. E., Goodall, K. F. Little, G. F. M, Davidson, F. P. (eds). 2011. *Law Making and the Scottish Parliament: The Early Years*. Edinburgh: Edinburgh University Press.
Swales, John. M. 1992. Language for Specific Purposes. In W. Bright (ed.), *International Encyclopedia of Linguistics*, Vol. 2, 300–302. New York, Oxford: Oxford University Press.
Swiggers, Pierre. 1997. *Histoire de la pensée linguistique*. Paris: Presses Universitaires de France.
Swiss Confederation. Federal Chancellery. 2015. *Rédaction législative*. [Online]. Available at: www.bk.admin.ch/themen/lang/04921/index.html?lang=fr.
Te Keti Ipurangi. 2015. *Thumbs Up! An Introduction to New Zealand Sign Language*. [Online]. Available at: https://nzsl.tki.org.nz/Introduction.
Terminology Coordination at the European Parliament. 2013. Luxembourg: European Parliament. Available at: http://www.termcoord.eu/wp-content/uploads/2014/01/TermNews_December_2013.pdf.
Thornton, Garth C. and Xanthaki, Helen (ed.). 2013. *Thornton's Legislative Drafting*. 5th edn. Haywards Heath: Bloomsbury Professional.

Tiersma, Peter. 1999. *Legal Language*. Chicago: University of Chicago Press.
Translation Centre for the Bodies of the European Union. 2015. *Revising Translations*. Luxembourg: Translation Centre for the Bodies of the European Union. [Online]. Available at: http://cdt.europa.eu/EN/whatwedo/Pages/Translation-annexes/Revising-translations.aspx.
Truffaut, Louis. 1997. *Traducteur tu seras. Dix commandements librement argumentés*. Brussels: Éditions du Hazard.
Truss, Lynne. 2005. *Eats, Shoots & Leaves*. London: Profile Books.
Tytler, Alexander Fraser. 1907. *Essay on the Principles of Translation*. London: J. M. Dent & Sons; New York: E. P. Dutton & Co.
UCL 2015. *What Is a Standard Language? History of the Dutch Language*. [Online]. Available at: www.ucl.ac.uk/dutchstudies/an/SP_LINKS_UCL_POPUP/SPs_english/language_history/pages/stand_lang.html.
UNESCO. 1996. *Universal Declaration on Linguistic Rights*. World Conference on Linguistic Rights Barcelona, Spain, 9 June 1996. [Online]. Available at: www.unesco.org/cpp/uk/declarations/linguistic.pdf.
Upton, Clive, and Widdowson, John D. A. 2006. *An Atlas of English Dialects*. 2nd edn. London: Routledge.
Vaillancourt, François, Coche, Olivier, Cadieux, Marc Antoine, Ronson, Jamie Lee. 2012. *Official Language Policies of the Canadian Provinces Costs and Benefits in 2006*. Studies in Language Policy Vancouver: Fraser Institute. [Online]. Available at: www.fraserinstitute.org/sites/default/files/official-language-policies-of-canadian-provinces-rev.pdf.
Van de Horst, J. M. 2011. *A Brief History of the Dutch Language. The Low Countries. 1996–1997*. Jaargang 4. dbnl digitale biblioteek voor de Nederlandse letteren. 163–172. [Online]. Available at: www.dbnl.org/tekst/_low001199601_01/_low001199601_01_0023.php.
Venuti, Lawrence. 1995. *The Translator's Invisibility. A History of Translation*. London and New York: Routledge.
Voss, Hans-Peter. *History of Schleswig Holstein*. 2000. [Online]. Available at: www.hans-peter-voss.de/gen/e/history.htm.
Vuorinen, Erkka. 2011. *Quality Assurance and Legislative Translation*. Brussels: European Commission. [Online]. Available at: http://ec.europa.eu/dgs/translation/workwithus/candidatecountries/documents/quality__assurance__legislative__translation_en.pdf.
Walker, David M. 2001. *The Scottish Legal System: An Introduction to the Study of Scots Law*. 8th edn. Edinburgh: W. Green/Sweet and Maxwell.
Weston, Martin. 1991. *An English Reader's Guide to the French Legal System*. New York, Oxford: Berg.
Wilson, Colin. 2007. *Drafting against a Background of Differing Legal Systems: Scots Law and the UK Statute Book*. [Online]. Available at: www.opc.gov.au/calc/docs/Loophole_papers/Wilson2_Jul2007.pdf.
Wilson, J. F. 2004. *Law Drafting*. [Online]. Available at: www.lawdrafting.co.uk/.
Wright, Sue Ellen and Budin, Gerhard (eds). 1997. *Handbook of Terminology Management. Vol. 1. Basic Aspects of Terminology Management*. Amsterdam/Philadelphia: John Benjamins Publishing Company.
Yearbook of International Organizations.[Online]. Available at: www.uia.org/yearbook.
Yen, Tony. 2010. *Bi-lingual Drafting in Hong Kong*. [Online]. Available at: www.opc.gov.au/calc/docs/Loophole_papers/Yen_Apr2010.pdf.
Yerushatenu. 2012. *Ki Tissa: Moses' Horns: Not a Mistranslation*. Our Heritage. Torah Commentary. Jewish History. [Online]. Available at: http://rabbiartlevine.com/Home/tabid/2652/ID/840/Ki-Tissa-Moses-Horns-Not-a-Mistranslation.aspx.
Yule, George. 2014. *The Study of Language*. 5th edn. Cambridge: Cambridge University Press.
Zulu & San Click Language. 2010. [Online]. Available at: www.youtube.com/watch?v=MXroTDm55C8.

Websites

Asociación de Academias de la Lengua Española (Association of Spanish Language Academies): [Online]. Available at: www.asale.org/.
British Institute of International and Comparative Law. [Online]. Available at: www.biicl.org/.
Charles S. Peirce. [Online]. Available at: www.peirce.org/.
The Commonwealth. [Online]. Available at: http://thecommonwealth.org/.
Community Research and Development Information Service. (CORDIS) [Online]. Available at: http://cordis.europa.eu/.
Comparative Legilinguistics. [Online]. Available at http://legilinguistics.amu.edu.pl/.
Council of Europe. [Online]. Available at: www.coe.int/en/web/portal/home.
Court of Justice of the European Union. Official website. [Online]. Available at: http://curia.europa.eu/
Ethnologue. [Online]. Available at: www.ethnologue.com/.
European Legal Interpreters and Translators Association (EULITA). [Online]. Available at: www.eulita.eu/.
EUR-Lex. Access to European Union Law [Online]. Available at: http://eur-lex.europa.eu/homepage.html.
European Commission. DG Translation. [Online]. Available at: http://ec.europa.eu/dgs/translation/index_en.htm.
European Commission. Interpretation (SCIC). [Online]. Available at: http://ec.europa.eu/dgs/scic/.
European Court of Human Rights. [Online]. Available at: www.echr.coe.int/Pages/home.aspx?p=home.
European Economic Area. [Online]. Available at: www.efta.int/eea.
European Parliament. [Online]. Available at: www.europarl.europa.eu/.
European Parliament Legislative Observatory (Oeil). [Online]. Available at: www.europarl.europa.eu/oeil/home/home.do.
European Union. Official website. [Online]. Available at: http://europa.eu/index_en.htm.
European Union Publications Office. [Online]. Available at: http://publications.europa.eu/en/web/about-us/who-we-are.
Hague Conference on Private International Law. [Online]. Available at: www.hcch.net/.
IAFL (International Association of Forensic Linguists). [Online]. Available at: www.iafl.org/.
IATE (InterActive Terminology for Europe). [Online]. Available at: http://iate.europa.eu/SearchByQueryLoad.do?method=load.
International Cognitive Linguistics Association (ICLA). 2015. [Online]. Available at: www.cognitivelinguistics.org.
International Court of Justice. [Online]. Available at: www.icj-cij.org/homepage.
International Institute of Space Law. [Online]. Available at: www.iislweb.org/.
International Phonetic Alphabet. 2014. [Online]. Available at: www.internationalphoneticalphabet.org/.
Interparliamentary EU Information Exchange (IPEX) www.europarl.europa.eu/webnp/webdav/users/jribot/public/IPEX_leaflet_EN.pdf.
Japanese Law Translation. [Online]. Available at: www.japaneselawtranslation.go.jp/?re=02.
Judicial Systems in Member States. 2015. [Online]. Available at: https://e-justice.europa.eu/.
Justice Québec. [Online]. Available at: www.justice.gouv.qc.ca/english/accueil.asp.
London Institute of Space Policy and Law. [Online]. Available at: www.space-institute.org/.
Nederlandse Taalunie. 2015. The Dutch Language Union. [Online]. Available at: http://taalunie.org/dutch-language-union.
N-LEX. A common gateway to national law [Online]. Available at: http://eur-lex.europa.eu/n-lex/index_en.htm.
The Number of Countries in the World. [Online]. Available at: http://geography.about.com/cs/countries/a/numbercountries.htm.
Oxford Dictionaries. [Online]. Available at: www.oxforddictionaries.com.
Uniform Law Conference of Canada. [Online]. Available at: www.ulcc.ca/en/uniform-acts-en-gb-1/546-drafting-conventions/66-drafting-conventions-act.

United Nations. [Online]. Available at: www.un.org/.
World Federation of the Deaf. [Online]. Available at: http://wfdeaf.org/.

National constitutions

Constitution of Austria. 1920 (reinstated 1945). [Online]. Available at: www.constituteproject.org/constitution/Austria_2009.pdf.
Constitution of Belgium. 1831 [Online]. Available at: www.senate.be/doc/const_fr.html#t1.
Constitution of France. 1958. [Online]. Available in English at: www.france.fr/en/institutions-and-values/constitution-fifth-republic.html.
Constitution of Ireland. 1937. [Online]. Available at: www.irishstatutebook.ie/en/constitution/index.html#part1.
Constitution of the Principality of Liechtenstein. 1921. [Online]. Available in English at: www1.umn.edu/humanrts/research/liechtenstein-constitution.pdf.
Constitution of the Grand Duchy of Luxembourg. 1868. English version [Online]. Available at: www.constituteproject.org/constitution/Luxembourg_2009.pdf.
Constitution of Malta. 1964. [Online]. Available at: www.constitution.org/cons/malta/chapt0.pdf.
Constitution of the Portuguese Republic. 1976. [Online]. Available in English at: http://www.wipo.int/wipolex/en/details.jsp?id=5452.
Constitution of the Republic of South Africa. 1996. (Act No. 108 of 1996). [Online]. Available at: www.acts.co.za/constitution-of-the-republic-of-south-africa-act-1996/index.html?6_languages.php.
Constitution of the Russian Federation. 1993. (with the Amendments and Additions of 30 December 2008). [Online]. Available at: www.wipo.int/edocs/lexdocs/laws/en/ru/ru003en.pdf.
Constitution of Spain. 1978. [Online]. Available in English at: www.congreso.es/portal/page/portal/Congreso/Congreso/Hist_Normas/Norm/const_espa_texto_ingles_0.pdf.
Federal Constitution of the Swiss Federation. 1999. [Online]. Available at: www.wipo.int/wipolex/en/text.jsp?file_id=179791.

Treaties, agreements and legislation

International charters, treaties and agreements

Agreement Governing the Activities of States on the Moon and Other Celestial Bodies. New York, 5 December 1979. [Online]. Available at: https://treaties.un.org/Pages/ViewDetails.aspx?src=IND&mtdsg_no=XXIV-2&chapter=24&lang=en.
Charter of the United Nations. 1945. [Online]. Available at: www.un.org/en/documents/charter/.
Constitutive Act of the African Union. 2015. [Online]. Available at: www.au.int/en/about/constitutive_act.
United Nations. Decision of the General Assembly in its Resolution 3190 (XXVIII) of 18 December 1973. Inclusion of Arabic among the official and the working languages of the General Assembly and its Main Committees. [Online]. Available at: www.un.org/en/ga/search/view_doc.asp?symbol=a/res/3190(xxviii).
United Nations. General Assembly Resolution 2(1) of 1 February 1946. Rules of Procedure concerning Languages. [Online]. Available at: www.un.org/documents/ga/res/1/ares1.htm.
United Nations. Rules of procedure of the General Assembly. [Online]. Available at: http://www.un.org/en/ga/about/ropga/.
United Nations Treaty Series Online Collection. [Online]. Available at: https://treaties.un.org/pages/UNTSOnline.aspx?id=1.
Vienna Convention on Diplomatic Relations 1961. [Online]. Available at: http://legal.un.org/ilc/texts/instruments/english/conventions/9_1_1961.pdf.
Vienna Convention on the Law of Treaties 1969. [Online]. Available at: https://treaties.un.org/doc/Publication/UNTS/Volume%201155/volume-1155-I-18232-English.pdf.

Bibliography

Council of Europe conventions and charters

Convention for the Protection of Human Rights and Fundamental Freedoms. 1950. [Online]. Available at: www.echr.coe.int/Documents/Convention_ENG.pdf.

Council of Europe. Complete list of the Council of Europe's treaties. [Online]. http://conventions.coe.int/Treaty/Commun/ListeTraites.asp?CL=ITA&CM=8.

European Charter for Regional or Minority Languages. Strasbourg. 5 XI.1992. [Online]. Available at: www.coe.int/t/dg4/education/minlang/ and also at: http://conventions.coe.int/Treaty/EN/Treaties/Html/148.htm.

European Union legislation

Agreement on the European Economic Area. 1994. [Online]. Available at: www.efta.int/eea.

Charter of Fundamental Rights of the European Union. 2000. Official Journal of the European Communities. No. C 364/1 of 18 December 2000. [Online]. Available at: www.europarl.europa.eu/charter/pdf/text_en.pdf.

Consolidated version of the Rules of Procedure of the Court of Justice of 25 September 2012 [Online]. Available at: http://curia.europa.eu/jcms/upload/docs/application/pdf/2012-10/rp_en.pdf.

Council Regulation (EC) No. 44/2001 of 22 December 2000 on jurisdiction and the recognition and enforcement of judgments in civil and commercial matters. Official Journal L 12, 16.1.2001, pp. 1–23 [Online]. Available at: http://eur-lex.europa.eu/legal-content/EN/TXT/?uri=celex:32001R0044.

Court of Justice of the European Union. Rules of Procedure. (OJ L 265, 29.9.2012), as amended on 18 June 2013 (OJ L 173, 26.6.2013). [Online]. Available at: http://eur-lex.europa.eu/legal-content/EN/TXT/HTML/?uri=URISERV:ai0049&from=EN, and http://curia.europa.eu/jcms/upload/docs/application/pdf/2012-10/rp_en.pdf.

Interinstitutional Agreement of 22 December 1998 on common guidelines for the quality of drafting of Community legislation (OJ C 73, 17.3.1999, p. 1). [Online]. Available at: http://eur-lex.europa.eu/legal-content/EN/ALL/?uri=CELEX:31999Y0317(01).

Protocol (No. 3) on the Statute of the Court of Justice of the European Union. Official Journal of the European Union. C 83/210 of 30 March 2010. [Online]. Available at: http://curia.europa.eu/jcms/upload/docs/application/pdf/2008-09/statut_2008-09-25_17-29-58_783.pdf.

Regulation No. 1 of 15 April 1958 determining the language to be used by the European Atomic Energy Community, Official Journal 17, 6.10.1958. pp. 401/58.

Regulation No. 1 of 15 April 1958 determining the languages to be used by the European Economic Community. Official Journal OJ 17, 6.10.1958, pp. 385–386. [Online]. Available at: http://eur-lex.europa.eu/legal-content/EN/ALL/?uri=CELEX:31958R0001.

Regulation (EU, Euratom) 2015/2422 of the European Parliament and of the Council of 16 December 2015 amending Protocol No 3 on the Statute of the Court of Justice of the European Union (OJ L 341, 24.12.2015, p. 14–17). [Online]. Available at: http://data.europa.eu/eli/reg/2015/2422/oj.

Treaty on European Union. 1992. [Online]. Available at: http://eur-lex.europa.eu/legal-content/EN/TXT/?uri=celex:12012M/TXT.

Treaty on the functioning of the European Union. 2007. [Online]. Available at: http://eur-lex.europa.eu/legal-content/EN/TXT/?uri=celex:12012E/TXT.

National legislation

The Age of Legal Capacity (Scotland) Act 1991. [UK] [Online]. Available at: www.legislation.gov.uk/ukpga/1991/50/contents.

Charter of the French Language 1977. [Canada] [Online]. Available in English at: www2.publicationsduquebec.gouv.qc.ca/dynamicSearch/telecharge.php?type=2&file=/C_11/C11_A.html.

De gecoördineerde wetten van 18 juli 1966 op het gebruik van de talen in bestuurszaken; Loi sur l'emploi des langues en matière administrative coordonnée le 18 juillet 1966, Koordinierte Gesetze über den Sprachengebrauch in Verwaltungsangelegenheiten. 18 July 1966 [Law Governing the Use of Languages in Administrative Matters Coordinated on 18 July 1966 as amended] [Belgium].

Gaelic Language (Scotland) Act 2005. [UK] [Online]. Available at: www.legislation.gov.uk/asp/2005/7/contents.

Grundgesetz (Basic Law) 1995. [Germany] [Online]. Available at: www.bundestag.de/bundestag/aufgaben/rechtsgrundlagen/grundgesetz/gg_01/245122.

Interpretation Act 1978. [UK] [Online]. Available at: www.legislation.gov.uk/ukpga/1978/30/contents.

Inuit Language Protection Act, SNu 2008 c.17. [Canada] [Online]. Available at: www.canlii.org/en/nu/laws/stat/snu-2008-c-17/latest/snu-2008-c-17.html.

Lawburrows Act 1429. [Scotland] [Online]. Available at: www.legislation.gov.uk/aosp/1429/20/paragraph/p1.

Loi du 24 février 1984 sur le régime des langues. [Luxembourg] [Online]. Available at: http://eli.legilux.public.lu/eli/etat/leg/loi/1984/02/24/n1.

Loi sur l'emploi des langues en matière administrative coordonnée le 18 juillet 1966 (as amended in particular in 2002). [Belgium] [Online]. Available at: www.axl.cefan.ulaval.ca/europe/belgique66.htm.

National Assembly for Wales (Official Languages) Act 2012. [Wales] [Online]. Available at: www.senedd.assembly.wales/mgIssueHistoryHome.aspx?IId=3011.

New Zealand Sign Language Act 2006. [New Zealand] [Online]. Available at: www.legislation.govt.nz/act/public/2006/0018/latest/whole.html.

Official Languages Act (R.S.C., 1985, c. 31 (4th Supp.))/Loi sur les langues officielles [Canada] [Online]. Available at: (L.R.C. (1985), ch. 31 (4ᵉ suppl.)): http://laws-lois.justice.gc.ca/eng/acts/O-3.01/page-1.html#h-1.

Official Languages Act 2003. [Ireland] [Online]. Available at: www.irishstatutebook.ie/eli/2003/act/32/enacted/en/html.

Official Languages Act for Nunavit, SNu. 2008, c.10. [Canada] [Online]. Available at: www.canlii.org/en/nu/laws/stat/snu-2008-c-10/latest/snu-2008-c-10.html.

Special Statute for Trentino-Alto Adige: Modified text of the Constitution of the 'Trentino – Alto Adige' Region and the Provinces of Trento and Bolzano. 1972. [Italy] [Online]. Available in English at: https://democraziadirettatrento.files.wordpress.com/2015/05/statuto-taa_english-version.pdf.

Treaty of Waitangi. 1840. [New Zealand] [Online]. Available at: /www.teara.govt.nz/en/treaty-of-waitangi.

Welsh Language Act 1967. [UK] [Online]. Available at: www.legislation.gov.uk/ukpga/1967/66/enacted.

Welsh Language Act 1993. [UK] [Online]. Available at: www.legislation.gov.uk/ukpga/1993/38.

Cases

Adams v Lindsell. (1818) 1 B & Ald 681. [Online]. Available at: www.bailii.org/ew/cases/EWHC/KB/1818/J59.html or http://archive.is/e30Y.

Case C-265/03: *Reference for a preliminary ruling from the Audencia Nacional: Igor Simutenkov v Ministerio de Educación y Cultura, Real Federación Española de Fútbol*. European Court Reports 2005 p. I02579.

Index

African Union (AU) 72–3, 81
Aitchison, Jean 25, 96, 100
alignment and equivalence of texts:
  equality 199; identical texts 12, 153,
  199; revision 172; terminology 118, 161;
  translation 154–62, 165, 182, 200
Allan, Keith 104
amendment 25, 51, 61–2, 67, 69, 83, 156
analysis *see* framework for analysis and
  understanding
The Atlas of the World's Languages 9, 10
Austin, John 36
Austria 75, 122
authentic texts 55, 66, 68, 80, 82, 166

bad or foul language 16–17
Baltic countries, Russian in 120, 122
Barav, Ami 106
barristers 32
Belgium 5, 15, 83; Constitution 12, 78; Dutch
  5, 78; federal states 78; French 5, 75, 78,
  122; German 5, 78; minority and lesser
  languages 208
Bennion, Francis 66
Bhatia, Vijay 109
Bible 3, 37, 41, 163
bilingual communities 11–12, 13, 77–8,
  84, 207–8
biology of language and sound production
  25–6, 96
boundaries 28, 42–3, 47, 93, 96, 136, 144,
  204, 207
brain and language 96
branches of law 25, 32, 43–5, 63, 75, 84, 95,
  113–14, 147, 204
Breton 120
Brochet, Philip 79
Budin, Gerhard 107

Cabré, M Teresa 107
Canada 5, 77–9, 83–4; bilingual legal
  system 11–12, 13; civil law systems 56, 77;
  co-drafting 54, 77, 79; common law systems
  56, 77; drafting 54, 77, 79, 167; English 5,
  78–9; federal states 78–9; French 5, 78–9;
  indigenous people 79; minority and lesser
  languages 208; official federal languages 5
case law *see* court cases and case law;
  precedent
Chambers Dictionary 106
Champollion, Jean-François 3
Chandler, Daniel 109, 129
changes to languages 9, 73–5, 109, 210
Chinese 109–10; changes 74; English 153;
  logograms 94–5; phonology 98; Pinyin 97
Chomsky, Noam 102
circles, concept of 25, 96, 111
civil law systems 31, 36, 41–5, 147; co-drafting
  77; indigenous communities 16; legal roles
  33; literary sources and legal literature 57;
  precedent 54
classification of languages by use and
  status 8, 44, 113, 195, 206, Appendix IV;
  comparative approach 195; context 119–20;
  dead languages 121–2; legal purposes,
  languages for 26, 113, 118–23, 124, 206;
  official language 118–21, 123; oral societies
  123; shared languages 122; table of
  classification 26, 121–2; terminology 118,
  119–23, 195, 198, 205; transition stages 198;
  universalism 195
co-drafting 65, 77, 79, 167
Collins Robert French Dictionary 106
common law systems 31, 44–5, 147;
  co-drafting 77; drafting 63; equity 59;
  indigenous communities 16; law, definition
  of 37; legal roles 33; precedent 55–6
Commonwealth 75, 122
comparative approach: education and
  training 195; horizontal dimension 110,
  124; legal purposes, languages for 124–5;
  linguistics 105, 110; research 187, 201; rules
  and practice 195; text issues 199; vertical
  dimension 110; viewpoints of law 31
compositionality, principle of 104
computerization *see* technology and tools

conflict of laws 55
consolidation 51, 67
context 26, 43, 196–9, 204–6; classification of languages by use and status 119–20; discourse analysis 108; drafting 63, 206; interpretation 65; legal texts 25, 62, 69; literary sources and legal literature 57; pragmatics 108; semiotics 134; substantive and procedural law 114; text issues 198–9; translation 153, 163–5, 167–8, 206
contract and agreements 5, 196–8; capacity 44–5; context 198; drafting 56; EU 43, 203; international law 60–1, 80–1, 196; postal rule 56; social contract 60; treaties and conventions 60–1
cooperation and coordination 3, 42, 104, 156
Cornu, Gérard 106
corporations 6, 94, 196–7
costs 163, 178, 200, 207
court cases and case law 197–8; EU 208–9; national laws 77–9; overturning and reversal 67; semiotics 135; sources of law 55–7; translation 77–8, 159, 164
creation of legal texts 15, 31, 51, 197–8
Crystal, David 9, 102
culture 7, 108, 117: context 206; education and training 185–6; identity 205; indigenous people 79; law, definition of 33–4; matrices 203–5; oral language 93; revision 171; rules and principles 40; semantics 145; semiotics 92, 129, 131–6; sites of engagement 142–3; technology and tools 178; translation 91–2, 155–6, 158, 165, 181, 186
Curzon's Dictionary of Law 38–9
custom 15, 39–40, 57–8, 60–1, 80, 123

Danish 9, 83–4
databases 23, 81, 177–8, 200, 209; EUR-Lex 160, 179, 181; IATE (InterActive Terminology for Europe) 107, 148, 180; SDL Trados 180; terminology 164, 166–7, 180, 186, 198, 206–7; translation 185
dead/dying languages 8–9, 120–2, 188, 206–7
definition of language *see* language, definition of
definition of multilingual law 1–15
descriptions 21
devolution 47, 79
dialects 9, 11; language distinguished 9, 76; monolingual communities 207–8; spelling 75–6, 123; terminology 76
dictionaries: classification of languages by use and status 118; interpretation 66; law, definition of 34; legal language 116; lexicology 106–7, 148; literal meaning 145; policy and planning 124; standardisation 73; technology and tools 180; terminology 198
Dictionary of Languages 8

Dictonnaire des Langues 8–9
discourse analysis 108
distributive justice 36
drafting: branches of law 45, 63; checklist for multilingual acts 173, 195, Appendix V; co-drafting 65, 77, 79, 167; context 62–3, 206; contracts 56; documents 56; education and training 185–7; EU 62–3, 154, 173, 179, 181; guidance 59, 65, 67, 73, 76, 194–5, Appendix III; in-house lawyers 33; international law 80, 82; interpretation 63, 81–2, 207; legal language 145–6; legal-linguistics 195; legal orders 62–3; legal purposes, languages for 113–14; legal texts 25, 51, 62–5, 69; official languages 118; quality control 195; revision 170, 173, 187; rhetoric 109; rules and practice 59, 65, 67, 73, 76, 194–5, Appendix III; same language shared by different legal systems 75; semiotics 129; sites of engagement 62–5; styles and formats 63; technology and tools 178–82; text issues 199; translation 64, 154, 156, 159, 163, 166–7; type and status of acts 63–4
drafting and revision checklist for multilingual acts 173, 195, Appendix V
Dudley-Evans, Tony 109
Dutch: Belgium 5, 78; changes 74; Dutch Language Union 74–5; EU 161
dynamic dimensions 23

education and training 4, 38, 184–9, 200; comparative approach 195; costs 207; culture 185–6; drafting 185–7; EU 185, 209; experts 34; international law 185; language skills 185, 186, 200, 209; legal linguistics 184, 200; legal purposes, languages for 119; legal skills 186, 200; literary sources and legal literature 57; national laws 185; professional skills 184–5, 189; questions on law and legal language 184–5, Appendix VII; research skills 184, 187–8; revision 170, 187; rules and practice 194–5; source texts and target texts 185, 186; specialist knowledge and skills 184–9, 209; standardisation 73; technology and tools 27–8, 182, 184–5, 187, 206, 209; terminology 185, 186–7, 200; translation 158, 163, 185, 186, 195, 200; vocational training 184, 189
EEA Agreement 206
EGIDS (Expanded Graded Intergenerational Disruption Scale) 119
emotion 4, 35, 122
enforcement 25, 35, 40, 45, 62, 68–9

Index

English: Canada 5, 73–5, 78–9; Chinese 153; Commonwealth 122; contracts 60; custom 40; English as a Special Language (ESP) 109; EU 157, 159, 161; Ireland 5; law, definition of 37–8; lingua franca 9, 27; New Zealand 17, 92, 122; Old English 37; Scots law 9, 74–5, 210; shared languages 122; sources of law 59; translation 153, 157; United Kingdom 79–80, 98; United States 98, 122
equality 14, 36–7, 65, 199, 208
equity 58–9
equivalence *see* alignment and equivalence
errors 117, 159, 170–2, 178
Ethnologue 8–11, 22–3, 26, 119–20, 195
EURAMIS 181
EUR-Lex 160, 179, 181
European Charter for Regional or Minority Languages 1992 9, 120, 123–4, 195, 197, 207
European Convention on Human Rights 54–5, 73, 82–3
European Union: accessions 76, 108, 122, 165–6, 206; Brussels I Regulation 68–9; Charter of Fundamental Rights 36; classification of languages by use and status 198; contracts 43, 203; Court of Justice 53–6, 59, 157, 173, 179, 208–9; direct effect 69; directives 50, 54, 63, 83, 167; drafting 62–3, 173, 179, 181; education and training 185, 209; EEA Agreement 206; enforcement 68–9; EURAMIS 181; EUR-Lex 160, 179, 181; European Court Reports 179; freedom of movement 10; harmonisation 31; historical linguistics 110; IATE (InterActive Terminology for Europe) 107, 148, 180; institutions 63, 83, 95, 173, 179; Interinstitutional Agreement 63, 179; Interinstitutional Style Guide 95; international law 43; Internet 188; interpretation 66; Joint Practical Guide 63, 154, 162, 179; lawyer-linguist concept 5, 7, 27, 173–4; literal meaning 145; literary sources and legal literature 57; negotiations 208; new terms 181; non-native speakers, revision 171–2; number of languages 12–13, 67; Official Journal 54–5, 57, 67, 179; official languages 6, 13, 54–5, 61, 75, 83, 156, 165–6; recitals 63; recommendations and opinions 54, 83; regulations and decisions 54, 83; research skills 188; revision 170–4; rules about language, law as making 15; semantics 145; standard clauses 115; supranational law 43, 47, 59–62, 68–9, 83; synoptic approach 13, 143; technology and tools 28, 177–82, 206; terminology 107–8, 122, 181, 206; translation 181–3; treaties 13, 53–4, 59–61, 66, 83; viewpoints 147 *see also* translation and the EU
evidence 25, 52, 62, 67–8, 69
experts: branches of law 45; education and training 34; native speakers 27; new terms 148; oral language 93; presentations or writing papers on multilingual legal languages, making 185, 195; revision 170–3; technology and tools 178, 180; translation 162–4, 180

facts 25, 52, 62, 67–8, 69, 142, 146
false friends (faux amis) 153, 181
federal states 47, 77, 78–9
Ferrara, M 21
field of enquiry 5–8
foreign law 164–5
framework for analysis and understanding 18, 20, 28, 193–201, 202–3 Appendix VIII; field of enquiry, structuring the field of 23–4; legal-linguistic modelling 20–3, 25, 28, 46–8, 119, 194, Appendix II; list of countries 209; models 20–8; translation 168, 197, 200–1; viewpoints 32, 201
French: Africa 122; Alsace-Lorraine 77; Belgium 5, 75, 78, 122; Breton 120; Canada 5, 78–9; case law 35; Constitution 40, 77; contracts 60; dictionaries 106; EU law 157–9, 161; Italian 153; law, definition of 38; legal systems 42; lingua franca 27; Luxembourg 122; morphology 99; shared languages 122; sources of law 59; Switzerland 5; translation 153, 157–8
Frydman, B. *Le Sens des Lois* 21
fuzziness 159, 207

Gaelic 80, 118–19, 124
Gaglioti, AR 21
genres 25, 109, 172–3, 198–9
German: Alsace-Lorraine 77; Austria 75, 122; Belgium 5, 78; changes 74; EU 157, 161; law, definition of 38; morphology 99; same language shared by different legal systems 75; Schleswig-Holstein 83–4; shared languages 122; South Tyrol 75, 122; Switzerland 5; translation 157
Germanic languages 9, 76
Gloag, WM and Henderson, RC. *The Law of Scotland* 44
glossaries 107, 148, 180, 186, 198
grammar 101–3, 110, 116
graphology 95
Greek 3, 95, 101
Groffier, Ethel 106
Grundnorm 36, 39

habit 40, 57–8, 60–1
Harris, JW 35–6

Henderson, RC 44
hieroglyphics 3, 94–5
historical linguistics 74, 96, 109–10
homogeneity 207–8
Hong Kong 117
horizontal dimension 15, 17–18, 110, 113, 120, 124, 153
human law 35–6
human rights 36, 54–5, 73, 82–3, 201

ignorance of the law is no excuse 35
immigrants 3, 10, 37, 79
impartiality 36, 135–6, 199
indigenous communities 16, 79, 122–3
in-house lawyers 33
intention 65–6, 148, 199
InterActive Terminology for Europe (IATE) 107, 148, 180
international conferences 165–6
International Court of Justice (ICJ) 55, 58–9, 80
international law 42–3, 72–3, 80–2, 84, 196; contracts and agreements 60–1, 196; custom 58, 80; dialects 76; education and training 185; equity 59; international organisations 80–2; interpretation 66, 80; official languages 80, 116; research skills 187; state practice 80; states and legal orders 46–7; terminology 205; translation 186
international organisations 5–6, 80–2; creation 80; international agreements 60–1, 80–1; legal-linguistic modelling 48; number of organisations 81; official languages 80–1; treaties and conventions 60–1 see also particular organisations
International Phonetic Alphabet (IPA) 95, 97
Internet 179, 187–8
interpretant 132–4, 148–9, 159, 161–2, 165–7
interpretation: absurdity or unreasonableness 66; aids to construction 65–6; authentic language versions 66, 82; barristers 32; comparative approach 124; conflicts 66; context 65; costs 207; custom 58; dictionaries 66; drafting 63, 81–2, 207; education and training 185; equivalence 199; equity 58–9; golden rule 65; good faith 66; guidance 59, 65, 67, 73, 76, 194–5, Appendix III; history of legal interpretation 21; intention 65–6, 199; international law 66, 80, 82; interpreters 91, 156; legal language 114, 146; legal philosophy 36; legal texts 25, 51, 65–7, 69, 142; legislation 54; literal meaning 65, 145; matrices of laws 204–5; mischief rule 65; multiple language versions 199; official languages 82, 117; ordinary meaning 66; penal provisions, strict interpretation of 66; precedent 55–7; rules and practice 59, 65, 67, 73, 76, 194–5, Appendix III; semiotics 92, 133–5, 201; sites of engagement 62, 65–7; syntax 101; texts, terms and meanings 141; translation 82, 157, 161–2
intertextuality 25, 40, 67, 75, 134–5, 144–5, 171–2, 185
Ireland: court cases 78; English 5, 64, 77–8; Irish 5, 64, 77–8; multiple languages, drafting in 64; official languages 5, 77–8
Italian: EU 161; false friends 153; South Tyrol 75, 84, 122; Switzerland 5; translation 153, 157

Japanese: hiragana 95; kanji 94–5; katakana 95; romaji 97
judgments, enforcement of 52, 68
justice 36–7, 66–7, 208

Kelsen, Hans 39

language, definition of 15–17, 90, 92–3
language skills 185, 186, 200, 209
language, viewpoints of see viewpoints of language
languages for legal purposes 113–25; classification of use and status 26, 113, 118–23, 124, 206; *langue* and *parole*, difference between 113; legal language 114–16, 124; LSP 26, 113, 124; official language, concept of 11, 26, 116–20, 124; policy and planning 26, 119–20, 124; substantive and procedural law 113–14, 124; table of classification 26
langue and *parole*, difference between 25–6, 92, 96, 100, 103, 105, 111, 113, 115–16
Latin 3, 41, 76, 80, 101, 107, 121–2, 210
law and language 15–18
law, definition of 15–16, 24–5, 31–2, 34–8
law of languages 72–85; choice of language, regulation of 25, 72; international law 72–3, 80–2, 84; linguistic regimes 25, 76–84; regulation of language by law and legal rules 25, 72, 73–4; supranational law 72–4, 82–3, 84; use of language, regulation of 25
The Law of Scotland. Gloag, WM and Henderson, RC 44
law, viewpoints of see viewpoints of law
lawyers, role of 8, 178–9, 183
legal language: core legal concepts and terms 114–15; legal purposes, languages for 114–16, 124; meaning 141, 145–6; official languages 11; sites of engagement 141, 142; texts, terms and meanings 141, 145–6

268 Index

legal-linguistics 13–18, 111, 194; drafting and revision checklist for multilingual acts 195; education and training 184, 200; lawyer-linguist concept 5, 7, 27, 28, 173–4, 182; matrices 55, 76; monolingual communities 13; oral language 93; revision 27, 156, 173–4, 187
legal orders 25, 34, 46–7, 62–3, 194
legal philosophy 24–5, 31, 33, 35–9, 48
legal purposes, language for *see* languages for legal purposes
legal skills 184–6, 200
legal systems 5, 31, 34, 37, 42–3, 199; legal-linguistic modelling 21, 46; legal texts 69; one system of law in different language codes 117; rules and practice 194; semiotics 41, 132; substantive and procedural law 46 *see also* civil law systems; common law systems; international law; national laws; supranational law
legal texts 51–69; acts or instruments 25, 51; amendment 25, 51, 67–8, 69; application 51; boundaries 144; context 25, 62, 69; creation 51, 197–8; drafting 25, 51, 62–5, 69; enforcement 25, 62, 68–9; EU 69, 115; facts, evidence and proof 25, 52, 62, 67–8, 69; formal aspects 144; genres 25, 109; interpretation 25, 51, 65–7, 69, 142; linguistics 144–5; meanings 141, 146, 149; official languages 116; oral language 51; preparatory phases 198; procedure 52; repeal 25, 51, 67–8, 69; revision 171–3; rhetoric 109; sites of engagement 51, 62–7, 69, 141–3; sources of law 25, 51, 52–61, 69; translation 153–68; types of text 51, 61–2, 69, 197–8; viewpoints 146–8
legal theory 7, 17, 22, 25, 31, 35, 38–9, 51, 58, 69, 111
legislation: context 198; drafting 33; EU 50, 53–4, 63, 83, 167; interpretation 54; sources of law 53–5; statute law 37; types 197
Legiswrite 179
lesser languages *see* minority or lesser languages
lexicography 106–7
lexicology 65, 104, 106–7, 148, 180
LGP (language used for general purposes) 4–5, 73, 90, 103
lingua franca 4, 9, 27, 118, 188
linguistics 95–111; applied linguistics 4–5, 14, 84, 93, 96, 111, 184; cognitive linguistics 96; comparative linguistics 96, 105, 110; combined with other fields 110–11; fore-grounding and back-grounding 91; historical linguistics 96, 109–10; language, definition of 92; neurolinguistics 96; phonetics 96–7, 102, 110; phonology 97–8, 102–3, 110; regimes 25, 76–84; research skills 187–8; revision 171–4; role of linguistics 28, 179–82, 183; rules and practice 76; scripts 95, 179; semantics 102–5, 110; semiotics 91–2, 111, 132, 136, 143–4; syntax 100–1, 102, 110; texts, terms and meanings 141, 144–5, 149; variations in regimes 83–4; viewpoints 25, 90–2, 95–111
literary sources and legal literature 57
literary theory 109, 129
loanwords 107, 130
local and regional languages: dialects 123, 207; indigenous people 122; official languages 116, 120, 122; province law 47; shared languages 122–3; state, concept of the 77; translation 165–6; vocabulary 122
LSP (language used for special purposes) 4–5, 26, 33, 73, 90, 93, 103, 107, 113, 124, 173
Luxembourg 75, 78, 122

Mac Aodha, Máirtín 106
Malta 77, 78
Maltese 6, 19, 77–8
mathematical models 21
matrices 203–5; interpretation 204–5; legal-linguistic matrix 55, 76; sources of law 55; time 205; translation 27
Mattila, Heikki ES 6
McLeod, I 66
meaning 26, 65, 141–9, 159, 199
mental element 26, 129–36
metaphor 104
minority or lesser languages 207–8; knowledge 37; official languages 37, 120, 124; recognition 37, 118–20; research skills 187–8; size of a language 206–7; terminology 186–7
models 5, 201; definition 21–2; field of enquiry, structuring the 23–4; hybrid models 47; legal-linguistic modelling 20–3, 23, 25, 28, 47–8, 119, 194, Appendix II; mathematical models 21
monolingual communities: bilingual communities 207–8; dialects 207–8; different languages in one community 13–14, 77; foreign influences 203; integration 208; multilingual law, definition of 13–14, 203; official languages 77, 123; research skills 187; semantics 103; semiotics 131; translation 164–6; unifying factor, single language as 37; unitary states 77
morphology 96, 98–103, 124, 153
multilingual law, definition of 11–15, 203
multinationals 94, 196–7
multiple languages 10, 12–14, 64, 67, 77, 117, 199

NASA (National Aeronautics and Space Administration) website 23
national laws 46–7, 60, 77–80, 82, 116, 167, 185
native speaker experts 27
natural law 35–6, 37–8, 58, 66, 208
natural or scientific phenomenon as a law 37
negotiations 159, 165, 208
Netherlands *see* Dutch
new terms 148, 156–7, 166, 181, 186, 198
New Zealand: English 17, 92, 122; Maori 17, 92–3, 122; oral language 93; sign language 84, 92; Treaty of Waitingi 122
non-governmental organisations (NGOs) 6
non-literate societies 123
non-native speakers, revision 27, 171–2
non-verbal communication 16–17, 92
norms 25, 32, 36, 38–42, 48
Norway 9, 93
noun, law as a 16
number of languages 8–12, 198; dialects 9, 11; EU 12–13; lower limit 13; official languages 5, 11–14, 23, 37, 54, 75–83, 194; statistics 10–11; undiscovered languages 9; upper limit 12

obiter dicta 55
object 124, 130–6, 141, 145, 148–9, 159–62, 165–7
objectification of the subjective 26, 135–6
official languages 5–6, 22, 28, 76, 118–21, 193–4; classification of languages by use and status 118–21, 123; codes 116–17; constitutions 118; EU 6, 13, 54–5, 61, 75, 83, 156, 165–6; federal states 5, 12, 78–9; historical dimension 117–18; horizontal dimension 117–18; informal use 120; international organisations 80; interpretation 82, 117; *langue* and *parole*, difference between 116; legal purposes, languages for 11, 26, 116–20, 124; list of countries 209, Appendix I; literary sources and legal literature 57; minority or lesser languages 120, 124; monolingual communities 37, 77, 123; more than one language 11, 117; non-official languages 123, 206–7; number of languages 5, 11–14, 23, 37, 54, 75–83, 194; one system of law in different language codes 117; oral languages 116; power relations between languages 117–18; recognition 37, 118–20; regional and local languages 116, 122; relationship between languages 118–19; rules and practice 194, 201; state, concept of the 23, 46; supranational law 116, 122; translation 118–19, 166; unifying factor, single language as 37; vocabulary 117; writing 116
O'Grady, William 103–4

Old English 37
Old Norse 37
oral language: customs 123; indigenous cultures 123; language, definition of 90, 92; legal language 141; legal meaning 145; legal texts 51; linguistics 95; memorisation 93; official languages 116; phonetics 97; phonology 98; revision 172; rule, definition of 40; texts, terms and meanings 141; translation 27; writing 25–6, 93–5, 111
Ostler, Nicholas 3, 9
ought statements 36
Oxford Dictionaries Online 9, 16, 21, 38–9, 41, 105, 107, 180
Oxford English Dictionary 106

Peirce, Charles Sanders 26, 124–5, 132–5, 143
Philips, Christian 106
phonetics 96–7, 102
phonology 96–8, 101–3, 110, 115, 124
police 16, 37
policy and planning 26, 63–4, 115, 119–20, 124, 195
political dimension 203
Poole, Stuart C 99
Portuguese 75
postal rule 56
power relations 52, 117–18
pragmatics 96, 108
precedent: binding precedent 55; civil law systems 54; common law systems 55–6; conflict of laws 55; contracts and documents, drafting 56; hierarchy of courts 55; interpretation 55–7; judges 32; *obiter dicta* 55; *ratio decidendi* 55; Scottish courts 55–6; sources of law 55–7; *stare decisis* 55; Supreme Court of the UK 55; technology and tools 179; text issues 199, 201
presentations or writing papers on multilingual legal languages 185, 195, Appendix VI
private individuals 6
private law 6, 196–7
problems and solutions 200–1, 208–9
procedures 52, 196–8
processes 21, 27, 155–6, 162–4
professions 5, 16, 33, 37, 84–5, 189
proof 25, 52, 62, 67–8, 69
proofreading 82, 171–2, 228
proportionality 154
pros and cons of multilingual law 207–8
proscription of languages 119
prosecutors 33
psychological dimension 10
public law 5–6
punctuation 95, 116, 118, 124, 148, 162, 170–2
punishment 35

270 *Index*

quality 27, 163–6, 170–1, 173, 195
questionnaires 209

ratio decidendi 55
reasonable man in law 104–5
Reboul, Olivier 109
recitals 63, 154, 162
Reed, David 106
regional languages *see* local and regional languages
religion: Bible 3, 37, 41, 163; legal philosophy 35–6; natural law 35–7; noun, law as a 16; sacred texts 3; semiotics 133; sources of law 53
repeal 25, 51, 62, 67–8, 69
representamen 132–4, 148–9, 159, 161–2, 165–7
research: areas for study and research 209; comparative law 201; human rights 201; presentations or writing papers on multilingual legal languages, making 185, 195, Appendix VI; skills 184, 187–8; technology and tools 187
respect 208
revision 170–4; checklist 173, 195, Appendix V; culture 171; drafting 170, 173; education and training 170, 187; errors 170–2; EU 27, 170–4; experts 170–3; first phase of translation 27; legal-linguistic revision 27, 156, 173–4; legal texts 171–3; linguistics 171–4; native speaker experts 27; non-native speakers 27, 171–2; oral language 172; proofreading 171–2; quality 170–1, 173; role of revisers 179–82, 206; rules and principles 40–1; second phase of translation 27; semiotics 201; skills 187; source texts and target texts 171–2; specialist texts 170, 172–3; style 170–2; terminology 170, 172; translation 27, 156, 167, 170–4, 180, 206, 208; viewpoints 27, 170–1
rhetorics 109
Roman law 43, 53
Romansh 5
Rosetta Stone 3
Rousseau, Jean-Jacques 60
rules and practice: comparative approach 195; creation of law 15; difference between rules and principles 38, 41; drafting 59, 65, 67, 73, 76, 194–5, Appendix III; education and training 194–5; facts, evidence and proof 68; guidance 59, 65, 67, 73, 76, 194–5, Appendix III; interpretation 59, 65, 67, 73, 76, 194–5, Appendix III; linguistic regimes 76; models 194; official languages 194; principle, definition of 41; rule, definition of 39–40; sources of law 59, 65, 67, 73; states, languages and official languages 201; syntax 100–1; viewpoints 25, 32, 38–42, 48

Russian: Baltic countries 120, 122; changes 74; same language shared by different legal systems 75

Sager, Juan C 107
same language, legal texts between countries using the 122–3
Šarčević, Susan 154
Saussure, Ferdinand de 14, 24–6, 92, 96, 100, 103, 113, 116, 124–5, 129–34
scientific language 107
Scotland: changes 210; civil law systems 43–4; common law systems 43–4; contractual capacity 44–5; custom 58; dialects 207; drafting 63; English 9, 74–5, 210; equity 58; European Charter for Regional or Minority Languages 9; Gaelic 80, 118–19, 124; historical linguistics 110; legislation 53–4; literary sources and legal literature 57; precedent 55–6; same language shared by different legal systems 74–5; sources of law 52–7, 59; Supreme Court of UK 55; viewpoints of law 34
scripts 94–5, 117, 204; alphabetical scripts 95; alternative scripts 117; change 74; graphology 94; hieroglyphics 3, 94–5; ideographic scripts 94–5; linguistics 95, 179; logograms 94–5; morphology 99; more than one script 76; semiotics 143, 145; Sumerian cuneiform 94; technology and tools 181–2; translation 153; transliteration 97
SDL Trados 180
second languages 10, 91, 100, 102, 188
secularism 36
semantics 96, 101–5, 110; codes 102–3; concept, definition of 103–4; co-operative principle 104; culture 145; EU 145; *langue* and *parole*, difference between 103, 105; legal meaning 145; legal purposes, languages for 124; lexicalisation 104; linguistics 102–5, 141, 145; metaphor 104; single-language codes 103; unicity of meaning 115
semiotics (theory of signs) 4, 74, 129–36, 196; alphabet, letters of the 143–4; comparative law 124; concepts, words as linked to 130; contracts 60; culture 92, 129, 131–6; drafting 129; iconic, indexical or symbolic 143; ideas 130; imagined signs 135–6; interpretant 132–4, 148–9, 159, 161–2, 165–7; interpretation 92, 133–5, 201; legal meaning 145–6; legal purposes, languages for 125; legal systems 41, 132; linguistics 91–2, 111, 132, 136, 143–4; mental element 26, 129–36; models 5, 21–2, 24; monolingual societies 131; new signs, creating 135; object 124, 130–6, 141, 145, 148–9, 159–62, 165–7; objectification

of the subjective 26, 135–6; overlapping words 130; policy and planning 124; primary and secondary term formation 26; representamen 132–4, 148–9, 159, 161–2, 165–7; reproduction of ideas and concepts 26; revision 201; same ideas and concepts; scripts 143, 145; semiosis 26; semiotic object 130, 132, 145–6, 148–9, 162; signified/signifiers 130–2, 148–9, 159, 161–2, 165–7; specialisms 188; synonyms 130; target and source languages 134; terminology 26, 148–9, 187; texts and terms 26, 141, 143–4, 149; three elements of signs 26, 132–4, 136; translations 133–4, 153, 158–9, 161–2, 165–7, 201; two elements, signs as comprising 26, 129–32, 134, 136; variations 161
shared languages 11, 73–8, 122–3, 207
sign language 17, 90, 92
signatures 115
signs see semiotics (theory of signs)
single-language communities see monolingual communities
sites of engagement 51, 62–7, 69; facts 62, 142; interpretation 62, 65–7; repeal 62, 67; texts and terms 26, 141, 143–4, 149
size of a language 206–7
Slavic languages 76
social contract 60
software 178, 179, 182, 200
solicitors, notaries or law agents 33
solutions and problems 208–9
sounds 97–100
source texts and target texts: classification of languages by use and status 118; education and training 185, 186; equivalence 154–9; knowledge 200; multiple languages, drafting in 64; revision 171–2; semiotics 134; technology and tools 179–81; terminology 205; translations 64, 162, 164, 166, 179–80, 200, 208
sources of law 25, 51, 52–61, 69, 73, 114; contracts 60–1; creation 53; custom 57–8; equity 58–9; extraneous sources 59; formal sources 52–9; historical sources 53; judicial precedents and case law 55–7; legal texts 25, 51, 52–61, 69; legislation 53–5; literary sources and legal literature 57; material sources 53; religion 53; rules and practice 59, 65, 67, 73; social, political, economic or moral sources 53; substantive and procedural law 52, 114
South Africa 15, 54: Constitution 116, 123; multilingual law, definition of 12; official languages 79; oral languages 116, 123
South Tyrol 75, 84, 122
Spanish 75

specialisms 4, 22, 34, 136; applied linguistics 84; boundaries 207; education and training 184–9, 209; language as specialist knowledge 7; law as specialist knowledge 7; legal roles 33; literatures 188–9; matrices of laws 204; models 22, 24; revision 170, 172–3; semiotics 188; technology and tools 177, 178–83; translation 153, 155–6, 162, 164, 167, 173
spelling 15, 64, 72–6, 94–5, 98, 116–17; change 109, 124; dialects 75–6, 123; historical linguistics 109; reforms 124; spellchecks 181; translation 181; variations 122
sports, rules in 16, 37
standardisation 42, 198; dictionaries 73; drafting 63; EU 115; grammar 101; one system of law in different language codes 117; rigidification 206; technology and tools 178, 206; terminology 63, 107, 123; translation 166–7; writing 116
states 22, 28, 193–4, Appendix I; concept of the state 23, 77; federal states 47, 77, 78–9; hybrid states 77, 79–80; legal orders 46; list of countries 209, Appendix I; local and regional dimensions 77; multinationals 194; power 53; questionnaires 209; rules and practice 201; state practice 80; unitary states 47, 77
status of languages see classification of languages by use and status
Stroud's Judicial Dictionary of Words and Phrases 106
styles and formats 16–17, 26, 63, 170–2, 179
subjective, objectification of the 26, 135–6
subsidiarity 154
substantive and procedural law 52, 113–14, 124
supranational law 42–3, 72–4, 82–4, 198; accession 122; contracts 60; education and training 185; equity 59; EU 43, 47, 59–62, 68–9, 83; European Convention on Human Rights 73, 82–3; official languages 43, 47, 59–62, 68–9, 83; states and legal orders 46–7; terminology 122, 205; translation 186
Swedish 9
Switzerland: Constitution 12; French 5, 75; German 5; Italian 5; minority and lesser languages 208; official languages 5; Romansh 5; rules about language, law as making 15
synonyms 130
synoptic approach 13, 143
syntax 100–3, 115, 118, 124; translation 153, 162, 168; viewpoints of language 96, 100–1, 102, 110
Systran 180

target texts *see* source texts and target texts
technology and tools 3–4, 177–82, 183; aids 178–82, 200; analogue tools 178, 200; back-up, support and training 27–8; computer-assisted tools (CAT) 167; computing language 16–17, 93; costs 178, 207; dictionaries and glossaries 180; digital technology 178, 200; document transmission 178; drafting 178–82; education and training 182, 184–5, 186–7, 200, 206; email 178; errors 178; EU 28, 177–82, 206; experts 178, 180; glossaries 186; grammar 102; Internet 179, 187–8; lawyer-linguists, role of 28, 182; lawyers, role of 28, 178–9, 183; linguists, role of 28, 179–82, 183; maintenance and repair of machines 177–8; management 177; mechanisation 177–80, 206; minority and lesser languages 186–7; new terms 186; official languages 188; precedents and styles 179; questionnaires 209; revisers, role of 179–82, 206; scripts 181–2; semiotics 187; software 178, 179, 182, 200; source text and target text 179–81; specialisation 177, 178–83; standardisation 178, 206; terminology 180; translation 163–4, 166–7, 171, 179–83, 206; viewpoints 177–8
see also databases
terminology 197–9; classification of languages by use and status 118, 119–23, 195, 198, 205; co-drafting 65; databases 164, 166–7, 180, 186, 198, 206–7; definition 107; dialects 76; dictionaries 198; domains 198–9; equivalence 161; EU 107–8, 122, 148, 165–6, 181, 206; glossaries 107, 148, 198; international law 205; lexicography 107, 148; local and regional languages 122; new terms 148, 198; official languages 117; primary term formation 107; problems and solutions 208; revisions 170, 172; scientific language 107; secondary term formation 107; semiotics 26, 148–9; shared languages 122; source language and target language 205; specialisms 185; standardisation 63, 107, 123; supranational law 122, 205; syntax 118; texts and terms 141, 148–50; translation 107–8, 148, 154, 159, 161–3, 165–7, 186; viewpoints 107–8; vocabulary 123, 205
texts 141–9; comparative law 199; context 26, 198–9; contrary to actual wording, meaning as 26; creation of legal meaning, sites of engagement for 26, 141; drafting 199; genres 198–9; interpretation 141; issues 198–9, 200–1; precedents 199, 201; semiotics 26, 141, 143–4, 149; sites of engagement 26, 141, 142–3, 149; terminology 141, 148–9; translation 148–9; viewpoints 26–7, 141, 146–8 *see also* legal texts

thesauruses 106, 116, 130, 186
time 205
tools *see* technology and tools
training *see* education and training
transition stages 198
translation 73, 153–68; anonymity of translator 154; authentic translations 80, 166; automatically generated texts 180; co-drafting 167; contexts 153, 163–5, 167–8; costs 163, 207; court cases 77–8, 159, 164, 208–9; creativity 154; culture 91–2, 155–6, 158, 165, 181, 186; definition of translation 27, 155–62; discourse analysis 108; drafting 64, 154, 156, 159, 163, 166–7; education and training 158, 163, 185, 186, 195, 200; equivalence 154–62, 165, 182, 200; errors 159; experts 162–4, 180; external source texts 166; false friends 153, 181; first phase of translation 27; foreign law 164–5; freelancers 164; fuzziness in texts 159; glossaries 107; horizontal dimension 153; hybrid fields 96; international conferences 165–6; international law 186; interpretation 82, 156–7, 161–2; invisibility 154; legal matrix 27; legal purposes, languages for 113, 124; legal texts 153–68; Legiswrite 179; linguistics 91–2; literal translations 153–4, 159, 161; monolingual systems 164–6; morphology 98–9, 153; negotiations 159, 165, 208; new terms 156–7, 166; notes and explanations 155, 156; official translations 118–19, 166; organizational process 163–4; process, as 27, 155–6, 162–4; quality 27, 163–6; recitals 154, 162; revision 27, 156, 167, 170–4, 180, 187, 206, 208; role of translators 179–83; same language shared by different legal systems 75; scripts 153; semiotics 133–4, 153, 158–9, 161–2, 165–7, 201; seven scenarios 27, 164–8; source texts and target texts 64, 155–9, 162, 164, 166, 179–80, 186, 200, 208; specialisms 153, 155–6, 162, 164, 167, 173; spirit or idea of texts 154; standardisation 166–7; subjectivity 159; substantive and procedural law 46; supranational law 186; syntax 100–1, 153, 162, 168; technology and mechanisation 163–4, 166–7, 171, 179–83, 206; terminology 107–8, 148, 154, 159, 161–3, 165–7, 186; text factories 163; texts and terms 148–9; translation memory approach 180; transposition 167; treaties and conventions 166; variations 159–61, 208; viewpoints 153–68, 170–1; vocabulary 156, 168; written texts 27, 156
see also translation and the EU
translation and the EU 155–68, 172, 208–9; accessions 165–6; Court of Justice 159–60;

drafting 154; equivalence 161; finalisation process 156; IATE (InterActive Terminology for Europe) 107, 148, 180; in-house translation 164, 165–6; institutions 156, 165–7; Joint Practical Guide 154, 162; national laws 167; negotiations 165; official languages 156, 165–6; recitals 162; Regulation on the EU language regime 160–1, 172; semiotics 134; technology and tools 181–3; terminology 165–6; variations 159–61
transliteration 97
treaties and conventions: contracts 60–1; EU 13, 53–4, 59–61, 66, 83; international organisations 80–1; translation 166; Vienna Convention on the Law of Treaties 66, 80
Turkish 74

understanding *see* framework for analysis and understanding
undiscovered languages 9
unitary states 47, 77–8
United Kingdom: common law systems 63; devolution 47, 79; drafting 63; English 79–80; federal states 47; Germanic languages 9; hybrid states 47, 79–80; Internet 179; legal philosophy 35; recitals 63; Supreme Court 55; unitary states 47; Westminster Parliament 47, 53–4, 79
United Nations (UN) 43, 72–3; authentic languages 82; Charter 81–2; Chinese texts 109–10; drafting 82; historical linguistics 109–10; interpretation 81–2; legal philosophy 35; official languages 5–6; organs 81–2; plurality 9–10; specialised agencies 82; spelling 98; table of states and languages 23; translation 82
United States: English 98, 122; immigration 37; integration 208; single official language as unifying factor 37; spelling 98
Universal Declaration of Human Rights 36
Universal Declaration on Linguistic Rights (UNESCO) 36
universalism 195
updating of rules 40–1
use of force 52
use of languages *see* classification of languages by use and status
utilitarianism 37

vertical dimension 15, 110, 113, 116, 124
Vienna Convention on the Law of Treaties 66, 80
viewpoints 199, 201; combined viewpoints 17–18; education and training 184–5, 188; models 22, 24; relativization 26; revision 170–1; semiotics 131; syntax 96, 100–1, 102, 110; technology and tools 177–8; translation 153–68, 170–1
viewpoints of language 14–15, 17, 89–111; biology of language and sound production 25–6, 96; brain and language 96; circles, concept of 25, 96, 111; codes 26, 90–1; context 26; gestures 90; grammar 101–3, 110; historical linguistics 109–10; language, definition of 90, 92–3; language theory 25; *langue* and *parole*, difference between 25–6, 92, 96, 100, 111; lexicology 106–7; linguistics 25, 90–2, 95–111; list of topics 25; morphology 98–100, 102; official languages 194; oral and written utterances 25–6, 93–5, 111; phonetics 96–7, 102; phonology 97–8, 102–3, 110; semantics 102–5, 110; syntax 100–1, 102, 110; terminology 107–8; texts and terms 26–7, 141, 146–8; vocabulary 105–6
viewpoints of law 14–15, 17, 31–48; branches of law 32, 43–5; creation of legal texts 31; law, definition of 24–5, 31–2, 34–8; legal-linguistics 5, 14–15; legal orders 25, 34, 46–7; legal philosophy 24–5, 31, 48; legal roles 31–2; legal systems 34, 42–3; legal viewpoints 32–4; real-life concept 31–2; rules, norms and principles 25, 32, 38–42, 48; states and legal orders 25, 46–7; structure of law and legal systems 31; substantive and procedural law 32, 45–6, 47
vocabulary 105–6; definition 105; grammar 101; knowledge 105; legal language 115–16; lexemes and lexical items 106; local and regional languages 122; official languages 117; terminology 123, 187, 205; translation 156, 168

Walker, David M 43–4, 45, 52–3, 57–9, 65
Welsh 80, 84, 118, 124
wordprocessing 178, 181–2
Wordsmith Tools software 179–80
Wright, Sue Ellen 107
writing: language, definition of 90, 92; legal meaning 145; oral language 25–6, 93–5, 111; presentations or writing papers on multilingual legal languages, making 185, 195, Appendix VI; standards 116; style 16–17 *see also* scripts

Yugoslavia: alternative scripts 117; break-up 76; Cyrillic and Latin alphabet 76; EU, accessions to 76; Serbo-Croat 117
Yule, George 98–9, 102

Taylor & Francis eBooks

Helping you to choose the right eBooks for your Library

Add Routledge titles to your library's digital collection today. Taylor and Francis ebooks contains over 50,000 titles in the Humanities, Social Sciences, Behavioural Sciences, Built Environment and Law.

Choose from a range of subject packages or create your own!

Benefits for you
- Free MARC records
- COUNTER-compliant usage statistics
- Flexible purchase and pricing options
- All titles DRM-free.

Benefits for your user
- Off-site, anytime access via Athens or referring URL
- Print or copy pages or chapters
- Full content search
- Bookmark, highlight and annotate text
- Access to thousands of pages of quality research at the click of a button.

REQUEST YOUR FREE INSTITUTIONAL TRIAL TODAY

Free Trials Available
We offer free trials to qualifying academic, corporate and government customers.

eCollections – Choose from over 30 subject eCollections, including:

Archaeology	Language Learning
Architecture	Law
Asian Studies	Literature
Business & Management	Media & Communication
Classical Studies	Middle East Studies
Construction	Music
Creative & Media Arts	Philosophy
Criminology & Criminal Justice	Planning
Economics	Politics
Education	Psychology & Mental Health
Energy	Religion
Engineering	Security
English Language & Linguistics	Social Work
Environment & Sustainability	Sociology
Geography	Sport
Health Studies	Theatre & Performance
History	Tourism, Hospitality & Events

For more information, pricing enquiries or to order a free trial, please contact your local sales team:
www.tandfebooks.com/page/sales

 The home of Routledge books

www.tandfebooks.com